THE PSYCHOLOGY
OF LEARNING AND MOTIVATION

Advances in Research and Theory

VOLUME 18

CONTRIBUTORS TO THIS VOLUME

Marilyn Jager Adams

Martin D. S. Braine

Lee R. Brooks

Matthew Erdelyi

Peter C. Holland

Robert Holson

Donald Homa

Larry L. Jacoby

Donald F. Kendrick

Brian J. Reiser

Mark Rilling

Barbara Rumain

Gene P. Sackett

Thomas B. Stonebraker

THE PSYCHOLOGY OF LEARNING AND MOTIVATION

Advances in Research and Theory

EDITED BY GORDON H. BOWER

STANFORD UNIVERSITY, STANFORD, CALIFORNIA

Volume 18

1984

ACADEMIC PRESS, INC.

(Harcourt Brace Jovanovich, Publishers)

Orlando • San Diego
New York • London • Toronto • Montreal • Sydney • Tokyo

ACADEMIC PRESS, INC.
Orlando, Florida 32887

United Kingdom Edition published by
ACADEMIC PRESS, INC. (LONDON) LTD.
24/28 Oval Road, London NW1 7DX

LIBRARY OF CONGRESS CATALOG CARD NUMBER: 66-30104

ISBN 0-12-543318-2

PRINTED IN THE UNITED STATES OF AMERICA

84 85 86 87   9 8 7 6 5 4 3 2 1

CONTENTS

THE RECOVERY OF UNCONSCIOUS (INACCESSIBLE) MEMORIES: LABORATORY STUDIES OF HYPERMNESIA

Matthew Erdelyi

ORIGINS OF BEHAVIOR IN PAVLOVIAN CONDITIONING

Peter C. Holland

DIRECTED FORGETTING IN CONTEXT

Mark Rilling, Donald F. Kendrick, and Thomas B. Stonebraker

EFFECTS OF ISOLATION REARING ON LEARNING BY MAMMALS

Robert Holson and Gene P. Sackett

ARISTOTLE'S LOGIC

Marilyn Jager Adams

SOME EMPIRICAL JUSTIFICATION FOR A THEORY OF NATURAL PROPOSITIONAL LOGIC

Martin D. S. Braine, Brian J. Reiser, and Barbara Rumain

CONTRIBUTORS

Numbers in parentheses indicate the pages on which the authors' contributions begin.

Marilyn Jager Adams, Bolt Beranek and Newman Inc., 10 Moulton Street, Cambridge, Massachusetts 02238 (255)

Martin D. S. Braine, Department of Psychology, New York University, New York, New York 10003 (313)

Lee R. Brooks, Department of Psychology, McMaster University, Hamilton, Ontario L8S 4K1, Canada (1)

Matthew Erdelyi, Department of Psychology, Brooklyn College of The City University of New York, Brooklyn, New York 11210 (95)

Peter C. Holland, Department of Psychology, University of Pittsburgh, Pittsburgh, Pennsylvania 15260 (129)

Robert Holson, Department of Psychology, Regional Primate Research Center, University of Washington, Seattle, Washington 98195 (199)

Donald Homa, Department of Psychology, Arizona State University, Tempe, Arizona 85281 (49)

Larry L. Jacoby, Department of Psychology, McMaster University, Hamilton, Ontario L8S 4K1, Canada (1)

Donald F. Kendrick, Department of Psychology, Middle Tennessee State University, Murfreesboro, Tennessee 37130 (175)

Brian J. Reiser, Department of Psychology, Carnegie-Mellon University, Pittsburgh, Pennsylvania 15213 (313)

Mark Rilling, Department of Psychology, Michigan State University, East Lansing, Michigan 48824 (175)

Barbara Rumain, Department of Psychology, New York University, New York, New York 10003 (313)

Gene P. Sackett, Department of Psychology, Regional Primate Research Center, and Child Development and Mental Retardation Center, University of Washington, Seattle, Washington 98195 (199)

Thomas B. Stonebraker, Department of Psychology, Greenville College, Greenville, Illinois 62246 (175)

NONANALYTIC COGNITION:
MEMORY, PERCEPTION, AND CONCEPT LEARNING

Larry L. Jacoby and Lee R. Brooks

McMASTER UNIVERSITY
HAMILTON, ONTARIO, CANADA

I. Introduction

For the past 20 years, cognitive theorizing has operated within a framework that has now outlived its heuristic usefulness. In this framework, tasks that require generalizing to new events were assumed to be accomplished in an essentially different way than tasks that require remembering unique past events. Perceptual identification and categorization, for example, are tasks that ask for generalization across trivial variations in detail; the subject's job is to identify the word *house* as essentially the same word despite its being presented in different typefaces or to identify two different dogs as being the same type of animal. In the traditional framework, these generalizing tasks are accomplished by coding the new events in terms of general procedures and stable units that have been abstracted from past experiences. The new event is analyzed into relevant and irrelevant elements, with the relevant elements being used to identify the more abstract, higher level units that constitute most of our stable, "semantic" knowledge. A string of letters, for example, would be identified as a particular word using the relevant letter features or graphemes, but not the nominally unpredictive cues from typeface or ink color.

1

THE PSYCHOLOGY OF LEARNING
AND MOTIVATION, VOL. 18

In contrast, recent treatments of tasks that require memory for specific episodes have emphasized the importance of specificity and variability in both encoding and retrieval. Tulving's principle of encoding specificity (e.g., Tulving & Thompson, 1973) states that one does not simply store a replica of a to-be-remembered item, but rather, encodes the item in a much more variable manner, a manner that is specific to the context in which it occurred. For retrieval, the similarity of the retrieval cues and the encoded trace is important, making it necessary to consider encoding and retrieval jointly rather than in isolation. This approach does not emphasize the stability and recombinability of component units, but rather the tightly integrated and interactive encoding of both conceptually relevant and irrelevant aspects of the episode. Along with the specificity and variability of encoding, the importance of differences in processing has been a central theme in recent theorizing about memory. Kolers (1979) emphasizes the importance of processing by referring to remembering operations rather than memory traces. Similar to the intent of the encoding specificity principle, Kolers stresses the uniqueness of the way an item is treated in a processing episode; good transfer depends on the similarity of the specific operations required at test to those that were applied earlier.

There is a contrast, then, in the usual treatment of generalizing tasks and the recent treatment of explicit episodic memory tasks. The processing usually thought to underlie generalizing tasks emphasizes the stability of units and identification procedures, probably in order to facilitate analytic generalization. Recent treatments of explicit episodic memory tasks, such as recognition and recall, emphasize the variability and specificity of processing, with little emphasis on the recombinability of component units. This contrast has encouraged the use of different experimental materials and procedures as well as different theoretical expectations for the two types of tasks. As a result, possible differences among the ways such tasks as recognition memory, perceptual identification, and conceptual categorization are normally accomplished have been emphasized to an unjustified extent. In contrast, we shall argue that the continuities among these tasks are far more impressive than their discontinuities.

An essential element in our argument is the distinction between analytic and nonanalytic generalization. As outlined above, the traditional cognitive approach to generalization relies on isolating, across many episodes, the features that individually help to predict a higher level unit, such as a grapheme, word, logogen, prototype, or semantic unit. Since this type of generalization requires breaking the original stimulus into stable relevant and irrelevant features, we shall refer to it as *analytic generalization*. The generalizing tasks of categorization and perception, however, can also be performed by reference to specific prior episodes, just as is the obviously specific task of remembering those episodes. Instead of relying solely on the analytic generalization of recombinable units, generality could come from treating similar situations analogously. By this process, a word could be identified by reference to a previous occurrence of a word in a similar context, from a similar source and in a similar format, rather than by reference to a generalized representation of the word, such as a logogen. A dog could be identified by reference to a similar, already-known animal rather than by reference to a general prototype of the species. Since this does not require breaking the current stimulus into separate relevant and irrelevant features, we will refer to it as *nonanalytic generalization*.

Nonanalytic generalization gains its validity from the high probability that an extremely similar previous episode represents an occurrence of the same generalized word or category as does the current episode. Furthermore, this form of generalization relies on the same interactive, context-specific organizations of the stimulus that have proven important in the recent literature on memory for particular episodes. With this type of organization, we should expect to see perceptual and categorical performance that would reflect tight integration among content, form, and source, that is, among the nominally relevant and the nominally irrelevant aspects of a processing episode. As we shall demonstrate, there is much in the recent literature that supports this suggested continuity between generalizing and episodic memory tasks.

In this article we shall describe evidence that challenges major points in the usual, divergent treatment of perception, categorization, and episodic memory. Specifically:

1. Perceptual and categorical processing cannot be assumed to depend on high-level units that change only over many trials and that are relatively independent of context. Rather, such processing seems to be as vulnerable to changes in context and task as is memory for individual episodes.

2. The effect of attentive processing need not be to systematically discard information about surface characteristics; many perceptual and conceptual judgments depend upon nominally irrelevant information about source and format. Depending on the processing selected by the task and context, these aspects of the processing episode can be integrally involved and therefore can affect later processing of closely similar material in both generalizing and explicitly episodic tasks.

3. Both generalizing and explicitly episodic memory tasks can be accomplished in several different ways. The analytic extreme, emphasized in the usual cognitive framework, depends solely on definitionally relevant information. A nonanalytic procedure depends on tightly integrated combinations of definitionally relevant and irrelevant (including adventitiously

correlated) information. How any of these tasks will be done, then, depends partly on how integral the previous processing of the probe stimulus was. Since there are so many variations in the way that an item can be processed, we expect many different relations among the generalizing and explicitly episodic tasks.

In short, we shall argue that we have no reason to believe that perceptual identification and conceptual judgments are any less variable or context dependent than explicit memory for episodes has proven to be. This, of course, is not an argument that categorical and perceptual judgments are never analytic. In perception, as in memory, it all depends on the particulars of processing.

II. The Parallel between Perceptual, Categorical, and Episodic Memory Tasks

In the following sections, we shall examine the effects on perception and categorization of manipulations that have traditionally been employed in investigations of explicit episodic memory tasks. Parallel effects would suggest that generalizing tasks often rely on memory for prior episodes rather than mainly on abstract representations such as logogens or schema.

A. PERCEPTUAL IDENTIFICATION

1. *Priming as Opposed to Memory for Prior Episodes*

The effect of the long reign of the traditional analytic and abstractive framework in cognition has been to build its assumptions nearly invisibly into the paradigms and terminology of the field. An excellent example of this is the use of the term *priming* to refer to the effect of a single presentation of an item on its later speed of processing or probability of correct identification. Priming is not a theoretically neutral term, but rather, is derived from the view that perception relies on abstract representations of knowledge such as schemata and logogens (e.g., Friedman, 1979; Morton, 1979). Morton (1969, 1979), for example, used the term to refer to a temporary reduction in the threshold of a logogen, that is, in the amount of information that must be collected for the subject to decide that a particular word has occurred. In contrast to the temporary effect of priming, Morton suggested that permanent effects on perception are gained only through a large number of repetitions of a word. These repetitions would combine to determine relatively permanent differences in the threshold of logogens so that logogens corresponding to high-frequency words would have a lower threshold than those for low-frequency words. This pooling of repetitions, of course, would not preserve information that is unique to any single presentation of a word. By a logogen view, then, a single prior presentation of a word would have almost no permanent influence on perception but could serve as a source of priming by temporarily lowering the threshold of a preexisting logogen.

The notion of priming, in general, implies that the memory system underlying perception differs from the episodic memory responsible for recognition memory in the magnitude and persistence of effects of a single presentation of a word. Large and persistent effects of a single presentation are predicted for a test of recognition memory but not for a test of perception. Recent experiments, however, have in fact yielded evidence of large and persistent effects of a single prior presentation of a word on its later perceptual identification. In fact, the effects of infrequency in the language can be greatly diminished by a single presentation of words in the experimental setting (e.g., Jacoby & Dallas, 1981); that is, a single presentation of a low-frequency word is sufficient to largely overturn a long history of differential exposure to high- and low-frequency words. Furthermore, the effects of a prior presentation persist over at least 5 days in visual perceptual identification (Jacoby, 1983a) and have been shown to last for a year in an investigation of reading inverted text (Kolers, 1976). To account for these persistent effects, it cannot simply be assumed that a single presentation of a word is sufficient to permanently lower the threshold of its corresponding logogen. Since threshold is itself an abstractive notion, it becomes meaningless when used to account for large and persistent effects of a single presentation.

The persistence of perceptual enhancement that comes from limited prior study trials suggests that perception relies on memory for prior episodes, the same type of memory that underlies performance on recognition and recall tests. As further evidence of this, even a single presentation of a pseudoword is sufficient to produce substantial facilitation of perceptual identification (Feustel, Shiffrin, & Salasoo, 1983; Hayman, 1982). Apparently working against this conclusion, however, is the finding that perceptual enhancement has been found to be independent of recognition memory performance. Even when a person does not recognize a word as having been previously presented, prior presentation of a word enhances its later tachistoscopic identification (Jacoby & Witherspoon, 1982), the completing of a fragmented version of the word (Tulving, Schacter, & Stark, 1982), and the speed of reading an inverted version of the word (Kolers, 1976). Tulving (1983) has interpreted the persistence of such enhancement effects as evidence that "priming" does not reflect an influence on semantic memory, for example, a reduction in the threshold of a logogen. Furthermore, he takes the independence of perceptual enhancement and recognition memory as evidence that perceptual enhancement does not rely on episodic memory.

Having eliminated these two forms of memory as a basis for perceptual enhancement, Tulving suggests that a third, rather poorly specified, form of memory is responsible. As will be discussed later, we believe Tulving was premature in dismissing the possibility that perceptual enhancement relies on the same form of memory as does performance on recognition memory and recall tests.

2. The Role of Attention

The effects of attention are another criterion that might be used to suggest that perceptual identification and episodic memory tasks are based on different memory systems. Generally, when assessed by explicit episodic memory tests, little or no memory has been found for items that were unattended during their prior presentation. As an extreme example, Moray (1959) presented words to the subject's unattended ear 35 times during a shadowing task and still found only chance recognition memory for those unattended items. Similar effects of attention have been found when items are visually presented. Fisk and Schneider 1984) found that recognition memory and frequency judgments of words that had served as nontargets were higher when the target words had been specified on the basis of meaning than on the basis of graphic characteristics, corresponding to an effect of levels of processing. Although effects of this sort are not sufficient to allow the conclusion that attention is necessary for memory, they do serve to relate attention, defined as differences in processing, to memory performance (Johnston & Heinz, 1978). Results from another condition reported by Fisk and Schneider provide more direct support for the necessity of attention for memory. In that experiment, subjects searched for target numbers among numbers presented at the corners of displays while being instructed to ignore words presented in the center of displays. The presentation rate of the displays was too fast to allow eye movements, resulting in foveal presentation of the to-be-ignored words. Later recognition memory of the previously ignored words was at chance level. Using a variety of procedures, other investigators have also reported evidence and arguments to support the conclusion that attention is required to produce memory.

Thinking of perceptual identification as being subject to the same influences as explicit episodic memory tasks, then, we would expect perceptual identification to also be affected by attentional variations in prior processing episodes. There are reasons to suspect, however, that attention plays no role in the effect of a prior presentation on later perceptual identification. First, effects on perceptual identification apparently are less reliant on variations in the type of prior processing than are recall or recognition memory. Whereas recall and recognition are influenced by level-of-processing manipulations (Craik & Tulving, 1975), superficial prior processing of a word (searching through the word for a target letter) does as much to enhance its later identification as does processing the meaning of the word (Jacoby & Dallas, 1981). Of course, in both the surface-feature judgment and the meaning-judgment conditions, the words were probably perceptually identified, which may be the only form of attention necessary for later enhancement of perceptual identification. This, however, raises a second possible basis for distinguishing perceptual and episodic tasks on the basis of memory: The forms of processing that are required for the perceptual enhancement effect may be automatic, that is, carried out without the necessity of attention. There is evidence that both the meaning (Marcel, 1983) and the phonemic characteristics (Humphreys, Evett, & Taylor, 1982) of a visually presented word are activated even under conditions that do not allow the person to report the word that has been presented. Activation of this sort might persist and act as the basis for the repetition effect in later perceptual identification.

A series of experiments carried out by the first author was designed to directly manipulate attention in a visual search task and observe its effect on subsequent perceptual identification. In the first phase of each of the experiments, words were presented at a rapid rate (e.g., 300 msec/word) at the same visual location so that words were subject to both forward and backward masking. Subjects were instructed to search through these words for members of a specified target category (e.g., animal names). The phenomenological experience in this task is not one of actively searching through a list of words but rather of members of the target category "jumping out" or being seen clearly against a background of visual noise that comes from the presentation of nontarget words. This experience of only seeing the target words has been attributed to there being an attentional response to the target words but not to the nontarget words (Shiffrin & Schneider, 1977). The notion seems to be that both targets and nontargets are fully processed but only target words gain awareness. In a second phase of each experiment, words that had previously served as targets and those that had served as nontargets were mixed with new words and presented for a test of perceptual identification. For this test, words were flashed for a short duration (e.g., 35 msec), followed by a mask, and subjects were to report the word that had been flashed.

If attention plays a role in producing the effect of repetition in perceptual identification, the probability of identifying words that served as targets during the first phase of the experiment should exceed that of identifying words that served as nontargets. Prior target words, however, may gain an advantage due to repetition of the category in addition to any advantage gained from repetition of the particular words representing that category.

That is, an advantage in later identification of prior target words may be due to attention to their category rather than being due to attention to the particular words. In support of this possibility, Fisk and Schneider (1983) have employed a visual search task and found substantial transfer from searching for a given set of targets to searching for new targets from the same taxonomic category. To check the sufficiency of this possibility, some of the words that were new on the identification test were taken from the target category, making it possible to separate effects of category repetition from those of repeating particular words.

In the first experiment, subjects were instructed to search through a rapidly presented list of 40 items for either animal names or clothing names. Both animal names and clothing names were included in the list so that members from the one category served as nontargets while those from the other category served as targets. The 40-word list comprised 6 target items, 6 nontarget items, and 28 fillers. Half of both the target and nontarget items were high-frequency words and the other half were low-frequency words. After the list had been presented, subjects were asked to recall the target items that had appeared in the list. In a second phase of the experiment, a test of perceptual identification was given. New words on this test were equated in number, category membership, and frequency in the language with old words, words presented in the first phase. The probability of perceptual identification served as the primary dependent variable.

The results of the first experiment are displayed in Table I. In line with the results of prior experiments, high-frequency words were more likely to be correctly identified than were low-frequency words, and words that were old were more likely to be correctly identified than were words that were new on the perceptual identification test. More important, the effects of prior presentation were larger for words that had served as targets in the prior "search" phase than for words that had served as nontargets. That

TABLE I

PROPORTION CORRECT PERCEPTUAL IDENTIFICATION AS A FUNCTION OF PRIOR ATTENTION

| | Category | | | |
| | Target | | Nontarget | |
Frequency	Old	New	Old	New
High	.86	.69	.76	.72
Low	.53	.40	.46	.44

is, the effect of previously presenting a word on its later identification did depend on attention to that word during its prior presentation. Furthermore, the effects of prior presentation were restricted to the particular target words that had been presented rather than generalizing to new members from the target category. Items from the target category were not identified any more readily than were new members from the nontarget category. Later experiments in this series confirmed the advantage of the target words over nontargets and furthermore demonstrated that the gain was actually at the expense of the nontargets, a further confirmation of the effect of attention in a prior episode on later perceptual identification.

In combination, these experiments strongly support the notion that attention on a single prior trial does affect perceptual identification. The marked effect of attentional variations during a single prior episode certainly does not suggest that the perception of a word is largely based on an automatic process that changes only across many trials. Rather it provides another area in which there is a clear continuity between the bases of perceptual identification and explicit episodic memory tasks.

3. The Effect of Variability in Prior Processing Episodes

More qualitative variations in attention in a prior processing episode also affect perceptual enhancement. The experiments described in this section demonstrate that variability in processing due to manipulations of context and task play a role in determining perceptual effects that are comparable to that observed in recognition memory and recall. And, as with these explicit episodic memory tasks, the effects in perception critically depend on the compatibility of the study processing with that demanded at the time of test.

Variability in perceptual processing is evident in the research designed to specify the unit of processing that underlies speech perception or reading. McNeill and Lindig's (1973) findings for speech perception provide a clear example. They note that Savin and Bever (1970) required listeners to detect the presence of phonemes or syllables in a list of syllables; they used the shorter detection latency of syllables to conclude that syllables are the unit of speech perception. The important extension of this finding reported by McNeill and Lindig is that minimum reaction times occur whenever the linguistic level of the target and that of items in the search list are the same. Phonemes are detected most rapidly in a search list comprising phonemes; syllables are detected most rapidly in a search list comprising syllables; etc. It is the match between the target and search lists rather than the particular level of the unit that is important. Thus, no one level of unit is more "real" or fundamental than is any other level.

In a parallel to the data used as evidence for the encoding specificity principle, the match between the unit of study processing and that of test has also been shown to be important for the effects of training on later perception. In their investigations of the reading of inverted text, Kolers and Magee (1978) required students to either name letters or read text as training for subsequent letter naming or text reading. Transfer was maximal when the units presented for test matched those of earlier training. Practice in reading text was good training for reading text but provided less transfer to letter naming than did prior practice naming letters. Similarly, reading of text benefitted more from practice reading text than from practice naming letters. Letters in a textual context are apparently processed differently than are letters in isolation, and the similarity of processing at study and test is important for transfer.

Effects that can be attributed to a mismatch in unit size have also been found in investigations of perceptual identification of words. Osgood and Hoosain (1974) report that presenting wordlike nominal compounds such as *peanut butter* did not enhance later tachistoscopic identification of the individual words in the compound. In contrast, presenting nouns in ordinary noun phrases (e.g., copper block) was found to result in later enhanced identification of the nouns in isolation. They interpret their results as evidence that the meaning of the individual words in nominal compounds is lost in the larger unit and that this change in meaning is responsible for the lack of an influence on later identification of the individual words. Perceptual identification is seen as utilizing feedback from central mediational processes concerned with meaning. The use of nominal compounds, however, is not the only means of finding an influence of context change on later perceptual identification. Monsell and Banich (1983) presented words either individually or embedded in a sentence during training and then presented words individually, intermixed with nonwords, for a lexical decision test. The effect of the prior presentation on later lexical decisions was reduced when the words were presented in sentences rather than individually.

Jacoby (1983b) has also demonstrated processing specificity effects in perception resulting from variations in the amount of data-driven or conceptually driven processing during the prior presentation. In his experiments, a word was presented to be read either in isolation (xxxx *cold*), or in the context of its antonym (*hot cold*), or was not presented to be read but was generated from its antonym as a cue (*hot* ???). Later tachistoscopic identification of the target word (*cold*), presented individually, was highest when the word had previously been read in isolation, next highest when the word had been read in context, and poorest when the word had previously been generated but not read. An opposite ordering of conditions was found when a recognition memory rather than a tachistoscopic identification test was given. Presumably, conceptually driven processing of target words was dominant when they were generated in the first phase of the experiment, whereas data-driven processing was dominant when words were read in isolation. In agreement with prior research, recognition memory improves from increases in "deeper," conceptually driven processing, the processing of meaning (e.g., Craik & Lockhart, 1972). Effects in perceptual identification are reliant on prior processing as are those in recognition memory. For perception, however, it is the extent of data-driven rather than that of conceptually driven processing that is the important determinant of later performance.

These effects due to variations in level and size of unit suggest a way to retain the notion of abstract units that is a key part of the logogen model. One could propose that the units at each of the levels have corresponding thresholds that can be temporarily lowered by their prior use. Effects in perception of the sort that would be taken as evidence of encoding specificity in investigations of memory can then be explained as being due to a mismatch between study and test of the activated units of perception. In contrast to the extreme variability in processing that is thought to be reflected by recognition memory performance, variability in perceptual processing would be constrained to differences in the units that are processed. By proposing units at a number of different levels, however, the number of representations is greatly increased and the generality of at least some of those representations is decreased, which diminishes the attractive simplicity of the model. In addition, this still leaves the difficulty, discussed earlier, with retaining the key notion of a temporary lowering of thresholds. Rather than being temporary, the effects of a prior presentation are so persistent as to cause problems for a logogen model and other hierarchical, abstracted unit models such as that proposed by McClelland and Rummelhart (1981). Further difficulties for a logogen view are created if the visual appearance of a word that is read is remembered and influences its later perceptual identification. Since a word can assume an essentially infinite number of shapes prior to its presentation, there is potentially no representation of its word shape whose threshold can be lowered. Evidence that changes in "surface characteristics" such as the visual details of a word reduce the effect of prior study on later perception is reviewed in Section II,A,4.

In summary, perceptual identification is strongly influenced by variations in the type of processing that occurs on single prior processing episodes. This supports treating much of perception as relying on the same type of memory as do explicit episodic memory tasks. Notice, however, that this does not force us to predict that performance on recognition memory and perceptual identification will always be correlated. Both the Jacoby and

Dallas studies (1981) and the Jacoby (1983b) study show that the two measures can rely on different aspects of the processing in the prior processing episode.

4. Memory for Surface Characteristics

By the traditional cognitive framework, the memory underlying the tasks of recognition memory or recall is more specific than that underlying perception. For recognition memory, a person must remember the time and place that an event occurred along with the superficial details of that prior event such as who said what and the particular words that were said. The memory underlying perception, in contrast, has been described as being more general, the superficial details that distinguish one member of a class of events from another having been discarded. In light of this contrast, it is important for us to demonstrate that effects of prior experience on later perception reflect memory for supposedly superficial characteristics of that prior experience.

In trying to make this argument for the effect of superficial details in perception, we must avoid a trap. If we demand that effects in perception be specific to superficial characteristics of an event before being willing to conclude that memory for prior episodes is involved, then we would be demanding that perception reflect more detailed episodic memory than does recognition memory, a task that, by definition, relies on memory for prior episodes. In fact, of course, explicitly episodic tasks often do not reveal an effect of changing supposedly superficial characteristics of an item between its study and test. Even when there are effects on recognition memory of changing the type font of an item (Kirsner, 1973), the speaker's voice (Craik & Kirsner, 1974), or the syntactic form of a sentence (Sachs, 1967), they are often small and sometimes short lived. Although changing environmental context between study and test does have an effect on recall, it does not influence recognition memory (Eich, 1980). Based on this evidence of weak memory for details in episodic tasks, there has been a push toward proposing representations that are at a higher level of abstraction for recognition memory as well as for perception. This emphasis on lack of memory for surface characteristics has led to the claim that it is only memory for meaning that is retained over the long term. The possibility, however, that memory primarily relies on abstract representations has been substantially refuted in a thorough review by Alba and Hasher (1983). In our view, the abstractive notion overlooks the very wide variance among different processing episodes.

Our claims, then, are (1) there is no reason to believe that there is necessarily a difference in the role of abstraction between explicitly episodic tasks and generalizing tasks and (2) the prevalance of abstraction has been overestimated in explicit episodic memory tasks. According to these claims, both kind of tasks can show many effects of surface details. To support these claims, we first shall discuss the factors that vary the importance of surface characteristics in recognition memory tasks. Next, we shall argue that the same factors are important for finding evidence that perception can rely on the details of memory for a prior episode.

Novelty or distinctiveness is one factor that influences retention of surface characteristics as measured by a test of recognition memory or recall. For example, McDaniel (1981) reported better memory for the surface characteristics of the more complicated self-embedded form of sentences than for that of more standard forms. The orientation of text is better remembered if the text was inverted or in some other unusual orientation during study rather than being in a normal orientation (Kolers, 1976). The influence on recognition memory of changes in type font between study and test is larger for nonwords than for words (Hock, Throckmorton, Webb, & Rosenthal, 1981). It seems that surface characteristics are most likely to be remembered in areas in which people have little expertise, resulting in their dealing extensively with the surface characteristics.

The claim that memory for surface characteristics is enhanced when people lack expertise with a particular type or material or task implies that gaining expertise always results in poorer memory for details such as type font, voice, or modality. Characteristics of this sort, however, are so relevant to some tasks that gaining expertise at those tasks should result in better, not poorer, memory for supposedly superficial characteristics. As an example, the interpretation of a sentence sometimes depends on its syntactic form, the particular words that are said, and whether the sentence is spoken by a male or by a female. In this vein, subjects maintain relatively accurate memory of surface characteristics when sentences are high in interpersonal content, leading to surface characteristics having an influence on the pragmatic inferences that are drawn (e.g., Keenan, MacWhinney, & Mayhew, 1977). Memory for the sex of the speaker is also relatively well remembered when the sex of the speaker influences the interpretation of a sentence (Fisher & Cuervo, 1983). Similarly, Hock *et al.* (1981) manipulated the task that subjects engaged in during study such that the type font of a presented item was made relevant to the task under one set of conditions but irrelevant under another set of conditions. A change in type font between study and test produced a larger reduction in later recognition performance when type font had been relevant for the prior task. In essence, if you use it, you don't lose it.

The effects of changing surface characteristics between training and a later perceptual identification test generally parallel those observed in recognition memory tasks. A change in environmental context does not reduce the influence of a prior presentation of a word on its later perceptual identification (Jacoby, 1983a). The effects of changes in type font are small and restricted to words that are tested in lower case. For words tested in lower case, previously reading the word in upper case produces less enhancement than does having read the word in lower case; significant facilitation, however, as compared to new items, is still observed (Jacoby & Witherspoon, 1982). Morton (1979) reports that reading words in a handwritten format confers as much benefit to later tachistoscopic identification of those words presented in a typed format as does having previously read the words in a typed format. Previously reading a word, however, does more to enhance its later visual perceptual identification than does either having previously heard the word (e.g., Jacoby & Dallas, 1981; Morton, 1979) or having previously generated the word as a response to some cue (Jacoby, 1983b; Winnick & Daniel, 1970) in the experimental setting. Transfer is only reduced, not eliminated, by a change in modality; previously generating (Jacoby, 1983b) or hearing (Kirsner, Milech, & Standen, 1983) a word sometimes does act as a source of transfer for later visual perceptual identification. Transfer between the visual and auditory modality is asymmetrical, being larger for visual to auditory identification of words than for the converse. This asymmetry in transfer might be due to subjects saying words to themselves that are presented to be read during study (Postman & Rosenzweig, 1956). That is, the asymmetrical transfer may be due to differential ease of translation in the direction from the written to the spoken form of a word as compared to the spoken to written form. Although with more difficulty and, perhaps, less reliability, hearing a word does sometimes result in access to the visual form of the word (Seidenberg & Tannenhaus, 1979). It has not yet been determined what proportion of the transfer across modalities, if any, is due to translation between surface forms rather than being due to the involvement of some abstract representation of meaning that is shared by auditory and visual forms of a word. But conversely, there is the same doubt about the necessity of assuming the mediation of abstract representations.

When subjects are required to engage in a novel perceptual task, changes in surface characteristics between practice and test have a substantial impact on perceptual performance. In his investigations of the reading of transformed text, Kolers and his colleagues have found that the effects of prior training are specific to the orientation of the text read during practice; changes in orientation between practice and test typically produce a substantial reduction in the amount of transfer that is observed. Even after a year, there is an advantage in reading speed for sentences that were previously read in the unusual orientation as compared to new sentences read in the same orientation (Kolers, 1976). Furthermore, transfer to reading sentences in an unusual orientation is specific to the typeface and spacing of letters read during training. Kolers, Palef, and Stelmach (1980) report that skill at reading text improved more from practice naming letters as the order of approximation to English of the letters was increased, but only if the letters were aggregated rather than being widely spatially separated. Furthermore, transfer was substantially reduced if the typeface of letters that were named was different from that of the text that was to be read. Kolers interprets his data as evidence that people remember the operations that they carried out so that no distinction can be made between surface characteristics and meaning; that is, knowledge is always source dependent.

The arguments that surface characteristics can affect perception and that the effect depends on task demands at study were supported in a recent series of experiments of our own. The notion underlying these experiments was that the effect of changing surface structure between practice and a perceptual test, like effects observed in recognition memory, would depend on whether subjects had been required to make use of the surface structure during the prior practice. The perceptual task that was employed was that of requiring subjects to name a degraded version of a picture. This choice of tasks was inspired by the evidence that amnesics are able to name a degraded version of a picture better if they had previously named an intact version of the same picture (Milner, Corkin, & Teuber, 1968). This influence of prior experience on the naming of pictures by amnesics is nearly as large as that shown by normals, although after having named a degraded version of the picture, amnesics profess to have no memory of having earlier named an intact version of the picture. It seemed to us that it is important to find out how specific the influence of prior experience on picture naming is in order to gain an understanding of the memory deficit suffered by amnesics. It could be that the amnesics' transfer only depends on a previously presented picture having the same name as does the later-presented degraded picture. If surface structure is not remembered, practice on the same picture that is to be tested may provide no advantage over practice with a different picture that has the same name. In support of this possibility, Milner (1970) suggests that effects in picture naming revealed by amnesics do not reflect new learning. Rather, the prior presentation of the intact version of the picture is seen as priming its name, information that is already in memory. Alternatively, transfer may be specific to the particular picture that was named during practice. Specificity of this sort would provide evidence that the amnesics are capable of remembering the particular new pictures that they are shown even though they may not be aware that they are doing so. In keeping with one of the main points of this section, we would also expect that this ability would depend on task demands at the time of study.

Our initial experiments were with normals and were aimed at developing procedures that would give us a fine-grained picture of the role of task demands in the specificity of transfer in both normals and amnesics. The test procedure that we developed uses a digitizer in combination with an Apple computer to vary the degree of degradation of presented pictures. This presentation procedure builds a picture by illuminating point locations on a television monitor. To produce degraded pictures, a portion of the points constituting a plot of a picture were intermixed with noise, points that were extraneous to the plot of the picture. The pictures presented at the beginning of a test trial were extremely degraded; very few points from the picture were presented and were intermixed with a large amount of noise. By pressing the return key on the computer, a subject could clarify the picture by increasing the ratio of points from the picture to noise points. A subject was to continue pressing the return key until he or she could name what was pictured. The number of key presses prior to a correct response along with the total amount of time that elapsed served as measures of perceptual identification performance.

Pictures in the test sequence were either identical to a picture that had been previously presented (identical), shared the name of a previously exposed picture but were not identical to that picture (name match), or were unrelated to any previously presented picture (new). The number of key presses required to identify a picture plotted across these three types of test picture corresponds to a transfer gradient. Extreme specificity in transfer would be evidenced by facilitation of the identical pictures and no facilitation of the name pictures as compared to new pictures. A lack of memory for the surface structure of pictures would be evidenced by no difference in the identification of pictures in the identical and name match conditions.

Several training conditions were run in order to investigate the effect of task demands on the specificity of the transfer. In one condition, subjects were simply instructed to name the presented pictures during this practice phase of the experiment. For subjects in a second condition, pictures were presented in a slightly degraded form and subjects went through a very abbreviated version of the clarification procedure that would be employed for the later test of perceptual identification. The procedure was abbreviated in that it took very few key presses to fully clarify the picture. Subjects in this abbreviated clarification condition were required to clarify the picture until they could name it. After they had correctly named the picture, it appeared fully clarified on the screen. The abbreviated clarification procedure was expected to require subjects to deal more extensively with the visual details of the picture than would simply naming the picture presented originally in a fully clarified form. Because of this differential processing of detail, transfer to the later test phase was expected to be more specific to the picture previously presented for subjects in the abbreviated clarification condition as compared to subjects in the condition that simply named pictures in the first phase of the experiment. That is, having previously clarified the picture should result in more transfer to identical pictures and less transfer to name match pictures than would having previously named the pictures. The results of this experiment are displayed in Table II.

In line with our expectations, the specificity of transfer did reflect the differential processing of pictures during their prior presentation. For subjects who only named fully clarified pictures in the first phase, the perceptual identification measure returns little evidence of memory for surface structure. The number of key presses required for identification did not differ greatly for identical and name match pictures. Test pictures of both sorts required fewer key presses for their identification than did new pictures. In contrast, there is more evidence that surface structure was remembered when subjects engaged in an abbreviated clarification procedure while viewing pictures in the first phase of the experiment. In that condition, identical pictures were identified after fewer key presses than were name match pictures. The difference between conditions in the identification of identical pictures might be attributed to the operations required by the test procedure being more similar to the operations required by the abbreviated clarification procedure than to those required to simply name the picture during its prior presentation. Later experiments in the series showed, however, that instructions to prepare for a forthcoming recognition memory test facilitated later identification of identical pictures nearly as much as did requiring subjects to engage in an abbreviated clarification procedure. Furthermore, requiring subjects to go through a prior full clarification procedure that was identical to that required for the later test did not enhance identification of identical test pictures any more than did requiring subjects to go through only an abbreviated clarification procedure. Results produced by recognition memory instructions and those produced by prior experience viewing a picture by means of going through the full clarification procedure were nearly identical to the results displayed in Table II for the abbreviated clarification condition. Thus, although there was certainly an effect of task demands on

TABLE II

CLARIFICATION STUDY: NUMBER OF BUTTON
PRESSES BEFORE IDENTIFICATION

	Identical	Similar	New
Name	37.3	40.7	55.4
Clarify	34.2	45.5	56.2

the specificity of transfer, there was not the specific dependence on the particular extent of clarifying operations that we would have liked.

In a related experiment, Warren and Morton (1982) first presented a set of pictures and then compared the tachistoscopic identification of identical pictures, pictures that only shared the same name as a previously viewed picture (name match), and new pictures. Similar to our results from the abbreviated clarification condition, Warren and Morton found that identical pictures were more likely to be correctly identified than were name match pictures, although both types of picture were more accurately identified than were new pictures. Warren and Morton interpret their results as evidence that perceptual identification of pictures partially relies on an abstract representation of the appearance of objects sharing a name. This abstract representation is termed a *pictogen* and is seen as being similar to the logogens said to underly word perception. The identification of name match pictures reflects the priming of a pictogen. To account for the advantage in identifying identical pictures over name match pictures, Warren and Morton suggest that memory for the particular picture that was previously viewed as well as the threshold of a pictogen can contribute to later perceptual identification.

A hybrid model of the form proposed by Warren and Morton encounters some difficulty accounting for the results of our experiment. Their model does not allow for an influence of task demands during practice on later identification. Some effects of task demands, however, could be easily incorporated by their model. It could be claimed that requiring more attention to the visual detail of a picture resulted in better memory for the particular picture but had no further influence on the threshold of the relevant pictogen. These assumptions would be sufficient to account for any facilitation in the identification of identical pictures that came from requiring subjects to further process visual detail. Requiring further processing of visual detail during the first phase of our experiments, however, not only enhanced the identification of identical pictures but also slowed the identification of name match pictures. This reduction in transfer to name match pictures is difficult to explain within the context of Morton's model since there seems to be no reason to believe that further processing of a picture should raise the threshold of its corresponding pictogen. Warren and Morton admit the possibility that repeated exposure to a picture results in a new pictogen being developed. Rather than number of exposures being the important factor, our results suggest that it is task demands that control memory for detail. One could claim that it is possible to create a new pictogen with a single prior presentation of a picture under some circumstances, but this eliminates the difference between a pictogen model and an instance-based model of transfer. Work that is currently going on in our labs is aimed at finding manipulations of task demands that have a larger influence on the specificity of later transfer. Manipulations of this sort are seen as being important for understanding the performance of normals as well as that of amnesics.

In general, the view that we are advocating is that the role of "surface" characteristics in memory will depend on the prior processing conditions and their match with processing conditions at retrieval. There is neither reason to believe that details are always important at some stages nor that later stages necessarily drop them. And, in keeping with our general point, the variable role of the details of prior processing episodes are visible in perceptual identification as well as in explicit episodic memory tasks.

B.   CONCEPTUAL CATEGORIZATION

Concept learning has traditionally been the bastion of analytic and abstractive thinking. For most of its history, in both the hands of the behaviorists and those of the information processors, this field was construed as the study of how people acquired the stable, context-free resources that allow generalization to novel situations. Regardless of whether these resources took the form of prototypes, schemata, frames, diagnostic rules, or even differential habit strength, there was an almost exclusive concentration on the abstraction of the "relevant" (individually correlated with the category) features from the "irrelevant" or "surface" features in the learning instances. In the terms presented earlier in this article, this was a concentration on analytic generalization; generalization based on identifying units by means of relevant features. Recently, however, there has been interest in schemes of concept learning based on nonanalytic generalization, that is, based on the close similarity of new events to whole past events (Brooks, 1978; Hintzman & Ludlam, 1980; Medin and Schaeffer, 1978; Medin & Smith, 1981; Medin & Schwanenflugel, 1981). In line with this literature, our aim in the current section is to show that conceptual categorization does not have to be, and possibly is not usually, dependent on abstract units that change only slowly with experience. We shall also show a dependence on the processing of specific prior episodes comparable to that documented in the previous sections for perceptual identification.

We shall start with a recent experiment from our lab (to be reported in Brooks, Jacoby, & Whittlesea, 1984) that was designed to compare the relative importance of category prototypes and specific experience in determining the ease with which familiar objects could be categorized. Subjects were shown a set of 12 slides (initial study, IS): three cups, three bottles, three glasses, and three "other" glass items, all presented on a plain background. The subjects' task was to rapidly answer one of three categorical questions that immediately preceded the presentation of each slide: "Is it [the object in the up-coming slide] a cup?'', ''Is it a glass?'', ''Is it a bottle?''. In a continuous sequence, the subjects were then asked to perform the same task with a test sequence of 38 slides. Three of these slides were category prototypes for the three categories, that is, examples that the subjects after the test series rated as highly typical of the category. If the subjects' categorical judgments were being determined by typicality, by some form of closeness to the prototype, then these prototypes (or at least near prototypes) should be categorized more rapidly than the more deviant examples used throughout the rest of the experiment. And indeed, as is shown in Table III, the prototypes (P) were categorized more rapidly than either the initial items or a set of new items (new different, ND) that were mixed randomly into the test sequence with the prototypes. The ND slides were drawn from the same pool of items as were the IS items, all of which were selected to be easily distinguishable from one another. Thus, the conditions of the experiment were sufficient to obtain the usual classification advantage for more typical members of a category over less typical new items.

The intent of the study, however, was to show the effect of specific experience within the immediate experimental context. Twelve of the test slides were repeats (IS_2) of the IS items, and these items were classified faster than were the prototypes. So far this merely repeats the advantage of specific training exemplars that has been reported from the beginning of the work on prototypes (e.g., Posner & Keels, 1968). The result of major interest, however, is the effect on the categorization times of items that were only similar (new similar, NS), rather than identical, to the IS items. These NS items were selected to be clearly distinguishable from, but also clearly similar to, one member of the IS set; for example, one IS item was a child's yellow cup with a lion painted on it; the corresponding NS item was a blue cup of the same shape that had a dog painted on it and was

TABLE III[a]

VERIFICATION TIMES FOR YES RESPONSES (MSEC)

	Study phase	Test phase			
	IS_1	IS_2	NS	P	ND
Immediate	268	214	225	237	278
24-hour delay	301	207	211	218	245

[a] IS_1, First presentation of initial study items; IS_2, test presentation of initial study items; P, prototypes, items rated as very typical; NS, new similar items, similar to IS items; ND, new different items.

lying on its side. Another pair was two demitasse cups, similar in ornateness, but clearly differing in color, type of decoration, and fluting on the rim. The categorization times of these NS items were in fact facilitated over the ND items. The facilitation of the NS items from one prior presentation of a similar item was sufficient to put them in the vicinity of the prototypes. Again, the major result is that items that only resembled examplars previously seen *once* in the current experimental context were categorized at least as rapidly as items that presumably were receiving the benefit of many hundreds of exposures to cups, bottles, or glasses.

So far the results could be produced by the temporary modification, some form of priming, of stable categorical identification procedures. If so, then these results would require only a mild modification of the view that attributes the lion's share of processing variance to a stable cognitive prototype. The results of a test series, however, that was run 24 hours after the 12-slide IS series were the same in the order of comparisons mentioned above. The duration of the effects suggests specific learning rather than a temporary, rapidly decaying modification of an essentially stable identification routine, such as a prototype or pictogen. Whatever is different about the experimental context and whatever is distinctive about the items as presented on the slides are sufficient to weigh impressively against any stable structures that might be operating. Both this study and the picture clarification study shown in Table II show the same strong effect on picture categorization of the supposedly irrelevant aspects of prior processing episodes. These results are also reminiscent of the finding that one prior trial of a words presentation (in Jacoby & Dallas, 1981) essentially wiped out a word frequency effect; word frequency, like the current effect of typicality, presumably is based on many hundreds of trials of accumulated prior experience. None of these studies rules out the possibility that under some circumstances there is a general abstracted form of knowledge available for the categorization of new objects. But they do demonstrate that this form of knowledge does not operate in a clear field; the lessons of specific experience are impressive competitors with material that is well within the range acceptable for testing prototype theories.

The object identification study, just described, and the clarification studies were originally aimed at different literatures and probably reflect the different backgrounds of the two authors. The clarification study is focused on variations in the processing of the same stimulus due to task demands, a characteristic of recent memory research. The cups–bottles–glasses experiment, in keeping with the concept-learning literature, is primarily concerned with the basis of transfer to new stimuli. Yet they both demonstrate the importance of individual prior processing episodes for picture identification. This type of convergence reinforces our belief that the processing episode perspective encourages cross-talk among areas often seen as separate: in this case, incorporating processing variations in concept-learning studies and concern about the structure of a transfer space in studies originating in memory problems.

The importance of considering variations in the processing of individual items was shown in a set of concept-learning studies that debated the conditions under which one would expect analytic as opposed to nonanalytic generalization. The studies, reported by Reber and Allen (1978), and, in reply, Vokey and Brooks (1983), all used strings of consonants, such as *TTXMT* and *VXM*. The order of the letters in these strings were sequenced according to an artificial grammar whose existence was mentioned to the subjects only after a set of the strings had already been studied. Reber and Allen proposed that presenting the strings as the stimuli in paired-associate learning (*TTXMT–Denver, VXM–Boston*), as had been done by Brooks (1978), would encourage subjects to differentiate the strings and would subsequently allow only nonanalytic transfer to new strings; that is, a new string would be categorized as having been generated by the same set of rules used for the study items only if it had close overall resemblance to at least one of the study strings. But if the subjects were merely to observe strings as they were being shown at a 5-sec-per-item rate, then conditions would be sufficiently nondirective that *implicit* abstractive mechanisms would be free to operate. Under this condition, then, Reber and Allen expected subjects to show analytic transfer, that is, categorization based on the grammaticality of the new items rather than their overall similarity to individual old items. Their results showed that subjects in the observation condition were, if anything, more accurate at categorizing than were those in the paired-associate condition. If one expected better nonanalytic transfer when the items were learned better, then this result would suggest that something other than nonanalytic transfer was operating; it was the observation condition, which produced less accurate recognition memory for the old items, that showed more accurate classification of the new items.

Vokey and Brooks argued that these results did not require hypothesizing that the subjects were unconsciously abstracting the grammar. Instead, as a result of differences in item processing among the study conditions, the old items might be generalizing to different ranges of new items. The old stimuli in the paired-associate conditions could be so differentiated that they would seem similar to few of the new items. As a result, responding to the new items would show few false alarms in recognition memory and few "grammatical" responses; only a small number of the new items would be seen as similar enough to any of the old items to be judged as probably having been generated by whatever rules had generated the old items. The items studied under the observation condition would be expected to show more false alarm recognitions and more classifications as "grammatical." Since in a rule system of this sort the grammatical items might be expected to resemble one another more than they resemble the ungrammatical items, responding with the laxer criterion of similarity used by the observation, subjects would be expected to produce more correct responses than would the more stringent criterion used by the paired-associate subjects. An even more stringent shift in criterion was expected in an additional condition in which subjects were given mnemonics for the study items (*VXM* = virgins expect miracles). To evaluate these possibilities, test items were used in which grammaticality and similarity to old items were unconfounded. For example, *VXR* differs in just as many letters from *VXM* as does *VXT,* but *VXT* violates the grammar that generated all of the study items and *VXR* does not; using both of them as test items allows us to unconfound the two variables that are normally confounded in the world and experiments alike. The results showed that a large majority of the variance was accounted for by the hypothesized shift in criterion of similarity to old items, leaving little, if any, reason in these data to hypothesize implicit abstraction. As in previous studies discussed in this article, the intent is not to claim that abstractive, analytic transfer never occurs. But these results do show the importance of nonanalytic transfer as well as the usefulness of considering variations in the processing of individual items in concept-learning experiments.

Again, this Vokey and Brooks study has an interesting parallel with the clarification study (Table II). In both cases the major manipulation was designed to vary the specificity of processing at study. In both cases greater specificity of processing of the study items decreased the range of categorical generalization, that is, no facilitation of the perception of other pictures in the same category and fewer judgments of "grammatical" for similar items. Thus, both pictorial identification and judgments of "well-formedness" showed sensitivity to a processing variable that normally has been associated with explicit episodic memory tasks. And finally, both studies were directed against the same type of claim: Implicit grammars and prototypes are the same sort of abstract resource as the logogens and semantic nodes on which human cognition was supposed to have routinely depended.

The variability of processing and its later effects on conceptual categorization raises a problem: The training conditions embedded in the common paradigms may be giving us a one-sided picture of generalization—a residual bias because of cognitive psychology's long emphasis on analytic generalization. Both the rule tradition (Bruner, Goodnow, & Austin, 1956; Bourne, 1974) and the "fuzzy category" tradition (Rosch, 1978; Posner & Keele, 1968) often use training conditions that do not encourage reasonably well-integrated processing of training items: Many similar stimuli are presented for few trials per item, with little information unique to the individual items. Even when unique information is given, it often simply adds to the load already imposed by the original volume of categorical information. Such training conditions are quite natural to select if the investigator already is thinking of concept learning as an analytic process, as normally being a shortcut that learners use to avoid having to learn about all of the variants of a category. But these experimental conditions are exactly those that might provide a strong motivation for the learners to reduce their learning load by analysis, by isolating a few predictive features. Even in experiments in which signs of nonanalytic transfer have been found, it often seems to result from the classification rule being so complicated that the subjects are virtually forced into individuating the items (Brooks, 1978; Medin & Schaffer, 1978; Vokey & Brooks, 1983). These considerations suggest that there are normal, even common, learning conditions that are not being represented in the concept-learning literature. For example, we often have relatively extensive interactions with a few instances of a new category before we are exposed to large numbers of them. A child's exposure to the family dog or furniture, or an adult's exposure to new equipment are examples. Furthermore, these exposures are likely to be confounded with particular contexts, a fact that suggests the possibility of context-specific generalization. The point is, a consideration of the conditions of processing at study could be very important in the concept-learning literature as well as in perception and memory.

One of the properties of nonanalytic transfer that has not been appreciated in psychology until recently is that it will produce many different patterns of results when applied to domains with different structures. Hintzman and Ludlam (1980) demonstrated that a strictly instance-based model could simulate results that have been taken as strong evidence for prototype theories. For example, previously unseen prototypes would be responded to at the same or better level than the old items from which they presumably had been derived, and the advantage of the prototype increased over time—presumably as the details of the individual instances were forgotten. These results arise in a theoretical stimulus space in which the training instances are clustered around the center, the prototype, of the distribution. If, in the instance model, the new items are responded to better the closer they are to an old item, then new items near the middle of a centrally clustered distribution will be responded to best. The central clustering of the old instances, argued by Rosch (1978) to be typical of natural categories, also means that if an item on the periphery is forgotten, then the effect on subsequent classification will be more severe than will be the forgetting of an item in the center where there are other neighboring old items. The results of Hintzman and Ludlam's simulation, in which an instance-based model simulated abstractionist results, suggest the same type of caution in attributing observed consistency to a single, central abstraction that we have been urging throughout this article.

With different distributions of study items and with different degrees of integration in processing, however, a nonanalytic model can in principle produce a variety of outcomes other than the classic abstractionist patterns. This is well illustrated in a series of experiments by Whittlesea (1983) for both conceptual categorization and perceptual identification. Whittlesea's materials were pseudowords generated as variations from two prototypes: *nobal* and *furig*. Some of the variations on the *furig* prototype are shown in Fig. 1. The pseudowords could vary in the number of letters by which they differed from the prototype; all of the pseudowords on the second ring, for example, differ from the prototype by two letters. They could also independently differ from a training item by various numbers of letters; if

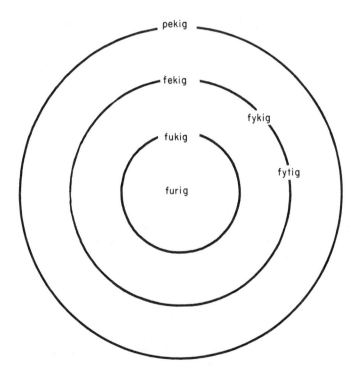

Fig. 1. Schematic representation of one set of stimuli from Whittlesea's experiments (1983). *Furig* is the prototype for this set. *Fekig, fykig,* and *fytig* all differ by two letters from the prototype. If *fekig* is a training item, then *fykig* and *fytig* would be test items that differ from it by one and two letters, respectively. These stimuli were used to unconfound distance from old and distance from the prototype.

fekig were a training item, then *fykig* and *pukig* would differ from it by one and two letters while still being only two letters from the prototype. In the perceptual identification studies, training simply consisted of three trials of copying down the training items as they appeared one at a time on the screen. The perceptual identification measure was the number of letters correctly reported in position in a rapid, masked presentation of the pseudoword. In the classification studies, the subjects were told that they would be shown two classes of pseudowords, some of which were nouns and some of which were verbs. Training consisted of three trials of copying down the pseudowords that were labeled as nouns with an -*ism* affix, *fekigism* from *fekig*; or, those labeled as verbs with an -*ing* affix, *notyling* from *notyl*. The dependent variables were the accuracy and confidence of classification of the same test series used in the perceptual identification studies.

Since the results were essentially the same for both the perceptual and the classification studies, they will be discussed together. If training consisted of three trials apiece on a few items (five from each prototype) on the second ring, then new test items from the first ring (closer to the prototype) were classified and seen better than items on the third ring—a simulation of the prototype results. The *new* items on the second ring, however, were responded to better if they were one away from the nearest training item than if they were two away, which suggests that analogy to the old items was important. But if the training items were moved out to the third ring, then there was little facilitation of response to the items on the first ring, even though the nominal prototypes, *furig* and *nobal,* were still the centers of the distributions. In this case one would expect a much smaller advantage for being close to the apparent prototype, an expectation that was confirmed. For example, a one-away (from closest old) item on the fourth ring was seen and classified better than a two-away item on the third ring; in this case, closeness to the apparent prototype was outweighed by closeness to the training item. The general picture given by these results was confirmed in detail in several other studies and analyses.

The point of these experiments is that nonanalytic transfer is observed when the encoding of items is reasonably well integrated, as presumably was assured by the subjects' prior experience with word pronunciation [which itself could be due at least partially to analogy (Glushko, 1979; McClelland & Rumelhart, 1981)]. Experiments in progress are designed to vary the degree of integration of the processing at study and hopefully produce the variations in ranges of transfer shown in the Vokey and Brooks studies. The hope here is to continue in the direction that we have been advocating in this article, namely, varying the type of processing at study in order to change the type of generalization. There is no reason to assume that all generalization is analytic, based on units abstracted over a large number of previous trials.

Finally, we would like to make two additional comments about nonanalytic transfer. The first is that the conditions under which abstraction, be it deliberate or automatic, provides an effective approximation to the complexity of the world are far more circumscribed than is generally appreciated. It strains credulity that people can do some of the pieces of analysis that they would have to do to produce the various unconscious orthographies, grammars, social systems, and game strategies that abstractionist theories attribute to them. Nonanalytic generalization can simulate these structures without requiring incredible feats of analysis, as demonstrated, for example, by the ability of McClelland and Rummelhart's (1981) interactive model to simulate English letter sequence rules without having any such rules directly represented. In addition, nonanalytic transfer is, by its very nature, likely to be very sensitive to local variations in complicated domains. This sensitivity to local variations could be important for fast, accurate perception as well as for conceptual categorization. The point is, under some circumstances, nonanalytic generalization is the process of choice, particularly if one is trying to account for where the cognitive resources came from (Brooks, 1983).

Our second comment is that we have been speaking as if nonanalytic transfer involves only the single most similar instance or episode. In fact, the context model of Medin and his colleagues (Medin & Schaffer, 1978; Medin & Smith, 1981), Hintzman's Minerva II model (Note), and Whittlesea's high metric (1983) all allow an effective influence of several similar items. This has the effect of computing a very local average at the moment of test, a local "chorus of instances." Since it is local, it would have some of the advantages of (small sample) averaging and yet still be able to simulate a complicated domain.

C. A Summary of the Parallel: A Processing
Episode View of Generalization

In the preceding sections, we have argued that the generalizing tasks of perception and categorization are as susceptible to the influences of individual prior episodes as are the explicitly episodic memory tasks, such as recognition and recall. We have attempted to document parallels between the two types of tasks on characteristics that traditionally were supposed to distinguish them. Both types of task show a long-term effect of individual prior episodes, not just the temporary priming that was supposed to be distinctively true of perception. They both show selective effects of attention and of the quality of encoding in single prior processing episodes. And they both show specific and variable effects of the nominally irrelevant surface features of an item's presentation.

In this preceding discussion, we were arguing against the abstractionist framework that has long dominated cognitive psychology. In that framework generalization was supposed to be carried out almost exclusively by means of units that were abstracted across nominally irrelevant surface information. Since that framework sought to understand cognition by means of a stable architecture, it tended not to look for variation due to changes in the specific situation. This encouraged premature conclusions about the invariability of processing; that is, it suppressed the search for different relations among tasks. In our view there are a variety of ways various cognitive tasks can be accomplished, and consequently there are probably a variety of relations among tasks. In attempting to understand the relationships among these tasks, we are arguing for the heuristic value of paying close attention to the type of processing carried out at study and the compatibility of the prior processing with that demanded at the time of test.

In the following section, we shall apply both sides of this approach to topics in episodic memory. That is, we shall try to document relationships among different tasks that are too variable to encourage interpretation in terms of stable systems. And we shall illustrate the heuristic value of close attention to processing conditions for topics that have not normally been treated this way.

III.   Nonanalytic Processing in Explicit Episodic Memory Tasks

Abstractionist assumptions have had an effect on theorizing about explicit episodic memory tasks as well as on the generalizing tasks discussed in the preceding section. In this section, we shall discuss two issues for which we believe an approach that stresses the explanatory value of variable processing yields a wider perspective than does the traditional view.

A.   Separate Memory Systems and Memory for Source

Failure to remember the source of information that is itself remembered has recently become an important topic in memory research. In its mild form, examples of this phenomenon are commonplace; we often remember having previously heard some opinion or argument being expressed without remembering who expressed the opinion or made the argument. At an extreme, forgetting the source of a message takes the form of remembering without awareness; people's performance provides evidence for memory of a prior experience even though they deny being able to remember it at all. Amnesics provide the most dramatic examples of source amnesia simply because their explicit, reflective memory performance is so bad. For example, amnesics show gains from practice of a pursuit-rotor task (Corkin, 1968), despite claiming that they don't remember having ever performed the task before. In a more cognitive task, amnesics show the effect of a prior reading in their speed of reading inverted text (Cohen & Squire, 1980). In another clearly verbal task (Jacoby & Witherspoon, 1982), amnesics gave more low-frequency spellings of homophones (e.g., *reed* rather than *read*) when they had recently *heard* the homophone in a question that biased its meaning toward the low-frequency spelling ("Name a musical instrument that employs a reed"). This effect in spelling was independent of recognition memory for the previously heard homophones. Similar types of dissociations have also been found with normals. For example, the influence of a prior presentation of a word on its later perceptual identification can be statistically independent of recognition memory of the word (Jacoby & Witherspoon, 1982; in addition to similar evidence in Jacoby & Dallas, 1981; and the Jacoby, 1983b, studies described earlier). Effects of prior experience with words in the completion of word fragments (Tulving *et al.*, 1982) and the reading of inverted text (Kolers, 1976) have also been found to be independent of recognition memory.

The dissociation of memory for source and memory for content is usually attributed to the two types of information being represented in different memory systems. The preserved memory for content in amnesics is said to rely on semantic memory (Kinsbourne & Wood, 1975), procedural memory (Cohen & Squire, 1980), or some other memory (Tulving, 1983). Memory for source, as tested by recognition memory or recall tests, is supposed to rely on a separate memory system: episodic (Tulving, 1983) or declarative memory (Cohen & Squire, 1980). These proposals of separate memory systems encounter problems similar to those faced when proposing separate logogen systems or different units of analysis to describe interactions between memory for surface and that for meaning. In the face of specificity of effects, such as those reviewed earlier in this article, one is forced to increase the number of logogens, the levels of units, or the memory systems proposed. As the number of abstract representations is increased, the difference between a purely episodic view and an abstract representational view is reduced. If one tries to limit this proliferation by allowing some combination of memory for prior episodes and more abstract representations to mediate cognitive behavior, then the factors that choose the level of representation that is most important for a particular combination of study and test circumstances must be specified. Specifying these factors seems to necessarily involve examining interactions among tasks, materials, and subject differences—the approach that we advocate as a starting point. The point is that such a hybrid of abstractions and particulars does not achieve the situational independence, the prediction of function from the nominal task that was once a selling point for an abstractive view.

Another major difficulty for these accounts is that the relationship between memory for source and memory for content is a variable one. Although effects of prior study in perceptual identification and recognition memory are sometimes independent of one another, dependence is also sometimes found. For example, Witherspoon (Jacoby & Witherspoon, 1982) found independence between perceptual identification and recognition memory of words, but found dependence between these measures when pseudowords were used. Again, if one were to try to explain these variable relationships by saying that sometimes the systems were sensitive to the same factors and sometimes they were independent, one would have to specify increasingly complex situational variables, an approach, we suspect, that will not turn out to be sufficiently flexible.

We expect variable relations between measures of source and content in memory for the same reasons we used to understand the variable relations between memory for surface information and memory for meaning. In fact, by our view, the problem of source amnesia is identical to that of forgetting surface characteristics. Although not usually described as such, the finding that a change in voice between study and test has no influence on recognition memory could as well serve as an example of source amnesia as an example of forgetting of voice information. Memory for the voice in which a communication was heard constitutes a part of the memory for the source of the communication as does memory for the particular words and syntactic form that were used to convey the communication. When source is identified with memory for a prior episode, as is done by employing tests of recognition memory, memory for surface characteristics is clearly implicated. The particular aspects of surface characteristics that are thought to be important usually are not specified. But when they are, it is usually memory for the time or the location of the prior presentation of an item that is said to be important. It seems to us that time and location do not differ in kind from other surface characteristics such as typeface or syntactic form.

By identifying source with surface characteristics, Tulving and Kolers can both be seen as taking too extreme a position on the relationship between memory for source and memory for content. By our reading of Tulving's position, his claim is that content is always remembered separately from its source, since the two involve separate memory systems. The content along with its surface characteristics constitute an episode that is retained in episodic memory, whereas the content stripped of its surface characteristics is represented by an abstract representation in semantic memory or some other memory system. It is this abstract representation that is said to be responsive to "priming" and whose existence allows effects in perception to be independent of recognition memory judgments. By Kolers' view, in contrast, content is never remembered separately from its source since it is the operations by means of which the knowledge was acquired that are remembered. In view of the variable memory for surface characteristics shown in investigations of recognition memory and perceptual identification, both positions appear to us to be too extreme. It seems that sometimes source is remembered separately from content, sometimes forgotten although the content is remembered, and sometimes largely ignored; that is, analytic processing is possible. On the other hand, source and other surface characteristics are sometimes very well remembered and are not easily separated from memory for content. That is, processing is sometimes nonanalytic in the sense that source and content are not treated as being separate dimensions.

In our view, the details of prior processing are critical in determining the relationship between performance on tests of explicit memory for source and effects of varying source between study and test. Of particular importance is whether source and content were treated as being separate or as being more integral during the prior processing episode. As an example, consider memory for a seminar that one has attended (cf. Keenan *et al.,* 1977). Interpreting a comment or a theoretical argument made by a participant in the seminar is the processing episode. One could treat the speaker and his comments as separate aspects of the episode. If so, we would expect that presenting the comments for test in the same or a different voice would have little influence on recognition memory or perceptual identification. If the content were remembered separately from its source, then memory or perceptual judgments about content would not rely on the accessibility of memory for source. Even though manipulations of source between study and test had no effect, however, an explicit test of memory for source could still show that source was remembered. The source was an aspect of the same processing episode as was the content, allowing the content to be used as a cue for recall of the source. But this recall of the source would *follow* recognition memory or perceptual identification of the content rather than being integrally involved in that recognition memory or perceptual identification. When source and content are treated as being separate during the prior processing episode, identification of source on an explicit memory test would be expected to be independent of effects of maintaining versus changing the source when requiring memory or perceptual judgments. We would interpret this independence as evidence that processing had been analytic with regard to memory and source in the prior processing episode rather than as evidence that different memory systems were involved.

Our analysis would be favored, if not compelled, by the contrasting case of integration of source and content. For example, the speaker's comments might have been high in interpersonal content, so that the content of the communication could not easily be interpreted separately from its source (Keenan *et al.*, 1977). As a result of this more nonanalytic processing, presenting the comments in the same rather than a different voice for test would result in a person being more likely to claim to have heard the comments before or later being more able to interpret a perceptually degraded version of the comments (identifying words in the comments when they are later played through noise, completing word fragments, tachistoscopic identification, etc.). Not having been separated during prior processing, memory for source would contribute to memory and perceptual tests of content rather than being accessed after the content is recognized or perceptually identified. After nonanalytic processing, we expect dependence between recognition memory or perceptual judgments and explicit memory for source, since source and content cannot be initially accessed separately from one another. Effects of source on judgments, however, can still be accompanied by a failure to show explicit memory for source. Indeed, an increase in dependence between recognition memory or perceptual judgments and explicit reports of source might even be accompanied by a reduction in the overall accuracy of explicit reports of source. When given a test of explicit memory for source, subjects are being asked to treat memory for source separately from memory for content. The tighter the integrality of the prior processing of source and content, the more difficult it would be to later separate them. Increasing the integrality of the prior processing of source and content, then, could have the apparently paradoxical effects of increasing the effects in recognition memory or perceptual identification of manipulating source between study and test while decreasing the probability that a person will show evidence of explicit memory for source by being able to report the source, isolating the source from the content. When people encounter difficulty isolating memory for source from that for content, it seems possible that they abandon attempts to do so, and they employ a more nonanalytic basis for responding even when a given explicit tests of memory for source. That is, rather than attempt to isolate memory for source from that for content, subjects may use a basis for responding that reflects the combined effects of memory for source and that for content. We consider this possibility in the next section.

B. Nonanalytic Judgments in Explicit Memory Tasks

To this point, we have argued that the generalizing tasks of perceptual identification and conceptual categorization can be performed in two general ways: analytically and nonanalytically. The difference between analytic and nonanalytic judgments can be characterized as the extent to which subjects rely solely on definitionally relevant information. When subjects are asked to categorize a new object, they are being asked to assess whether this object has the characteristics that generally determine membership in the category selected. If this is accomplished by noting that the new object has great overall resemblance to a known member of the category, then the definitionally relevant and definitionally irrelevant information are not being analyzed apart. Similarly, if the person is asked to identify a word, he or she is not being asked directly to assess the similarity of the item to its occurrence in a prior processing episode. Basing the identification on a particular prior processing episode is again not fully analyzing the definitionally relevant from the nominally irrelevant details.

Our argument has been that cognition has consistently emphasized analytic processing, with consequent limitation of perspective in experimental designs and theorizing. We now apply the same argument to explicit episodic memory tasks. In tasks such as recognition memory, the subject is asked to judge prior occurrence. Any information that links the item to a specific prior episode is definitionally relevant for the task. But the judgment could also be made by a fluency heuristic, namely, "If I can process this item so much more easily than other items in the list, I must have seen it before." If recognition memory is accomplished by a heuristic such as this, one that does not separate definitionally relevant from irrelevant information, then it is being accomplished in a way that is nonanalytic in the same sense that we used for the generalizing tasks. In this case also, we believe that there has been too strong a tendency to treat these tasks as if they could only be done using definitionally relevant information. In the following sections, this analysis will be applied to three types of tasks for which prior episodes are definitionally relevant. Again, we shall argue that considering the heuristic, nonanalytic ways in which the task can be done will result in a broader perspective on the problems. And, as with the generalizing tasks, the mode of processing at the time of judgments will depend heavily on details of the prior processing, details that are too variable to encourage treating memory judgments as reflecting the operation of discrete, independent memory systems.

1. Nonanalytic Judgments of Recognition Memory: A Fluency Heuristic

Mandler (1980), as well as others (e.g., Atkinson & Juola, 1974), has suggested that recognition memory judgments can be based either on familiarity or on the retrieval of study context. The retrieval of context is the more analytic and the more conservative basis for recognition memory in that the context in which the test item occurred is definitionally relevant for a test of prior occurrence in a particular, usually the current, context. For analytic memory judgments, such as the reconstruction of an event, a person can engage in more analytic processing to gain external justification. In contrast, recognition on the basis of familiarity can be seen as being a nonanalytic judgment that is similar to judgments made in concept-learning experiments that are attributed to intuition. In concept-learning experiments, classification on the basis of overall similarity, which we have characterized as nonanalytic judgments, result in the relevant dimensions not being isolated from definitionally irrelevant ones; consequently, a decision cannot be justified by specifying the defining dimensions. If pressed for justification, the learner is likely to claim that his or her classification was based on intuition or, simply, a guess. This combination of above-chance classification performance accompanied by the claim that classification performance is based on guessing or intuition is a relatively common one and is reminiscent of the dissociation shown by amnesics. When presented with word fragments as cues for recall of words in a previously studied list, amnesics are able to correctly complete the fragments although they claim to be only guessing (Weizkrantz & Warrington, 1975). A claim of a feeling of familiarity as a justification of memory recognition, like a claim of intuition in categorization, is sometimes deemed unsatisfactory, barely differing from a guess. In general, recognition memory based on the feeling of familiarity has several aspects in common with intuitive categorization. For both, the judgment is relatively rapid, not easily justified, and subject to error.

If familiarity were a directly accessible attribute of an item in memory, then judging on the basis of familiarity would still have a considerable quality of analytic processing. We would prefer, however, to view familiarity as an attribution rather than an attribute. Some items on a recognition memory test are processed more fluently than others, and this difference in processing can be used as a heuristic for the recognition memory decision. Recognition memory judgments based on judgments of relative fluency are nonanalytic in that the definitionally relevant dimensions relating to the prior presentation of an item in the experimental setting are not isolated from definitionally irrelevant aspects of an item that contribute to its fluency of processing. For example, frequency in the language influences ease of word identification but is not definitionally relevant to a recognition memory judgment. Also, whether the item is written in the same format is definitionally irrelevant to whether the item itself had occurred previously, but it could contribute to ease of processing and a recognition judgment based on it.

This use of fluency of processing to judge prior occurrence is similar to using the availability heuristic to estimate probabilities (Kahneman & Tversky, 1973). When using the availability heuristic, a person infers that a class of events is a probable one if an instance of that class can readily be brought to mind. When using the fluency heuristic, the person infers that an item must have occurred before if it can be processed relatively more easily. In both cases, subjects in principle also have recourse to means of making judgments that are more analytic. Contrary to one's expectations, if only a nonanalytic heuristic were being employed, judgments of recency and judgments of frequency (probability) can apparently be based on different information, being relatively independent of one another (Underwood, 1969). Our account of the fluency heuristic differs from that of an availability heuristic in placing greater emphasis on variability in encoding and retrieval processes than did Kahneman and Tversky. That is, we attempt to explicate differences in fluency by referring to current theorizing about memory and concept formation.

Reliance on a fluency heuristic for recognition memory judgments would result in a correlation between ease of perceptual identification and the probability of calling an item "old." That is, words that are readily perceived should be judged to be old. Feustel, Shiffrin, and Salasoo (1983) have presented data that shows such a correlation between perceptual fluency and recognition memory judgments is sometimes obtained. Their procedure for testing perceptual identification involved intermixing the presentation of a word and that of visual noise; the visual signal-to-noise ratio of the printed word was slowly increased so that the presented word appeared to clarify across time. The increase in clarification continued until the presented word could be named, providing a measure of identification time. After a presented word had been named, it appeared fully clarified and subjects were required to judge whether the word had been presented previously. In this procedure, words that were readily perceived were likely to be judged as being old. The correlation between identification time and the false alarm rate was −.78, showing more rapid perceptual identification of words that gave rise to false alarms as compared to those that were correctly rejected. For "hits," the correlation between identification time and the hit rate for items on their second presentation was −.84. For both hits and false alarms, then, subjects were likely to judge words that were readily perceived as being old. Conceivably, this correlation could be interpreted as resulting from words that were mistakenly judged as being old being processed in a faster, less cautious manner. We think, however, that it is more reasonable to interpret the correlation as arising from a tendency to judge items that are readily perceived, for whatever reason, as being old.

Despite the high correlation between identification time and recognition memory judgments evidenced by their data, Feustel *et al.* express doubt that judgments of perceptual fluency play an important role in recognition memory decisions. They note that perceptual fluency is an unreliable cue for recognition memory and that some variables produce differential effects in recognition memory and perceptual identification, which suggests that performance on the two types of test can be independent of one another. It is the variable relationship between perceptual identification and recognition memory, however, that we have stressed and that we see as being important for differentiating our view from that of theorists who claim that recognition memory and effects in perceptual identification rely on separate memory systems (Tulving, 1983). Familiarity derived from differences in perceptual fluency is only one of the bases a subject could use to judge prior occurrence.

As mentioned in Section III,A, we expect that a subject's willingness to rely on nonanalytic judgments will vary with materials and task demands. Some materials provide relatively little opportunity for analysis as a means of arriving at a recognition memory judgment and so encourage nonanalytic judgments. For example, Witherspoon (Jacoby & Witherspoon, 1982) found that recognition memory performance was independent of perceptual identification for words, whereas for nonwords, dependence in performance on the two measures was found. The independence observed with words was interpreted as evidence that recognition memory can rely on retrieval of study context, a form of processing that is not important for perceptual identification of words tested out of context. Because of their lack of meaning and the consequent reduction in relationships among study items, recognition memory of nonwords was said to rely more heavily on the use of the fluency heuristic, producing dependence of perceptual identification and recognition memory judgments. Further evidence of the importance of materials comes from an experiment by Johnston, Dark, and Jacoby (1984). They used a procedure similar to that employed by Feustel *et al.* (1983) to examine the relationship between identification time and recognition memory judgments but, like Witherspoon, examined the relationship for nonwords as well as for words. In agreement with the results of Feustel *et al.,* they found a correlation between identification latency and the probability of an "old" recognition memory decision. Classifying on the basis of recognition memory decisions, hits and false alarms were identified with a shorter latency and more accurately than were misses and correct rejections—words responded to as being new. This correlation between ease of identification and the probability of an old recognition memory decision was higher for nonwords than for words.

The correlational data are consistent with the claim that a perceptual fluency heuristic is used as a basis for recognition memory judgments. A correlation between identification latencies and recognition memory judgments could arise, however, from sources other than the application of a fluency heuristic. Two types of data are required to provide more firm support for the conclusion that subjects sometimes employ a fluency heuristic when making recognition memory judgments. First, it would be useful to show that the magnitude of the correlation between identification time and recognition memory varies across tasks and materials in a predictable manner. The experiments by Johnston *et al.* provide evidence of this sort. Second, if judgments of fluency do serve as a basis for recognition memory decisions, it should be possible to manipulate fluency by a means other than prior presentation of an item and to find effects in recognition memory judgments. This possibility suggests an experiment that is the converse of that done by Whitherspoon and Allan (1984). Witherspoon and Allan found that a prior presentation of a word influenced the judged duration of its later presentation. Conversely, differences in true duration may also influence recognition memory judgments. If recognition memory decisions are based on an evaluation of overall ease of processing, subjects may misattribute true differences in duration to differences in prior study. That is, one can tamper with the validity of the cues offered by differences in overall processing and examine effects in recognition memory judgments. Experiments of this sort are planned.

2. Nonanalytic Judgments for Meaning and for Surface Characteristics

When a subject is asked to judge whether a current item means the same thing as a previously seen item, changes in surface characteristics such as syntax or synonyms are nominally irrelevant. As discussed earlier, the abstractionist view is that meaning is remembered separately from surface structure and, therefore, can be isolated as a basis for judgments. This view also claims that memory for surface structure is lost very rapidly so that only meaning is retained over the long term. If processing is nonanalytic, however, we expect changes in surface structure to influence judgments of meaning. Earlier, we briefly reviewed the results of experiments that demonstrated that surface structure can be retained over the long term and that meaning and surface structure are sometimes integrated to an extent that does not allow one to easily treat the one dimension in isolation from the other. In this section we shall discuss the effect of the nonanalytic judgments of surface and meaning information.

A recent experiment by Masson (1983) is an excellent demonstration of judgments of meaning being influenced by variations in surface structure. Following Kolers (1979), Masson presented words in either a normal or an inverted typography to be read in the first phase of his experiment. In the second phase of the experiment, both the orientation of previously read sentences and their wording was manipulated. Sentences read in the second phase were either in the same or a different orientation and were either a verbatim or a paraphrased version of a sentence that had been read earlier. After subjects read a sentence in this second phase, several judgments were required. First, they were to judge whether the sentence had the same meaning as did a sentence that they had previously read. If they judged that the sentence did have the same meaning, they were to judge whether the sentence was in the same or a different orientation and whether it was a verbatim or paraphrased version of the earlier read sentence. An important finding was that both the manipulation of orientation between study and test and the manipulation of wording influenced judgments of meaning. Subjects were more likely to judge a sentence as being the same in meaning if it was a verbatim repetition read in the same orientation as it was during its prior reading. Judgments of orientation and judgments of verbatim as opposed to paraphrase were also not independent of one another. A paraphrased version of a sentence presented in the same orientation as its previously read counterpart was more likely to be judged as being a verbatim repetition than if orientation was changed between study and test. A change in orientation was less likely to be detected if the sentence presented at test was a verbatim rather than a paraphrased version of a previously read sentence.

The pattern of results reported by Masson is important in that it shows a lack of independence between judgments of surface structure and those of meaning. Prior experiments have shown that a verbatim version of a sentence can be identified more rapidly than a paraphrased version as being the same in meaning (e.g., Begg & Wickelgren, 1974; Hayes-Roth & Hayes-Roth, 1977). Effects of paraphrasing, however, are not necessarily due only to an influence of surface structure. Paraphrasing can produce subtle changes in meaning, producing effects that are due to a change in meaning rather than a change in surface structure. It is difficult to make a comparable claim when interpreting the influence of changes in orientation on judgments of meaning. The orientation of a sentence that is read is clearly definitionally irrelevant to its meaning. Effects in judgments, however, produce evidence that subjects were unable to isolate the nominally relevant dimension of meaning from the nominally irrelevant dimension of surface structure. That is, judgments of meaning were nonanalytic.

Other results reported by Masson can be taken as evidence that subjects judged meaning by using a fluency heuristic of the sort described for recognition memory. Subjects might rely on judgments of their fluency of reading sentences as a heuristic for recognition memory judgments. That is, subjects might expect sentences that mean the same as a sentence read earlier to later be read more easily and faster and use differences in reading fluency as a heuristic for judgments of recognition memory for meaning.

If subjects were relying on a fluency heuristic, sentences that were read faster at test should be judged to be old rather than new in meaning. The procedure of requiring subjects to read test sentences prior to making the required judgments allowed Masson to look at the relationship between reading speed and recognition memory judgments of meaning. In line with the possibility that subjects relied on a fluency heuristic, sentences that were judged to be old in meaning were read faster than those judged to be new. Classifying sentences on the basis of judgments of recognition memory for meaning, both hits (18.77 sec) and false alarms (18.48) were read faster than were misses (22.57 sec) and correct rejections (20.66 sec). Similar to results taken as evidence of a fluency heuristic for recognition memory of words, there was a correlation between reading speed of sentences and judgments of their meaning.

Fluency of reading might also be used as a heuristic for other judgments of meaning. A possibility that we find particularly interesting is that students might judge their comprehension of reading assignments or lectures by a nonanalytic means that is similar to a fluency heuristic. When talking to students, one gains the impression that they use their lack of "stumbling" as a criterion for judging their comprehension of material. If they can read through a chapter without being forced to backtrack, they are convinced that they understand the material and are then outraged when they do poorly on a classroom examination covering that material. By our view, the classroom examination requires evidence of more analytic processing as a measure of comprehension than did the nonanalytic measure that students employed to assess their comprehension when reading the material.

3. Nonanalytic Judgments of Source

Marcia Johnson and her colleagues have pointed out that accurate memory for source is necessary for people to monitor reality—to discriminate between memory for external events (perception) and memory for internal ones (thoughts). Johnson and Raye (1981) provided a summary of research on reality monitoring and a framework for its interpretation. Several experiments that they reviewed provided evidence that subjects can discriminate between memories obtained from an external source, such as reading, and memory obtained from an internal source, such as memory for an answer that subjects generated themselves. In line with our own observations, Johnson and Raye note that the relationship between recognition memory and memory for source is a variable one. Recognition memory and memory for source in some cases respond in the same way to experimental variables and in other cases appear to be affected in opposite ways (Johnson, Raye,

Foley, & Foley, 1981). To explain this variable relationship, they suggest that judgments of source rely on attributes of memory for an event such as memory for the speaker's voice or a person's memory for how a thought of his own related to his other thoughts or his goals in a situation. The variable relationship is supposed to result from the attributes of memory that are important for judgments of source not necessarily being the same attributes that subjects rely on when making judgments of recognition memory.

Although we agree that memory for source can rely on analytic judgments involving the isolation of attributes of a memory, we believe that judgments that are less analytic may also play an important role. For example, Johnson and Raye report a general finding that when subjects felt that a completely new item was familiar (a false positive), they were much more willing to attribute it to an external source than to say that they had generated it. That is, subjects expect self-generated information to have an advantage in memory and may be biased toward claiming that they generated items that they remember well. A bias of this sort is similar to the fluency heuristic that we have described for recognition memory judgments. The correlation between identification latency and recognition memory judgments could also be described as being due to a comparable bias. Subjects are biased toward calling items "old" that they can identify very readily.

Describing effects of this sort as being a bias, however, carries the risk of overlooking the potential validity of differences in ease of identification as a basis for recognition memory judgments. A single prior presentation of a word does have large and persistent effects on its later identification so differences in perceptual identification can serve as a valid cue for recognition memory decisions. Similarly, subjects are correct in their belief that self-generated material has an advantage in memory (e.g., Jacoby, 1978; Slamecka & Graf, 1978). Differences in "familiarity" generally provide a valid cue for judgments of source, although as we repeatedly encounter and work with somebody else's ideas, we may take them on as our own, forgetting the real source and being guilty of unintentional plagiarism. Describing nominally irrelevant dimensions as producing bias and nominally relevant cues as influencing sensitivity may be a separation of dimensions that is descriptive of the experimenter's behavior but not that of the subject's. The subject may not isolate the two types of dimensions but rather make nonanalytic judgments that reflect their combined effects.

The accuracy of nonanalytic judgments of source is likely to depend on the extent that source and content were processed interdependently during prior study. As an example further to those mentioned in the memory for source section, sex of the speaker may contribute to the intepretation of the message with the result that information about source is not remembered separately from the content of the message. If so, the message will later be interpreted more easily if it is delivered by the same speaker rather than a different one. In this circumstance, judged ease of interpretation, a nonanalytic judgment, will provide a partially valid basis for judgments of source. In contrast, if source and content were previously processed separately from one another, nonanalytic judgments of source should be particularly prone to error. A repeated message delivered from the same source as it was earlier will not be processed any more readily than would be the same message delivered from a different source; differences in ease of processing will not serve as a valid cue for judgments of source.

C. THE IMPORTANCE OF NONANALYTIC PRIOR PROCESSING FOR MEMORY

The nature of prior processing is as important for the relations among later tests of memory as it is for concept learning. The processing assumed in the traditional accounts of analytic generalization in concept learning parallels that assumed by theories that view memory for an event as being a collection of attributes (e.g., Underwood, 1969), both in the idea of a fixed set of features and in their lack of integration. We share Kolers and Smythe's (1983) reluctance to speak in terms of a fixed set of attributes. The notion of a fixed set of attributes shares a major problem with that of a fixed number of levels of unit size or number of memory stores, that of not providing a convenient means of describing variability across situations. Regardless, if one does choose to describe memory for an event as a collection of attributes, it is clearly necessary to specify the relationships among those attributes. Integral processing of attributes provides a basis for nonanalytic memory judgments as well as a basis for nonanalytic classifications in a concept-learning task. In contrast, relatively separate processing disposes toward later analytic judgments and probable independence of generalizing and explicitly episodic memory tasks. We believe that dependence in performance among these two types of tasks (e.g., Jacoby, 1983b; McKoon & Ratcliff, 1979) is at least as common and as important as is the normally assumed independence. Furthermore, we believe that theories of memory necessarily contain assumptions, albeit sometimes hidden in a semantic memory, about the nature of concept learning. Proposing an episodic memory that is separate from semantic memory corresponds to a hybrid model of concept learning that describes both memory for prior episodes and more abstract representations as playing a role in classification judgments. Accordingly, the earlier discussion directed at those theories of concept learning is also relevant to theories of memory. By our view, both memory judgments and classification judgments depend heavily on the details of prior processing, details that are too variable to encourage treating judgments as reflecting the operation of discrete, independent representational systems that differ in their level of abstraction.

IV. Summary and Conclusions

Taking nonanalytic cognition into account has considerable heuristic value. From this perspective many of the standard relationships and questions change drastically. In traditional analytic cognition, acts of perception, memory, and concept learning are generally discrete stages that often occur in a fixed order. First an item is perceived, then the person searches through memory for a match, and then categorizes the item, if required. In nonanalytic cognition, both perception and categorization are acts of memory that can rely on one or more prior episodes. By our view, memory for episodes is not something that can only be searched after perception of a test item but, rather, memory for episodes contributes to the perceptual identification of the test item; perception and memory are not discrete acts. The same flexibility discussed in connection with interactive models, well illustrated by McClelland and Rummelhart (1981), also is gained by emphasizing the importance of nonanalytic processing of item and context. Most important to us, however, is that an emphasis on nonanalytic processing encourages cross-talk among areas that are typically considered to be separate. Manipulations and materials that have been largely restricted to one area can be equally applicable to other areas. An example is the relevance for concept learning of manipulations of task demands common in investigations of memory. Task demands interact with characteristics of the material and those of the learner to choose between analytic and nonanalytic processing with the choice having important consequences for memory, perception, and concept learning.

An emphasis on nonanalytic cognition also has implications for training in applied settings, the choice among educational practices. Kemler (1983), studying children's judgments of change, has shown that children are more likely than adults to make nonanalytic judgments, to classify items on the basis of overall similarity, rather than isolating a dimension to be judged. For example, although differences in the size of stimuli are nominally irrelevant to judgments of their color, children sometimes respond as if color is not conserved across variations in size. Rudimentary analytic abilities are seen as being sharpened through experience, with their application being reliant on task demands. In contrast to this apparently natural developmental sequence, current educational practices often stress analytic approaches from the outset, attempting to provide the student with a set of rules, such as spelling or pronunciation rules, for analyzing a problem or for generating its solution, although the rules may apply only within a very limited domain. Perhaps treating similar situations analogously, via nonanalytic cognition, plays an important role in at least the earlier stages of learning. Given the prevalence of the nonanalytic effects reviewed earlier, however, we have little reason to assume that nonanalytic cognition is always simply an untutored basis for judgments. Rather, it may also be a way of exploiting the very local predictors provided by nominally irrelevant details, which may be the basis for true expertise in some areas.

We intend to continue to investigate the possibilities of nonanalytic cognition, exploring implications, seeking to recruit allies, and trying to differentiate our views from those of still others. We do not claim to have made any truly unique contribution, although we hope that we have pointed out the similarities among the work in several different areas. The prevalance of these types of results guarantees that there are people that we should have referenced but did not because of space limitations or oversight. If our work is seen as being only an elaboration of a new Zeitgeist, one that redresses the overemphasis on analytic processing, we shall not object.

Acknowledgments

Many of the themes in this article benefitted from the discussion at a recent conference, The Priority of the Specific, held at Elora, Ontario, June, 1983. Support for this conference by the National Science and Engineering Research Council of Canada and by McMaster University is gratefully acknowledged. The authors were also supported by individual grants from the National Science and Engineering Research Council.

References

Alba, J. W., & Hasher, L. Is memory schematic? *Psychological Bulletin,* 1983, **93,** 203–231.

Atkinson, R. C., & Juola, J. F. Search and decision processes in recognition memory. In D. H. Krantz, R. C. Atkinson, R. D. Luce, & P. Suppes (Eds.), *Contemporary developments in mathematical psychology* (Vol. 1), *Learning, memory and thinking.* San Francisco, California: Freeman, 1974.

Begg, I., & Wickelgren, W. A. Retention functions for syntactic and lexical vs. semantic information in sentence recognition memory. *Memory & Cognition,* 1974, **2,** 353–359.

Bourne, L. E., Jr. An inference model for conceptual rule learning. In R. L. Solso (Ed.), *Theories in cognitive psychology: The Loyola symposium.* Potomac, Maryland: Erlbaum, 1974.

Brooks, L. R. Non-analytic concept formation and memory for instances. In E. Rosch & B. Lloyd (Eds.), *Cognition and categorization.* Hillsdale, New Jersey: Erlbaum, 1978.

Brooks, L. R. *The insufficiency of analysis.* Paper submitted for publication, 1983.

Brooks, L. R., Jacoby, L. L., & Whittlesea, B. W. A., 1984, submitted.

Bruner, J. S., Goodnow, J. J., & Austin, G. A. *A study of thinking.* New York: Wiley, 1956.

Cohen, N. J., & Squire, L. R. Preserved learning and retention of pattern-analyzing skill in amnesia: Dissociation of knowing how and knowing that. *Science,* 1980, **210,** 207–210.

Corkin, S. Acquisition of motor skill after bilateral medial temporal-lobe excision. *Neuropsychologica,* 1968, **6,** 255–266.

Craik, F. I. M., & Kirsner, K. The effect of speaker's voice on word recognition. *Quarterly Journal of Experimental Psychology,* 1974, **26,** 274–284.

Craik, F. I. M., & Lockhart, R. S. Levels of processing: A framework for memory research. *Journal of Verbal Learning and Verbal Behavior,* 1972, **11,** 671–684.

Craik, F. I. M., & Tulving, E. Depth of processing and the retention of words in episodic memory. *Journal of Experimental Psychology: General,* 1975, **104,** 268–294.

Eich, J. E. The cue-dependent nature of state-dependent retrieval. *Memory & Cognition,* 1980, **8,** 157–173.

Feustel, T. C., Shiffrin, R. M., & Salasoo, A. Episodic and lexical contributions to the repetition effect in word identification. *Journal of Experimental Psychology: General,* 1983, **112,** 309–346.

Fisher, R. P., & Cuervo, A. Memory for physical features of discourse as a function of their relevance. *Journal of Experimental Psychology: Learning, Memory, and Cognition,* 1983, **9,** 130–138.

Fisk, A. D., & Schneider, W. Category and word search: Generalizing search principles to complex processing. *Journal of Experimental Psychology: Learning, Memory, and Cognition,* 1983, **9,** 177–195.

Fisk, A. D., & Schneider, W. Memory as a function of attention, level of processing and automatization. *Journal of Experimental Psychology: Learning, Memory, and Cognition,* 1984, **10,** 181–197.

Friedman, A. Framing pictures: The role of knowledge in automatized encoding and memory for gist. *Journal of Experimental Psychology: General,* 1979, **108,** 316–355.

Glushko, R. J. The organization and activation of orthographic knowledge in reading aloud. *Journal of Experimental Psychology: Human Perception and Performance,* 1979, **5,** 674–691.

Hayes-Roth, B., & Hayes-Roth, F. Concept learning and the recognition and classification of exemplars. *Journal of Verbal Learning and Verbal Behavior,* 1977, **16,** 321–338.

Hayman, C. A. G. *A task analysis of lexical decisions.* Unpublished Ph.D. thesis, McMaster University, 1982.

Hintzman, D. L. *"Schema abstraction" in a multiple-trace memory model.* Paper read at the Priority of the Specific conference, Elora, Ontario, June, 1983.

Hintzman, D. L., & Ludlam, G. Differential forgetting of prototypes and old instances: Simulation by an exemplar-based classification model. *Memory & Cognition,* 1980, **8,** 378–382.

Hock, H. S., Throckmorton, B., Webb, E., & Rosenthal, A. The effect of phonemic processing on the retention of graphemic representations for words and nonwords. *Memory & Cognition,* 1981, **9,** 461–471.

Humphreys, G. W., Evett, L. J., & Taylor, D. E. Automatic phonological priming in visual word recognition. *Memory & Cognition,* 1982, **10,** 576–590.

Jacoby, L. L. On interpreting the effects of repetition: Solving a problem versus remembering a solution. *Journal of Verbal Learning and Vebal Behavior,* 1978, **17,** 649–667.

Jacoby, L. L. Perceptual enhancement: Persistent effects of an experience. *Journal of Experimental Psychology: Learning, Memory, and Cognition,* 1983, **9,** 21–38. (a)

Jacoby, L. L. Remembering the data: Analyzing interactive processes in reading. *Journal of Verbal Learning and Verbal Behavior,* 1983, **22,** 485–508. (b)

Jacoby, L. L., & Dallas, M. On the relationship between autobiographical memory and perceptual learning. *Journal of Experimental Psychology: General,* 1981, **3**, 306–340.

Jacoby, L. L., & Witherspoon, D. Remembering without awareness. *Canadian Journal of Psychology,* 1982, **36**, 300–324.

Johnson, M. K., & Raye, C. L. Reality monitoring. *Psychological Review,* 1981, **88**, 67–85.

Johnson, M. K., Raye, C. L., Foley, H. J., & Foley, M. A. Cognitive operations and decision bias in reality monitoring. *American Journal of Psychology,* 1981, **94**, 37–64.

Johnston, W. A., Dark, V., & Jacoby, L. L. Perceptual fluency and recognition judgments. *Journal of Experimental Psychology: Learning, Memory, and Cognition,* 1984, in press.

Johnston, W. A., & Heinz, S. P. Flexibility and capacity demands of attention. *Journal of Experimental Psychology: General,* 1978, **107**, 420–435.

Kahneman, D., & Tversky, A. On the psychology of prediction. *Psychological Review,* 1973, **80**, 237–251.

Keenan, J. M., MacWhinney, B., & Mayhew, D. Pragmatics in memory: A study in natural conversation. *Journal of Verbal Learning and Verbal Behavior,* 1977, **16**, 549–560.

Kemler, D. G. Holistic and analytic modes in perceptual and cognitive development. In T. J. Tighe & B. E. Shepp (Eds.), *Perception, cognition and development: Interactional analyses.* Hillsdale, New Jersey: Erlbaum, 1983.

Kinsbourne, M., & Wood, F. Short-term memory processes and the amnesic syndrome. In D. Deutsch & A. J. Deutsch (Eds.), *Short-term memory.* New York: Academic Press, 1975.

Kirsner, K. An analysis of the visual component in recognition memory for verbal stimuli. *Memory & Cognition,* 1973, **1**, 449–453.

Kirsner, K., Milech, D., & Standen, P. Common and modality-specific processes in the mental lexicon. *Memory & Cognition,* 1983, **11**, 621–630.

Kolers, P. A. Reading a year later. *Journal of Experimental Psychology: Human Learning and Memory,* 1976, **2** (5), 554–565.

Kolers, P. A. A pattern-analyzing basis for recognition memory. In L. S. Cermak & F. I. M. Craik (Eds.), *Levels of processing and human memory.* Hillsdale, New Jersey: Erlbaum, 1979.

Kolers, P. A., & Magee, L. E. Specificity of pattern-analyzing skills in reading. *Canadian Journal of Psychology,* 1978, **32**, 43–51.

Kolers, P. A., Palef, S. R., & Stelmach, L. B. Graphemic analysis underlying literacy. *Memory & Cognition,* 1980, **8**, 322–328.

Kolers, P. A., & Smythe, W. E. Symbol manipulation: Altenatives to the computational view of mind. *Journal of Verbal Learning and Verbal Behavior,* 1983, in press.

Mandler, G. Recognizing: The judgment of previous occurrence. *Psychological Review,* 1980, **87**, 252–271.

Marcel, A. J. Conscious and unconscious perception: Visual masking, word recognition and an approach to consciousness. *Cognitive Psychology,* 1983, **15**, 197–237.

Masson, M. E. J. Memory for the surface structure of sentences: Remembering with and without awareness. *Journal of Verbal Learning and Verbal Behavior,* 1983, in press.

McClelland, J. L., & Rumelhart, D. E. An interactive activation model of context effects in letter perception: Part 1. An account of basic finding. *Psychological Review,* 1981, **88**, 375–407.

McDaniel, M. A. Syntactic complexity and elaborative processing. *Memory & Cognition,* 1981, **9**, 487–495.

McKoon, G., & Ratcliff, R. Priming in episodic and semantic memory. *Journal of Verbal Learning and Verbal Behavior,* 1979, **18**, 463–480.

McNeill, D., & Lindig, K. The perceptual reality of phonemes, syllables, words, and sentences. *Journal of Verbal Learning and Verbal Behavior,* 1973, **12**, 419–430.

Medin, D. L., & Schaffer, M. M. Context theory of classification learning. *Psychological Review,* 1978, **85,** 207–238.

Medin, D. L., & Schwanenflugel, P. Linear separability in classification learning. *Journal of Experimental Psychology: Human Learning and Memory,* 1981, **7,** 355–368.

Medin, D. L., & Smith, E. E. Strategies and classification learning. *Journal of Experimental Psychology: Human Learning and Memory,* 1981, **7,** 241–253.

Milner, B. Memory and the medial temporal regions of the brain. In K. H. Pribram & D. E. Broadbent (Eds.), *Biology of memory.* New York: Academic Press, 1970.

Milner, B., Corkin, S., & Teuber, H. L. Further analysis of the hippocampal amnesia syndrome. *Neuropsychologia,* 1968, **6,** 215–234.

Monsell, S., & Banich, M. T. *Lexical priming: Repetition effects across input and output modalities.* Paper presented at the 23rd annual meeting of the Psychonomic Society, in Minneapolis, Minnesota, 1983.

Moray, N. Attention in dichotic listening: Affective cues and the influence of instructions. *Quarterly Journal of Experimental Psychology,* 1959, **11,** 56–60.

Morton, J. Interaction of information in word recognition. *Psychological Review,* 1969, **76,** 165–178.

Morton, J. Facilitation in word recognition: Experiments causing change in the logogen model. In P. A. Kolers, M. E. Wrolstal, & H. Bonma (Eds.), *Processing of visible language i.* New York: Plenum, 1979.

Osgood, C. E., & Hoosain, R. Salience of the word as a unit in the perception of language. *Perception & Psychophysics,* 1974, **15,** 168–192.

Posner, M. I., & Keele, S. W. On the genesis of abstract ideas. *Journal of Experimental Psychology,* 1968, **77,** 353–363.

Postman, L., & Rosenzweig, M. R. Practice and transfer in the visual and auditory recognition of verbal stimuli. *American Journal of Psychology,* 1956, **69,** 209–226.

Reber, A. S., & Allen, R. Analogic and abstraction strategies in synthetic grammar learning. A functionalist interpretation. *Cognition,* 1978, **6,** 189–221.

Rosch, E. Principles of categorization. In E. Rosch & B. Lloyd (Eds.), *Cognition and categorization.* Hillsdale, New Jersey: Erlbaum, 1978.

Sachs, J. S. Recognition memory for syntactic and semantic aspects of connected discourse. *Perception & Psychophysics,* 1967, **2,** 437–442.

Savin, H. B., & Bever, T. G. The nonperceptual reality of the phoneme. *Journal of Verbal Learning and Verbal Behavior,* 1970, **9,** 295–302.

Seidenberg, M. S., & Tanenhaus, M. K. Orthographic effects on rhyming. *Journal of Experimental Psychology: Human Learning of Memory.* 1979, **5,** 546–554.

Shiffrin, R. M., & Schneider, W. Controlled and automatic human information processing: Perceptual learning, automatic attending, and a general theory. *Psychological Review,* 1977, **84,** 127–190.

Slamecka, N. J., & Graf, P. The generation effect: Delineation of a phenomenon. *Journal of Experimental Psychology: Human Learning and Memory,* 1978, **4,** 592–604.

Tulving, E. *Elements of episodic memory.* London and New York: Oxford Univ. Press, 1983.

Tulving, E., Schacter, D. L., & Stark, H. A. Printing effects in word-fragment completion are independent of recognition memory. *Journal of Experimental Psychology: Learning, Memory, and Cognition,* 1982, **8,** 336–342.

Tulving, E., & Thomson, D. M. Encoding specificity and retrieval processes in episodic memory. *Psychological Review;* 1973, **80,** 352–373.

Underwood, B. J. Attributes of memory. *Psychological Review,* 1969, **76,** 559–573.

Vokey, J. R., & Brooks, L. R. Taming the clever unconscious: analogic and abstractive strategies in artificial grammar learning. *Cognition,* 1983, in press.

Warren, C. E. J., & Morton, J. The effects of priming on picture recognition. *British Journal of Psychology,* 1982, **73,** 1117–130.

Weiskrantz, L., & Warrington, E. K. The problem of the amnesic syndrome in man and animals. In R. L. Isaacson & K. H. Pribram (Eds.), *The hippocampus,* (Vol. 2). New York: Plenum, 1975.

Whittlesea, B. W. A. *The representation of concepts: An evaluation of the abstractive and episodic perspectives.* Unpublished Ph.D. thesis, McMaster University, 1983.

Winnick, W. A., & Daniel, S. A. Two kinds of response priming in tachistoscopic recognition. *Journal of Experimental Psychology,* 1970, **84,** 74–81.

Witherspoon, D., & Allan, L. *Time judgments and the repetition effect in perceptual identification,* 1984, in preparation.

ON THE NATURE OF CATEGORIES

Donald Homa

ARIZONA STATE UNIVERSITY
TEMPE, ARIZONA

I. Introduction

Tangible and naturally occurring categories, such as objects in the environment that are readily available to the senses, or more ethereal cate-

THE PSYCHOLOGY OF LEARNING
AND MOTIVATION, VOL. 18

gories, such as artistic style, are comprehended by experience. As a general rule, these experiences are gained from contact with the members or examples of a category, and, as a consequence, our conception of that category evolves. To state that information from a category is abstracted is to imply that our mental representation of the category has been modified by the combining or integrating of experiences provided by its exemplars, with the end result that general knowledge of the category has been acquired. For example, a novice listener develops the ability to recognize an unfamiliar musical selection once sufficient experience with other passages by the same composer has been provided ("it sounds like Vivaldi").

Historically, no topic has received more attention than the issue of how ideas are formed from raw sensory experiences. Plato spoke of ideal forms that were embodied in sensible objects, and Aristotle partitioned the environment into 10 global categories. The British empiricists debated whether ideas were the end result of abstracting out the essential properties of categories or whether ideas were represented by the particular and specific experiences available to the observer. Experimentally, category abstraction was studied at the turn of the century (Kulpe, 1904), and today, research on classificatory principles has been expanded into such diverse areas as medical diagnosis and the computer recognition of speech.

The laboratory investigation of human concept acquisition has witnessed a number of major trends. One was the shift in emphasis from introspective analyses of concepts (Fisher, 1916; Moore, 1910) to more objective and quantitative approaches (Hull, 1920; Kuo, 1923). Another was the departure from research employing categories whose members contained a physically invariant component to categories that permitted active hypothesis-testing strategies (Bruner, Goodnow, & Austin, 1956; Smoke, 1932). A third trend involved the dichotomy of categories into well-defined and ill-defined types (Neisser, 1967).

For the purposes of the present article, the last trend is the most important. According to Neisser (1967), the members of well-defined categories typically contained a critical, invariant feature, exemplar variability was usually limited, and the dimensions underlying the categories could be specified precisely. Much of the research that explored the acquisition of well-defined categories supported the view that the subject proceeded through a series of hypothesis-testing stages until the classificatory rule for a category was discovered (Bourne, 1966; Levine, 1975). Major issues included the effect of rule complexity, number of relevant and irrelevant dimensions, the information conveyed by positive and negative instances, and memory demands on concept acquisition. In a sense, the classificatory rule *was* the abstraction, since only the rule was invariant among the category members.

In contrast, ill-defined categories were characterized by Neisser as categories whose members were infinitely variable and whose dimensions were frequently obscure. At least part of the motivation for dividing categories into well-defined and ill-defined types arose from problems encountered in pattern recognition by computer analyses: The automatic recognition of machine-printed letters was a solvable problem; the automatic recognition of hand-scripted letters was not. The major difference between these two types of categories was one of pattern variance; machine-printed letters are virtual copies of each other and can be recognized by a template-matching program; hand-scripted letters are never identical, and identification remains a problem today (e.g., Backer, 1974).

There is a growing consensus that many categories, and perhaps most, are essentially ill defined (Neisser, 1967) or fuzzy (Zadeh, 1965). Unfortunately, the recent proliferation of studies in conceptual learning has produced little consensus on how the human organism encodes, catalogs, integrates, and utilizes categorical information. Thus, mental representations based on discovered rules, transformational distance, abstracted prototypes, diagnostic feature sets, and individual exemplars have each been offered as explanations for classificatory performance. Similarly, results have been obtained which suggest that the human organism stores all (Medin & Schaffer, 1978), stores none (Franks & Bransford, 1971), or stores some (Posner & Keele, 1970) of the specific stimulus information that is used to define the various categories. The memorial representation of acquired categories is further complicated by studies suggesting that the internal representation of a category is modifiable by additional exemplar experience (Homa, Cross, Cornell, Goldman, & Shwartz, 1973) and the passage of time (Fisher, 1916).

The existence of antagonistic models that purport to explain the same phenomena suggests that 60 years of intensive, experimentally oriented research have uncovered few general principles of classification. Conceivably, models of classification based on abstracted prototypes, feature sets, and intact exemplars converge to a common set of laws. Alternatively, these models may represent categorical knowledge but at different stages of formation. Another possibility, and the one favored here, is that these models may be appropriate to different kinds of categories. By ignoring the possibility that categories may be of qualitatively different types, or that categories may possess different kinds of structure, investigators may have improperly extended their explanations to phenomena that warrant different principles. Thus, variables important in learning one type of category may be relatively unimportant in learning other types. The premise that all categories are processed in fundamentally similar ways is almost certainly false. The fact that some categories have defied solution after 25 years of intensive research (e.g., computer recognition of speech), whereas other types of categories lend themselves to simple explanations (e.g., definition of club membership based on discrete valued attributes) strongly suggests that categories may differ in fundamentally important ways.

PURPOSE OF THE PRESENT ARTICLE

Precisely how categories differ is part of the focus on the present article. To this end, a general taxonomy of category types is proposed, specifically directed toward the dichotomy of categories into ill-defined and well-defined types. Hopefully, the proposed taxonomy of category types will allow results to be summarized and interpretative discrepancies to be isolated. For example, recent models of classification (e.g., Hayes-Roth & Hayes-Roth, 1977; Medin & Schaffer, 1978) can only be properly evaluated with this distinction in mind. The proposed taxonomy may also help systematize important findings from diverse areas that are essentially concerned with categorical problems, for example, medical diagnostics and the acquisition of finite-state grammars. The taxonomy is based on a set of four criteria that seem to have some intuitive appeal. In addition, most previous research, including early experimental work in this area (e.g., Fisher, 1916; Gengerelli, 1927; Hull, 1920; Kuo, 1923) seems readily classifiable by these criteria.

A second major focus is the emphasis on learning variables and the critical role they play in the shaping and modification of concepts. To state that concepts evolve with experience is to make an inference about the changing mental status of a concept. It is an inference, however, that must be dependent upon the demonstrated importance of learning variables on the acquisition, transfer, and retention of concepts. For example, generalization gradients may be altered (Homa, 1978) and perceived structure may be modified (Homa, Rhoads, & Chambliss, 1979) by the prior manipulation of learning variables. Learning variables often interact in important ways to affect later transfer performance; the acquired breadth of a category is an interactive function of category size and stimulus distortion (Homa & Vosburgh, 1976). The view that concepts evolve with experience is hardly new; objective (Hull, 1920) and introspective (Fisher, 1916) evidence for the evolution of concepts has been available for some time. Nonetheless, a common shortcoming of current research is the tendency to theorize from a data base that is devoid of influences from variable manipulations. Specifically, the levels of potentially important variables are rarely manipulated but are held constant and accorded the status of an extraneous variable such as room temperature or ambient noise. A number of recent findings in diverse categorical areas is presented, in which it is shown that variable manipulations critically determine the interpretation. Included are studies on the long-term retention of categorical information by children, perceptual processing, and categorical decision making. In addition, the importance of variable manipulations on the learning of ill-defined problems is shown; here, the boundaries function as principles to be inferred, where the stimuli approximate, rather than illustrate, the principle.

Finally, results are presented which focus on the changing composition of concepts as a function of experience. Although a formal model of category learning is not attempted, the utility of viewing category learning in terms of stimulus sampling from the category domain is discussed.

II. Models of Categorization

A. PROTOTYPE MODELS

The view that all concepts are represented by prototypes, abstractions, or ideal forms has historical roots in the writings of Plato and Aristotle, and later, by the British empiricist, John Locke. For Plato, general concepts or ideals had objective reality that were embodied in sensible objects. The particulars of the sensible world depended upon ideal forms for their existence, and the ideal forms existed in a real but invisible and intangible world. In his formulation, the sensible world was a mere shadow of a separate world of ideal forms, in which reality was composed of three levels: (1) the ideal; (2) the tangible; and (3) the copy (as in art). In Book 10 of *The Republic,* he argued that knowledge can only be obtained by understanding ideal forms.

Aristotle rejected the Platonic view that ideal forms had objective reality, while accepting the view that knowledge was of the universal. Primary substance was, for Aristotle, always of the particular thing, whereas the species or genus of the particular was considered substance of a secondary kind. Experiential factors were important in understanding the universal: "As a result of seeing the same thing happen many times we would look for the universal and have a proof; the universal becomes clear from a number of particular instances" (*Posterior Analytics,* Chapter 31, Book 1). In the "Categories," Aristotle enumerated 10 global and heterogeneous categories that were mutually exclusive and jointly exhaustive of reality: (1) substance (or being); (2) quantity; (3) qualification; (4) relation; (5) where; (6) when; (7) being in a position; (8) having; (9) doing; and (10) being affected. If the categories are interpreted as dimensions, the Aristotelian system appears to describe a coordinate system in which particulars of the world occupy unique locations. It has been suggested that Aristotle may have arrived at his list of 10 categories by noting the kinds of questions that may be asked about something (Ackrill, 1967).

The British empiricists vigorously debated the existence of abstract or general ideas. According to John Locke, the mind forged general ideas from directly experienced particulars. He noted that the higher mental processes such as reasoning and communicating were unattainable unless the multitude of sensations could be reduced to general classes or concepts. Both physical similarity ("nature, in the production of things, makes several of them alike") and pure invention were the means by which general ideas were framed. Locke also thought it highly implausible that the human mind was capable of retaining each distinct impression: "It is beyond the power of human capacity to frame and retain distinct ideas of all the particular things we meet with: every bird and beast men saw, every tree and plant that affected the senses, could not find a place in the most capacious understanding" (Locke, 1690).

Current versions of prototype theory have usually posited that the memorial representation of a category includes the central tendency (or abstracted prototype) which is a result of exemplar averaging (Reed, 1972) or information integration (Anderson, 1972). The end result is that the abstracted prototype functions to guide subsequent classification or recognition, that is, that generalization gradients are primarily anchored to the prototype and less to individual exemplars (Homa, Sterling, & Trepel, 1981). Adherents of prototype theory have generally stressed that the abstracted prototype is not the sole memory representation of a category (Posner & Keele, 1970). Specific information about some individual exemplars may be retained (although subject to decay), as well as knowledge about the allowable distortion for the members of the category (e.g., Bartlett, 1932).

B.   Exemplar Models

Exemplar models assume that intact stimuli are stored in memory and that classification or recognition is determined by the degree of similarity between a stimulus and the stored exemplar. This model shows a close similarity to simple models of classical conditioning, in which the magnitude of a conditioned response (likelihood of category membership) is determined by the similarity of the test stimulus (new exemplar) to a conditioned stimulus (stored exemplar).

Although formal modeling based on stored exemplars is relatively recent (Brooks, 1978; Hintzman & Ludlam, 1980; Medin & Schaffer, 1978), exemplar models share an obvious similarity to the views of Berkeley and Hume on conceptualizing. Berkeley and Hume accepted the view that categorical meaning was derived from direct experience, but disputed the existence of abstract ideas. They argued that the meaning of a word or category was obtained by the remembrance of singular experiences: "a word becomes general by being made the sign, not of an *abstract* general idea, but of several particular ideas, any one of which it indifferently suggests to the mind" (Berkeley, 1708).

Hume was even more explicit on this point, arguing that experience is never general but specific, and thus, conceptions must be specific as well:

> Everything in nature is individual, and that it is utterly absurd to suppose a triangle really existent, which has no precise proportions of sides and angles. If this, therefore, be absurd in fact and reality, it must also be absurd in idea; since nothing of which we can form a clear and distinct idea is absurd and impossible. (Hume, 1739)

How does the mind avoid misrepresentation of a concept, such as might arise if an atypical impression is retrieved? By retrieving *many* particulars associated with a word:

> the hearing of that name revives the idea of one of the objects, and makes the imagination conceive it with all its particular circumstances and proportions . . . when a quality becomes very general, and is common to a great many individuals, it leads not the mind to any one of them; but, by presenting at once too great a choice, does thereby prevent the imagination from fixing on any single object. (Hume, 1739)

For Hume, memory was simply a passive storehouse of sensations, unable to alter the order or context of its impressions. The imagination was given the power to transpose the order and form of the original impressions.

Hume did allow for one interesting form of generalization that could be used to classify a totally novel sensation. If an individual had experienced all colors of the spectrum but for one shade of blue, and if all shades but this one were ordered and placed before him, he should, through his imagination, be able to "supply this deficiency." Hume, however, felt this situation was rare and "scarce worth our observing."

As might be anticipated, the dispute over abstract ideas has had its adherents and adversaries in the time period following Hume:

> I will begin with Berkeley. The note, so bravely struck by Berkeley, could not, however, be well sustained in the face of the fact patent to every human being we *can* mean color without meaning any particular color, and stature, without meaning any particular height. James Mill, to be sure, chimes in heroically in the chapter on Classification of his "Analysis"; but in his son, John, the nominalistic voice has grown so weak that, although "abstract ideas" are repudiated as a matter of traditional form, the opinions uttered are really nothing but a conceptualization ashamed to call itself by its own legitimate name. (James, 1890)

The most interesting experimental questions for exemplar models are whether generalization gradients can be shown to be anchored to individual stimuli (as opposed to a prototype or some central tendency) and whether

individual exemplars can maintain their memorial integrity as the number
of experiences relevant to a category is increased dramatically (a view disputed by John Locke).

C. FEATURE MODELS

Feature models are typically characterized by treating the memorial representation of category members in terms of their component features or
parts. In effect, intact stimuli are not preserved but the sampling distribution of features is. Classification or recognition of a stimulus is typically
mediated by computing the feature similarity of the current stimulus to the
stored representation of features for the various categories being considered. The features of a stimulus may be either specific values on a single
dimension (Rosch & Mervis, 1976), higher order combinations of stimulus
values (Hayes-Roth & Hayes-Roth, 1977), or a purely hypothetical construct (Homa & Chambliss, 1975).

Historically, the definition of concepts in terms of features or constitu-
ent parts has had few adherents. For example, Aristotle provides a lengthy
and complicated treatise on features, designating them as either accidental
or essential. Accidental features refer to those properties or attributes that
are not critical to the meaning of a category, such as "whiteness" when
applied to man. In contrast, essential attributes refer to those attributes that
are always part of the concept, such as two-legged as part of man. Nonetheless, even the essential features appear to be treated as a derivative or
by-product of the category, not part of its primary being, since *being* a man
results in his two-leggedness: "In the case of all things that have several
parts and in which the whole is not like a heap, but is a particular something
besides the parts, there is some uniting factor" (Book Eta of the *Metaphysics*). Throughout the *Metaphysics,* Aristotle refers to categories in terms
of the destiny or "what it is to become" of its members, which is why man
is not "a mere aggregate of things, such as an animal plus a biped." Regardless, feature models have received widespread popularity among psychologists and researchers in artificial intelligence.

D. SIMILARITIES AMONG THE MODELS

A number of similarities among the three basic models can be identified.
Exemplar models mirror the predictions of feature models if the entire stimulus is considered as a feature or if the dimensions underlying the stored
exemplar take on variable weights (e.g., Medin & Schaffer, 1978). Thus, if
it is argued that the entire stimulus is stored, but some dimensions receive

a zero or minimal weight, then the stored stimulus is effectively a subset (or feature) of the nominal stimulus.

Feature distribution and prototype models share a number of similarities as well. In both models, individual stimuli are forged into a composite representation, and a central tendency (mode or mean) of category members may influence later classification. Prototype models, however, preserve stimulus information that can vary *continuously* along several dimensions. In contrast, feature distribution models assume that the stimulus can be decomposed into a collection of discrete features. The question of how discrete features are extracted from continuously variable stimuli has not been dealt with. Rather, investigators (e.g., Elio & Anderson, 1981; Hayes-Roth & Hayes-Roth, 1977) have generally explored feature models by employing stimuli that are composed of *identical,* rather than *similar,* features. A prototype model, based on averaging mechanisms, can generate a central tendency that is based on information that is not precisely mirrored in any particular exemplar. Thus, a modal prototype, derived from a feature distribution, is composed of those features which both occur most often but which are specifically contained in its exemplars; an average prototype, however, may be represented by stimulus information that is not specifically embodied in any particular form. An interesting example of exemplar averaging for complex stimuli was devised by Galton (1879) with his discovery of composite photography. One of Galton's interests was the discovery of criminal types. A criminal stereotype was produced by superimposing photographs of individual criminals. The final product of this averaging process was a composite photograph of those individuals who were, supposedly, genetically predisposed toward crime. When the technique was applied to individuals of the same family, the outcome was a striking photograph that clearly showed the prominent details common to the bloodline, for example, nose shape, with some blurring around the edges. Although no individual had this average nose, the relationship of particular noses to the "bloodline" nose was striking. Interestingly, Galton noted that the composite photograph was more handsome than any of the particular individuals who constituted the composite, since the imperfections of each member were washed out in the composite. In Galton's composite photograph, the prototype would be the average face outline and the prominent details, and the allowable distortion may correspond to the range of blurring produced by individual faces from the mean value.

Conceptually, the three basic models may be easily distinguished; if the subject stores specific categorical experiences and abstracts nothing, then support for a pure exemplar model would be obtained; if the subject extracts and stores components of these experiences, then a feature model is supported; and if a subject integrates specific categorical experiences, then a prototype model would be favored. Unfortunately, the search for a most appropriate model of human conceptual behavior is predicated on the implicit assumption that all categorical information is processed in a fundamentally similar manner.

III. The Components of Categorization

Disputes over the representation of concepts have dominated recent laboratory investigations. Nonetheless, a number of ancillary, but potentially critical, issues warrant comment. To illustrate these issues, consider some of the interrelated components of categorization shown in Fig. 1.

A structured, objective categorical space (1) is assumed, knowledge of which is gained by experience (2). The nature of this experience may be in the form of definition or, more generally, through encounters with the members of the categories. Generally, these experiences can be defined by the levels exhibited along a number of critical dimensions or variables (3). The internal representation of categories (4) is shaped by these experiences and, with extreme levels of experience, begins to approximate the characteristics inherent in the objective categories.

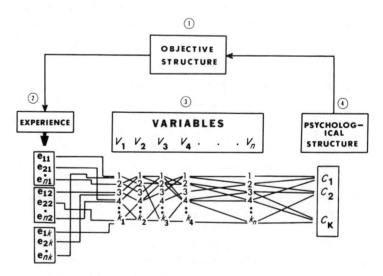

Fig. 1. The component of categorization e_{ij} is the ith experience of category j; V_{ij} is the ith level of variable j; C_j is the representation of category j.

A. DEFINITION OF A CATEGORY

An issue of fundamental importance concerns the definition of a category itself. In the simplest and most inclusive case, a category may be defined by the assignment of a common name to an arbitrary collection of stimuli. No algorithm exists for designating additional stimuli as members of the category, and the members need not share an obvious similarity relationship with each other. A number of recent studies has used such categories, where the intent is to provide a model of some generality (e.g., Elio & Anderson, 1981; Hintzman & Ludlam, 1980; Medin & Schaffer, 1978).

A more restrictive definition requires that the members sharing a common name also be generated by a specifiable rule or algorithm (e.g., Evans, 1967; Homa, 1978; Posner, Goldsmith, & Welton, 1967). The criticality of a genetic plan or rule that binds members together is clearly intended in the definition of a category by the ancient philosophers: "In general, those things are really united which must be conceived by the same formula for their essential being" (Aristotle, Book Delta in the *Metaphysics*). Even invented categories had an abstract plan that governed members: "The craftsman, in making either of these articles of furniture, keeps his eye upon the idea and so makes the beds or tables which we use accordingly, and so with other things" (Plato, Book 10 of *The Republic*). Potential processing distinctions for arbitrary collections lacking an algorithm versus collections generated by an algorithm or plan have not received empirical attention.[1] Support for examplar-based and prototype-based models, however, may be contingent upon this distinction.

B. CATEGORICAL STRUCTURE

Categorical information is not acquired in a vacuum or in isolation from other categories. A child cannot adequately learn about dogs without also learning about other categories such as cats. Similarly, an adult unfamiliar with classical music cannot be expected to identify musical selections by Brahms unless exposure to other, similar musical styles is provided. Categories are learned relative to each other, and both within-category variance and between-category distinctiveness shape this knowledge.

Categorical structure reflects both of these latter properties. In the biological realm, species not only share a similarity relationship with each other,

[1]Markman (Markman, 1978; Markman & Seibert, 1976) has shown developmental differences between the processing of nonarbitrary collections and classes, where collections are based on spatial proximity (e.g., a forest) or organized activity (e.g., a team). Although decisions about a novel object's membership in such a collection are possible, they cannot rely on criteria independent of the object's relation to the members.

but the members of a species are allowed to vary within the dictates of a genetic plan. A similar perspective exists for other kinds of categories. For example, the stimulus information contained in a spoken word is shaped, in part, by the physical configuration of the laryngeal tract, the oral cavity, and the positioning of the lips and tongue. The unique shape of the vocal apparatus precludes identical voicing among individuals. Even for the same individual, repetition of a word produces endless variety, since the placement of lips and tongue, stress, duration, and intensity can never be exactly duplicated. The end result is an infinity of stimuli, each having the same name. These variations on a theme make it clear that, for many categories, each exemplar of a category reflects both an algorithm (or plan, constraint, production system) plus some allowable distortion.

Regardless of internal representation (exemplars, features, prototypes), the learner's task is almost always the same—to learn to recognize the endless variation of stimuli for a number of related categories. An unresolved issue is how to best capture this information. Multidimensional scaling (Kruskal, 1964; Shepard, 1962) holds promise as one means of displaying the magnitude of within- and between-category similarity. A laboratory example of a categorical space is shown in Fig. 2, which represents 30 distorted forms belonging to three different categories. Each category was represented by the prototype and three examples from each of three distortion levels.[2] Recent experiments indicate that the overall degree of constraint in a multidimensional space can predict later ease of learning (Homa & Cultice, 1984). Furthermore, numerical taxonomists (Sneath & Sokal, 1973) have turned increasingly to multidimensional scaling techniques, since these methods allow an assessment of similarity without prior commitment to assumptions of common ancestry. Wood (1983) has shown that the resulting multidimensional configuration of 17 species of storks, where similarity was based on skeletal properties, mirrored that obtained when behavioral traits were used (courtship dances, reactions to threat, etc.).

This perspective, in which the observer must cope with endless variation for a number of related categories, also makes it clear why laboratory research with single categories (e.g., Franks & Bransford, 1971; Neumann, 1974) is inadequate; such studies may provide useful information on similarity processing, but the results are not extendable to multiple category situations. In particular, category distinctiveness is excluded as a variable

---

[2]Overall constraint has been defined previously as $S = d_w/d_b$, where S indexes the overall degree of structure of a space containing members from multiple categories, d_w is the average within-category scaled distance of stimuli to members of the same category, and d_b is the average between-category scaled distance for stimuli belonging to different categories (Homa et al., 1979).

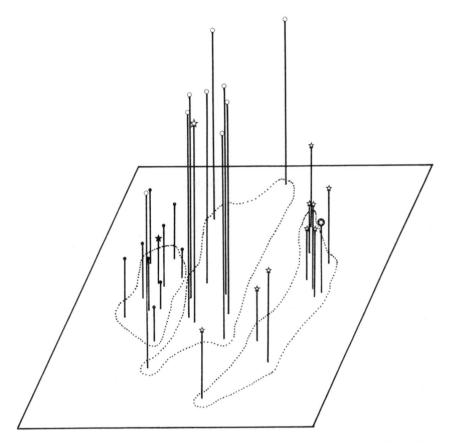

Fig. 2. An example of a categorical space containing three categories with 10 members each. Prototypes of each category are indicated by the major stars.

of importance, and the effect of between-category similarity on within-category processing cannot be determined.

C. EXPERIENCE

A category can be defined in terms of familiar words (Reed, 1946), by analogy with known categories (Rumelhart & Abrahamson, 1973), or by exposure to examples of the category. In Fig. 1, each experience is a sample of potential experiences from the environment. Thus, e_{ij} would be the ith instance of category j. In the natural environment, the encountering of category members is haphazard; in structured (teaching) situations, the exemplars may be organized in such a manner to presumably optimize comprehension (selection of typical members, block presentation). Hull (1920) found that concepts were better comprehended if training proceeded from simple to complex examples rather than the reverse.

Three issues are important. First, the encountered exemplars of a category constitute a sample whenever the population is infinitely large, and, therefore, the nature of that sample determines the form of the concept. Second, the number and similarity of experienced exemplars probably determines their later recognition. Finally, the definition of an exemplar can be extended to a myriad of situations, including those in which the stimulus information is not static in time and place. For example, the schoolboy who works five math problems may be considered to have encountered five exemplars of a category if these problems illustrate the use of a particular concept. In a more complex vein, the apprentice plumber may encounter a vast set of variable problems within a work day; problem A may involve devising a system whereby water is pumped up a hill to a distant house; problem B may require thawing out the water (and not the gas) pipes located in the crawlspace of a house, etc. Each problem may be considered an example of hydraulic principles (gone wrong), where the critical information may be collected across time and place.

D.   VARIABLE DEFINITION

Each category experience (e_{ij}) can be expressed in terms of levels on a number of variables or dimensions. To see this in the case of an experiment, suppose five categories, each represented by 10 different exemplars, are to be learned. Both the number of exemplars per category and the number of categories to be learned are variables. Furthermore, each category member must vary in terms of its distortion or goodness of example of the category, and the five categories must have some form of similarity relationship to each other. Categorical similarity and stimulus distortion are therefore also variables.

To date, laboratory investigation has identified seven variables that modify the form of a category, as determined by performance on a later transfer test: (a) category size (or number of different exemplars per category); (b) stimulus distortion (variance); (c) number of categories; (d) category similarity; (e) type and availability of feedback; (f) memorial set and decisional influences; and (g) the passage of time. With the exception of the last variable, these variables can be grouped into three classes: within-category variables (a and b), between-category variables (c and d), and situational variables (e and f). Within-category variables are primarily responsible for defining common information of a category, as well as marking the boundary of the category. Between-category variables are instrumental in isolating distinctions among categories. Together, these variables define the degree of structure of the categorical space (average within- to between-category similarity). Situational variables affect the learner's disposition, since it is the learner that ultimately controls the scanning, selection, and utilization of information contained in the learning stimuli.

The impact of these variables on category learning and transfer is undoubtedly interactive; that is, the importance of a given variable on learning or subsequent transfer is modulated by selected levels on the remaining variables. Figure 3 summarizes a number of results from our laboratory; panel A shows that reaction times to novel stimuli are reduced by increasing levels of category size, regardless of the distortion level of the stimulus (Omohundro & Homa, 1981); panel B shows that classification accuracy is en-

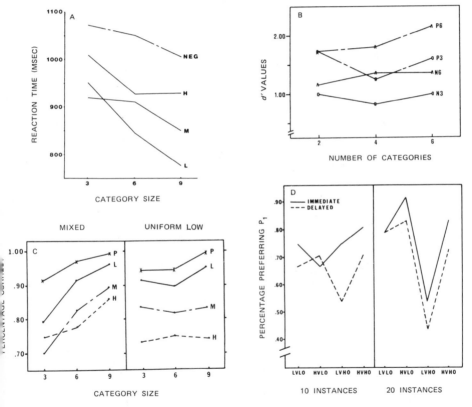

Fig. 3. Summary of results showing the effects of variable manipulations. (A) Reaction time as a function of category size; (B) d' measures as a function of number of categories learned; (C) proportion correct as a function of training level distortion and category size; (D) preference for modal (P_f) prototype, as a function of category size, overlap, and variability.

hanced by the number of categories learned; panel C shows the effect of training-level distortion and category size on transfer; and panel D shows the effect of category similarity (overlap) on preference for a modal-feature prototype.

The importance of these variables is not diminished for naturally occurring situations. Each of the above variables exists in these situations as well, since each experience must have an occurrence number, a similarity relationship to other experiences, and so on.

E. CATEGORICAL KNOWLEDGE AND THE DATA BASE

Suppose knowledge of a category is determined by only two variables, the distortion level of the experienced stimuli and the category size. A theoretical transfer surface in three dimensions is defined, where the first two dimensions identify the two variables and the third dimension indexes performance on the transfer stimuli (Fig. 4). An experiment that manipulates

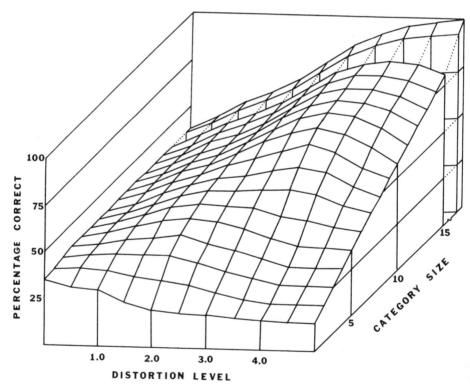

Fig. 4. Hypothetical transfer surface as a function of category size and distortion level.

neither of these variables provides transfer data that estimates a single point on this surface. If one variable is held constant and the other is manipulated over a reasonable range, then performance for slice through the transfer space can be estimated. When both variables are factorially manipulated across a reasonable range, the shape of the entire surface space can be estimated.

The complexity of human concepts is far greater than this two-variable example. With a minimum of seven important variables, the transfer space requires eight dimensions for definition. The implication for any successful model is obvious: The data to be accounted for must be generated from the influence of critical variables, since the transfer surface is the best indicator of a subject's knowledge. Current quantitative models (e.g., Elio & Anderson, 1981; Medin & Schaffer, 1978) have the virtue of precise description and prediction. Yet current models are notable for their failure to generate a data base produced by variable manipulations. As such, the percentage of data accounted for in terms of the hypothetical transfer surface is negligible or zero.

IV. Variable Manipulation

In the last section, the importance of seven variables on category processing was mentioned. In this section, recent results are presented which show the pervasive impact of some of these variables in a variety of categorization tasks.

A. CATEGORY SIZE AND DELAY: LONG-TERM RETENTION OF ACQUIRED CONCEPTS BY CHILDREN

The vast majority of our studies has employed college students as subjects. We were interested in whether children (age 10) would be similarly affected by category size and whether these acquired concepts would systematically decay across lengthy retention intervals. In this task (Homa & Little, unpublished), children sorted form stimuli to near-errorless criterion (0 or 1 error on a trial of 18), where the categories contained 3, 6, and 9 different stimuli. The transfer test contained old, new, prototype, and unrelated stimuli, where the new stimuli were at one of three levels of distortion (low, L; medium, M; high, H). The transfer test was administered immediately, 1 week later, and 1 month later. The transfer results are shown in Fig. 5.

Although the patterning of results was somewhat erratic, category size was a potent determinant of transfer for children. A striking result was the

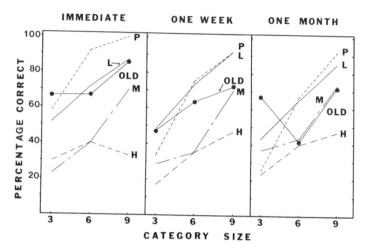

Fig. 5. Classification performance by children as a function of category size and delay of test. P, Prototype; L, low; M, medium; H, high.

near-perfect classification of the prototype belonging to the largest-sized category, even after a month's delay. A very similar task has been run with college students, in which identical learning and transfer stimuli were used. Overall, college students outperformed the children by 12%. The benefits of category size, however, were greater for the children; performance improved by 20% across category size for the adults versus 32% for the children. Thus, children may be even more sensitive to this variable than adults.

B.   CATEGORY SIZE: PERCEPTUAL DISCRIMINATION
        AND CLASSIFICATION

It has been suggested that all perception is the end product of a categorization process (Burner, 1957). Given the significant impact of increasing category size on categorical knowledge, we were interested in determining whether this variable affected categorical perception. In this study (Homa & Omohundro, unpublished), subjects classified 30 different stimuli into categories defined by 3, 9, and 18 different stimuli. On the perceptual discrimination task, a novel stimulus that belonged to one of the three learned categories was briefly shown (50 msec), followed by a mask and two forced-choice stimuli. The subject had to identify which of two stimuli had been tachistoscopically presented, where the foil was a pattern from the same category as the presented stimulus. On half the trials, the subject was further cued before the trial regarding the category to be shown. On the perceptual classification task, the subject simply had to identify the category which contained the briefly exposed stimulus. Figure 6 shows the performance on the two types of perceptual test, as a function of category size. Increasing the degree of prior category abstraction, inferred from having categories defined by varying numbers of exemplars, facilitated the rapid perceptual analysis for the classification of stimuli. In contrast, increasing levels of prior category abstraction slightly degraded the perceptual discrimination of stimuli belonging to the same category, especially when the category was cued beforehand. These results suggest that shape dominates features, at least in the early stages of perceptual processing, and that a variable known to enhance categorical knowledge (category size) affects perceptual analysis.

C. FEEDBACK AND DISTORTION LEVEL: ACQUISITION OF CATEGORICAL STRUCTURE

A number of researchers have argued that categorical information can be acquired in the absence of feedback (Gibson, 1969; Smallwood & Arnoult, 1974). There is little dispute that some categorical information can be acquired without feedback (e.g., Bersted, Brown, & Evans, 1969; Brown & Evans, 1969; Evans & Arnoult, 1967). The efficiency, magnitude, and scope of learning in the absence of feedback is unclear, however.

In a recent study (Homa & Cultice, 1984), subjects attempted to learn categories defined exclusively by low-, medium-, high-, or mixed-level distortions, in the presence or absence of corrective feedback. Our major con-

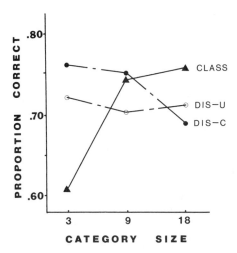

Fig. 6. Percentage correct in the perceptual discrimination and classification as a function of category size. U, Uncued; C, cued.

cern was whether corrective feedback is ever deleterious to category learning and whether boundary conditions can be identified that require feedback for learning.

Acquisition performance is shown in Fig. 7, which shows accuracy of classification across trials for the feedback (left panel) and no feedback (right panel) subjects. What is most apparent is the consistent and powerful effect of corrective feedback on learning and the near absence of category learning when feedback was omitted; only the minimally distorted stimuli were learnable in the absence of feedback. The learning materials were subsequently scaled, and measures of conceptual structure (Homa *et al.*, 1979) were computed for each condition. A lawful relationship was observed between ease of learning and degree of categorical structure, a relationship that may prove to be general across different types of categories and materials.

Generally, these results suggest that the extraction of structure is not automatic and that feedback may promote learning by the reduction of choice (number of categories to be considered), especially in ambiguous situations. We are currently investigating whether feedback need always be available (100%) or whether full benefits may accrue when a small percentage of

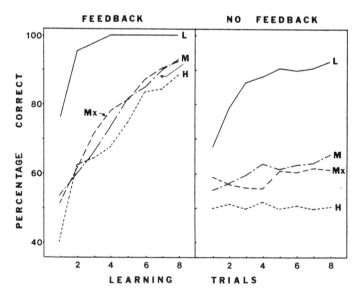

Fig. 7. Percentage correct as a function of learning trials and feedback condition. L, Low; M, medium; H, high; Mx, mixed.

stimuli is associated with feedback. In a similar vein, how much erroneous information can be tolerated before a category loses its integrity?

D. DECISIONAL SET, DISTORTION LEVEL, AND CATEGORY
SIZE: THE EFFECT OF INSTRUCTIONAL SET
ON CHOICE DIFFICULTY

Logically, classification involves more than simply matching the current stimulus to an internal array of categories. In addition, the goodness of the match must be evaluated, and factors such as expectancy, global strategies, and payoffs should affect the decisional stage. In general, subjects naturally exhibit conservative or liberal strategies; conservative subjects tend to avoid classification by assigning a large percentage of transfer stimuli into an available "none" category unless they are reasonably certain of their choice; liberal subjects exhibit an opposite strategy, ignoring the "none" category, even when their confidence of being correct is low.

We were interested in manipulating variables that would mimic a situation whereby degree of categorical experience, difficulty or choice, and type of strategy would exist. For example, an experienced radiologist, recently made cautious (perhaps by a suit brought against the hospital), might exercise caution in a selective manner: Only those choices that were difficult ones would come under additional scrutiny, such as requiring additional laboratory tests. In contrast, a less experienced radiologist might exercise caution more generally, such that decisions at all levels of difficulty would be affected.

In this study (Homa, Burruel, & Field, unpublished), degree of experience was manipulated by variations in category size (3, 6, 9), and ease of choice was defined by degree of pattern distortion. Half the subjects classified transfer patterns under a conservative strategy and half under a liberal strategy. The results for one of the conditions is shown in Fig. 8.

First, the benefits of category size were evident on the classification of new stimuli at all levels of distortion (choice difficulty), and, overall, the hit rate for liberal subjects exceeded that of the conservative subjects. Second, the effect of each of the variables (category size, stimulus distortion, instructional set) on transfer was additive. This suggests that the boundary of the category was not contracted under conservative instructions, since this strategy would have produced an interaction between distortion level and set. Rather, all stimuli were affected equally by changes in instructional set, suggesting that the effect of set was pervasive rather than selective. We are currently exploring this question under conditions of extreme category size learning, where additivity might be expected to break down.

Donald Homa

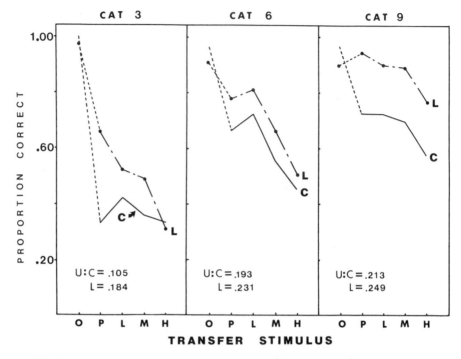

Fig. 8. Percentage correct as a function of instructional set, category size, and distortion level. C, Conservative; L, liberal; U:C, false alarm rate, conservative; U:L, false alarm rate, liberal.

V. The Handyman Space: Ill-Defined Problems with Well-Defined Boundaries

A final line of research was concerned with what we have termed the *handyman's knowledge*. First, consider the suggestion that 10 years are needed to become an expert or skilled technician (Simon, 1982). Although this estimate is based on some dubious calculations (50,000 needed chunks over 10 years at 10 sec a chunk requires 2 min a day for expert training), there is little doubt that most persons develop one major livelihood. Most persons, however, become competent in a variety of other activities. At a minimum, we learn how to push things to make them slide rather than tip over, to grasp without crushing, and to pour without splashing. The more adventuresome may become adept in repairing leaky pipes, wiring a room, or tinkering with the family auto.

What distinguishes a skilled technician from a handyman? One difference is between experience and knowledge of formal causes: "Men of experience discern the fact 'that,' but not the reason 'why'; whereas experts know the reason why and explanation" (Aristotle, Book Alpha of the *Metaphysics*). Failure to grasp formal cause need not be deterrent to productive action, however:

> Now experience seems in no respect inferior to art in a situation in which something is to be done. On the contrary, we see experienced men succeeding even better than those who know the reasons, but who lack experience. The reason is that experience, like action or production, deals with them generally. Thus, a physician does not cure 'man' but he cures Callias, Socrates, or some other individual with a proper name, each of whom happens to be a man. (Book Alpha)

The distinction of interest here can be made clear with an example. The Tower of Hanoi is a favorite problem of researchers in artificial intelligence, in part because of the problem's simplicity: The rules are clear, the steps required for solution can be specified, and variation in the problem is minimal (the number of pegs and disks can be varied). If human problem solving is logical and orderly, then the Tower of Hanoi problem appears to tap into the very fabric of complex cognition. Now consider an alternative problem, here called "The Plumber's Dilemma," which has numerous variations. One version might require the installation of a pump so that an adequate amount of water is pushed up a steep rise to a house located a considerable distance away. The particulars of this problem are never repeated; the distance and hill rise can vary endlessly, and other peripheral aspects to the problem guarantee its uniqueness (variations in tree cover, terrain, etc.). Technically, the water pump problem is a problem in hydraulics, in which variables such as the hill rise, distance to the house, diameter of the water pipe, and the power of the pump must be considered. In actuality, the plumber is unlikely to solve any formal equations before proceeding. First, the distance and hill rise will probably have to be estimated rather than measured directly, thus complicating solution to the formal problem. Second, the plumber is unlikely to know how to solve the problem in a formal manner (Jack Webster, personal communication). That the problem can be rectified (the installation of a workable system) suggests that the answer is still knowable.

How solutions can be effected without knowledge of formal causes was the concern of two preliminary studies. Consider Fig. 9, which shows a space segmented into four regions. Assume that the regions represent different states of an event, determined by the values along a set of dimensions (e.g., various states of matter or meteorological states as a function of temperature and pressure; tearing and stretching in metals as a function of stress and temperature). When an event or stimulus has one combination of values, it belongs to one state; a different combination of values, and it belongs to a different state, etc. We have termed this kind of space the

Donald Homa

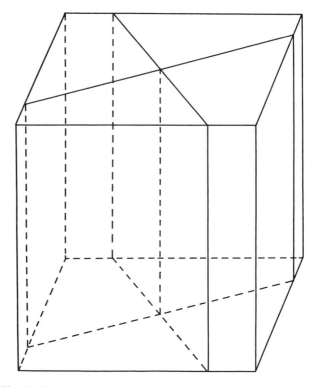

Fig. 9. The handyman space. Each region represents a different state.

handyman's space, because precise relationships or principles are specified at the boundaries, yet state prediction is not precluded by ignorance of the principles. In the pump example, the two variables might be hill rise and distance, and the regions may correspond to the horsepower needed to drive an adequate amount of water. Two properties of the handyman's space are apparent: (1) there exists an infinity of "exemplars" and a finite number of states; and (2) the problem space is a categorical one. Specifically, one set of stimuli (events) is associated with one name (state), a second set with a different name, and so on. Unlike the categorical spaces considered so far, critical information exists at the boundaries rather than at the centroid.

Two preliminary studies have been conducted. In the first, type of presentation was varied for its effect on ease of acquisition. In the random condition, stimuli (rectangles varying in width and height) were presented haphazardly from three segmented regions of a two-dimensional space. In the blocked and blocked/description conditions, examples were presented consecutively by region (subjects in the blocked/description condition were told to imagine that the regions corresponded to different medical symptoms). In the contrasting-pairs condition, pairs of stimuli occupying directly opposite positions in two regions were shown, a procedure intended to highlight the boundaries and reveal the most difficult discriminations. A study-test procedure was used (3 sec/stimulus in the random, blocked, blocked/description conditions and 6 sec/pair with contrasting pairs); the acquisition results are shown in Fig. 10.

Contrary to our expectations, random presentations produced the fewest errors and contrasting pairs the most, with the two blocked conditions intermediate. One explanation is that systematic presentation induced an analytical or hypothesis-testing approach, and the random presentation fostered a more synthetic approach. A similar conclusion was proposed by Reber and Allen (1978), who studied the effects of different presentation modes on the acquisition of a finite-state grammar.

In the second experiment (Homa & Thorn, unpublished), the effects of category size were investigated. The problem space was quadrasected (see Fig. 9) in three dimensions, with two dimensions relevant. The stimuli were faces, with eye and mouth length relevant and nose length irrelevant. The locations of the study and test stimuli, when projected onto the two relevant dimensions, are shown in Fig. 11. In the 4-instance condition (large black dots), each region was represented by four stimuli; in the 11-instance con-

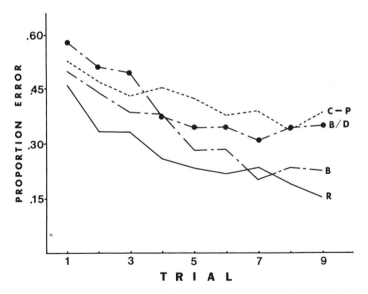

Fig. 10. Acquisition performance for a handyman space as a function of mode of presentation. R, Random; B, blocked; B/D, blocked with description; C-P, contrasting pairs.

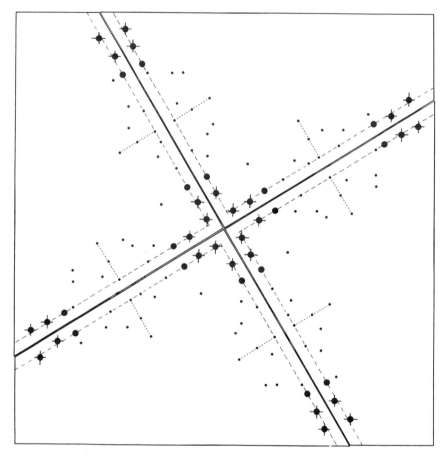

Fig. 11. Location of learning and transfer patterns for the handyman space (large dots, learning stimuli; small dots, transfer).

dition (large black dots + large black dots with crosses), the additional 7 stimuli occupied the extreme regions of the boundary, in hopes of better highlighting the boundary. On the transfer test (small dots), novel stimuli possessed values such that they were at one of four distances from a particular old (training) stimulus and at one of five values from the boundary. The only exception was the transfer stimuli bisecting the boundary (a condition, for the 11-instance subjects, analogous to Berkeley's notion of inferring a gap in a continuum); these stimuli (small dots connected by a dotted line) were moderately distant from any of the training stimuli.

A random presentation was employed in the learning phase, and the transfer results are shown in Fig. 12 (only those subjects who exhibited

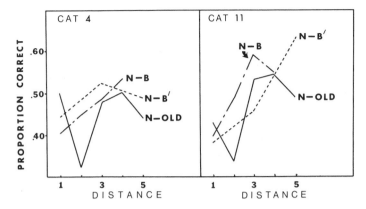

Fig. 12. Percentage correct as a function of distance of new patterns from old stimuli and the boundary. N-B, distance of new to boundary; N-OLD, distance of new to old; N-B', distance of new to bisected boundary.

significant learning—about 50%—had their transfer data analyzed). First, subjects exposed to a greater number of different exemplars during learning were more accurate on the transfer test, an outcome consistent with more traditional category abstraction tasks. Second, the distance of a new stimulus to an old one was not a systematic predictor of classification accuracy; the distance of a new stimulus from the (inferred) boundary was a significant predictor, however, especially for the 11-instance categories. This last result mimics that of the handyman—being able to generate solutions and functioning *as if* the boundary were comprehended. None of the subjects in either experiment was able to articulate explanations involving the boundary.

The results of this second study are in need of replication with better controls and different types of material (including mechanical problems). Nonetheless, these results may be germane to some curious findings reported by McCloskey (1983) on naive physics. In one task, subjects who had recently completed a course in physics, and who could solve textbook problems involving Newtonian principles, oftentimes gave erroneous predictions to simple physical problems, for example, predicting a straight, rather than curved, path of an object dropped by a moving body. McCloskey provided a number of explanations for his curious results (e.g., reference frames), yet a simple explanation may be offered: In natural settings, objects generally do fall straight down because the dropped object is usually stationary in the horizontal plane rather than moving. Critical tests of Newton's principles are rarely put to test in natural settings. The restricted variations, combined with high levels of frequency, may determine the belief.

VI. Internal Composition of Categories

The dramatic effect of variable manipulations during the learning phase on subsequent classification performance guarantees that knowledge of the category has been altered. In most studies, a global dependent measure, such as percentage correct or latency of response, is used to gauge these changes. These measures are too general, however, to reveal the internal composition of categories. In this section, the internal composition of categories is defined, and changes in the internal composition are described as a function of prior variable manipulations.

A. MAGNITUDE AND PURITY

The composition of a category may be defined by the kinds and amounts of information it contains. Two components, magnitude and purity, define the composition of a category, and magnitude- and purity-shift index the changing composition of a category due to variable manipulations.

The magnitude of a category refers to its size, expressed as a proportion of the number of stimuli it should contain in a given situation. For example, a category that should contain 50 stimuli in a given situation has a magnitude of .80 if only 40 stimuli are assigned to it. The purity of a category refers to the accuracy of information sorted into the category. If only 20 of the 40 sorted stimuli actually belong to that category, then the purity of the category is .50.

Magnitude- and purity-shift refer to changes in the magnitude and purity as a result of variable manipulations relevant to that category. For example, being made liberal should affect the magnitude, and perhaps the purity, of a category. If 60 stimuli are assigned to the category under liberal instructions, then the magnitude and magnitude-shift would be 1.200 and .500, respectively. If 27 of these stimuli actually belong, then the revised purity and purity-shift would be .450 and .350, respectively. The purity-shift indexes the purity of information entered into (or extracted from) a category because of variable manipulations.

B. AN EXPERIMENT

The composition of a category was computed for four conditions, determined by two levels of category size (3, 9) and two levels of instructional set (liberal, conservative). The transfer stimuli contained old, new, prototype, and unrelated stimuli, with the new stimuli having one of three levels of distortion. Figure 13 shows the composition of a category for these four conditions; the height of each column corresponds to the hit rate for each item type, and the width refers to the objective proportions of each item

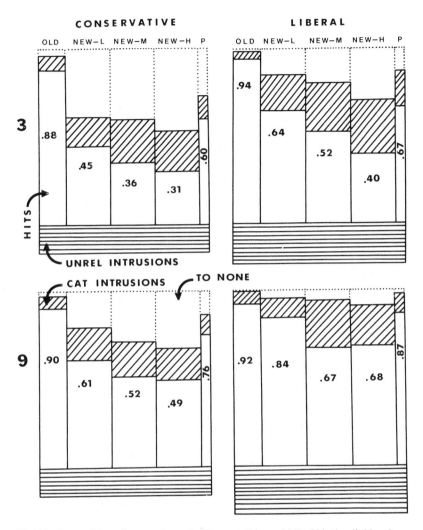

Fig. 13. Composition of categories under four conditions. OLD, Old stimuli; New-L, new, low-level distortions; New-M, new, medium-level distortions; New-H, new, high-level distortions; P, prototype.

type (old items occurred three times per category, each type of new occurred five times per category, and the prototype occurred one time per category).

A number of results are illuminating. First, the magnitude of a category is greater when it was defined by an objectively greater number of instances in the learning phase (Mag-3 = .932; Mag-9 = 1.073), although the magnitude-shift was comparable for both types of categories (MS-3 = .305;

MS-9 = .299). Second, the purity was greater for the larger-sized categories (P-3 = .570; P-9 = .642), as was the purity-shift due to instructional set (PS-3 = .521; PS-9 = .574). If the old stimuli are excluded from these analyses, the magnitude shift is relatively larger but comparable for each category size (MS-3 = .357; MS-9 = .356). Both the purity and purity-shift values drop when the old instances are excluded, especially for the three-instance categories, since the latter are more dominated by old instances (P-3 = .497; P-9 = .594; PS-3 = .498; PS-9 = .570). Third, a greater number of unrelated stimuli were sorted into the nine-instance categories. The proportion of stimuli sorted into a category that was unrelated, however, was comparable for the three- and nine-instance categories (.205 and .194, respectively). Finally, the composition of the unrelated stimuli can also be computed (not shown in Fig. 13). The purity of the unrelated category was, overall, greater for the nine-instance category (.362 versus .508); under liberal instructions, the purity of the unrelated category was relatively unaffected for the three-instance categories (.352 under conservative and .373 under liberal), whereas the purity was substantially improved under liberal instructions for the nine-instance category (.447 versus .570).

What these analyses and Fig. 13 show is a more complicated picture of how the internal representation of a category changes due to variable manipulations. The poorer performance associated with the smaller-sized categories is not due to hesitancy on the subject's part to sort stimuli into these categories, since the purity and purity-shift are much poorer for the smaller categories. The higher false alarm rate for the larger-sized categories conceals the fact that these stimuli constitute a small percentage of the category's composition and that the proportion of unrelated stimuli is no greater for the larger-sized categories. The over-sized magnitude of the nine-instance category indicates that the breadth of these categories is overextended, and even greater levels of category size would probably not diminish this fact. Manipulations that supposedly sharpen the boundary of a category (e.g., increasing the number of categories to be learned or category similarity or both) should reduce the magnitude (overextension) and perhaps increase the purity of the category. Future research should indicate whether this kind of analysis is fruitful and whether variable manipulations can be more sensitively monitored.

VII. A Taxonomy of Categories

Although it may be a fruitless task to attempt to identify the information contained in an individual stimulus (microstructure), some properties about the stimuli within a category can be unambiguously identified (macrostructure), for example, whether the stimuli belong to a category of infinite variation. It will be argued that some types of categories possess an internal structure sufficiently different from that of other categories that qualitatively different mental representations and processing assumptions must be considered.

A taxonomy of categories may be constructed from a variety of viewpoints. One approach is to simply consider the types of stimulus materials that have been employed in studies on category learning and to then group these materials according to obvious criteria. The diversity of categories that has been investigated is impressively varied: artificial categories such as dot patterns (Posner *et al.*, 1967), distorted forms (Homa, 1978) and histoforms (Evans, 1967); Chinese characters (Hull, 1920; Kuo, 1923); geometric forms (Medin & Schaffer, 1978); schematic faces (Goldman & Homa, 1977; Reed, 1972); alphanumeric symbols (Kabrisky, 1970) and handwritten numerals (Backer, 1974); speech (Lowerre, 1976; Reddy, 1976) and speaker characteristics (Atal, 1976; Rosenberg, 1976); poetic (Lindauer & Arcamore, 1974) and artistic (Hartley & Homa, 1981) style; social stereotypes (Cantor & Mischel, 1977; Perloe, 1978); optical illusions (Ginsburg, Carl, Kabrisky, Hall, & Gill, 1974); artificial grammars (Brooks, 1978; Reber & Allen, 1978); natural categories (Rosch *et al.*, 1976); imaginary animals (Brooks, 1978; Sokal, 1974); chest X rays (Harlow & Eisenbeis, 1973); and brain lesions (Meyer & Weissman, 1974). Another approach is to generate a list of categories that come to mind, and again, seek grouping criteria that simplify the list.

The taxonomy shown in Fig. 14 blends both of these considerations and is based on four primary criteria:

1. Is the category deterministic or probabilistic in nature?
2. Is the stimulus domain composed of a finite or an infinite membership?
3. Does each stimulus have an invariant component that can mediate classification?
4. If an invariant component exists, is the remaining (or complementary) information in the stimulus correlated with the invariant component?

The complete listing in Fig. 14 contains 16 globally different kinds of categories, only some of which have been explored in experimental designs. Included in Fig. 14 is a designation of categories into well-defined and ill-defined types, as well as examples of stimulus materials that illustrate the types of categories that have been studied. Thus, the taxonomy would consider the artificial categories employed by Posner and Keele (1968, 1970) as ill defined, whereas the categories used by Hayes-Roth and Hayes-Roth

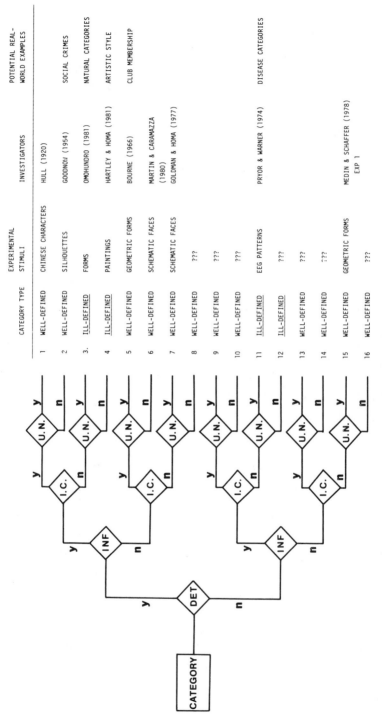

	CATEGORY TYPE	EXPERIMENTAL STIMULI	INVESTIGATORS	POTENTIAL REAL-WORLD EXAMPLES
1	WELL-DEFINED	CHINESE CHARACTERS	HULL (1920)	
2	WELL-DEFINED	SILHOUETTES	GOODNOW (1954)	SOCIAL CRIMES
3.	ILL-DEFINED	FORMS	OMOHUNDRO (1981)	NATURAL CATEGORIES
4	ILL-DEFINED	PAINTINGS	HARTLEY & HOMA (1981)	ARTISTIC STYLE
5	WELL-DEFINED	GEOMETRIC FORMS	BOURNE (1966)	CLUB MEMBERSHIP
6	WELL-DEFINED	SCHEMATIC FACES	MARTIN & CARAMAZZA (1980)	
7	WELL-DEFINED	SCHEMATIC FACES	GOLDMAN & HOMA (1977)	
8	WELL-DEFINED	???		
9	WELL-DEFINED	???		
10	WELL-DEFINED	???		
11	ILL-DEFINED	EEG PATTERNS	PRYOR & WARNER (1974)	DISEASE CATEGORIES
12	ILL-DEFINED	???		
13	WELL-DEFINED	???		
14	WELL-DEFINED	???		
15	WELL-DEFINED	GEOMETRIC FORMS	MEDIN & SCHAFFER (1978) EXP 1	
16	WELL-DEFINED	???		

Fig. 14. A taxonomy of category types. DET, Deterministic; INF, infinitely variable; I.C., invariant component; U.N., uncorrelated noise.

(1977) would be well defined. Medin and Schaffer (1978) used the term ill defined to describe their categories, yet it is appropriate to view their categories as well defined but lacking an invariant component. For example, the stimuli used by Medin and Schaffer were drawn from a finite population, and stimulus variation was minimal. In fact, the stimuli were virtually identical to those previously used by Bourne (1966) and Bruner *et al.* (1956), for example, geometric forms varying in color, number, location, where the different values fall along discrete points on easily verbalized dimensions.

A. DETERMINISTIC AND PROBABILISTIC CATEGORIES

Most categories that have been experimentally studied have deterministic properties. That is, each stimulus belongs, with 100% certainty, to one and only one of the available categories in question. In the simplest case, a defining attribute (e.g., red) or an invariant component characterizes the category; in more complex cases, the stimulus may be statistically generated from a prototypical pattern such that the generated pattern is always more similar to the category prototype than to any other category. In general, the question of importance is this: Given the population of category members for a number of different categories, does there exist an algorithm (however complex) that allows for perfect classification? If the answer is yes, then the category is said to be deterministic.[3]

Relatively few investigators have explored probabilistic categories, although Bruner *et al.* (1956) provided some preliminary data on the learning of categories with probabilistic cues, and Medin and Schaffer (1978) used both probabilistic categories as well as categories that could not be defined by identification of a critical dimension. Reed (1973, Chapter 8) summarizes a number of studies that required the assignment of stimuli to multiple categories, based on probabilistic cues. Still, the study of probabilistic categories has been largely investigated outside the experimental realm, such as the recent attempts to identify medical abnormalities using computer-assisted analyses (Donaldson, 1974; Ingram & Dickinson, 1974). Obviously, the identification of features that predicted a classificatory outcome with 100% accuracy would implicate a deterministic category. Even when categories appear to possess a probabilistic structure, it may be the case that

---

[3]Some hedging is probably necessary. For the most part, deterministic categories should not have members that overlap with the members of other categories. The likelihood of an algorithm producing an extreme-level distortion or highly atypical exemplar cannot be excluded, however. With our distorted form stimuli, involving a total of 20 different form prototypes, we have yet to produce a stimulus that was closer to some other prototype. Still, infinite generation guarantees such an outcome.

cues (or information) that provide for categorization with certainty may exist but have eluded detection. Agassiz (1863) provides a number of interesting examples from zoology in which organisms were reclassified once their internal structure was analyzed more carefully.

A summary of categorical spaces which illustrates different kinds of deterministic and probabilistic categories is shown in Fig. 15. In the simplest case (15a), the categorical space is partitioned into N subsets which are mutually exclusive. Furthermore, category membership is determined by a singly necessary and sufficient property along a specific dimension. Classification by color coding, by height, or by weight would exemplify this

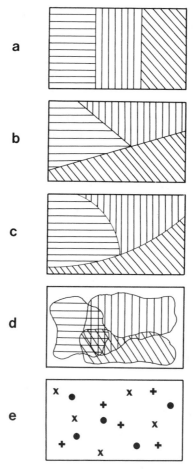

Fig. 15. A summary of category spaces showing deterministic and probabilistic types.

type of structure. This case can be extended to conjunctive and disjunctive categories involving two or more dimensions, the important point being that one or more relevant dimensions partition the space into two or more nonoverlapping subsets. Much of the previous work in category learning which involved well-defined categories (e.g., Bourne, 1966) is of this type.

A more complicated categorical space is shown in Fig. 15b. Here, the categories are mutually exclusive and separable by a series of linear discriminant functions (Sebestyen, 1962). Unlike case 15a, however, the assignment of a stimulus to a category cannot be completely determined by possession of a critical value along a particular dimension. An example of a categorical space having the properties shown in Fig. 15b would be relational categories, where category A contained all objects that are longer than they are wide.

A similar kind of space is shown in Fig. 15c, where the categories are again mutually exclusive, but the categories are bounded by nonlinear functions. The various states of a physical medium (liquid, gas, solid), as affected by temperature and pressure, exemplifies this kind of space. Again, each exemplar has an unambiguous membership.

A probabilistic category space is shown in Fig. 15d, where the categories have overlapping boundaries. This kind of space has received some attention in areas such as medical diagnostics, where the categories are separable only if the medical outcome is considered (e.g., diseased versus nondiseased state). For example, medical researchers have attempted to predict rheumatic heart disease from symptoms such as pulmonary artery mean pressure, total pulmonary resistance, etc. (Pryor & Warner, 1972). It should be noted that the categories in medical diagnostics are separable if the disease is considered as an attribute rather than as a state to be predicted.

Finally, the space in Fig. 15e is a random space in which no categorical boundaries exist. A paired-associate list, in which the stimulus terms are unrelated and the response terms are repeated (e.g., 15 stimuli, 5 of which have the response term A, 5 of which are B, and 5 are C), is an example of a random space.

The five classes of categorical spaces permit a division of deterministic and probabilistic categories. Clearly, case 15a is deterministic and case 15e is probabilistic, since membership is either perfectly determined by possession of a single attribute (15a) or imperfectly determined by any collection of attributes (15e). Although cases 15b and 15c are probabilistic when dimensions are considered singly, it seems preferable to consider these kinds of categories as deterministic; in both cases, an algorithm exists which permits perfect classification, since the categories have nonoverlapping boundaries. Case 15d is probably the fundamental probabilistic categorical space, since boundaries overlap and unequivocal membership cannot be determined.

B. POPULATION SIZE AND STIMULUS VARIATION

One of the primary criteria for distinguishing between well-defined and ill-defined categories is whether the stimulus domain contains members that are infinitely variable. Obviously, if the stimuli have the potential for infinite variation, then the stimulus domain contains an infinite number of stimuli. In effect, the category is ill defined if it is impossible to catalog the stimuli by listing each individual member (and the category lacks an invariant component).

It is useful to exclude from ill-defined categories those categories whose membership is very large but finite in number, and those categories whose membership is infinite due to trivial and minute distortions of finite set. With regard to the former, it is technically possible to write a computer program that can recognize *all* machine-printed letters. The estimated number of fonts, about 300,000, would require an enormously large computer memory, but the program for recognizing any of 300,000 possible fonts is logically reducible to the program for identifying a much smaller number (Young & Calvert, 1974). These programs typically involve the matching of a template for each possible stimulus. This approach fails, however, when the number of potential stimuli is infinitely large, as witnessed by the inability to write a program to recognize handscript (Backer, 1974). With regard to the latter concern, it is clear that even copies of the same stimulus are never exactly identical. Minor imperfections, such as stray marks and minor distortions of the stimulus, are impossible to avoid. Still, the population of stimuli in a category should be considered as finite in size if cleanup and normalizing operations (Neisser, 1967) result in a finite number of stimuli that may be matched with an equivalent number of templates. Only when it is impossible to provide a finite number of templates that produce exact or near-exact matches with all stimulus members may it be concluded that the domain is infinitely large. For example, the form stimuli used by Homa (1978) are sampled from an infinitely large population, whereas the biographical descriptions employed by Hayes-Roth and Hayes-Roth (1977) are drawn from a population of finite size. In the experiments by Medin and Schaffer (1978), the entire population consisted of 16 stimuli, derived from four binary-valued dimensions.

Although determination of the size of the category domain is usually straightforward, there are two cases that warrant comment. The intent of using population size as one determinant for deciding ill-defined and well-defined categories is really predicated on the concept of variance. Although it is true that populations of infinite size will have infinite variety, it is not always true that stimulus components will have infinite variety. Thus, number sequences of indeterminant length belong to a population of infinite size. Here, however, the components have restricted variance. Similarly, the number of grammatical sentences is infinitely large. Although the spoken and written pool of allowable sentences contains unlimited stimulus variety, the potential pool can be transformed such that the components are not variable, for example, typing all sentences with a common font. The sense of the definition of "ill-definedness" would consider the former case to be ill defined, whereas the latter transformed pool to be well defined. Thus, ill-definedness is reserved for populations of infinite size where the components have infinite variation as well.

The second case relates to the manner in which most well-defined categories are constructed. Typically, the experimenter selects a finite number of levels from N dimensions to form the stimulus pool, where the total population size is equal to (number of levels of Dimension 1) $\times$ (number of levels on Dimension 2) $\times$ etc. As represented in a categorical space, the members of a category would be represented as a finite collection of points, rather than regions. If, however, the experimenter chose to sample the levels of each dimension, then the number of potential stimuli in a given category would be infinitely large. With the exception of an occasional study (e.g., Rosch, 1975), investigators have generally ignored the *sampling* of values along stimulus dimensions. According to the criteria adopted here, such a practice would result in categories having ill-defined properties.

C. INVARIANT COMPONENTS AND CORRELATED NOISE

The last two criteria are considered together, since illustrations of these criteria can be demonstrated in a single stimulus. If each stimulus of a category has an invariant component, then it may be further asked whether the stimulus context is correlated with the invariant component. For example, in both Hull's (1920) and Kuo's (1923) study, the stimuli were modified Chinese characters, where each stimulus of a category contained an embedded invariant radical. The population for each category in these studies was infinitely large, however, because the context containing the embedded and invariant component was free to vary. Since neither of these investigators manipulated the stimulus context containing the invariant component, the noise was uncorrelated with the component. That is, the concept *was* the invariant component, and the remainder of the stimulus was irrelevant. The importance of the uncorrelated noise, however, was shown by two curious results obtained by Hull (1920): (1) transfer to new patterns was *not* enhanced by simply learning the common radical; and (2) when subjects were periodically stopped during the learning phase and asked to draw each concept, the subjects' drawings of the common radical clearly changed with increasing learning to better approximate the invariant radical. These results suggest that the common radical became functional only after viewing the radical embedded in irrelevant noise, that is, the irrelevant noise acted to free the invariant component. Nearly all of the early experimental research employed stimuli having an invariant radical or component (e.g., Gengerelli, 1927; Hull, 1920; Kuo, 1923), as did much of the more recent research in concept discovery (e.g., Bruner et al., 1956). Thus, defining a concept as consisting of all red triangles effectively asks the subject to treat as irrelevant all other dimensional information. Unlike the early experimental research, which sampled from a potentially infinite population, most of the rule-discovery research employed stimuli from finite populations.

When the members of a category lack an invariant component, the entire stimulus must represent the category and no noise exists. Experimental examples of categories with an infinite population which lack an invariant component would include the distorted dot-pattern stimuli of Posner (Posner et al., 1967), the related form stimuli (Homa, 1978), and paintings (Lindauer & Arcamore, 1974). Similarly, the categories employed by Medin and Schaffer (1978) and Elio and Anderson (1981) lacked an invariant component, where the category population was finite in size. Most natural categories probably lack an invariant component, as do most esthetic categories.

With the exception of a study by Goodnow (1954), there is no research on categories that have an invariant component and the noise is correlated with the category. Some categories have this property; the legal definition of murder or bribery has an invariant component (someone was killed or bribed). In addition, correlated stimulus information (circumstantial evidence?) is usually available. For murder, a weapon is usually used, the assailant is usually male, etc.

The division of category types into those having an invariant component (with correlated or uncorrelated noise) versus those lacking an invariant component permits a contrast of two views of category abstraction. According to one view, abstraction consists of the isolation of the essential properties of a category, free of the particular context in which the category appeared. This is essentially the view of James (1890). By observing examples of a category in a variety of contexts, the concept becomes synonomous with the invariant property and independent of the specific and idiosyncratic context. By context, James (1890), and presumably others, meant the environment. According to an alternative view, the concept is embodied in the stimulus but not separable from it, that is, the concept cannot be parceled out. Plato embraced this view, as did Locke and others. This is apparently the crux of the discussion between Socrates and his pupil, Menon, who initially attempted to understand the concept of virtue by seeking to discover that invariant component in each virtuous act. Socrates' line of questions ultimately teaches Menon that the invariant component sought is illusory. This argument was made explicit by Smoke (1932) in his criticism of Hull and others who employed stimuli having an invariant component: "What is the 'common element' in 'dog'? Is it something within the visual stimulus pattern? If exact drawings were made of all the dogs now living, or even of those with which any given child is familiar, would they 'contain certain strokes in common' which could be 'easily observed imbedded in each'?'' Smoke likened the experiments by Hull, Kuo, and Gengerelli to one of detection of a camouflaged element in a stimulus complex and argued that such stimuli failed to capture the variance among members of a category.

These two views of abstraction would share more apparent similarity if continuously distorted forms were embedded in uncorrelated noise, the uncorrelated noise functioning like the irrelevant context (environment).

D. CATEGORY TYPES AND MODELS

Only a handful of the category types shown in the taxonomy has received experimental attention, with most of the evidence obtained on five basic types: (1) deterministic categories having a finite population and an invariant component, in which the complementary stimulus information is uncorrelated with the category; (2) deterministic categories having a finite population and lacking an invariant component; (3) deterministic categories having an infinite population and an invariant component, in which the complementary stimulus information is uncorrelated noise; (4) deterministic categories from infinitely large populations which lack an invariant component; and (5) probabilistic categories drawn from an infinite population. Most of the current hypothesis-testing research (e.g., Bourne, 1966; Levine, 1975) characterizes the first type, whereas the second type reflects more recent concerns in which categories lack defining properties (e.g., Medin & Smith, 1981). Much of the early experimental research falls in the third type (e.g., Hull, 1920; Kuo, 1923), and research employing materials generated from a prototypical stimulus (e.g., Omohundro, 1981) belongs to the fourth type. Computer analyses of speech, handscript, and medical symptoms (e.g., Backer, 1974; Reddy, 1976) generally characterize the last type. Of the remaining category types, some have unusual but not impossible properties. For example, categories can have an invariant component but still be probabilistic, since other categories may also contain the same invariant component.

A systematic evaluation of processing differences for the various category types has not been made. There exists, however, a reasonable correspondence in the literature between category types and mode of categorical representation. For example, prototype models have been favored when the population size is infinite and invariant components are lacking; when the component is invariant but well camouflaged, a mixture of prototype (Hull, 1920; Kuo, 1923) and rule-discovery (Smoke, 1932) strategies has been reported. In contrast, prototype models have rarely received support whenever the categories have a finite population. For these category types, hypothesis-testing and exemplar-based models have been favored; the former when an invariant component also exists (e.g., Levine, 1975) and the latter when an invariant component is lacking (Medin & Schaffer, 1978; Medin & Schwanenflugel, 1981; Medin & Smith, 1981).

Recently, evidence has been obtained for deterministic categories having a finite population, where an invariant component exists and the noise is correlated with the category. Martin and Caramazza (1980, Experiment 2) obtained support for hypothesis testing with component features, whereas Kellogg (1980, 1981) proposed a hybrid model based on both feature frequency and hypothesis testing. The difference in complexity of the invariant component may explain these differences; in the Martin and Caramazza study, a conjunctive rule was used, whereas a more difficult biconditional rule was employed by Kellogg (1980).

Currently, it is unclear whether the correspondence between category types and category models is real or specious. If reliable, the taxonomy may help explain the diversity of theoretical conclusions: Different category types breed different kinds of stimulus processing, resulting in different kinds of categorical representation. In effect, the *type* of category is what is important, not its appearance or material form.

The taxonomy may also help sharpen two other issues. First, the taxonomy is biased toward those categories that have been used in laboratory research. It would be useful to know which of these category types have analogs in the natural environment and which might be inventive creations of researchers (Smoke, 1932). Second, the different models may, ultimately, derive from the ease with which critical variables (Section III) are allowed to function. When the population is infinite in size, these variables can function in an unconstrained manner. When the population is finite, variable definition is restricted, oftentimes severely.

VIII. Stimulus Sampling and the Evolution of Concepts

For us, the most interesting kinds of categories are those whose membership is infinitely large and whose features are never exactly repeated. These types of categories are probably the most common in the natural environment, and they may be the most common of the invented categories, such as social stereotypes or artistic style. For example, to label an individual as cowardly is to ascribe traits to an individual that have been revealed by specific behaviors (a set of exemplars) in the past. Not coincidentially, these categories have also proven most resistant to solution by researchers in artificial intelligence.

For these categories, the acquisition and utilization of conceptual information may be broadly conceived as a problem in sampling theory, in which the organism attempts to comprehend the meaning of a category by sampling its members from the category domain. Two related principles probably underlie the acquisition of ill-defined categories and the subsequent generalization to novel experiences: sampling from the stimulus domain pertinent to a category and making inferences about the parent population, given the properties of the stimulus sample used to define a category. It is likely that variables like category size, category similarity, number of categories, and stimulus distortion are important to subsequent generalization *because* these variables are critical to making accurate judgments about the membership of novel stimuli.

The following statements summarize some of the more important properties of a sampling perspective:

1. Information about the environment is accrued by sampling (encountering exemplars) from the stimulus domains of categories.

2. The degree of preexisting structure in each category domain is unknown and probably variable for natural and invented categories, but presumably it is not zero.

3. Stimuli from each category domain differ from each other and in terms of how well they represent a category.

4. Each stimulus conveys information about its own category, and, to a lesser extent, about other categories as well.

5. Each stimulus may be viewed as a kind of informational vector, in which the exemplar is partially defined by the levels of variables it contains, for example, stimulus i is the nth example of this category, in which m categories are under consideration, it is of distortion value k, occurring after t units of time have elapsed since the last member, etc.

6. The breadth, central tendency, and perhaps the sampling distribution of the category become increasingly well described as exemplar sampling increases.

These basic tenets leave open the question of the nature, and even the existence, of potential integrative mechanisms which may operate on the stored exemplars that represent a category.

The sampling perspective sketched here does not so much explain category abstraction as to identify the conditions under which abstraction should be investigated. For example, to answer the question of whether generalization occurs to specific stored examples requires that the variable conditions that define the learning situation be given serious consideration. The answer to this question may be "yes" but only when exemplar sampling is minimal and an immediate test is administered (Homa *et al.*, 1981) or when the category space is relatively unstructured (e.g., Medin & Schaffer, 1978). The answer may be "no," otherwise.

Since sampling models have not been systematically investigated in human categorization paradigms, it follows that they may prove to be unsatisfactory. Nonetheless, until agreed-upon criteria for distinguishing among category types have been established, it is a virtual certainty that contradictory results and conflicting models will flourish in this area.

ACKNOWLEDGMENTS

I would like to thank Julie Omohundro for her extensive comments on each section of the article and Jeff Hartley for reviewing the final version. I would also like to thank David Goldman, who provided comments and references in the area of medical diagnostics and Carl Homa for his assistance with philosophical viewpoints. Finally, I would like to thank Sara Carolyn Fisher for her helpful comments on the purpose of this article.

REFERENCES

Ackrill, J. L. *Aristotle's categories and De Interpretatione.* London and New York: Oxford Univ. Press, 1967.

Agassiz, L. *Methods of study in natural history.* Boston: Houghton, 1863.

Anderson, N. H. *Information integration theory—a brief survey.* (Tech. Rep. CHIP 24) San Diego, California: Univ. of California, Center for Human Information Processing, April, 1972.

Aristotle. *Metaphysics,* R. Hope (trans.). Ann Arbor, Michigan: Univ. of Michigan Press, 1968.

Aristotle. *The philosophy of Aristotle,* R. Bambrough (Ed.). New York: New American Library, 1963.

Atal, B. S. Automatic recognition of speakers from their voices. *Proceedings of the IEEE,* 1976, **64,** 460–475.

Backer, E. Two-step discrimination of hand-written numerals. In J. Rose (Ed.), *Advances in cybernetics and systems* (Vol. 1). London: Gordon & Breach, 1974.

Bartlett, F. C. *Remembering: A study in experimental and social psychology.* London and New York: Cambridge Univ. Press, 1932.

Berkeley, G. A treatise concerning the principles of human knowledge, 1708. In A. J. Ayer & R. Winch (Eds.), *British empirical philosophers.* New York: Simon & Schuster, 1968.

Bersted, C. T., Brown, B. R., & Evans, S. H. Free sorting with stimuli clustered in a multidimensional attribute space. *Perception & Psychophysics,* 1969, **6,** 409–413.

Bourne, L. E. *Human conceptual behavior.* Boston, Massachusetts: Allyn & Bacon, 1966.

Brooks, L. Nonanalytic concept formation and memory for instances. In E. Rosch & B. B. Lloyd (Eds.), *Cognition and categorization.* Hillsdale, New Jersey: Erlbaum, 1978.

Brown, B. R., & Evans, S. H. Perceptual learning in pattern discrimination tasks with two and three schema categories. *Psychonomic Science,* 1969, **15,** 101-103.

Bruner, J. S. On perceptual readiness. *Psychological Review,* 1957, **64,** 123-152.

Bruner, J. S., Goodnow, J. J., & Austin, G. A. *A study of thinking.* New York: Wiley, 1956.

Cantor, N., & Mischel, W. Traits as prototypes: Effects on recognition memory. *Journal of Personality and Social Psychology,* 1977, **35,** 38-48.

Donaldson, F. W. Computers in problem oriented medicine. In J. Rose (Ed.), *Advances in cybernetics and systems* (Vol. 2). London: Gordon & Breach, 1974.

Elio, R., & Anderson, J. R. The effects of category generalizations and instance similarity on schema abstraction. *Journal of Experimental Psychology: Human Learning and Memory,* 1981, **7,** 397-417.

Evans, S. H. Vargus 7: Computed patterns from markov processes. *Behavioral Science,* 1967, **12,** 323-328.

Evans, S. H., & Arnoult, M. D. Schematic concept formation: Demonstration in a free sorting task. *Psychonomic Science,* 1967, **9,** 221-222.

Fisher, S. C. The process of generalizing abstraction; and its product, the general concept. *Psychological Monographs,* 1916, **21,** (whole No. 90).

Franks, J. J., & Bransford, J. D. Abstraction of visual patterns. *Journal of Experimental Psychology,* 1971, **80,** 65-74.

Galton, F. Generic images. *Proceedings of the Royal Institution,* 1879, 161-171.

Gengerelli, J. A. Mutual interference in the evolution of concepts. *American Journal of Psychology,* 1927, **38,** 639-646.

Gibson, E. J. *Principles of perceptual learning and development.* New York: Appleton, 1969.

Ginsburg, A. P., Carl, J. W., Kabrisky, M., Hall, C. F., & Gill, R. A. Psychological aspects of a model for the classification of visual images. In J. Rose (Ed.), *Advances in cybernetics and systems* (Vol. 3). London: Gordon & Breach, 1974.

Goldman, D., & Homa, D. Integrative and metric properties of abstracted information as a function of category discriminability, instance variability, and experience. *Journal of Experimental Psychology: Human Learning and Memory,* 1977, **3,** 375-385.

Goodnow, R. E. *Utilization of partially valid cues in perceptual identification.* Unpublished Ph.D. thesis, Harvard University, 1954.

Harlow, C. A., & Eisenbeis, S. A. The analysis of radiographic images. *IEEE Transactions Computers,* 1973, **C-22,** 678-689.

Hartley, J., & Homa, D. Abstraction of stylistic concepts. *Journal of Experimental Psychology: Human Learning and Memory,* 1981, **7,** 33-46.

Hayes-Roth, B., & Hayes-Roth, F. Concept learning and the recognition and classification of exemplars. *Journal of Verbal Learning and Verbal Behavior,* 1977, **16,** 321-338.

Hintzman, D. L., & Ludlam, G. Differential forgetting of prototypes and old instances: Simultation by an exemplar-based classification model. *Memory & Cognition,* 1980, **8,** 378-382.

Homa, D. Abstraction of ill-defined form. *Journal of Experimental Pschology: Human Learning and Memory,* 1978, **4,** 407-416.

Homa, D., Burruel, L., & Field, D. *The role of decisional factors in category abstraction.* Unpublished manuscript.

Homa, D., & Chambliss, D. The relative contributions of common and distinctive information on the abstraction from ill-defined categories. *Journal of Experimental Psychology: Human Learning and Memory,* 1975, **1,** 351-359.

Homa, D., Cross, J., Cornell, D., Goldman, D., & Shwartz, S. Prototype abstraction and classification of new instances as a function of number of instances defining the prototype. *Journal of Experimental Psychology,* 1973, **101,** 116-122.

Homa, D., & Cultice, J. Role of feedback, category size, and stimulus distortion on the acquisition and utilization of ill-defined categories. *Journal of Experimental Psychology: Learning, Memory, and Cognition,* 1984, **10,** 83–94.

Homa, D., & Little, J. *The abstraction and long-term retention of ill-defined categories by children.* Unpublished manuscript.

Homa, D., & Omohundro, J. *The perception of abstracted form.* Unpublished manuscript.

Homa, D., Rhoads, D., & Chambliss, D. The evolution of conceptual structure. *Journal of Experimental Psychology: Human Learning and Memory,* 1979, **5,** 11–23.

Homa, D., Sterling, S., & Trepel, L. Limitations of exemplar-based generalization and the abstraction of categorical information. *Journal of Experimental Psychology: Human Learning and Memory,* 1981, **7,** 418–439.

Homa, D., & Thorn, L. *Performance on a quadra-sected space.* Unpublished manuscript.

Homa, D., & Vosburgh, R. Category breadth and the abstraction of prototypical information. *Journal of Experimental Psychology: Human Learning and Memory,* 1976, **2,** 322–330.

Hull, C. L. Quantitative aspects of the evolution of concepts. *Psychological Monographs,* 1920, **28** (whole No. 123).

Hume, D. A treatise of human nature, 1739. In A. J. Ayer & R. Winch (Eds.), *British empirical philosophers.* New York: Simon & Schuster, 1968.

Ingram, D., & Dickinson, C. J. A preliminary study of the use of a digital computer model of the heart, circulation, body fluid compartments and kidneys to determine the changes in intrinsic cardiac contractility after a heart attack. In J. Rose (Ed.), *Advances in cybernetics and systems* (Vol. 2). London: Gordon & Breach, 1974.

James, W. *The principles of psychology* (Vols. 1 & 2). New York: Holt, 1890.

Kabrisky, M. A theory of pattern perception based on human physiology. In H. T. Welford & E. H. Houssiadas (Eds.), *Contemporary problems in perception.* London: Francis & Taylor, 1970.

Kellogg, R. T. Feature frequency and hypothesis testing in the acquisition of rule-governed concepts. *Memory & Cognition,* 1980, **8,** 297–303.

Kellogg, R. T. Feature frequency in concept learning: What is counted? *Memory & Cognition,* 1981, **9,** 157–163.

Kruskal, J. B. Multidimensional scaling by optimizing goodness of fit to a nonmetric hypothesis. *Psychometrika,* 1964, **29,** 1–27.

Kulpe, O. Versuche ueber Abstraktion. *Bericht ueber den IoKongress fuer experimentelle Psychologie in Giessen,* 1904, 56–68.

Kuo, Z. Y. A behavioristic experiment on inductive inference. *Journal of Experimental Psychology,* 1923, **6,** 247–293.

Lindauer, M., & Arcamore, A. Concept identification and the identification of poetic style. *Psychological Reports,* 1974, **35,** 207–210.

Levine, M. J. *A cognitive theory of learning: Research on hypothesis testing.* Hillsdale, New Jersey: Erlbaum, 1975.

Locke, J. An essay concerning human understanding, 1690. In A. J. Ayer & R. Winch (Eds.), *British empirical philosophers.* New York: Simon & Schuster, 1968.

Lowerre, B. T. *The HARPY speech recognition system.* Unpublished doctoral dissertation, Carnegie-Mellon University, 1976.

Markman, E. M. Empirical versus logical solutions to part-whole comparison problems concerning classes and collections. *Child Development,* 1978, **49,** 168–177.

Markman, E. M., & Seibert, J. Classes and collections: Internal organization and resulting holistic properties. *Cognitive Psychology,* 1976, **8,** 561–577.

Martin, R. C., & Caramazza, A. Classification in well-defined and ill-defined categories: Evidence for common processing strategies. *Journal of Experimental Psychology: General,* 1980, **109,** 320–353.

McCloskey, M. Intuitive physics. *Scientific American,* 1983, **248,** 122–130.

Medin, D. L., & Schaffer, M. M. Context theory of classification learning. *Psychological Review*, 1978, **85**, 207–238.

Medin, D. L., & Schwanenflugel, P. J. Linear separability in classification learning. *Journal of Experimental Psychology: Human Learning and Memory*, 1981, 7, 355–368.

Medin, D. L., & Smith, E. E. Strategies and classification learning. *Journal of Experimental Psychology: Human Learning and Memory*, 1981, 7, 241–253.

Meyer, A. U., & Weissman, W. K. Computer-aided localization of lesions in the nervous system. In J. Rose (Ed.), *Advances in cybernetics and systems* (Vol. 2). London: Gordon & Breach, 1974.

Moore, T. V. The process of abstraction: An experimental study. *University of California Publications in Psychology*, 1910, **1**, 73–197.

Neisser, U. *Cognitive psychology.* New York: Appleton, 1967.

Neumann, P. G. An attribute frequency model for the abstraction of prototypes. *Memory & Cognition*, 1974, 2, 241–248.

Omohundro, J. Recognition vs. classification of ill-defined category exemplars. *Memory & Cognition*, 1981, 9, 234–331.

Omohundro, J., & Homa, D. Search for abstracted information. *American Journal of Psychology*, 1981, **94**, 267–290.

Perloe, S. I. *Representativeness and distinctiveness in the formation of cognitive prototypes and social stereotypes.* Paper presented to the Eastern Psychological Association, Washington D.C., 1978.

Plato. *Great dialogues of Plato.* E. H. Warmington & P. G. Rouse (Eds.). New York: The New American Library, 1956.

Posner, M. I., Goldsmith, R., & Welton, K. E., Jr. Perceived distance and the classification of distorted patterns. *Journal of Experimental Psychology*, 1967, **73**, 28–38.

Posner, M. I., & Keele, S. W. On the genesis of abstract ideas. *Journal of Experimental Psychology*, 1968, **77**, 353–363.

Posner, M. I., & Keele, S. W. Retention of abstract ideas. *Journal of Experimental Psychology*, 1970, **83**, 304–308.

Pryor, T. A., & Warner, H. R. Some approaches to computerized medical diagnosis. In A. J. Jacquez & C. C. Thomas (Eds.), *Computer diagnosis and diagnostic methods.* Springfield, Illinois: Thomas, 1972.

Reber, A. S., & Allen, R. Analogic and abstraction strategies in synthetic grammar learning: A functionalist interpretation. *Cognition*, 1978, **6**, 189–221.

Reddy, D. R. Speech recognition by machine: A review. *Proceedings of the IEEE*, 1976, **64**, 501–553.

Reed, H. B. Factors influencing the learning and retention of concepts. I. The influence of set. *Journal of Experimental Psychology*, 1946, **36**, 71–87.

Reed, S. K. Pattern recognition and categorization. *Cognitive Psychology*, 1972, 3, 382–407.

Reed, S. K. *Psychological processes in pattern recognition.* New York: Academic Press, 1973.

Rosch, E. The nature of mental codes for color categories. *Journal of Experimental Psychology: Human Perception and Performance*, 1975, **1**, 303–322.

Rosch, E., & Mervis, C. B. Family resemblances: studies in the internal structure of categories. *Cognitive Psychology*, 1975, **7**, 573–605.

Rosch, E., Mervis, C. B., Gray, W. D., Johnson, D. M., & Boyes-Braem, P. Basic objects in natural categories. *Cognitive Psychology*, 1976, **8**, 382–439.

Rosenberg, A. E. Automatic speaker verification: A review. *Proceedings of the IEEE*, 1976, **64**, 475–487.

Rumelhart, D. E., & Abrahamson, A. A. A model for analogical reasoning. *Cognitive Psychology*, 1973, **5**, 1–28.

Sebestyen, G. S. *Decision-making processes in pattern recognition*. New York: Macmillan, 1962.

Shepard, R. N. The analysis of proximities; Multidimensional scaling with an unknown distance function: I. *Psychometrika,* 1962, **27,** 125-140.

Simon, H. A. *The sciences of the artificial* (2nd ed.). MIT Press: Cambridge, Massachusetts, 1982.

Smallwood, R. A., & Arnoult, M. D. A comparison of simple correction and dunctional feedback in schema learning. *Perception & Psychophysics,* 1974, **15,** 581-585.

Smoke, K. L. An objective study of concept formation. *Psychological Monographs,* 1932, **42,** (whole No. 191).

Sneath, P. H. A., & Sokal, R. R. *Numerical taxonomy*. San Francisco, California: Freeman, 1973.

Sokal, R. R. Classification: Purposes, principles, progress, prospects. *Science,* 1974, **27,** 1115-1123.

Wood, D. S. A phenetic assessment of the ciconiidae (aves) using skeletal morphology. *Annals of the Carnegie Museum,* 1983, **52,** 79-112.

Young, T. Y., & Calvert, T. W. *Classification, estimation, and pattern recognition*. New York: American Elsevier, 1974.

Zadeh, L. S. Fuzzy sets. *Information and Control,* 1965, **8,** 338-375.

THE RECOVERY OF UNCONSCIOUS (INACCESSIBLE) MEMORIES: LABORATORY STUDIES OF HYPERMNESIA

Matthew Erdelyi

BROOKLYN COLLEGE OF THE CITY UNIVERSITY OF NEW YORK
BROOKLYN, NEW YORK

I. Hypermnesia for Subliminal Inputs

In 1917, Otto Pötzl, a professor of psychiatry and neurology at the University of Vienna, published the first experimental study of the retrievability of subliminal inputs. The study, in fact, probably constitutes the first experimental investigation of subliminal perception, or subception, along modern lines.

The background of this work was Pötzl's involvement with a number of patients suffering brain damage in the visual cortex. What particularly intrigued Pötzl about these cases was that, in addition to suffering from a variety of expectable perceptual deficits, some of these patients also evidenced paradoxical enhancements of perceptual sensitivity.

Consider, for example, the case of Obszut, a patient of Pötzl's who had suffered a gunshot wound in the occipital area. Obszut was described as having unusually sensitive peripheral vision—he had, however, virtually no central vision left. At the same time, Obszut's central vision was hypersensitive in one respect: He was able, under certain circumstances, to perceive his blind spot. Another feature of Obszut's "enhanced" visual world was that he saw in double rather than in single images (*physiological diplopia*). Finally, and probably most intriguing to Pötzl, was a phenomenon he termed *delayed piecemeal delivery into consciousness:* When fixating on some complex stimulus, Obszut could see little or nothing; however, a short time after the removal of the stimulus (Pötzl doesn't specify how long after),

THE PSYCHOLOGY OF LEARNING
AND MOTIVATION, VOL. 18

Obszut would often experience the sudden crystallization in consciousness of some cohesive, previously unseen detail of the stimulus or its intrusion into a subsequent percept.

Since these types of perceptual "enhancements" resulted from destruction rather than any addition to the perceptual system, Pötzl quite logically reasoned that such heightened sensitivities had to result from the *destruction of inhibitory mechanisms* that normally blocked maladaptive hypersensitivities. In other words, all of us could, in principle, perceive our blind spot or see in double images, but some merciful inhibitory system intervenes (Pötzl termed it the *abstracting process*) to spare us from such embarrassment of perceptual riches. The clear implication of this reasoning is that much more of the input is registered and processed than is normally accessible to conscious perception (i.e., the subception hypothesis).

It occurred to Pötzl to wonder whether it might be possible to demonstrate such disinhibition effects—*release phenomena*—in normal, neurologically intact subjects. Pötzl, who was one of the few established academicians in Vienna to take a serious interest in psychoanalysis (for many years he was a member of the Vienna Psychoanalytic Society), finally settled upon dreams as the disinhibited cognitive medium in normal people that might yield effects similar to those of his brain-damaged patients. Pötzl finally carried out the following experiment with some dozen inmates at his mental hospital. Each subject was tested individually and, by means of a tachistoscope, shown a complex pictorial stimulus for 10 msec. The subject was then required to reproduce in a drawing everything that he had perceived. Much like Obszut (when he was centrally fixating upon a stimulus), the subject could report little if anything of the stimulus. The subject was then instructed to return to his room, have a dream that night, and return the next day to report his dream. Pötzl's finding, now known as the *Pötzl effect,* was that many undetected (i.e., subliminal) features of the stimulus emerged, often in disguised or transformed fashion, in the content of the subjects' dreams.

Pötzl presented his findings to the Vienna Psychoanalytic Society in 1917. Freud, who rarely saw value in laboratory experiments in psychology, was, for once, impressed. So much so, that he added the following footnote to his 1919 revision of the *Interpretation of dreams* (1900/1963):

An important contribution to the part played by recent material in the construction of dreams has been made by Pötzl (1917) in a paper that carries a wealth of implications. . . . The material that was taken over by the dream-work was modified by it for the purpose of dream-construction in its familiar "arbitrary" manner [i.e., primary process cognitive operations such as displacement, condensation, primitive symbolization]. The questions raised by Pötzl's experiment go far beyond the sphere of dream interpretation as dealt with in the present volume. (pp. 181–182)

Although enthusiastic, Freud was not particularly specific about the "wealth of implications" posed by the Pötzl study. At the minimum, the following points might be interpolated:

1. The study (insofar as it is valid) corroborates the reality of unconscious perception and memory.
2. It demonstrates the feasibility of recovering unconscious materials into consciousness, that is, hypermnesia.
3. It substantiates Freud's claim that "dreams are hypermnesic" (e.g., Freud, 1900/1963, pp. 11–17, p. 589).

Despite Freud's footnote and, indeed, the fundamental implications of the study, there was only scattered follow-up research on the topic (Allers & Teler, 1924; Malamud, 1934; Malamud & Linder, 1931) until Charles Fisher revived it in the mid 1950s, at the height of the New Look movement.

The Allers and Teler (1924) study is worth examining briefly, both because of its interesting theoretical perspective and because of a practical innovation. According to Allers and Teler, the Pötzl effect had nothing to do with disinhibition, the unconscious, or dreams per se; rather, the effect was to be understood in terms of a hypothesis put forth by Allers in 1922, according to which the psychological system comprised (roughly speaking) two partially dissociated subsystems: a pictorial and a verbal subsystem. Intentional memory reports tend to access information in the verbal subsystem; there exists, however, residual information in the pictorial or imagistic system, especially for items that are not "namable" or "word-near." These materials can be recovered by tapping the information in the picture system through a variety of imagistic productions, including—but not exclusively—dreams. Dreams, therefore, are not unique; the effect, as Allers and Teler demonstrated experimentally, could just as readily be obtained with waking imagery productions. Because of "the independence of the verbal process from the pictorial" (p. 146), each system contributes its own, often nonoverlapping information. Indeed, recoveries from one subsystem are often not recognized by the other (recall without recognition).

Although it is not clear whether the Allers and Teler reconceptualization is at variance, in a formal sense, with the notion of unconscious mentation [dissociation being a basic paradigm of unconscious processes (Erdelyi, 1984)] or, for that matter, with disinhibition (*secondary process functioning* tending, according to psychoanalytic theory to inhibit imagistic *primary process functioning*), the possibility of demonstrating the Pötzl effect in waking states made the phenomenon more accessible to standard laboratory procedures and substantially influenced subsequent experimental practices.

The more modern literature, which gradually incorporated a variety of crucial methodological refinements, has pervasively replicated the Pötzl effect, both with dreams as well as a spectrum of other fantasy media, such as daydreams, imagery, and free associations (e.g. Eagle, Wolitzky, & Klein, 1966; Fisher, 1954, 1956; Fisher & Paul, 1959; Fiss, Goldberg, & Klein, 1963; Giddan, 1967; Hilgard, 1962; Shevrin & Luborsky, 1958; for comprehensive reviews, see Dixon, 1981; Eriksen, 1962).

Nevertheless, there remained a fundamental conceptual issue which Charles Eriksen and Israel Goldiamond independently articulated in 1958. It was pointed out that subception effects, of which the Pötzl effect is a variant, were based on observed discrepancies between two *different* indicators of perception: (1) an *intentional report* and (2) (in the case of the Pötzl effect) some *fantasy* production. Such discrepancies might reflect intrinsic differences in the indicators rather than subception; that is, dissociation between indicators need not imply psychological dissociation—between conscious and unconscious. (A modern variant of this issue is to be found in the problem of interpreting the meaning of discrepancies between *recall* and *recognition* indicators of memory.) In the case of the Pötzl effect, for example, there is, at the simplest level, the problem of differential response output from the two indicators—very few or no responses in intentional reports of tachistoscopic inputs versus many lines or pages of responses in dream or fantasy reports (cf. Erdelyi, 1972). Or, there may be differences in amount or type of contextual elaboration (cf. Hilgard, 1962). Or, there may be subtle or unexpected effects, such as possible chance base-rate differences in item occurrence in intentional reports versus fantasy reports (cf. Johnson & Eriksen, 1961).

In response to these intractable problems, which probably no configuration of controls can fully resolve, Haber and Erdelyi (1967), borrowing from the work of Hilgard (1962), introduced a new strategy. If "fantasy" (dreams, daydreams, free associations, doodles, etc.) has the property of making contact with unconscious or dissociated information, then it is possible that some of this activated material might become accessible to a post-fantasy intentional recall. If this were true, then it would be possible to demonstrate the effect by comparing the same indicator (e.g., *recall*) before and after fantasy, bypassing the intractable problem of *inter*indicator comparisons. The approach is a simple extension of the Pötzl paradigm, which may be schematized as S–R–F, that is, stimulus, S, followed by recall, R, followed by fantasy, F, the effect being defined by the interindicator discrepancy $F > R$. Haber and Erdelyi simply appended a second, postfantasy recall test to the original paradigm: $S–R_1–F–R_2$. The critical comparison, however, was no longer $F > R$ but $R_2 > R_1$, the question becoming whether after a period of fantasy generation (some 40 min in Haber & Erdelyi) subjects would evidence hypermnesia rather than amnesia with the passage of time and mental activity.

The stimulus used (Fig. 1) was presented for 500 msec, enough for the detection of at least some of the items. The intentional reports (R_1 and R_2) were labeled drawings of everything seen and remembered from the stimulus. The fantasy task involved free associations to self-generated cue words. One of the two control groups employed engaged in an enjoyable sensorimotor task (dart throwing) between R_1 and R_2 instead of fantasy. A second control group, the "yoked" subjects, never actually saw the stimulus but instead copied the first drawing (R_1) of an experimental counterpart, free associated, and then tried to produce an improved R_2. The results were unambiguous. The fantasy subjects, unlike the control subjects, recalled more stimulus items after fantasy than immediately after the stimulus presentation but before fantasy, that is, $R_2 > R_1$. (Also, the fantasy material was shown to contain stimulus content retrieved in neither recall effort, replicating the traditional Pötzl effect.)

Two examples of pre- and postfantasy recall, in the form of drawings, are presented in Figs. 2 and 3. It will be seen that considerable stimulus

Fig. 1. The stimulus presented for 500 msec by Haber and Erdelyi (1967).

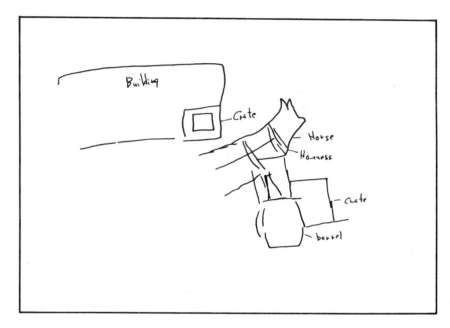

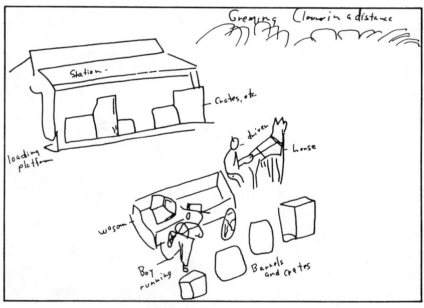

Fig. 2. Pre- and postfantasy recall of subject H. J.

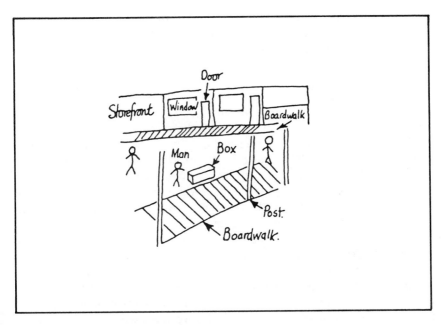

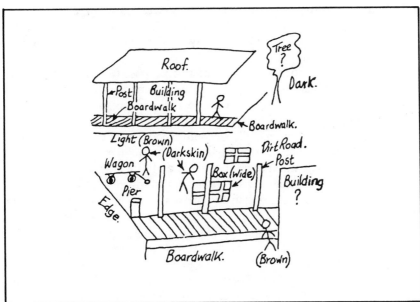

Fig. 3. Pre- and postfantasy recall of subject L. B.

material was recovered in the second recall effort after some 40 min of free associations. Neither of the control groups produced any similar recoveries. The statistical analyses bore out the recovery effect as well as the group differences. For example, a blind judge rated pairs of drawings without knowledge of which groups the pairs were drawn from, nor which was R_1 or R_2. Of the 20 experimental postfantasy recalls (R_2), all 20 were judged superior ($p = \frac{1}{2}^{20}$). On the other hand, no reliable discrimination was achieved between R_1 and R_2 for the control groups.

The study, therefore, succeeded not only in experimentally confirming the Pötzl effect (F > R) but also in demonstrating the derivative, methodologically less problematical, "recovery effect" ($R_2 > R_1$).

There remained, however, one methodological issue. Although the number of responses produced in the two recall trials did not grossly differ as it did between the two different indicators, recall versus free associations, there was nevertheless a discernable difference in response output between pre- and postfantasy recall (see Figs. 2 and 3). This small difference could, of course, reflect the subjects' superior recall of the stimulus after fantasy. An alternative possibility, however, is that the fantasy subjects resorted to laxer response criteria. This seemed an unlikely explanation since a very thorough and systematic prodding procedure was used in all recall trials and for all groups to ensure that everything detected was reported, short of outright guessing. Nevertheless, a formal investigation of this factor seemed necessary before it could be safely concluded that fantasy amplified subliminal memory traces.

Two converging tactics were used for this purpose (Erdelyi, 1970). One was to equate response number in R_1 and R_2 by forcing subjects to generate a set number of items in all recall trials, guessing if necessary. Thus, a shift was made from *free recall* to *forced recall* (forced in terms of response number, not response order). The second experimental tack was to make use, in some studies, of a recognition indicator of memory and directly compute d' for recognition memory before and after fantasy.

The outcome of this complex of studies was also—much to the author's chagrin—unambiguous. Although the original recovery effect was readily replicated, the effect was shown unmistakably to be a response criterion effect (β) and not a true memory effect (d'). Thus, the effect of free associations was not the *recovery of inaccessible memories* but the recovery of *unreported memories*.

In a follow-up study of the Pötzl-type design (F versus R), in which the number of fantasy responses (doodles) were equated with number of intentional recall responses (bona fide recalls plus forced guesses), it was shown that not only was fantasy not superior to intentional recall but that, on the contrary, intentional recall was actually superior to fantasy in reflecting stimulus content (Erdelyi, 1972).

Fantasy, free associative or imagistic, was not after all hypermnesic—at least not in these studies controlling response output. These findings were rather discomforting for the psychoanalytic hypothesis, at least as the author construed it. Freud (1900) had claimed that "dreams are the royal road to the . . . unconscious." It had been the author's assumption—congruent with Freud's conception of free associative fantasy—that fantasy was at least a noble path. These experiments suggested otherwise. Moreover, they raised questions about the claim of psychoanalysis that all kinds of unconscious memories are eventually recovered in psychoanalytic therapy. To the extent that these recoveries are not confabulations ["false recollections," "paramnesias" (cf. Freud, 1906)] might they merely be response bias effects?

The author was prepared to abandon this line of research. There remained, however, one last study to conduct—"last" because of the expectation, by this point, that it too would prove abortive.

II. Hypermnesia for Subliminal (Inaccessible) Memories

This study (Erdelyi & Becker, 1974) was informed by two considerations. The first of these was the gradual realization that the type of recoveries dealt with in psychoanalysis are not of tachistoscopic inputs; there exists, in fact, no claim in Freud's writings—his 1919 footnote on Pötzl's work is the closest he comes to suggesting it—that subthreshold tachistoscopic inputs are registered unconsciously, much less that they are recoverable. Freud does make such a claim for "incidental" or "unattended" inputs, but that is not the same claim. The recoveries of focal interest in psychoanalysis concern items that are subliminal, that is, unconscious, not because they are initially impoverished visually but because (excepting materials "primally repressed") they became, after being fully—often painfully—conscious, eventually inaccessible to conscious recollection. Thus, a critical change in strategy was to transpose the study from one of subliminal *perception* to one of subliminal, that is, inaccessible *memory*. In this new experiment, the stimulus was not a tachistoscopic flash but a superspan memory list.

The list consisted of 80 slides, each individually presented for 5 sec, consisting of 40 simply sketched single objects (e.g., watch, fish, boomerang, rat, feather) and 40 printed word labels for similar types of objects. (The word items were included in the study on the hunch that they, unlike the pictures, might be successfully activated or cued by the words generated in fantasy.) The words and pictures were interspersed randomly and presented individually for 5 sec each, for a total "stimulus duration" of about 7 min. The subjects were then administered a 7-min *forced*-recall test, in which they were required to produce a preset number of responses, guessing if necessary. The recall responses were all verbal, regardless of whether the items recalled were words or pictures. This first recall effort, R_1, was followed by a fantasy task, F, of 7 min duration, which, because subjects were tested in groups, was in written form (i.e., "automatic writing"). The fantasy task was then followed by a second forced-recall test, R_2, requiring the same number of responses as in R_1 and also 7 min in duration. Thus far the basic design is that of the Haber and Erdelyi study (except for the type of the stimulus, the *forced* nature of the recall, and the shortened fantasy interval). On the possibility that the original fantasy period might not be sufficient, another fantasy series was instituted, followed by a final forced-recall test. The basic design, then, may be schematized as follows: $[S]_{40P,40W}$ $-R_1-F-R_2-F-R_3$.

The second novel feature of this experiment was the inclusion of another experimental group, one which featured "concentration," instead of fantasy production. This new group was suggested by careful reading of the psychoanalytic literature, particularly Freud's early writings on the recovery of unconscious materials (Breuer & Freud, 1895). It turns out that with Freud's adoption of the free-association procedure there occurred a subtle but fundamental shift in emphasis in the consciousness-raising objective of the therapy (cf. Erdelyi, 1984). The starting point of psychoanalysis, Breuer's *cathartic technique,* was essentially a hypnotic hypermnesia procedure: The patient, under hypnosis, was required to recover the episodes—both the facts and the emotions—associated with the outbreak of the target symptoms. The recall of these events and the uninhibited expression of the accompanying emotions were thought to put an end to the hysterical symptoms, which Freud conceived of as *reminiscences* articulated in the recondition dialect—incomprehensible to the patient himself—of *organ speech* (Breuer & Freud, 1895). The therapeutic objective, then, was for the patient to recall the episodes consciously rather than unconsciously and indirectly (symptoms).

With the shift away from hypnosis to free associations, psychoanalysis retained its hypermnesic objective—C. G. Jung continued to refer to it at times as *hypermnesic therapy*—but the focus now shifted away from gaining consciousness for isolated past events to gaining consciousness for themes or patterns of events, that is, to gaining "insight." Since the types of recoveries under experimental investigation were of the former kind, it was thought desirable to explore in the experiment the earlier hypermnesic procedure. Instead of hypnosis, an intermediate technique was adopted which had been employed by Freud for a short period in his transition from hypnosis to free associations. This technique was one labeled *concentration* or *pressure* by Freud and consisted, roughly speaking, of hypnotic instruction without hypnotic induction. The subject was insistently told that regardless of its subjective implausibility, he would be able to remember; failure to recover the target memories was met with continued insistence for further concentration and effort (accompanied, at times, by Freud's laying his hand upon the recalcitrant patient's forehead, in the tradition of faith healing, with the repeated assurance that he would be able to recall under the "pressure" of his hand).

The concentration technique adopted in the experiment was a very mild variant of Freud's mnemonic badgering procedure. Instead of receiving free-association instructions between recall trials, subjects in this group were asked to close their eyes and continue silently "thinking" about the original list, without allowing their attention to wander for any prolonged period.

A third set of subjects, who engaged in no interpolated activities between recall trials but immediately proceeded from one trial to the next, served as controls.

The outcome of the study is summarized in Table I. It will be seen that, contrary to the author's original hunch, recall of words, regardless of treatment, remained constant over recall trials. The pattern of picture recall, however, was dramatically distinctive: Regardless of the nature of the interpolated activity, or its absence, picture recall increased with repeated recall effort.

Informal reactions to these data by the author's experimental colleagues were generally skeptical. Replication of the findings seemed essential. A modified new study was immediately undertaken. One new design feature was to make the pictures-versus-words condition a between- rather than a

TABLE I

AVERAGE RECALL SCORES[a]

Group	Pictures			Words		
	R_1	R_2	R_3	R_1	R_2	R_3
Free association	16.65	18.30	18.59	14.00	14.17	14.23
Think	15.76	17.76	18.94	16.35	16.82	17.00
No interval	15.82	17.11	18.05	13.41	12.47	13.00
Mean (all subjects)	16.08	17.72	18.53	14.59	14.49	14.74

[a] Erdelyi and Becker (1974, p. 163).

within-subjects treatment; that is, subjects viewed either just pictures (60 of them) or just words (the verbal labels corresponding to the 60 pictures). This modification was prompted by the outside possibility that in the previous recall procedure the subjects adopted differential response criteria for the pictures and words, resulting in the obtained picture–word differences. The second modification was one of economy. Since there was no hint that free associative fantasy had in any way augmented the picture hypermnesia effect—in fact, the free-association group had produced the numerically smallest picture recall increment—it seemed pointless to continue including this treatment. It appeared that free associative fantasy (see, also, Erdelyi, 1972) is not hypermnesic, at least no more so than concentrated retrieval effort, that is, thinking. Thus, there were four independent experimental groups: subjects who saw *pictures* or *words* crossed with subjects with interpolated *think* intervals between trials and subjects with *no intervals* between trials.

The experimental outcome (Fig. 4) fully replicated the first study: Picture recall increased over time and recall effort whereas word recall remained constant. Statistical analysis, moreover, showed that, as suggested by the

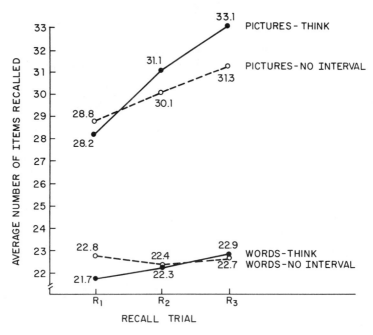

Fig. 4. Picture and word recall over recall trials with and without interpolated think intervals. (From Erdelyi & Becker, 1974, Study 2.)

recall patterns in Fig. 4, the interpolated think intervals enhanced the hypermnesia effect.

There is nothing mysterious about the effectiveness of the think intervals in enhancing hypermnesia. It appears that they simply function as *covert* counterparts of overt recall. This can be garnered from Fig. 5 (Erdelyi, 1977) which plots recall as a function of retrieval time in Study 2 of Erdelyi and Becker. Clearly, it makes no difference, at least in this study, whether retrieval is in the form of official recall trials or silent thinking; net recall of pictures (but not of words) increases with retrieval time, overt or covert (see also, Erdelyi & Kleinbard, 1978; Roediger & Thorpe, 1978; Shapiro & Erdelyi, 1974). From this vantage point, free associative fantasy may be viewed as inefficient retrieval effort. Of course, what may be an inefficient technique for recovering episodic events may yet prove to be effective for uncovering undetected coherences—themes or patterns—among events, that is, for gaining insight.

The Erdelyi and Becker (1974) studies, in any case, experimentally corroborated the existence of hypermnesia for subliminal items. This hypermnesia effect, however, involved not inaccessible perceptual inputs but inaccessible memories. It became a pressing concern at this point to connect

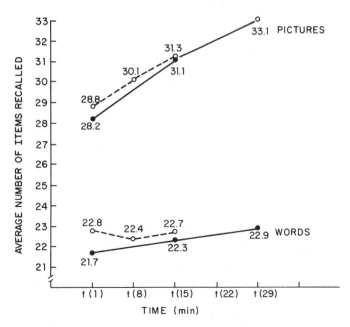

Fig. 5. Picture and word recall as a function of retrieval time, overt or covert, in Study 2 of Erdelyi and Becker. (From Erdelyi, 1977.)

up these findings, which had independently evolved from the subliminal perception tradition, with the already extant laboratory literatures on homologous memory effects. The most relevant literatures seemed to be those on reminiscence and hypnotic hypermnesia.

It is beyond the scope of this article to attempt a review of these substantive research traditions. Instead, three "facts" extracted by the author from these literatures will be briefly considered. Quotation marks are used advisedly since at least the last of these "facts" has recently become controversial.

First, the ostensible hypermnesic effects obtained in past memory work were controversial.

Let us take up reminiscence first. Ballard (1913), in an impressive series of studies, had demonstrated that children's recall of poetry actually increased rather than decreased with time, at least up to a few days. He called the recovery of hitherto inaccessible items, *reminiscence,* importing the term into psychology from Plato. The demonstration of memory improvement over time stirred wide interest in succeeding decades, in part because of its disturbing implications for the Ebbinghaus curve of forgetting (e.g., McGeoch, 1935; Williams, 1926). The phenomenon was soon mired in methodological controversy and difficulties of replication, however. Buxton (1943), in his classic review, was forced to conclude that after a sustained effort by experimental psychologists to discover the "effective conditions" (if any) for reminiscence (including age, sex, IQ, length of stimulus list, level of initial mastery, frequency of presentations), reminiscence remained a "now-you-see-it now-you-don't" phenomenon.[1]

---

[1]A comment about terminology is in order regarding *reminiscence* and *hypermnesia.* In practice, researchers have often used the two terms to refer to the same phenomenon. The author chose to adopt the term hypermnesia for several reasons. One of these was the semantic drift which had overtaken the concept of reminiscence. Although Ballard, who introduced the term, chose to treat *internal review* (thinking, covert retrieval) between recall tests as a component, albeit not a crucial one, of reminiscence (Ballard distinguished between *simple reminiscence,* which involved no review, and *compound reminiscence,* which did involve review), subsequent researchers (cf. Buxton, 1943) chose to treat review as an artifact which had to be eliminated for bona fide reminiscence to be demonstrated. Since the author's research, and probably most of the work on therapeutic and hypnotic hypermnesia did involve internal review, the term hypermnesia seemed more appropriate. Further, there exists a basic inconsistency regarding the phenomenon to which reminiscence actually refers. The early pages of Ballard's monograph, in which reminiscence is defined as "the remembering again of the forgotten without re-learning," suggest that he was in fact referring to *net* increases in recall of poetry over time, and this is how subsequent researchers in the field construed the term. A careful reading of Ballard shows, however, that he intended another phenomenon:

> It will be observed that I have so far spoken mainly of the improvement in the capacity to reproduce lines of poetry memorised, and have made but little reference to reminiscence proper. It might indeed be thought that since the improvement referred to is due

The hypnotic hypermnesia literature is no less inconclusive. A rough sampling of experimental studies reveals an approximate 50–50 split between successful and unsuccessful outcomes. (For a simple explanation of this unreliability, see Erdelyi, Dinges, Orne, & Orne, 1984.) Other ostensible hypermnesic phenomena, such as the Penfield effect, are likewise in doubt (cf. Neisser, 1967; Loftus & Loftus, 1980) as is, as has been seen, the purported power of dreams to recover lost memories.

The second basic "fact" common to past hypermnesia literatures is that they fail to control for response bias effects. No published experimental demonstration of hypnotic hypermnesia known to the author controls for this factor and so, even in the 50% of the cases where results are positive, it cannot be assumed that hypnosis in fact produced enhanced recall rather than merely enhanced responding and, therefore, more hits (cf. Klatzky & Erdelyi, 1984). This problem applies as well to virtually all published re-

---

to reminiscence, as according to my definition of the term it obviously is, the amount of improvement would indicate the amount of reminiscence. But this is not so. Suppose for instance a subject wrote correctly six lines at the primary test and six lines at the secondary test. One would naturally infer that the lines written at the two tests were identical. But a scrutiny of the actual papers reveals the fact that this is frequently not the case. What often happens is that the pupil loses one or more of the original six lines and remembers one or more that were not remembered at the primary test. In other words reminiscence has taken place. So it is when the pupil improves. The amount of reminiscence is frequently greater than the difference between the two measures. And not even when the pupil's record deteriorates does it follow that no reminiscence has taken place. (Ballard, 1913, pp. 17–18)

Thus, by reminiscence Ballard is referring to item recoveries from the first to second trial—"NC" (Tulving, 1964) or "01" items (Erdelyi, Finkelstein, Herrell, Miller, & Thomas, 1976)—and not to net increases in recall, i.e., "improvement." As Ballard stresses, reminiscence (NC, 01) tends to be countered by "oblivescence" (CN, 10) so that net recall often fails to reflect extensive reminiscence. But if this is what reminiscence constitutes, then it hardly is a "now-you-see-it now-you-don't phenomenon." In fact, it would be hard to think of a more robust one, the phenomenon of intertrial item variability being incontrovertibly established—and not just in children or with pictures or poems (Ballard, 1913; Erdelyi *et al.,* 1976; Roediger & Thorpe, 1978; Tulving, 1964).

This inconsistency in the meaning of reminiscence suggests a clarifying terminological distinction between reminiscence and hypermnesia which already seems to be on the way to adoption in the modern literature (Belmore, 1981; Roediger & Thorpe, 1978; Roediger *et al.,* 1982). Following Ballard (but not subsequent investigators of the phenomenon), *reminiscence* is taken to refer to item recoveries on succeeding memory trials irrespective of item losses. Thus, amount of reminiscence in multitrial memory tests consists of the cumulative number of items recovered beyond the initial trial, that is, $\text{Rem} = \text{cum } R_n - R_1$, where Rem, reminiscence, is the cumulative level of recall at the last (nth) trial, cum R_n, minus the number of item recoveries on the first trial, R_1. In contrast, *hypermnesia* (Ballard's "improvement") refers to increments in *net* recall across succeeding trials. Thus: $\text{Hyp} = R_n - R_1$, where hypermnesia, Hyp, is net recall on the last (nth) trial, R_n, minus net recall on the first trial, R_1.

ports on reminiscence (in the sense of hypermnesia—see Footnote 1). Thus, Ballard's children may have produced more correct lines of poetry because they produced more lines of poetry.

The third common denominator underlying the hypermnesia literatures, which at this point is more correctly to be regarded as a hypothesis than a fact, is that imagery is intimately associated with hypermnesia and may in fact be the key to hypermnesia (for earlier claims to this effect, see, Allers & Teler, 1924; Holt, 1964; Jung, 1935). This link is obvious in regard to dreams (the imagistic cognitive medium par excellence) and the Penfield effect. Also, it may be gleaned from Freud's early approach to eliciting hypermnesia in therapy (Breuer & Freud, 1895). Repeatedly, Freud speaks not just of memories but of "picture ideas" (p. 315), "memory pictures" (p. 343), and "memory images" (p. 345). When instructing his patients to try recovering lost memories, he urges them to "bring out pictures and ideas" (p. 193) and assures them, even if they draw a blank initially, that they will ultimately "see" before them "a recollection in the form of a picture" (p. 315). He prods their recall by asking: "Do you see this scene before your eyes?" (p. 153). "Go on looking at the [mental] picture; it will develop and become more specialized. . . . Be patient and just keep looking at the picture" (p. 158). Elsewhere: "When memories return in the form of pictures our task is in general easier than when they return as thoughts. Hysterical patients, who are as a rule of a 'visual' type, do not make such difficulties for the analyst as those with obsession" (p. 325).

Ballard (1913) also noted "the seeming preponderance of visual imagery" (p. 41) in reminiscence. He writes:

> good visualisers were able to see more lines or a more complete scene the second time, e.g.,
>
> J. T. improved from 15 to 21 lines in three days. Imagined she saw the lines in front of her.
>
> J. I. improved from 9 to 10 lines in two days, and from 19 to 21 lines in three days. Pictured the paper with the hectographed lines.
>
> W. R. improved from 13 to 16 lines in two days and from 25 to 26 lines in three days. Imagined the scene, but not the words.
>
> E. G. improved from 10 to 26 lines in two days. Visualised lines.
>
> J. P. improved from 3 to 11 lines in seven days. Pictured the words on the blackboard (the poetry in this case was learnt from the blackboard).
>
> B. G. improved from 9 to 13 lines in seven days. "As I began to write it, I could picture it on the paper before me." (Ballard, 1913, p. 40)

The hypnotic hypermnesia literature similarly tends to implicate imagistic processes. The classic experiment of White, Fox, and Harris (1940) is prototypic of the literature as a whole. Three types of stimuli were used: nonsense syllables, pictures, and poetry. Of these, nonsense syllables proved to be inert, whereas pictures and poetry yielded hypnotic hypermnesia.

Finally, there is the Erdelyi and Becker study, with its striking picture-word difference in hypermnesia.

Nevertheless, it is to be noted that part of the evidence is surmise rather than data. Although pictures in contrast to isolated words incontestably yield hypermnesia, it is also the case that certain kinds of verbal materials, notably poetry, seem to be effective. It is of course the case that poetry is a form of verbal discourse that is uniquely imagistic.

Along these lines, an interesting observation arises from an examination of *individual* recall patterns for words. Erdelyi and Becker noticed that whereas the *grouped* word-recall functions were inert, there was considerable individual variability; some subjects recalling words produced hefty hypermnesias over trials, which, however, were counterbalanced by other subjects' amnesic or inert word-recall functions. Halfway through their Study 2, Erdelyi and Becker began to query the word subjects, at the end of their last recall trial, about the kinds of coding strategies they had used at the time of the stimulus presentation. Three types of coding strategies were most often mentioned: (1) recoding the words into images, (2) conceptual organization of the words, and (3) silent repetition. A very clear relation emerged between coding strategy and hypermnesia. Three word subjects reported recoding the words into images, and all three, upon the scoring of their recall protocols, turned out to have produced hypermnesia. The other subjects, however, almost uniformly showed amnesia for words or no change over recall trials. Was it then the image code rather than the actual stimulus format that was responsible for hypermnesia? The question suggested a straightforward experiment, which was carried out by Erdelyi, Finkelstein, Herrell, Miller, and Thomas (1976).

The experiment involved a direct replication of the picture and word conditions (with interpolated thinking) in Study 2 of Erdelyi and Becker, with the addition of a third condition. Subjects in this latter group were treated identically to the word group, with one exception: These subjects were instructed, prior to the presentation of the word list, to try to form a picture of each verbal item as it was being shown. Figure 6 summarizes the obtained results.

As in Erdelyi and Becker, recall of the set of pictures (P) increased over recall trials, whereas recall of the word set (W) remained inert. On the other hand, recall of the words that had been imaged (IW) was hypermnesic like the recall of pictures (there being no statistical differences between the P and IW groups). These data suggest that the critical factor in hypermnesia is not the stimulus format (pictures) but the coding format (images). An internal correlational analysis performed on the W group, between magnitude of hypermnesia (R_3-R_1) and coding strategies (as reported by subjects in a postexperimental rating form), tended to replicate the experimental effects: Extent of *imagery recoding* correlated significantly $(r =$

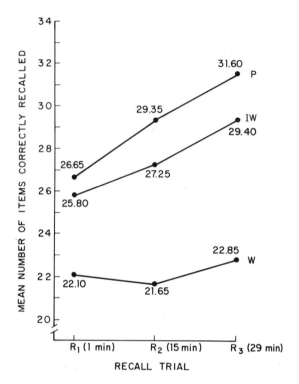

Fig. 6. Recall as a function of recall trials for a set of pictures (P), words (W), and imaged words (IW). (From Erdelyi *et al.*, 1976.)

.76) with magnitude of hypermnesia, but not with conceptual organization ($r = .15$) nor with *covert repetition* ($r = .37$).

Another correlational analysis was carried out, in this case to test whether higher initial recall level (R_1) determines magnitude of hypermnesia (for, usually, hypermnesic recall functions begin at a higher initial recall level than inert functions). For each of the three groups, the correlation between R_1 and R_3–R_1 proved null or negative ($r = .09$, .05, and $-.43$, for the W, IW, and P groups, respectively, the latter negative correlation probably reflecting a ceiling effect on R_3 for the picture group). As pointed out by Erdelyi (1982), these correlations are not likely to be null because of regression artifacts, since test–retest reliability (e.g., R_1 versus R_2) is in the order of $r = .90$. Initial recall level (R_1) does not appear to determine magnitude of hypermnesia (see also, Belmore, 1981, 1982; Erdelyi, 1982; Roediger, 1982).

The imagery hypothesis of hypermnesia was further tested by Erdelyi and Finkelstein (unpublished) who replicated the basic Erdelyi *et al.* (1976) image-recoding effect with auditory inputs and oral reports. Thus, subjects orally recalling a set of auditorily presented words failed to produce hypermnesia, whereas another group of subjects, instructed to form a visual image of each item heard, did produce hypermnesia.

Another approach to the imagery-coding hypothesis was pursued by Erdelyi and Finkelstein (1975). It has been noted by imagery researchers (e.g., Bugelski, Kidd, & Segmen, 1968; Paivio, 1971) that it takes about 1.5 to 2.5 sec to form an image from a word. If this is true, then imagery-recoding instructions such as used successfully by Erdelyi *et al.* (1976) should fail to produce hypermnesia if the stimuli were presented too rapidly for the imagery recoding to be effected. In the present study, the Erdelyi *et al.* experiment was repeated in every detail but for the rate of stimulus presentation: One item was presented every 1 sec rather than, as previously, every 5 sec. Would the image-recoding effect disappear? As Fig. 7 shows, imagery-recoding instructions fail to produce hypermnesia with words when the presentation rates are (presumably) too rapid for image-recoding processes to be effectively carried out.

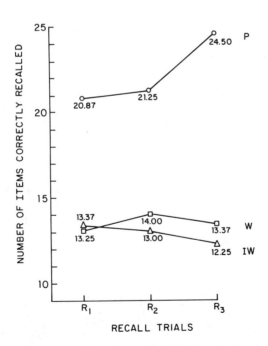

Fig. 7. Failure of imagery-recoding instructions to produce hypermnesia when the presentation rate (1 sec per item) is too fast for imagery recoding to be effected. Note that except for the rate of the stimulus presentation, this study was identical to the Erdelyi *et al.* (1976) experiment, in which a 5-sec-per-item rate was used. (From Erdelyi & Finkelstein, 1975.)

Although these data are highly consistent with the imagery hypothesis of hypermnesia, they are nevertheless not decisive. The problem is that the various treatments thought to influence imagery coding—for example, imagery instructions, speed of presentation—may, alternately, be influencing some other, more fundamental factor, such as depth of processing (cf. Belmore, 1981; Erdelyi, Buschke, & Finkelstein, 1977) or level of asymptotic cumulative recall (Roediger, Payne, Gillespie, & Lean, 1982). Unfortunately, it will not be easy—and perhaps impossible—to discriminate among certain classes of coding hypotheses (cf. Erdelyi, 1982; Popkin & Small, 1979; Roediger, 1982), since manipulations affecting one class (imagery) are likely to affect the other (e.g., depth of processing). At best, a great amount of converging discriminative evidence will have to be collected to warrant the espousal of one over the other.

A. LONG-TERM HYPERMNESIA

Thus far, the modern experimental work that we have been considering has been restricted to relatively short time frames, laboratory periods of about an hour. What might be expected from recall effort spanning real-life time scales—periods of hours, days, or weeks? Psychoanalytic psychotherapy, it might be noted, involves 50-min "trials," administered several times a week, for several years. What, if any, is the limit of the growth of recall with time and effort?

Erdelyi and Kleinbard (1978) investigated this issue by examining the course of recall over a period of approximately 1 week. In their first study, a single subject—Jeff Kleinbard—attempted to recall 40 pictures several times a day for 7 days. The subject–experimenter, J. K., did not know initially that he would be attempting to recall the pictures beyond the standard laboratory period (he thought he was getting first-hand experience in what it felt like to be a subject in the typical hypermnesia experiment, preparatory to his being an experimenter himself in a future study). J. K. attempted five recalls in a single laboratory period (with no interpolated think intervals), after which he was handed three dozen envelopes, each containing a recall protocol. He was instructed to fill out at least three recall protocols a day for the next week. He was to take 7 min for each trial and produce 40 nonrepeating responses, guessing if necessary. After the completion of a recall trial he was to seal the envelope (and, thus, never to consult a prior recall test). J. K. was encouraged to spend as much time as possible during the week thinking of and covertly retrieving the stimulus items. Thus, the formal recall tests reflect considerably more retrieval time than the official 7 min spent on each test.

Before turning to J. K.'s retention function, it might be instructive to reproduce another subject–experimenter's data on the course of memory over time, Hermann Ebbinghaus's (1885) classic curve of forgetting (Fig. 8).

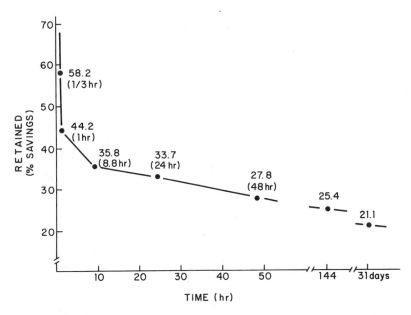

Fig. 8. Retention as a function of time. (Plotted from data reported by Ebbinghaus, 1885.)

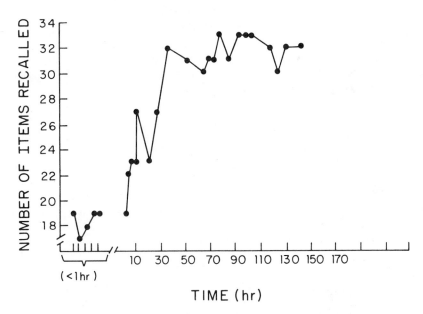

TIME (hr)

Fig. 9. Retention as a function of time and recall effort. (Erdelyi & Kleinbard, 1978, Study 1.)

Figure 9 shows J. K.'s retention curve (Erdelyi & Kleinbard, 1978, Study 1). It will be readily seen that J. K.'s recall of pictures increased rather than decreased with time (and retrieval effort). Important to note, of course, is that Ebbinghaus' curve is based on different procedures and stimuli—nonsense syllables versus pictures, method of savings versus recall, single retest versus repeated tests, no thinking about the stimuli versus extensive thinking.[2]

The point of this comparison is not that Ebbinghaus is not replicable, but that "decay" or "interference" is not the inevitable course of memory over time. For long-term memory, at least, external "clocktime" is not the relevant factor: Rather, the usual (but not inevitable) correlates of external clocktime, such as amount of interference, retrieval effort, recoding processes, determine levels of accessible memory (cf. Erdelyi, 1977; Erdelyi & Kleinbard, 1978). This point, it might be noted, is analogous to criticisms (e.g., Craik, 1983; Craik & Lockhart, 1972) of literalistic conceptions of memory stores in terms of unique time spans, codes, or localities. The critical factors (by no means fully understood) are the types of psychological processes to which information is subjected. Similarly, memory does not vary with time in a literal "tic-toc" sense but with "psychological time" (Erdelyi, 1977), that is, the type and amount of different psychological activities engaged in. Thus, the "clock" is not external but internal, and there may well be different internal clocks, each having different effects, sometimes contradictory ones, upon the resultant outcome. The picture is uncomfortably murky, not only theoretically but empirically as well (thus, memory may decay, increase, or stay the same with time).

Although one is inevitably tempted to provide a simple explanation, hypermnesia probably reflects a variety of processes. This may be gleaned from J. K.'s subjective experiences of the manner in which he recovered different items:

> During the early trials, I began to organize the words into small clusters of two or three items each. Without conscious direction or effort, I evolved a variety of clusters with no one type predominant. Among them were common associations (e.g., tree-snake and key-chain), physical word resemblances (e.g., snake, snail), functional resemblances (e.g., toothbrush, comb), and abstract sets (e.g., appliances: TV, iron, telephone).

> I made my hypermnesic recoveries in two distinctly different ways. The first, which occurred relatively early, was via environmental recognitions: e.g., feather—I was returning home from the lab on the first day of the experiment when I saw a feather lying on the ground and suddenly recognized it as one of the picture items; telephone—during

---

[2]It is interesting to note that in a summary of replications of the Ebbinghaus forgetting curve provided by Woodworth and Schlosberg (1954, p. 727), one function, that of Boreas (1930), fails to be progressively amnesic like the others. With poems as stimuli—but not with nonsense syllables—percentage savings actually increases for several days before resuming its downward course.

the very same trip, I recognized "telephone" as an item upon seeing a pay-phone in a subway station. This recognition had not occurred until 8 hours into the experiment although I had seen numerous telephones earlier in the day; key—particularly interesting is that I recovered this item via an auditory recognition; specifically, I heard the jingle of some keys and recognized "key" as a picture item. This occurred an hour after the lab period.

The second way in which I recovered items was less item-specific but ultimately more productive. By far, the most interesting subjective experience was getting a general "visual feeling" in my mind for a particular shape such as a length or roundness. I remember seeing a vague, oblong shape in my mind from which I was able to extract such items as gun, broom, and baseball bat; from an oval shape—football and pineapple; from an inverted cup form—bell, funnel, and bottle (the bottle in the stimulus resembled a bell-jar); from a rectangular box—table and book. Just before many of these recoveries, I often experienced what might best be described as a "tip-of-the-eye" (TOE) phenomenon, in which I was certain a particular item was on the verge of recovery but which would take its time before suddenly coalescing into an image in consciousness. (Erdelyi & Kleinbard, 1978, pp. 279–280)

Since their first study was based on the performance of a single subject, Erdelyi and Kleinbard (1978, Study 2) extended their investigation to a larger sample—six subjects: three subjects who repeatedly attempted to recall 60 pictures and three subjects who attempted to recall 60 words (the labels corresponding to the picture items). Figure 10 summarizes the course of recall for the picture and word groups. As in Study 1, picture recall continued to increase for several days ($p < .01$), whereas word recall was inert ($p > .10$).

Figure 11 depicts *cumulative* recall across the same trials. If we follow the terminological distinction suggested in Footnote 1, Figs. 9 and 10 correspond to *hypermnesia* functions, whereas Fig. 11 corresponds to *reminiscence* functions. It will be evident that cumulative recall (reminiscence)

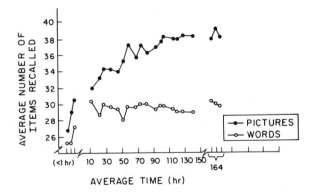

Fig. 10. Number of items (pictures or words) recalled in successive recall trials. (From Erdelyi & Kleinbard, 1978, Study 2, p. 282.)

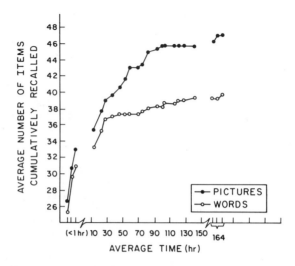

Fig. 11. Average number of items cumulatively recalled from the word and picture lists. (From Erdelyi & Kleinbard, 1978, Study 2, p. 283.)

continues to increase for *both* pictures and words (Fig. 11) even though net recall (hypermnesia) increases only for pictures (Figs. 9 and 10).

B.   Recognition Hypermnesia

All hypermnesia effects discussed thus far have been obtained with recall indicators. The question often arises whether hypermnesia is restricted to this form of memory or whether it can be obtained with other indicators, especially recognition. The question turns out not to be that easy to answer. It is not possible simply to substitute recognition tests for the usual recall tests because of the notoriously high recognition levels obtained with pictorial materials (Nickerson, 1965; Shepard, 1967; Standing, Conezio, & Haber, 1970). In a pilot study conducted by the author, recognition memory was measured for 120 pictures of the sort used in past hypermnesia studies. Subjects produced a 99% hit rate for a 1% false alarm rate. With such ceiling performance on an initial test, one could hardly expect any hypermnesia to be found on subsequent tests. Theoretically unpromising expedients for dampening recognition levels, such as very rapid rates of stimulus presentation or difficult or numerous distractors, showed little promise in pilot studies of yielding recognition hypermnesia. In two experiments, Bernbach, Roediger, and Payne (1981) found that verbal materials that produced recall hypermnesia (words that were imaged or semantically elaborated) failed to produce recognition hypermnesia—in one of the studies, in fact, a hefty amnesia pattern was observed instead.

Consonant with Erdelyi and Becker's (1974) model of hypermnesia, based on a two-stage (retrieve-recognize) approach to memory performance, it seemed to the author that the key to producing recognition hypermnesia was to find a recognition task where the retrieval component of recognition was not trivial or automatic, as in the usual laboratory recognition situation. Active retrieval, in any case, is probably a more common feature of real-life recognition tasks, where the item to be recognized is rarely identical to the original item and, often, is only a component of the original stimulus.

A recognition hypermnesia experiment was designed by Erdelyi and Stein (1981) in which the subject's task was to recognize not the original list of stimuli, but components of the stimuli. The stimuli employed were 180 cartoons with captions (see both left panels of Fig. 12). Subjects were tested not for their recognition of the whole cartoons (which pilot data showed

Fig. 12. Examples of the configured stimuli (two left panels) and the nonconfigured stimuli (two right panels) employed by Erdelyi and Stein (1981).

to be virtually perfect) but for either the *pictorial* or the *verbal* component of the cartoons. The rationale of the study was that initially unrecognized components would produce search for the complementary component which, if found, would reconstitute with the original component to form a configured—and easily recognizable—whole. Given this logic, it was assumed that components of *non*configured stimuli would not as likely yield retrieval of their complement or, when such retrieval did take place, recognition of the reassociated, but nonconfigured stimulus. To test this line of reasoning, a set of pseudocartoons was created by pairing captions with the wrong pictures (see the two right panels of Fig. 12). These pseudocartoons constituted the nonconfigured stimulus set, which was hypothesized not to yield recognition hypermnesia.

In summary, four groups of subjects were tested: subjects who saw 180 funny (configured) or 180 nonfunny (nonconfigured) stimulus items and who were then given recognition tests for either the captions or the pictures from the original stimuli. The recognition set consisted of 20 items randomly selected from the stimulus set (pictures or captions, depending on the group) and 20 distractors (again, pictures or captions) taken from other, never-shown cartoons. Three recognition tests were administered. Each test contained the same stimulus and distractor items, presented in the same order. Subjects were required to provide confidence ratings, from which ROC curves were extracted.

Figure 13 depicts the ROC curves for the three successive recognition tests for pictures when the pictures had originally been components of (a) funny cartoons (PICTURES/FUNNY) and (b) of pseudocartons (PICTURES/ NONFUNNY). As predicted, recognition memory (d') for pictures from

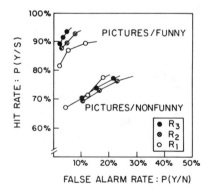

Fig. 13. The course of recognition memory, plotted as ROC curves, over three successive recognition tests (R_1, R_2, R_3) for *pictures* from configured (funny) and nonconfigured (nonfunny) cartoons.

the configured set was hypermnesic ($p < .01$), but recognition memory for the same pictures from the nonconfigured set failed to increase over recognition trials.

Figure 14 shows the corresponding ROC curves for the captions. In this case neither recognition triad was hypermnesic. Once again a picture–word difference arose, again unexpectedly. In a post hoc explanation of the failure of the CAPTIONS/FUNNY group to yield recognition hypermnesia, Erdelyi and Stein suggested that the reason was an asymmetry in the effectiveness of pictures and captions to serve as retrieval cues for their missing complements: The pictures from the configured stimuli tend to suggest the semantic domain of their corresponding captions, whereas the captions provide virtually no clues of the semantic domain of their missing picture complements. Although the pattern of the results is somewhat complex, inviting replication, Erdelyi and Stein's study is probably the first successful induction of recognition hypermnesia beyond fleeting short-term intervals [hypermnesia for face recognition having been reported for post-stimulus durations of under 90 sec by Milner (1968) and Wallace, Coltheart, and Forster (1970)].

It appears, then, that picture hypermnesia is obtainable with both recall and recognition indicators. Such findings suggest the need for caution in interpreting a wide variety of phenomena based on single, time-limited measures of memory accessibility [e.g., "availability heuristic" effects (Kahneman & Tversky, 1973)], and conclusions based on accessibility discrepancies produced by different indicators of memory (all subception effects, comparisons of recall and recognition performance, etc.). It has been suggested, for example (Tulving & Thomson, 1973), that the phenomenon of recall without recognition invalidates two-stage models of recall. The dynamism

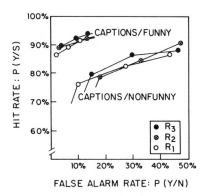

Fig. 14. The course of recognition memory over three successive recognition tests (R_1, R_2, R_3) for *captions* from (a) configured (funny) and (b) nonconfigured (nonfunny) cartoons.

of accessibility with time and effort tends to undermine such inferences; we now know that there is not only recall without recognition but also recognition without recognition (R_2 versus R_1)—as well as recall without recall, and recognition without recall.

C. RESEARCH IN PROGRESS

At this juncture, three basic issues are being pursued. The first of these is the question of the ultimate limit, if any, of recall, given sufficient time and effort. On the basis of preliminary work, it does not appear that extending the recall interval beyond 1 week will by itself yield hypermnesia substantially beyond the levels obtained by Erdelyi and Kleinbard (1978). One recently tested subject, B.B.B., attempting to recall 60 pictures for 3 months, settled in, after several days, into an altogether stable level of recall for the remaining period (Fig. 15). On the other hand, it might be noted that the subject made her gains rapidly and reached close to a perfect recall level (over 90% of the list items). Thus, a ceiling effect is likely to be operating here, masking possible long-term hypermnesia effects. Pilot work with several other subjects has focused on the introduction of free associations and other destructuring techniques during later phases of recall (e.g., beyond 2 weeks), the rationale being that after everything has been gained from a particular recall strategy, which gradually becomes routinized, a destructuring of frozen retrieval patterns might yield new recoveries. Preliminary results are promising but modest in magnitude.

The second research program in progress, which is related to the first, concerns the use of hypnosis to enhance hypermnesia. In conjunction with Martin T. Orne and his colleagues at the Unit for Experimental Psychiatry

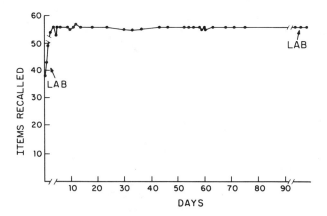

Fig. 15. The course of recall of 60 pictures over 90 days for subject B.B.B.

(of the Institute of Pennsylvania Hospital and University of Pennsylvania), a major experimental program is being undertaken to determine whether hypnosis does in fact have the power to enhance memory. As has been already suggested (p. 109), no convincing experimental evidence exists to date for the reality of hypnotic hypermnesia, even though there exists wide public belief in the phenomenon and a burgeoning application of hypnosis to forensic settings (Orne, Soskis, & Dinges, 1984). The question, obviously, is not the existence of hypermnesia but whether hypnosis adds anything to the phenomenon. Very preliminary data collected at the Unit for Experimental Psychiatry suggest that, on the contrary, hypnosis might actually interfere mildly with hypermnesia, at least in some circumstances. It should be stressed that these are very preliminary results. The pattern of outcomes may well look different within the next few years. Nevertheless, these earliest data do bring to mind the effect of free associative fantasy on hypermnesia, discussed earlier.

Finally, work is under way to explore the psychodynamic implications of hypermnesia. Thus, to what extent may the individual's motives (wishes, fears, defenses, attitudes, etc.) selectively determine which unconscious (inaccessible) memories—or complex of memories—will be subjected to "consciousness-raising." In Freud's terminology, may the "work of recollection" be "tendentious"?

Several experiments recently completed in the author's laboratory have thus far failed to turn up selective hypermnesia effects. Thus, subjects motivated (through instructions or monetary incentives) to think selectively of one category of items (e.g., animals) versus another (e.g., furniture) did not produce differential hypermnesia levels for items from the target categories. This has been puzzling. Roediger et al. (1982, Experiment 3), however, testing categories from semantic rather than episodic memory, succeeded in obtaining an unambiguous selectivity effect. Items from the targeted category increased substantially with time and effort, whereas items from other categories did not. The biased allocation of retrieval effort to some and not to other memory complexes probably accounts, at least in part, for repression-like effects in the real world. Some memory complexes may be relatively inaccessible not because they are actively pushed out of consciousness at the time of recall—though this too might happen—but because of the retrieval counterpart of selective inattention; the subject selectively allocates less retrieval effort to some memory complexes than to others, producing, over the long run, substantial differences in accessible memory (note, in the sense of d' not just of β).

This, as the author has stressed in previous works (e.g., Erdelyi, 1974, 1984; Erdelyi & Goldberg, 1979) is a pervasive, unifying theme in psychodynamic cognition: Bias begins at the beginning and ends only at the very end of information processing.

ACKNOWLEDGMENTS

This article was written during the author's tenure as a Fellow at the Center for Advanced Study in the Behavioral Sciences, Stanford, California from 1982 to 1983. The financial support of the John D. and Catherine T. MacArthur Foundation is gratefully acknowledged. Also gratefully acknowledged is the supplementary support provided by the City University of New York through a Scholar's Incentive Award, and of Grant No. 19156 of the National Institute of Mental Health, United States Public Health Service.

The author wishes to thank Martin and Emily Orne, David Dinges, Robert Crowder, Fergus Craik, Roberta Klatzky, and Thomas Trabasso for their valuable comments.

REFERENCES

Allers, R., & Teler, J. [On the utilization of unnoticed impressions in associations]. J. Wolff, D. Rapaport, & S. Annin (Trans.). *Psychological Issues,* 1960, **3**, Monograph 7, 121–154 (originally published, 1924.)

Ballard, P. B. Oblivescence and reminiscence. *British Journal of Psychology* (*Monograph Supplements*), 1913, **1**, (2).

Belmore, S. M. Imagery and semantic elaboration in hypermnesia for words. *Journal of Experimental Psychology: Human Learning and Memory,* 1981, **7**, 191–203.

Belmore, S. M. *Hypermnesia and recall level.* Paper presented at the 23rd annual meeting of the Psychonomic Society, Minneapolis, Minnesota, 1982.

Bernbach, H. A., Roediger, H. L., & Payne, D. G. *Hypermnesia: Effects of encoding and retrieval manipulations.* Paper presented at the 22nd annual meeting of the Psychonomic Society, 1981.

Boreas, T. Experimental studies of memory: Second preliminary communication. The rate of forgetting. *Praktika Akademia Athenes,* 1930, **5**, 382–396.

Breuer, J., & Freud, S. Studies on hysteria. In J. Strachey (Trans. & Ed.), *The standard edition of the complete psychological works of Sigmund Freud* (Vol. 2). London: Hogarth Press, 1955 (originally published, 1895).

Bugelski, B. R., Kidd, E., & Segmen, J. Image as a mediator in one-trial paired associate learning. *Journal of Experimental Psychology,* 1968, **76**, 69–73.

Buxton, C. E. The status of research in reminiscence. *Psychological Bulletin,* 1943, **40**, 313–340.

Craik, F. I. M. On the transfer of information from temporary to permanent memory. *Philosophical Transactions of the Royal Society, Series B,* 1983.

Craik, F. I. M., & Lockhart, R. S. Levels of processing: A framework for memory research. *Journal of Verbal Learning and Verbal Behavior,* 1972, **11**, 671–684.

Dixon, N. F. *Preconscious processing.* New York: Wiley, 1981.

Eagle, M. D., Wolitzky, D. L., & Klein, G. S. Imagery: Effect of a concealed figure in a stimulus. *Science,* 1966, **151**, 837–839.

Ebbinghaus, H. [*Memory*]. H. A. Ruger & C. E. Bussenius (Trans.). New York: Dover, 1964 (originally published, 1885).

Erdelyi, M. H. Recovery of unavailable perceptual input. *Cognitive Psychology,* 1970, **1**, 99–113.

Erdelyi, M. H. The role of fantasy in the Pötzl (Emergence) phenomenon. *Journal of Personality and Social Psychology,* 1972, **24**, 186–190.

Erdelyi, M. H. A new look at The New Look: Perceptual defense and vigilance. *Psychological Review,* 1974, **81**, 1–25.

Erdelyi, M. H. *Has Ebbinghaus decayed with time?* Paper presented at the 18th annual meeting of the Psychonomic Society, Washington, D.C., 1977.

Erdelyi, M. H. A note on the level of recall, level of processing, and imagery hypotheses of hypermnesia. *Journal of Verbal Learning and Verbal Behavior,* 1982, **21**, 656-661.

Erdelyi, M. H. *Psychoanalysis: Freud's cognitive psychology.* New York: Freeman, 1984 (in press).

Erdelyi, M. H., & Becker, J. Hypermnesia for pictures: Incremental memory for pictures but not words in multiple recall trials. *Cognitive Psychology,* 1974, **6**, 159-171.

Erdelyi, M., Buschke, H., & Finkelstein, S. Hypermnesia for Socratic stimuli: The growth of recall for an internally generated memory list abstracted from a series of riddles. *Memory & Cognition,* 1977, **5**, 283-286.

Erdelyi, M., Dinges, D. F., Orne, M. T., & Orne, E. C. *The stimulus and the test in hypnotic hypermnesia.* Manuscript in preparation, 1984.

Erdelyi, M., & Finkelstein, S. *Hypermnesia for imagistically recoded auditory verbal inputs.* Unpublished study, 1976.

Erdelyi, M., & Finkelstein, S. *Failure of imagery-recoding instructions to produce hypermnesia for words when rate of input is too rapid for effective recoding.* Unpublished study, 1975.

Erdelyi, M. H., Finkelstein, S., Herrell, N., Miller, B., & Thomas, J. Coding modality vs. input modality in hypermnesia: Is a rose a rose a rose? *Cognition,* 1976, **4**, 311-319.

Erdelyi, M. H., & Goldberg, B. Let's not sweep repression under the rug: Toward a cognitive psychology of repression. In J. F. Kihlstrom & F. J. Evans (Eds.), *Functional disorders of memory.* Hillsdale, New Jersey: Erlbaum, 1979.

Erdelyi, M. H., & Kleinbard, J. Has Ebbinghaus decayed with time? The growth of recall (hypermnesia) over days. *Journal of Experimental Psychology: Human Learning and Memory,* 1978, **4**, 275-289.

Erdelyi, M. H., & Stein, J. Recognition hypermnesia: The growth of recognition memory (d') over time with repeated testing. *Cognition,* 1981, **9**, 23-33.

Eriksen, C. W. Unconscious processes. In M. R. Jones (Ed.), *Nebraska Symposium on Motivation: 1958.* Lincoln, Nebraska: Univ. of Nebraska Press, 1958.

Eriksen, C. W. (Ed.). *Behavior and awareness.* Durham, North Carolina: Duke Univ. Press, 1962.

Fisher, C. Dreams and perception. *Journal of the American Psychoanalytic Association,* 1954, **3**, 380-445.

Fisher, C. Dreams, images, and perception: A study of unconscious-preconscious relationships. *Journal of the American Psychoanalytic Association,* 1956, **4**, 5-48.

Fisher, C., & Paul, I. H. The effect of subliminal visual stimulation on images and dreams: A validation study. *Journal of the American Psychoanalytic Association,* 1959, **7**, 35-83.

Fiss, H., Goldberg, F., & Klein, G. Effects of subliminal stimulation on imagery and discrimination. *Perceptual and Motor Skills,* 1963, **17**, 31-44.

Freud, S. [*The interpretation of dreams*]. J. Strachey (Ed. & Trans.). New York: Wiley, 1961 (originally published, 1900).

Freud, S. [My views on the part played by sexuality in the aetiology of the neuroses]. J. Bernays (Trans.). In P. Rieff (Ed.), *Freud: Sexuality and the psychology of love.* New York: Collier, 1963 (originally published, 1906).

Giddan, N. S. Recovery through images of briefly flashed stimuli. *Journal of Personality,* 1967, **35**, 1-19.

Goldiamond, I. Indicators of perception: I. Subliminal perception, subception, unconscious perception: An analysis in terms of psychophysical indicator methodology. *Psychological Bulletin,* 1958, **55**, 373-411.

Haber, R. N., & Erdelyi, M. H. Emergence and recovery of initially unavailable perceptual material. *Journal of Verbal Learning and Verbal Behavior,* 1967, **6,** 618–628.

Hilgard, E. R. What becomes of the input from the stimulus? In C. W. Eriksen (Ed.), *Behavior and awareness.* Durham, North Carolina: Duke Univ. Press, 1962.

Holt, R. R. Imagery: The return of the ostracized. *American Psychologist,* 1964, **19,** 254–264.

Johnson, H., & Eriksen, C. W. Preconscious perception: A reexamination of the Poetzl phenomenon. *Journal of Abnormal and Social Psychology,* 1961, **62,** 497–503.

Jung, C. G. *Analytical psychology: Its theory and practice.* New York: Random House, 1968 (originally published, 1935).

Kahneman, D., & Tversky, A. On the psychology of prediction. *Psychological Review,* 1973, **80,** 237–251.

Klatzky, R. L., & Erdelyi, M. The response criterion problem in tests of hypnosis and memory. *International Journal of Clinical and Experimental Hypnosis,* 1984 (in press).

Loftus, E. F., & Loftus, G. R. On the permanence of stored information in the human brain. *American Psychologist,* 1980, **35,** 409–420.

Malamud, W. Dream analysis: Its application in therapy and research in mental diseases. *Archives of Neurology and Psychiatry,* 1934, **31,** 356–372.

Malamud, W., & Linder, F. E. Dreams and their relationship to recent impressions. *Archives of Neurology and Psychiatry,* 1931, **25,** 1081–1099.

McGeoch, G. O. The conditions of reminiscence. *American Journal of Psychology,* 1935, **47,** 65–89.

Milner, B. Visual recognition and recall after right temporal lobe excision in man. *Neuropsychologica,* 1968, **6,** 191–209.

Neisser, U. *Cognitive psychology.* New York: Appleton, 1967.

Nickerson, R. S. Short-term memory for complex meaningful configurations: A demonstration of capacity. *Canadian Journal of Psychology,* 1965, **19,** 155–160.

Orne, M. T., Soskis, D. A., & Dinges, D. F. Hypnotically-induced testimony and the criminal justice system. In G. L. Wells & E. F. Loftus (Eds.), *Advances in the psychology of eyewitness testimony.* London and New York: Cambridge Univ. Press, 1984.

Paivio, A. *Imagery and verbal processes.* New York: Holt, 1971.

Pötzl, O. [The relationship between experimentally induced dream images and indirect vision]. J. Wolff, D. Rapaport, & S. Annin (Trans.). *Psychological Issues,* 1960, **3,** Monograph 7, 41–120 (originally published, 1917).

Popkin, S. J., & Small, M. V. Hypermnesia and the role of imagery. *Bulletin of the Psychonomic Society,* 1979, **13,** 378–380.

Roediger, H. L. Rejoinder. *Journal of Verbal Learning and Verbal Behavior,* 1982, **21,** 662–665.

Roediger, H. L., & Payne, D. G. Hypermnesia: The role of repeated testing. *Journal of Experimental Psychology: Learning, Memory, and Cognition,* 1982, **8,** 66–72.

Roediger, H. L., Payne, D. G., Gillespie, G. L., & Lean, D. S. Hypermnesia as determined by level of recall. *Journal of Verbal Learning and Verbal Behavior,* 1982, **21,** 635–655.

Roediger, H. L., & Thorpe, L. A. The role of recall time in producing hypermnesia. *Memory & Cognition,* 1978, **6,** 296–305.

Shapiro, S. R., & Erdelyi, M. H. Hypermnesia for pictures but not words. *Journal of Experimental Psychology,* 1974, **103,** 1218–1219.

Shepard, R. N. Recognition memory for words, sentences, and pictures. *Journal of Verbal Learning and Verbal Behavior,* 1967, **6,** 156–163.

Shevrin, H., & Luborsky, L. The measurement of preconscious perception in dreams and images: An investigation of the Poetzl phenomenon. *Journal of Abnormal and Social Psychology,* 1958, **56,** 285–294.

Standing, L., Conezio, J., & Haber, R. N. Perception and memory for pictures: Single-trial learning of 2,500 visual stimuli. *Psychonomic Science,* 1970, **19**, 73–74.

Tulving, E. Intratrial and intertrial retention: Notes towards a theory of free recall verbal learning. *Psychological Review,* 1964, **71**, 219–237.

Tulving, E., & Thomson, D. M. Encoding specificity and retrieval processes in episodic memory. *Psychological Review,* 1973, **80**, 352–373.

Wallace, G., Coltheart, M., & Forster, K. *Psychonomic Science,* 1970, **18** (6), 335–336.

White, R. W., Fox, J. F., & Harris, W. W. Hypnotic hypermnesia for recently learned material. *Journal of Abnormal and Social Psychology,* 1940, **35**, 88–103.

Williams, O. A study of the phenomenon of reminiscence. *Journal of Experimental Psychology,* 1926, **9**, 368–387.

Woodworth, R. S., & Schlosberg, H. *Experimental psychology* (2nd Ed.). New York: Holt, 1954.

ORIGINS OF BEHAVIOR IN PAVLOVIAN CONDITIONING

Peter C. Holland

UNIVERSITY OF PITTSBURGH
PITTSBURGH, PENNSYLVANIA

I. Introduction

In the past decade the study of animal conditioning has undergone a cognitive revolution. The recent literature is replete with empirical reports described as investigations of concept formation, the processes, contents, and structure of memory, the representation of events and event relations, and the like. And modern theories of learning are often laced with concepts and terminology borrowed from the literature of human cognition.

Common to most of these trends is the conviction that the most profitable subjects of inquiry are the mental events, structures, and processes that underlie conditioned behavior. Behavior itself is tolerated as a necessary index of learning processes, but its origins are seldom the subject of investigation. Instead, the domain of most modern theories of conditioning is one of constructs: Their predictions are couched in terms of variables like associative strength and salience rather than responding. The relation of these constructs to behavior is usually dismissed by a simple assumption of monotonicity of the relation between constructual and behavioral variables, and an occasional disclaimer that now-unspecified performance rules may follow.

This associative approach has been enormously successful in guiding important and exciting conditioning research and has helped regenerate en-

THE PSYCHOLOGY OF LEARNING
AND MOTIVATION, VOL. 18

thusiasm and interest in the study of simple learning processes. At the same time, however, some investigators have rejected this approach and have championed instead what may be called a functional–evolutionary model (e.g., Johnston, 1982; Plotkin & Odling-Smee, 1979). In the extreme these theorists argue that an account of learning that ignores behavior is primarily an exercise in sophistry. Behavior and behavior processes are shaped by mechanisms of evolution through natural selection, and only behavior—not associations, representations, or processors—makes contact with the selective pressures within the environment. Investigators holding this view frequently argue that conditioning represents only one mechanism of behavioral adaptation, albeit an important one. Behavior in conditioning experiments is thus more profitably viewed in a much broader context of adaptation in which associative processes may play important but perhaps not crucial roles. In fact, the behaviors observed in laboratory conditioning experiments may be at best unnatural subsets of adaptive responses of organisms' behavior systems. Or the tasks examined in the laboratory may reveal only "surplus" learning abilities which are related to true, ecologically valid learning abilities only in the way that pathological and normal development are related. From this perspective, the laboratory search for the origins of these truncated or ecologically irrelevant behavior patterns is no more than the determination of the amount and dimensions of difference between valid learning situations and the laboratory and is not particularly helpful to our understanding of behavior mechanisms.

In this article I argue that the study of the origins of conditioned behavior is best served by an appreciation of the views, methods, and data of both associative and functional–evolutionary perspectives. After a brief description of such a synthetic approach, I examine a sampling of research and speculation concerning the origins of conditioned behavior from traditional associationist perspectives, and then consider views that embrace both associative and evolutionary conceptualizations. Examples from a variety of species, response systems, and conditioning procedures are described, but most of the discussion is oriented around data from rats in Pavlovian appetitive conditioning experiments, many of which were conducted in my laboratory.

II. A Synthetic View of Conditioned Behavior

Pavlovian conditioning is an adaptive mechanism by which organisms adjust to relatively short-term variations in their environment, specifically, relations among events. However, that adaptation involves both the acquisition and processing of information and the use of that information in the production of responding in a variety of behavior systems. An adequate theory of conditional behavior must deal with both aspects of adaptation. Currently, popular associative models of conditioning (e.g., Mackintosh, 1975; Pearce & Hall, 1980; Rescorla & Wagner, 1972; Wagner, 1981) deal with only the operating characteristics of presumed underlying learning processes, but say little or nothing about the origins of conditioned behavior. Thus, by themselves these theories provide little promise of aiding our understanding of the origins of particular learned behaviors. Functional-evolutionary approaches offer more promise in dealing with the nature of a variety of behavior systems, but by ignoring the importance of studying the underlying associative processes these approaches also suffer shortcoming in dealing with the origins of conditioned behavior.

Evolutionary approaches often argue that since only performed behavior makes contact with environmental selection pressures, speculation about underlying, theoretical learning mechanisms is unimportant. Different performance characteristics of various behavior systems undergoing change must reflect differential adaptive learning processes. Thus, those approaches ignore learning–performance distinctions. But it is conceivable that many of an organism's behavior systems make use of similar underlying information of a representational, predictive, or associative nature. That is, there may be a relatively general learning process which provides information that is used in plastic changes in performance within a variety of different behavior systems. Hence, adaptive considerations may shape the manner in which various behavior systems make use of common learned information about the environment, rather than the way each behavior system "learns."

Consider the analogous relation between sensory systems and behavior. An organism may need visual information for a wide range of behavior systems such as those involved in defense, foraging, reproduction, and so forth. But we do not usually think of the organism as evolving a variety of separate visual systems (but see Johnston & Turvey, 1980). Of course, different activities may make use of visual information in different ways, for example, different perceptual features of objects may be more salient depending on the behavior system in which that information is being used. However, it is likely that there remains a substantial commonality in the behavioral and physiological operating characteristics of the underlying visual system.

It seems reasonable to make similar claims about an underlying, conceptual "learning system" which acquires and processes information about environmental events and event relations. Since the features of that system may often reflect some sort of adaptive compromise among the needs of a variety of behavior systems that make use of learning information, the system may not provide optimal solutions for each behavior system's problems, just as an organism that must use its feet for walking, feeding, climbing, social grooming, and fighting may not have feet ideally specialized for any of those functions. Apparent adaptive specializations evident in the learning performance within various behavior systems may be better understood as specialized uses of learned information of a more general sort. For example, information about the timing of two events would be used very differently by behavior systems that protect the eye from surface damage and those that protect the body from toxins. Similarly, differing adaptive constraints may permit some behavior systems to be able to afford the luxury of ignoring chance contiguities of events, demanding instead correlative information, while others cannot. Clearly, an understanding of the origins of conditioned behavior demands knowing both the nature of a presumed underlying associative process, and the ways in which various behavior systems make use of that information.

I shall argue that a major task of the learning theorist should be to determine whether differences observed in the learning performance in various behavior systems reflect differences in underlying associative mechanisms or in the differential use of common associative information by various behavior systems. I am not demanding that *all* plastic adaptations of behavior systems tap the same learning system; there may well be behavior systems with their own specially adapted learning systems. But the questions must be asked experimentally. Have different selection pressures on various response systems resulted in different learning processes or in different interactions of those processes with various behavior systems? Does the ontogeny of a particular learned behavior pattern reflect the development of an underlying learning ability that is tapped by a variety of response systems, or does it reflect learning only within that behavior system? Does differential learned performance in closely related species reflect evolutionary differences in underlying learning mechanisms or in the ways in which similar information is used in behavior? For the most part these kinds of questions have not been addressed. But their consideration is likely to greatly further our understanding of the origins of conditional behavior.

III. Accounts of the Origins of Conditioned Behavior

A. REFLEX TRANSFER ACCOUNTS

Although most current theories of conditioning are largely silent on the nature of the conditioned response, that silence is not universal. Perhaps the most frequently held view of conditioning has its roots in the physiological study of reflexes in the nineteenth century. Within this tradition,

Pavlovian conditioning is described as the substitution of a previously neutral stimulus into an existing reflex system, the transfer of control of an unconditioned reflex from the unconditioned stimulus (US) to the conditioned stimulus (CS). This view was encouraged by early observations which suggested that the conditioned response (CR) was a replica of the unconditioned response (UR). Furthermore, the notion that the CS acts as a substitute elicitor of the UR was consistent with both the "S-R" and "S-S" approaches to conditioning: UR-like CRs might be evoked either directly by associations of CS and UR or indirectly by the CS's activation of a US center that in turn evoked the UR.

This *reflex transfer* account was simple and deterministic: The origin of conditioned behavior was the unconditioned reflex. One need only possess knowledge of the existing, unconditioned reflex and the form of conditioned behavior would follow. Such an analysis also is amenable to physiological analysis: The physiological underpinnings of learning could be traced simply by tracing the activation of the unconditioned reflex system "upstream" toward the receptor pathways activated by the CS. Indeed, such an approach characterizes much recent physiological investigation of learning (e.g., Thompson, Berger, Berry, Clark, & Kettner, 1982).

The adequacy of a reflex transfer account in providing a full account of the origins of conditioned behavior was in a large part dependent on the somewhat limited range of conditioning situations examined early in the history of the field. As the range of conditioning preparations widened, as measurement techniques improved, and as researchers examined larger samples of their subjects' behavior, it became obvious that the CR and UR, although frequently similar, were seldom identical.

Often the CR lacked obvious features of the UR; for instance, swallowing and jaw movements were typically not observed in canine salivary conditioning (Sheffield, 1965; Zener, 1937), although those behaviors form a prominent part of the UR (but see Kierylowicz, Soltysik, & Divac, 1968). Or the CR included behaviors that were not part of the UR; many investigators (e.g., Liddell, 1934; Zamble, 1968; Zener, 1937) have observed substantial motor activity in response to CSs that signal food even though that activity is typically not evoked by food delivery itself. More recently, birds have been observed to approach and peck visual signals for USs that do not themselves evoke pecking, such as water delivered directly into the mouth (Woodruff & Williams, 1976) or heat (Wasserman, 1973b; Wasserman, Hunter, Gutowski, & Bader, 1975).

Some CRs even involve behavior changes opposite in direction to those engendered by the US. For instance, although delivery of foot shock usually elicits a jump and heart rate acceleration, a signal for that shock generally evokes freezing and heart rate deceleration (e.g., deToledo & Black, 1966).

The occurrence of so-called compensatory conditioned responses is especially prevalent when the US is the administration of toxic drugs (see Siegel, 1979, for a review). For instance, although the unconditioned response to the administration of lithium chloride to rats is increased drinking, the conditioned response to flavor cues signaling that substance is decreased drinking (e.g., Domjan & Gillan, 1977; Domjan, Gillan, & Gemberling, 1980). Similarly, although the UR to morphine injection in rats includes hyperthermia and analgesia, the conditioned response to signals thereof include hypothermia and hyperalgesia (e.g., Siegel, 1977). In fact, the occurrence of these compensatory CRs has been used as the basis of a conditioning theory of the acquisition of drug tolerances and addictions (Siegel, 1977, 1979).

Finally, the form of the CR often seems largely determined by the characteristics of the CS as well as those of the US. In Pavlovian defensive conditioning, for instance, features of the CS such as its modality, duration, or CS–US interval have been reported to reflect the form of paw flexion responses in cats (Wickens, Nield, Tuber, & Wickens, 1969), the form of eyelid closure CRs in rabbits (Smith, 1968), the occurrence of fear or leg flexion responses in dogs (Konorski, 1967), and freezing or flight responses in rats (Blanchard & Blanchard, 1969a,b; Bolles & Collier, 1976). Similarly, in appetitive conditioning, pigeons show conditioned pecking to localized visual stimuli paired with food delivery, but not to diffuse visual CSs or to auditory CSs (Rashotte, Griffin, & Sisk, 1977; Rescorla, 1980; Wasserman, 1973a), even though other measures of conditioning (see below) demonstrate substantial learning to those stimuli (Blanchard & Honig, 1976; Nairne & Rescorla, 1981).

The observation of CS determination of the form of conditioned behavior deserves special mention here. First, although it is inconsistent with simple reflex transfer schemes and was initially regarded as a somewhat unusual outcome (Holland, 1977), I shall suggest below that CS determination of response form may yet be recognized as a basic and important feature of many conditioning preparations that will yield important insights into the nature of conditioning. Second, variations in CR form as a consequence of differences in the nature of the CS are likely to have important implications for the measurement of association. Many independent variables that are thought to influence association processes may be viewed as manipulations that affect the nature of the CS and might have their primary effect on the form of responding rather than the amount of association. Third, much systematic research designed to discover the origins of CS-dependent differences in conditioned behavior also provides evidence concerning other problems with the reflex transfer notion. Consequently, I shall consider in detail a particular example of CS determination of CR form that I have studied over the past 8 years. Although I do not claim that the answers provided by experiments using this preparation apply to other situations (except when confirming data are available), certainly the methods and conclusions are of interest to investigators who use those other preparations.

Initial experiments using rather unsophisticated measures of appetitive conditioning suggested that different CR forms might be acquired to different CSs that signal the delivery of food to hungry rats. Holland and Rescorla (1975) noted that auditory CSs paired with food evoked large increases in general activity measured by a stabilimeter, but visual CSs similarly paired did not. Nevertheless, both visual and auditory CSs were capable of serving as reinforcers for subsequent, second-order conditioning of other auditory cues. Thus, although the stabilimeter gave no evidence of conditioning to visual CSs, those CSs were clearly conditionable. In an attempt to make sense out of this finding, I began observing the behavior of my subjects with television recording equipment.

Unless otherwise noted, all of the experiments from my laboratory used similar subjects, apparatus, and procedures. Consider an experiment that illustrates the basic finding of CS-dependent differences in CR form (Holland, 1977, Experiment 4). Eight Sprague-Dawley-derived albino rats maintained at 80% of their normal weights by limiting their food intake served as the subjects. The apparatus consisted of four standard but leverless Skinner boxes enclosed within sound-attenuating chambers. A window in each sound chamber permitted the observation of the rats' behavior via a low-light television camera and recording equipment. Background illumination was provided by jewelled 6-W lamps placed over the recessed food cup in each chamber. During each 80-min training session, the rats received two presentations each of four different 10.5-sec CSs. The four CSs were an 1800-Hz steady tone, a 250-Hz intermittent (2 Hz) tone, a steady localized light consisting of the illumination of a 6-W lamp mounted in front and above the transparent-topped Skinner box, and an intermittent (2 Hz) diffuse light consisting of a 14-cm tubular lamp contained within a translucent prism-shaped housing mounted along the top of one side of the outside of the Skinner box. In the first five sessions, all stimuli were presented without food reinforcement, randomly intermixed, in order to examine unconditioned behaviors to those stimuli. The subsequent nine sessions involved reinforced presentations of all four stimuli, again in random sequence. Reinforcement comprised the delivery of two 45-mg food pellets during the final .5 sec of each CS.

Behavior was scored from video tapes of the training sessions. Observations of the behavior of each individual rat were made at 1.25-sec intervals during CS presentations, paced by visual and auditory signals superimposed on the videotapes. In addition, the occurrence or nonoccurrence of a startle response during the first 1.25 sec after CS onset was recorded. Two observers agreed on behavioral category judgments on over 90% of the observations.

Figure 1 shows the results of this experiment. The form of conditioned behavior evoked by the auditory CSs differed considerably from that evoked by the visual CSs, the latter of which showed further differences among themselves. During the conditioning phase (right panels), the rats acquired *rear* (standing on hind legs) and *magazine* (standing motionless with head in the food magazine) behaviors during the two visual CSs, but *startle* (a rapid movement or jump resulting in a change in position) and *head jerk* (short, rapid horizontal or vertical movements of the head) behaviors, as well as some magazine behavior during the auditory stimuli. Furthermore, although rear behavior was more frequent than magazine behavior during the localized light, magazine behavior predominated during the diffuse light. Finally, the temporal distribution of behaviors within CS presentations differed: During visual CSs rear behavior occurred pri-

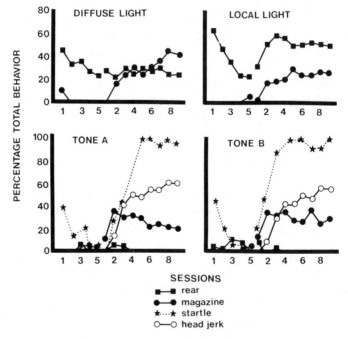

Fig. 1. Behaviors observed during the four stimuli in Holland (1977) experiment 4. The stimuli were not reinforced during the first five sessions (left portions of each panel), and were paired with food delivery during the last nine sessions (right portions of each panel). Percentage total behavior was computed by dividing the frequency of a target behavior by the total number of observations made.

marily during the first 5 sec and magazine behavior occurred mostly during
the second 5-sec period. Startle behavior occurred only immediately after
onset of auditory cues, but head jerk and magazine behaviors were relatively evenly distributed across the CS interval (Fig. 2). A subsequent phase
of the experiment (not described here) which reversed the intermittent-
steady nature of the stimuli found no significant role of that stimulus dimension.

Thus, visual and auditory stimuli which signaled food USs evoked CRs
of very different forms, forms disparate enough to produce all-or-none differences in a crude, but commonly used, stabilimeter measure of conditioning. Other experiments have shown the several dimensions and features
of CSs influence the pattern of conditioned behavior in this and related
conditioning situations, including the CS's modality, location, localizability, ease of contact, and CS–US interval (Boakes, Poli, Lockwood, &
Goodall, 1978; Cleland & Davey, 1982; Davey, Oakley, & Cleland, 1981;
Holland, 1977, 1980a,b; Peterson, Ackil, Frommer, & Hearst, 1972; Timberlake, 1983; Timberlake, Wahl, & King, 1982).

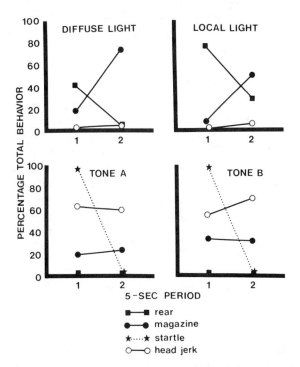

Fig. 2. Temporal distribution of the conditioned behaviors observed during the last two
sessions of Holland (1977) experiment 4.

For example, in one experiment (Holland, 1980b, Experiment 1) I examined rats' behavior in the presence of various 10-sec visual signals for food delivery. One CS was the illumination of a small circular patch on one side wall, another was the illumination of a larger rectangular swatch on that wall, and a third was the illumination of the entire wall. Rearing constituted 56% of the rats' total behavior during the first, most discrete, CS; 41% during the second; and 32% during the third, most diffuse, CS. Conversely, magazine behavior constituted 31, 55, and 62% of the behavior, respectively, during those three CSs. In another experiment (Holland, 1980b, Experiment 2), four small illuminated patches located various distances from the food magazine were individually paired with food delivery. Rearing was primarily directed toward the illuminated CS patch. Interestingly, the amount of rearing engendered by a CS was inversely related to its distance from the food magazine and the amount of magazine behavior directly related. (It is worth noting that with all CSs, virtually all terminal behavior was magazine behavior; thus there was no greater delay in receiving food for rearing in the presence of more distant cues.) Finally, a third experiment (Holland, 1980b, Experiment 3) showed that rats would contact, but not attempt to bite or chew, an illuminated 3.5-cm diameter lens that extended 3 cm into the chamber and was paired with food delivery.

B. "TRANSFER-PLUS" ACCOUNTS

The preceding challenges to a simple reflex transfer account of the origins of conditional behavior led to a demise of that account and a growing acceptance of more cognitive views of conditioning, which made little effort to specify the origins of CRs. However, one broad class of accounts accepted transfer of the unconditioned refex as the basic mechanism of conditioned response genesis, but proposed one or more additional sources of behavior which may influence the observed CR, perhaps concealing the strictly determined CR forms from view. Three kinds of such influences can be distinguished: instrumental reinforcement contingencies, US processing factors, and CS processing factors.

1. Instrumental Reinforcement

A common account for CR–UR dissimilarity has been to attribute the offending behaviors to instrumental contingencies embedded within the Pavlovian conditioning experiment. Since it has often been claimed that instrumental responses are less constrained by the nature of the US than are Pavlovian CRs (e.g., Rescorla & Solomon, 1967; Skinner, 1938), the observed variations between CR and UR forms may be more easily interpreted within the context of instrumental reinforcement.

One type of instrumental conditioning account claims that the supposed conditioned response represents an instrumental adaptation which allows an animal to most effectively receive or avoid the US. This preparatory responding (Perkins, 1968) or response shaping (Gormezano, 1972) argument could potentially tolerate any violation of CR–UR identity simply by assuming that the observed behavior in fact maximizes the value of the US. Unfortunately, there have been few attempts to show either that the conditioned behavior indeed serves that function, or that such a function is subsumed by instrumental conditioning contingencies (but see Prokasy, 1965). Furthermore, the notion is not particularly useful in accounting for CS-dependent differences in conditioned responding: It is hard to imagine why the act that most effectively alters receipt of the US should differ depending on the nature of the signal.

A second instrumental account attributes nonreflexive conditioned behaviors to "parasitic" or adventitious reinforcement contingencies. Since orienting, investigatory, or other behaviors occurring spontaneously during the CS are followed by USs capable of serving as instrumental reinforcers, those behaviors could increase in frequency as a consequence of response-reinforcer rather than stimulus–reinforcer pairings. Although these accounts are more straightforward when appetitive USs are involved (e.g., Konorski, 1967), analogous accounts have been advanced in cases of defensive conditioning as well (e.g., Wilson, 1964, 1969).

Adventitious operant explanations, on the surface at least, can readily account for many instances of CS-determined variations in CR form, simply by adding the assumption that different CSs initially evoke different unconditioned or orienting responses: Different forms of conditioned behavior reflect the learning of different discriminated operants. This account leads one to anticipate the form of alleged CRs to be related to the form and frequency of behaviors composing the unconditioned responses to CSs. In many conditioning preparations, including, for example, heart rate conditioning (e.g., Black, Carlson, & Solomon, 1962; Teyler, 1971; Wilson, 1964, 1969), autoshaping (e.g., Hearst & Jenkins, 1974), and conditioned suppression (e.g., Henderson, 1973), differences in CR form do seem to reflect differences in the forms of the unconditioned reactions to the CSs. That relation is especially obvious in the appetitive conditioning procedure for rats described above. Note in Fig. 1 that the to-be-conditioned rear behavior to visual CSs and startle behavior to auditory CSs occurred almost exclusively to those stimuli on the first nonreinforced preconditioning training session. Furthermore, the relative dominance of those behaviors within the conditioned response among CSs differing in localizability, location, or duration (Holland, 1977, Experiments 4 and 5; 1980a,b) mimics that observed during initial nonreinforced presentation of those stimuli.

Despite the fair amount of circumstantial evidence linking adventitious instrumental reinforcement contingencies to the occurrence of CR patterns unaccountable by simple transfer notions alone, the attribution of those behaviors to instrumental contingencies has been more based on the unsupported assumption that those behaviors could not be conditioned in Pavlovian fashion than on any experimental evidence. Until recently, little or no effort was made to disentangle the contribution of Pavlovian and instrumental contingencies in most conditioning preparations.

In the past several years, however, many investigators attempted such a separation in a number of conditioning preparations. For the most part (but not without exception), those investigators have found little role for instrumental response contingencies in Pavlovian conditioning situations (see Locurto, 1981; Williams, 1981, for recent reviews.) Investigations of appetitive conditioning in rats in my laboratory illustrate these efforts. In those experiments the acquisition of behavior patterns uniquely evoked by visual or auditory CSs was little affected by manipulations designed to minimize the involvement of instrumental contingencies. For instance, habituation of initial differential behaviors to various CSs prior to conditioning (so that all CSs evoked similar behaviors at the initiation of reinforcement contingencies) had no effect on the emergence of differential conditioned behaviors to those CSs (Holland, 1977). Similarly, rats that received simultaneous light + tone compounds paired with food showed differential behavior patterns to the light and tone elements when they were tested separately—in fact, the same differential behavior patterns shown by rats that received separate light–food and tone–food pairings (Holland, 1977; Ross & Holland, 1981). Since both sets of unconditioned behaviors occurred during compound presentations, within an adventitious instrumental account the same behaviors would be reinforced in the presence of the light and tone cues. Hence both stimuli should have controlled similar responding when tested alone.

Most important, CS-determined differences in CR form emerged even when an omission contingency was placed on the occurrence of CS-specific behaviors. In an omission contingency, the CS is followed by the US only on trials on which the CR does not occur. Thus CR–US pairings presumed to be involved in an adventitious instrumental account could not occur, although CS–US pairings would occur on trials on which a CR was not elicited. Several experiments (Holland, 1979a) examined the effects of placing omission contingencies on each of the behaviors observed to occur to visual and auditory CSs signaling food (see above). In each of those experiments, four groups of rats received six CSs in each of 20 75-min sessions. Rats that were assigned to the *omission* condition received a US after a CS presentation only if a particular target behavior did not occur on that trial. Behavior of a single subject was monitored continuously on line to make this decision. Other rats were *yoked* to omission subjects; that is, they received USs on the same trials as their partners in the omission group. Comparison of the performance of omission and yoked subjects then reflected the effects of the omission contingency, over and above the effects of introducing partial reinforcement and particular US patterning. Rats in an *unpaired* condition were also yoked to omission rats; they received US presentations at the same time as their yoked partners, but CS presentations were delayed until at least 3 min later. Finally, the rats in a *consistent* reinforcement group received a US after each CS presentation. Comparisons of omission and consistent subjects permitted addressing the question of whether omission contingencies would ever completely eliminate conditioned behavior. Behavior was scored as described above.

Figure 3 shows the effects on a target response of making US delivery contingent on the nonoccurrence of that target response. There were no detectable effects on startle behavior of placing an omission contingency on that behavior during pairings of auditory CSs with food and only small (but reliable) effects of imposing omission contingencies on head jerk or magazine behavior during the conditioning of auditory CSs. Similarly, the evocation of rear behavior during visual CSs was only moderately reduced by the imposition of an omission contingency on that behavior's occurrence. Interestingly, magazine behavior to visual CSs paired with food was completely eliminated when an omission contingency was placed on that behavior's occurrence. Regardless, the results of these experiments did not support the notion that differential CR forms to auditory and visual signals for food were the result of instrumental reinforcement contingencies. CS-specific behavior patterns emerged even when omission contingencies ensured that those behaviors were not adventitiously paired with food. In fact, the behaviors most unique to particular stimuli were least susceptible to omission contingencies.

2. Variations in US Processing

Strict transfer of the unconditioned response to the CS might also be salvaged as an account for the form of CRs if it is recognized that nominal USs may be processed as multifeatured events (e.g., Estes, 1969), each controlling components of the response which can be independently transferred to the CS. Early attempts to account for the nonidentity of CR and UR often relied on this notion (e.g., Hilgard & Marquis, 1940). For instance, swallowing might not be transferred to a CS signaling food in salivary con-

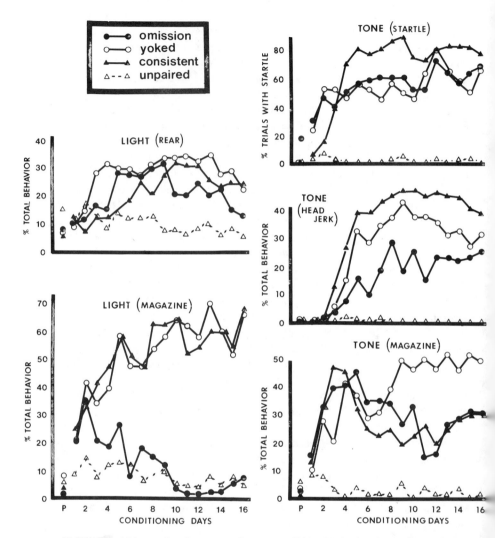

Fig. 3. Acquisition and maintenance of target conditioned behaviors in the five omission experiments in Holland (1979). The heading on each panel indicated whether the CS used was a light or a tone, and whether the target behavior of the omission contingency was rear, magazine, startle, or head jerk.

ditioning because that component of the complex of behaviors evoked by food delivery occurs too distant temporally from the CS. In fact, experiments in which food (Kierylowicz *et al.*, 1968) or water (Debold, Miller, & Jensen, 1965; Gormezano, 1972) is delivered directly to the oral cavity rather than to a dish frequently yield conditioned licking, swallowing, or jaw movement responses. Differences in CR form as a function of CS–US interval might also be anticipated since the CS might be in optimal temporal relations with different US features. More extreme cases of CR–UR dissimilarity might occur in the same way: Closer examination of some pharmacological URs (Domjan & Gillan, 1977; Domjan *et al.*, 1980; Wikler, 1973) shows them to be multiphasic, thus including the changes labeled as "opposite" or "compensatory." In fact, Schull (1979) and Solomon and Corbit (1974) argued that most USs might elicit both a primary reaction and a compensatory or opponent secondary reaction. Either of these reactions might be conditioned to antecedent CSs.

Application of a US-processing account to the cases of CS-dependent differences in CR form is less obvious. Perhaps existing qualitative relations among CS and US features render various CSs selectively more associable with different features of the US. Or, the presence of different CSs and their accompanying orienting responses at the time of US delivery might differentially modify the receipt of various properties of the US.

At least in some preparations, however, CSs that evoke very different CRs have been shown to be associated with similar properties of the US. Several types of evidence are available in the case of rats' appetitive conditioning. First, Holland (1977, Experiment 2) found that pretraining a CS that evoked one response enabled that CS to block conditioning of a very different response to another CS when the pretrained and new CSs were reinforced in compound. Most theoretical accounts of Kamin's (1968) blocking effect (e.g., Pearce & Hall, 1980; Rescorla & Wagner, 1972) and considerable data (e.g., Fowler, 1978; Holland, 1984; Dickinson & Mackintosh, 1979) suggest that blocking occurs only if the reinforcer delivered in the compound conditioning phase is predictable as a consequence of pretraining. If CS-dependent differences in CR form occurred because two CSs were associated with different features of the nominal US, then the effective US for the added CS would not be predicted by the pretrained CS. Thus, blocking of different response topographies should not occur. In Holland's (1977) experiment, three groups of rats received pairings of either a light, a tone, or no stimulus with food delivery. Then all rats received pairings of a light + tone compound CS with food. Finally, responding to the tone and light separately was examined in each group. Pretraining the light blocked the acquisition of startle and head jerk behaviors to the tone, even though the light never evoked those behaviors. Similarly, pretraining the tone blocked the acquisition of rear and magazine behaviors to the light, relative to performance in the no-pretraining group. Thus, it is unlikely that the light and tone CSs were associated with different features of the food US. Blanchard and Honig (1976) and Tomie (1981) noted similar findings in pigeon autoshaping: Prior conditioning of a diffuse cue which does not evoke pecking interferes with the acquisition of key pecking to a key light paired with food).

Second, communality of association regardless of response form is suggested by the observation that the form of responding to a second-order CS is unaffected by the form of the response evoked by its first-order reinforcer CS. Holland (1977, Experiment 3) found the same form of second-order conditioned responding to a tone CS regardless of whether it was paired with a previously conditioned light CS or a previously conditioned tone CS. Similarly, tones and key lights paired with food evoke very different conditioned behaviors in pigeons, but both establish pecking when they are in turn signaled by a key light (Nairne & Rescorla, 1981; Rashotte *et al.*, 1977). In addition, Holland (1980a) found that the form of second-order conditioned responding to visual or auditory CS was not affected by the duration of their reinforcer CSs, despite those latter CSs evoking very different conditioned behaviors. Third, the associative strengths of CSs that evoke very different CRs sum, even though the peripheral responses compete. Holland (1977, Experiment 3) compared the abilities of a light + tone compound and its individual elements to establish second-order conditioning to another auditory cue. Considerably more head jerk and startle behavior was established to the second-order CS if the compound was used as the reinforcer than if either element alone was used, even though that compound itself evoked less of those behaviors than the tone element alone. In a related unpublished experiment, I found that a light + tone compound blocked conditioning to added visual or auditory cues more than did either element alone. Finally, Rescorla and Holland (1977) found that a conditioned inhibitor established by nonreinforcing it in the presence of a CS of one modality was capable of inhibiting the very different conditioned behaviors evoked by CSs of other modalities. All of these data make it unlikely that the variations in CR forms discussed here are the consequence of different underlying learned information.

3.   CS-Processing Accounts

Members of this class of accounts attribute apparent violations of simple transfer principles to an additional contribution of various CS-processing mechanisms. Within these accounts the search for the origins of conditioned behavior beyond reflex transfer primarily involves the specification of the nature of CS events, of the organism's perceptual processes, and of the interaction of those processes with learning. This class of accounts is of special interest, first, because many current models of conditioning stress the role of CS-processing functions in conditioning and attempt to specify rules for variations in those functions (e.g., Mackintosh, 1975; Moore &

Stickney, 1980; Pearce & Hall, 1980), and, second, because they provide a natural framework in which to place the occurrence of CS-dependent differences in CR form. Two general types of CS-processing notions can be specified: those that claim that CS processing modifies the CR in performance and those that assume learned alterations in behavior.

   a.   Performance Accounts.   The simplest way that processing of the CS might modify the CR is by directly affecting performance at the time of response evocation. For instance, the observed CR might be a "compromise response" (Guthrie, 1940) that reflects the interaction of a UR-like CR and orienting, investigatory, or pseudoconditioned responses evoked by the CS unrelated to the occurrence of conditioning. Historically, such notions have played a frequent role in accounting for quantitative variations in CRs when different CSs are used. For instance, a number of researchers have noted that variations in CS intensity may affect performance more than learning, citing evidence that those variations alter responding in pseudoconditioning procedures as much as in conditioning procedures (e.g., Cohen, 1974) or that they affect only aspects of behavior that occur as orienting responses to the CSs, rather than "true CRs" (e.g., Kimmel, 1959; Walker, 1960). Furthermore, such accounts are especially well suited for explaining differences in CR form attributable to CS characteristics if those CSs evoke varying orienting or investigatory behaviors (as in the rat appetitive conditioning situation described earlier): Similar responses could be learned to different CSs, but the presence of different stimuli at the time of performance would modulate those common behaviors.

   Alternatively, perhaps the occurrence of particular components of a reflex depends on the presence of particular stimulus "supports" (Tolman, 1932) at the time the reflex is emitted. That it, chewing, swallowing, or pecking may not occur as part of the CR if there is nothing available to chew, swallow, or peck when the CR is evoked. Changing the nature of the CS would change the nature of the stimulus supports for behavior and hence would alter the form of conditioned behavior, just as modifying the water level in a maze after learning changes the form of the instrumental response from, say, swimming to wading (MacFarlane, 1930). Experiments in which "chewable" CSs have been used frequently have generated such behavior, superficially supporting that notion (e.g., Boakes *et al.,* 1978; Breland & Breland, 1966; Peterson *et al.,* 1972; Stiers & Silberberg, 1974; Timberlake *et al.,* 1982).

   A simple way to test the possibility that variations in CR form are generated in performance rather than in learning is to provide in testing stimulus supports that were absent in learning. For instance, Holland (1977, Experiment 1) examined rats' behavior during an auditory + visual compound stimulus after conditioning one of its elements. If the differential behaviors that these elements evoke when conditioned alone are due to the presence of different stimulus supports or to the occurrence of different unconditioned responses in performance, then responding to the compound should be the same regardless of which element had been trained, since that compound provides both auditory and visual supports. Rats first received discrimination training involving either reinforced tone and nonreinforced light CSs or reinforced light and nonreinforced tone CSs. Then all rats received nonreinforced test presentations of the light, the tone, and a light + tone compound. Figure 4 shows the results of the test phase. Clearly, behavior evoked by the compound CS was identical in form to that evoked by the previously conditioned element alone. A similar outcome has been obtained with autoshaped pecking in pigeons: Availability of a lighted key during presentations of auditory and diffuse visual stimuli that signal food does not result in pecking (e.g., Schwartz, 1973; Wasserman, 1973a). Thus, at least these cases of CS determination of response form are not solely performance effects.

A somewhat contrived but informative unpublished experiment showed somewhat more dramatically that the various conditioned behaviors in the rat appetitive conditioning situation were not engendered solely by the stimuli present at the time of performance. In this experiment, a tone + light

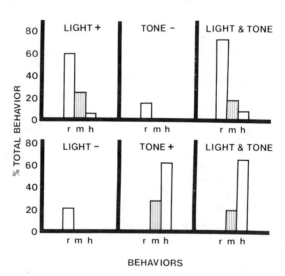

Fig. 4. Behavior during tests of the light, tone, and light and tone compound in Holland (1977) experiment 1. The top panels show responding of subjects who had previously received reinforced presentation of the light; the bottom panels show responding of subjects who had previously received reinforced tone presentations. r, Rear behavior; m, magazine behavior; h, head jerk behavior.

compound stimulus was present at all times in the experimental chambers except on CS trials. Some rats received food after the light was turned off for 10 sec and no food after the tone was turned off for 10 sec, whereas other rats received the reverse contingencies. Discrimination learning proceeded more slowly than when stimulus onset was paired with reinforcement (Holland, 1977), but eventually the rats that received light-off paired with food showed rear and magazine behavior during the light-off periods, and the rats that received tone-off paired with food showed startle and head jerk behavior during tone-off periods. Note that the stimulus actually present during tone-off was the light and that present during light-off was the tone. Thus the occurrence of rear behavior did not require the presence of visual "supports" nor did startle and head jerk behaviors require auditory supports.

b. *Learning Accounts.*   Learned changes in CS processing might also interact with a transferred UR to produce CR–UR similarity. Many investigators (e.g., Dykman, 1965; Maltzman, 1977; Patten & Rudy, 1967; Sokolov, 1963) have suggested that conditioning operations enhance orienting responses. The interaction of such learning-enhanced responses with transferred CRs could be responsible for a variety of CR–UR dissimilarity effects. Within this view, CS-dependent differences in CR form would emerge whenever the orienting responses evoked by CSs differed. A more general statement of this view could be made within attention theory: Conditioning operations may enhance attention (e.g., Mackintosh, 1975; Sutherland & Mackintosh, 1971), one consequence of which would be the augmentation of orienting responses.

A number of examples of CS-dependent variations in CR form are consistent with this notion. For example, in heart rate conditioning DeToledo (1971) found that postconditioning differences in CR form to noises differing in pulse rate correlated with preconditioning response differences. Similarly, Black *et al.* (1962) noted that the CS–US interval-dependent changes in response form might correlate with the multiphasic nature of orienting responses (ORs) to the CSs: Different intervals would ensure close contiguity between different portions of the OR and the US. I (Holland, 1977) favored a variation of such a view in accounting for the CS-determined variations in CR form that I have studied in my laboratory. In a variety of experiments investigating the nature of responding to stimuli differing in modality, location, localizability, and duration, the relative postconditioning frequencies of the two behaviors that primarily occur early in the CS intervals—rear and startle behaviors—were predictable from the relative frequencies of those behaviors prior to conditioning. Since orienting responses are often thought to be elicited by the onset of a stimulus (or by stimulus change, as in the experiment just described), it is just these early behaviors that might be expected to increase in frequency within the accounts now under consideration.

Because within this account the ability of CSs to evoke orienting responses depends on Pavlovian learning, it is superior to two other accounts that implicated a role for unconditioned or orienting responses to the CS. First, one would not expect the mere presence of certain stimuli or stimulus supports at the time of performance to substantially affect conditioned responding. Thus, the results of the stimulus compound test described above (Holland, 1977, Experiment 1) would be anticipated: Only the conditioned element would evoke ORs. Second, since the learning process involved is a Pavlovian one, features of the data that argued against the involvement of instrumental contingencies in enhancing the orienting response would be irrelevant.

A number of theorists have espoused a similar view. For example, Culler (1938) suggested that the animal must learn both to adjust to the CS itself and to the imminent US. Similarly, Dykman (1965) proposed that although late-CS behavior had its origins in the UR, early CS behavior was generated by a conditioning-dependent enhancement of the OR. And Maltzman (1977) has suggested that enhancement of ORs in human galvanic skin response conditioning procedures involves a very different learning process than that involved in generating other components of CRs.

It is worth noting that these notions imply some independence of CS-generated and US-generated behaviors, even though conditioning is responsible for both. Thus it might be possible to separately influence each class of behavior. For example, the use of relatively long CS–US intervals might be anticipated to minimize the importance of CS-generated behaviors, since the OR would occur in an unfavorable relation with the US. In fact, Holland (1980a) showed that responding to 1-min visual and auditory CSs paired with food differed very little in form and not at all during the later portions of the CS. Similarly, the occurrence of tone-specific startle and head jerk behaviors was substantially reduced by reducing the predictiveness of CS onset. In one experiment (Holland, 1980a, Experiment 4), 30-sec presentations of a tone were reinforced but 5-sec presentations were nonreinforced. Eventually the CS came to evoke little startle and head jerk behaviors but substantial magazine behavior. Note that this operation, which might be construed as removing the influence of the onset of the CS, resulted in responding that resembled closely the magazine responding evoked by food delivery itself. To ensure that the shift in response form did not occur simply because of a reduction in conditioning strength in that discrimination, the conditioning strength of that stimulus was evaluated independently of response form by using it as a reinforcer in second-order conditioning. The data showed the 30-sec stimulus to be a stronger reinforcer than another, 5-sec tone stimulus that evoked substantially more startle and head jerk behavior but had not been as frequently paired with food.

Other evidence which supports the independence of CS- and US-generated behaviors came from experiments in which features of either the US or CS were manipulated. Changes in the nature of the CS affected the nature of responding during early CS periods, but had little effect on late-CS behavior (Holland, 1980b). Conversely, the use of USs varying in quantitative and qualitative properties directly influenced US-related magazine behavior more than the CS-specific behaviors (Holland, 1979). In fact, conditioned rear and startle behaviors were observed even when weak-shock USs, which supported freezing in the later portions of CS–US intervals, were used. Shettleworth (1978) noted a similar potentiation of orienting responses in aversive conditioning in one experiment, but not in another similar one. In a related finding, Holland and Straub (1979) found that various devaluations of the US after conditioning had different effects on CS-specific and US-related behaviors (cf. Cleland & Davey, 1982). Similarly, Holland (1979) noted substantially greater effects of imposing US-omission contingencies on US-related magazine behavior than on CS-specific behaviors (cf. Davey et al., 1981). Finally, in unpublished experiments, both William Socker in my laboratory and Robert McCann working in Dr. Robert St. Claire-Smith's laboratory found conditioned inhibitors to have greater suppressive effects on US-related magazine behavior than on CS-specific behaviors.

Recently, Robert Ross and I (Holland & Ross, 1981; Ross & Holland, 1981, 1982) identified another way in which learned changes in CS processing may affect the form of conditioned behavior. We found that the occurrence of startle behavior to auditory cues for food depended on their being "surprising." Tones that were signaled by other cues (some of which themselves evoked startle behavior and some of which did not) did not evoke startle behavior, but did acquire head jerk and magazine behaviors. Furthermore, degrading the predictive ability of the signal cue by presenting that cue without the target auditory CS reduced the suppressive effects of signaling. All of these data are consistent with the notion that processing of CSs is a function of their predictedness (Wagner, 1978).

It should be emphasized that although the CS-specific and US-common responses can be separately influenced by various manipulations, a variety of evidence (noted above in Section III,B,2) showed that the learning underlying those two types of changes still must be substantially similar. Kaye and Pearce (1984), who also examined the appetitive conditioning of rats, make a somewhat different assumption. They claim that rear behavior evoked by localized visual CSs reflects not conditioning to those CSs, but rather attention. This distinction is important, since within the Pearce and Hall (1980) model of conditioning, attention and conditioning frequently do not covary. In fact, within that model attention to a CS is greater when that CS is a poor predictor of upcoming events than when it predicts it well. Thus, Kaye and Pearce (1984) predicted that rear behavior should decrease in frequency with extended training, increase again when the US is omitted (as in extinction), and be maintained whenever the CS is an ambiguous predictor of the US (as in partial reinforcement). They found all three effects. In a number of experiments, however, I have found no evidence for a substantial decline in rear behavior with continued reinforcement of visual CSs. The source of this discrepancy is unclear now, although it may be important that Kaye and Pearce observed the behavior of their subjects only twice within a 10-sec CS, at 4 sec and 9 sec after CS onset. Holland (1977) found that rear behavior occurred most frequently just after CS onset; relatively little of that behavior occurred during the second 5-sec interval of a 10-sec CS; in addition, the frequency of that behavior during later portions of the CS was observed to decrease with extended training. I attributed that loss, however, to the replacement of CS-generated rear behavior by US-determined magazine behaviors during the later portions of the CS. A similar process could account for our fragmentary observations that support Kaye and Pearce's other observations, the occurrence of more rear behavior with partial than continuous reinforcement, and an initial upward shift in rear frequency at the beginning of extinction: Extinction of magazine behavior could release early CS rear behavior from competition.

Regardless of the outcome of attempts to resolve the differences in our findings, Kaye and Pearce's notion is an important one: Learning-dependent changes in CS processing could affect the nature of CRs in ways that seem inconsistent with the effects of variations in CSs' associative strengths.

C.   NONTRANSFER ACCOUNTS

A second major class of accounts for the nature of conditioned behavior rejects the simple reflex transfer or stimulus substitution viewpoint. Instead of attempting to explain its failures by pointing to other sources of behavior, these accounts postulate alternative sources of behavior to which so much exception need not be taken. The classic alternatives to simple stimulus substitution models of conditioning are those that assume that conditioning primarily involves the learning of emotional responses (e.g., Mowrer, 1947, 1960) and those that assume that the primary function in conditioning is to establish an expectancy or anticipatory set (e.g., Tolman, 1932).

1. Conditioned Value Changes

A number of theorists have suggested that a major consequence of Pavlovian conditioning operations may be the establishment of new motivational significance or value to the CS. Indeed, that claim formed the basis of the tradition of two-process theory, which still lingers. Note especially that responding might be expected to be centered around the CS in some manner since that stimulus itself acquires value. Various sources of behavior can be postulated within such a notion. First, animals might act instrumentally in such a manner as to advantageously modulate receipt of the newly valued CS (e.g., Culler, 1938). Thus, conditioned behavior directed toward appetitively conditioned CSs might reflect instrumentally reinforced attempts to gain and maintain contact with those conditionally valued stimuli. Note that the many attempts to place omission contingencies on conditioned behaviors have ignored the potential role of such conditioned reinforcement.

I recently considered such a possibility in the case of signal-directed behavior in rats. The greater sensitivity to omission contingencies of behaviors evoked by visual cues for food than by auditory cues in my omission experiments (Holland, 1979a; above) encouraged the thought that, although instrumental contingencies between rearing and food delivery were not responsible for the emergence of the unique rear response, an instrumental contingency between rearing and optimal receipt of the visual CS may have been. The visual CS used in the above experiments, unlike the auditory cues, was quite localizable, above the conditioning chamber. The rear response could thus be construed as an approach response which maximized receipt of a conditioned reinforcer, the visual CS paired with food.

I considered this possibility in an unpublished experiment by examining the effects of making either US omission, CS termination, or both contingent on the occurrence of rear behavior (see Schwartz, 1972, for a related attempt to solve a similar problem in the case of autoshaped key pecking in pigeons). The US-only condition was identical to that of the previous experiments: Occurrence of rear behavior canceled the delivery of food but had no effect on CS duration. In the CS-only condition, rearing caused the immediate termination of the CS, but the scheduled US was delivered. In the CS + US condition, the occurrence of rearing both immediately terminated the CS and canceled US delivery. Six rats received training with visual CSs much like that in the omission experiment described earlier (Holland, 1979) except that each subject received two 16-session blocks under each of the three omission contingencies; the six blocks of training were presented in counterbalanced order across the subjects. In addition, each rat was yoked to a control rat that received the same pattern of CS and US presentations as the omission rat. At the end of each block of training, each rat received a single test session in which the visual CSs were presented nonreinforced for 10 sec. Thus the effects of all contingencies were evaluated under common test conditions. The outcomes of the test sessions were in all cases similar to the performance observed during the final four acquisition sessions in each training block. The data presented below are those from the test sessions.

As in Holland's (1979a) experiments, imposition of the US-only condition slightly reduced the frequency of rear behavior relative to controls (rear constituted 20% of the total behavior of the rats in the US-only condition versus 38% in their yoked partners). Conversely, response-dependent termination of the CS had no effects on the frequency of rearing (42% in the omission rats versus 37% in the yoked rats). Thus it seems unlikely that rear behavior is maintained by secondary reinforcement in this conditioning situation. It is interesting to note, however, that the CS + US omission contingency reduced rear behavior to levels below that observed with the US-only condition in five of the six subjects (17% omission versus 42% controls), even though the CS-only procedure had no effect. One possibility is that the CS termination procedure had subthreshold effects more easily observed at different response levels. That, however, seems unlikely given the range of behavior levels observed across subjects. But it is also possible that the termination of the CS served as a feedback cue, marking the rear response as responsible for the subsequent omission of the US (e.g., Lieberman, McIntosh, & Thomas, 1979). Regardless, this experiment gave no support to the notion that instrumental response contingencies are completely responsible for the behavior patterns displayed to visual CSs paired with food in this conditioning situation.

Conditioned value changes might also cause animals to respond to a conditionally valued CS in a consummatory fashion, that is, in a manner appropriate to a valued key light, tone, or so forth, rather than in a manner appropriate only to the US (Mowrer, 1947). For instance, rats presented with another rat signaling the impending delivery of food do not attempt to bite or chew the other rat (Timberlake, 1983; Timberlake & Grant, 1975) but rather engage in social contact appropriate to the CS animal. (The frequency of that social contact is much higher than with the presentation of another rat not paired with the US.) Similarly, rats faced with a prod that previously delivered shock often bury or barricade it rather than flee or freeze in its presence (e.g., Pinel, Treit, & Wilkie, 1980; Terlecki, Pinel, & Treit, 1979). Chicks peck key lights signaling heat lamp reinforcement rather than engaging in the behaviors the heat lamp evoked (Wasserman, 1973b). And the frequent approach and contact responses seen anticipatory to food delivery in a variety of preparations might be viewed as analogous to the approach and contact of unconditionally valued objects and events. Consideration of the role of acquired value in influencing CR form might be especially valuable in dealing with the frequent observation that animals approach sites of signals positively correlated with food (Hearst, 1975) or negatively correlated with shock (LeClerc & Reberg, 1980) but withdraw from signals positively correlated with shock (LeClerc & Reberg, 1980) or negatively correlated with food (Wasserman, Franklin, & Hearst, 1974). Finally, a particularly interesting example is Garcia's claim (Garcia, Kovner, & Green, 1970) that conditioned flavor aversions established using toxin USs involve *hedonic shifts,* that is, changes in the palatability of flavors that signal illness. Supporting this view is the observation that rats respond to an illness-paired flavor the same way they respond to a naturally foul-tasting substance, rather than in a manner similar to their responses to the toxins used (e.g., Grill, 1975).

2. Expectancy Theories

Expectancy theories have largely been silent on the determinants of the form of conditioned responding. Tolman (1932) suggested that the CR is determined by the *sign character* of the CS. That is, the CR is a response to the expectancy of the US, rather than an anticipatory version of the UR. As Liddell (1934) put it, there would be no particular reason to anticipate CR–UR similarity since the two highly integrated acts of expectation and consumption of a US may be quite dissimilar. Furthermore, as Tolman (1932) claimed, the nature of the CR might be appropriate not only to the sign properties of the CS but also its *discriminanda and manipulanda characteristics,* that is, its perceptual features, ability to be contacted, and so forth. Thus the nature of the CS would be expected to play a major role in the determination of the observed CR form; only in cases when the "behavior supports" provided by CS and US were similar would CR and UR be similar. Only when the supports were internal, that is, stimulus properties controlling glandular secretions and the like, would CS features not affect CR form. Thus, such a view has room for encompassing many of the data previously discussed. It is worth noting, however, that Tolman's account stressed that the CS-provided supports were effective in modulating behavior in performance only. Learned behavior did not differ regardless of CS features. Thus his particular view seems incompatible with many of the data discussed above showing that CS-dependent differences in CR form were not simply performance generated.

Formulations like Tolman's recognize that association and the determination of response form may be somewhat loosely related and that we must look elsewhere for the source of the particular form of CRs. To say that

CRs represent responses "appropriate to the expectancy" of the US adds little without some more detailed consideration of what is meant by such a phrase. A number of accounts have been suggested recently which attempt such a specification.

3. Behavior Systems Approaches

One frequent specification of what is meant by "behavior appropriate to the expectancy of the US" is the notion that the CS comes to evoke not a replica of the UR evoked by the particular US delivered but a more complex set of naturally occurring action patterns appropriate to that US. For instance, feeding is a complex activity containing many separate, sequentially organized action patterns ranging from food procuring to food consumption. Stimuli that are artificially arranged to precede terminal activities may come to release the whole feeding sequence or various portions of it, regardless of the behaviors evoked by the US itself. Williams (1972) and Woodruff and Williams (1976) suggested that CSs that signal food or water come to release preorganized action patterns related to seeking those substances. They noted the resemblance of the acquisition of conditioned behaviors in pigeon autoshaping experiments to the nature and development of "unconditioned" food-seeking behaviors. Furthermore, they distinguished between such an account and a reflex transfer or substitution account by demonstrating that food-seeking behaviors (e.g., approaching and pecking) occurred as conditioned responses to key lights paired with food or water even when those behaviors were excluded from the UR by delivering those substances directly into the subjects' mouths. Similarly, Hogan (1974) noted that key lights paired with heat stimulation (Wasserman, 1973b) may release action patterns related to nestling, which include pecking, even though the heat lamp used in Wasserman's experiments may not itself have elicited pecking.

Jenkins, Barrera, Ireland, and Woodside (1978) offered a more involved version of this notion. They observed that CSs paired with food came to evoke naturally occurring food-procuring behaviors in dogs, such as begging, hunting, and sign pointing (see also Liddell, 1934; Lorenz, 1969, p. 47). Jenkins et al. (1978) suggested that CSs come to substitute not for the US, but rather for "natural signals" for the subsequent receipt of food. Thus, as for Tolman, the CR is a response to an expectancy of food rather than to food itself. This formulation permits both greater latitude in the "acceptable" forms of the CR and greater advance specification of those forms. For instance, if the CS is substituting for a natural precursor of food, then conditioned behavior to that CS might be dependent on its resemblance to that precursor. Thus, localized and more general, diffuse CSs might evoke very different behaviors since dogs' food-procuring behaviors presumably would differ depending on whether the naturally occurring cues were localized (e.g., another dog in view). Similarly, different CS–US intervals might be anticipated to come to control different portions of the food-procuring–consumption sequence. Thus, within this type of formulation, the search for the origins of the CR centers around an investigation of the sequence of behaviors—and the stimuli naturally controlling those behaviors—involved in natural interactions with objects like those used as the US. It is a satisfying notion because it captures some of the spirit of both substitution theories (since unconditioned behavior patterns come under the control of new stimuli) and expectancy theories (since evoked behaviors are characteristic of the "expectancy" of the US, not of the response to the US itself).

Perhaps the best developed theory of the origins of conditioned responses is the *behavior system* approach offered by Timberlake (Timberlake, 1983; Timberlake *et al.*, 1982). As with the preceding notions, the behavior system approach assumes that there are species-specific preorganized behavior systems related to a variety of important activities such as feeding. Each of those systems is said to be composed of smaller modules that consist of responses that show particular probabilistic sequential relations and are elicited, controlled, and terminated by particular events. For instance, the feeding system may contain modules such as individual foraging, social approach behavior, investigation, predation, food handling, hoarding, ingestion, and rejection. Those modules may be organized linearly or hierarchically (or both); the basis of their identification and organization is the naturalistic observation of the behavior system in question. Most important, learning is said to be possible at several points, and at several levels, within a complete behavior system. Thus, learning may occur within modules, for instance, changing the relative frequency or timing of individual behaviors, or the development of control by particular stimuli, or it may occur between modules, altering the frequency, sequence, or other aspects of between-module organization. In a sense, the behavior system approach views *all* Pavlovian conditioning as involving the modulation of otherwise organized behavior patterns, just as traditional two-process theories viewed Pavlovian conditioned emotional responses as modulating ongoing instrumental behavior.

Given the temporal organization of behavior patterns, it is perhaps not surprising that the use of different CS–US intervals might produce somewhat differently formed CRs (e.g., Black *et al.,* 1962; Holland, 1980a, above; Konorski, 1967). A particularly interesting case is that of backward conditioning. Historically, the claim has generally been that conditioning does not occur with that stimulus arrangement (e.g., Mackintosh, 1974).

But typically we have looked for the occurrence of conditioned responses that usually occur as anticipatory behaviors. Indeed, most successful demonstrations of excitatory backward conditioning (e.g., Heth, 1976; Heth & Rescorla, 1973; Mowrer & Aiken, 1954) have used indirect assessment techniques in which conditioning is inferred by alterations in a cue's ability to serve as a conditioned reinforcer. A behavior systems approach encourages us to look instead for the development of postconsummatory behavior. (Of course, such a view is also consistent with a simple reflex transfer position.)

In an unpublished experiment, Dorothea LeDonne and I observed the behavior of rats that received backward food–tone pairings. Casual observations had suggested that, at least with certain reinforcers, rats often groomed after eating. Grooming never appeared as an anticipatory CR in earlier, forward-conditioning experiments, however. In each of four 60-min sessions, four rats in Group Backward received six presentations of .3 ml of 16% sucrose solution followed 5 sec later by a 5-sec, 1800-Hz tone; four rats in Group Forward received six presentations of the sucrose solution preceded by the 5-sec tone; and four rats in Group Unpaired received six sucrose and six tone presentations, explicitly unpaired. Finally, all rats received a test session which included six 5-sec presentations of the tone alone. In that test session, only the rats in Group Forward showed appreciable startle (83%), head jerk (52%), or magazine (21%) behavior. But the rats in Group Backward showed significantly more grooming behavior during the 60-sec interval initiated by tone onset (12%) than the rats in Group Forward (0%) or Group Unpaired (4%). In a similar vein, Keith-Lucas and Guttman (1975) conceived a backward-conditioning episode as a model of an unsuccessful predator attack. In their experiment, a toy hedgehog was thrown into the experimental chamber immediately after the rat subjects had received foot shocks. They found substantial backward conditioning, as indexed by a number of preference measures.

Consideration of postconsummatory behaviors also leads to the expectation that backward CSs would come to evoke responses that serve to physiologically readjust the organism (i.e., restore homeostasis) after a disruptive US (e.g., Hollis, 1982; Schull, 1979). Thus, one might anticipate backward CRs that are opposite in character to forward CRs and that would, of course, interfere with the latter CRs. It is interesting to speculate that the "conditioned inhibition" obtained with extended backward pairings (e.g., Heth, 1976) reflects quite different learning from that acquired in other conditioned inhibition procedures.

Perhaps what most distinguishes Timberlake's system from others is his use of that system to generate and test specific predictions. After a tentative "natural structure" of behavior modules is postulated, a variety of hypotheses concerning their appearance and interaction in learned behavior can be generated. Timberlake considers possibilities that can be loosely described as involving the independence of behavior modules (e.g., the separate elicitation of different modules by stimuli that differ in certain physical and temporal characteristics), the sequencing of behavior modules (e.g., the effects of artificially reordering the naturally occurring sequence by presenting signals for inappropriate sequences of conditioned behaviors under various experimental circumstances), and behaviors within modules (e.g., changes in the frequency, timing, vigor, or efficiency of modular behaviors).

Timberlake has conducted a number of experiments involving the conditioning of various aspects of the feeding system in rodents. For instance, the use of a rolling ball bearing as a CS signaling food delivery in rats resulted in a set of conditioned behaviors including such behaviors as contacting, retrieving, carrying, patting, and chewing the bearing (Timberlake *et al.,* 1982). Those behaviors were seen as deriving from naturally occurring behaviors related to predation, handling, and hoarding food. As in Jenkins's account, those behaviors, rather than food cup approach or other "US-related" behaviors, were observed because the CS type used resembled natural signals for subsequent food ingestion closely enough to tap into that aspect of the behavior system. That resemblance was both physical (i.e., the CS was chaseable, graspable, chewable, and retainable) and temporal (i.e., initially occurring remote from the time of consumption, but available during and after food delivery as well).

A more intriguing set of experiments conducted in Timberlake's laboratory involved conditioning of various aspects of the social module. Rats are social feeders, often approaching already feeding rats and attempting to grab food out of each others' mouths. A number of investigators have provided a fair amount of detail concerning the nature and role of this social component of feeding (e.g., Bayroff & Lard, 1944; Ewer, 1971; Galef & Clark, 1972). Within the behavior systems view, then, variations in the conditioning situation that mimic those that can occur in natural feeding situations should result in variations in the CR that mimic those seen in natural feeding behaviors.

In an initial experiment, Timberlake and Grant (1975) observed the behavior of rat subjects in the presence of various signals for food delivery. For one group of rats, food was signaled by the presentation of a live rat (strapped to a platform), and for another group food was signaled by the presentation of a rat-sized wood block. Rats whose food signal was the wood block showed substantial increases in orienting toward that stimulus, but showed no signs of social interaction. Rats whose signal was another rat exhibited a variety of behaviors including orienting, approaching, and more detailed social behaviors such as sniffing, crawling over, pawing, grooming, and poking their noses into the stimulus rat's mouth. Notably, although the authors reported some biting of the platform, the subjects did not attempt to bite or chew the stimulus rat, as would be expected from a reflex transfer position, and as they have been noted to do with lever insertion CSs (Peterson *et al.*, 1972). Furthermore, considerably less social behavior was noted in other subjects that received random presentations of food and a stimulus rat, or stimulus rat presentations alone. It is also worth noting that the distribution of various social behaviors as well as their frequency was altered by rat–food pairings: The most frequent baseline behaviors were not necessarily the most frequent conditioned behaviors. Related preliminary findings have been observed in pigeons by Rashotte (in Hearst, 1975).

As in many other experiments reported above, the nature of the CR observed differed drastically depending on the type of CS. The use of a CS much like a natural social cue for food led to the induction of a variety of conditioned social behaviors much like those observed in natural feeding situations. Subsequent experiments examined the effects of other variations in the CS that were suggested by consideration of natural social feeding patterns in rats.

Galef and Clark (1972) noted that juvenile rats approach and attend to feeding adult rats, as might be anticipated within an evolutionary view. A number of researchers have pointed to the important involvement of learning processes in food selection (e.g., Rozin & Kalat, 1971), and it seems reasonable that attending to the feeding of adults and learning to eat those foods in those locations would confer selective advantage. Similarly, by virtue of their rearing arrangements, juvenile rats tend to feed together. Conversely, Timberlake noted that it would hardly seem adaptive for adults to approach and feed with juvenile rats inexperienced at food selection. Thus, the patterns of conditioned social interaction observed should depend on the age of the subject and stimulus rats.

A second experiment (Timberlake, 1983) used a factorial design involving either adult or juvenile subjects and adult or juvenile stimulus rats. As suggested by knowledge of social interaction patterns in natural food consumption, adult subjects approached and made social contact with adult CSs, and juvenile subjects approached and made social contact with both adult and juvenile CSs, but adult subjects did not approach or contact juvenile CSs paired with food. Another experiment showed that although juvenile rats preferred social interaction with other juveniles to interaction with adults prior to conditioning, those same juveniles approached adults more than juveniles after conditioning. Thus, unlike the case of orienting in my experiments, observation of behaviors evoked intrinsically by the CS alone prior to conditioning gave little clue as to the relative dominance of behaviors after conditioning. That is, it is not the relative probability of juvenile and adult CSs of eliciting social contact that determines the likelihood of conditioned behavior, but rather the relative likelihood of adult and juvenile signals for food in the natural situation evoking such behavior.

Other experiments in that series investigated the effects of imposing various response contingencies (e.g., reward and omission) on social contact responses and of imposing various delays between CS presentation and food delivery. The logic of these experiments is that immediate presentation of the food would lead to the CS rat becoming a cue for investigative and food-handling modules which might interrupt the social module behaviors otherwise conditioned in these circumstances. On the whole, the results of those studies showed that the response contingencies affected the frequencies of conditioned behaviors, but had little or no effect on the topography of that behavior. Delivery of immediate reward reduced the duration of social contact. Nevertheless, that contact persisted several seconds after the US was delivered (thus delaying food receipt), indicating that behaviors within the social module are sufficiently integrated to withstand a fair amount of interruption.

Other experiments found that the nature of social interaction differed depending on whether a stimulus rat signaled food or water. Unfortunately, naturalistic data that might show correspondence (and powerful confirmation of the usefulness of the approach) were not available.

An unpublished experiment conducted in my laboratory examined another example of a behavior within a "social module" of feeding. Lore and Flannely (1977) observed that established rat colonies typically develop a fairly consistent pattern of feeding dominance if food access is limited to particular places and times: Particular individuals consistently gain first access, spend the most time eating, and gain the most weight. Interestingly, that feeding dominance is often unrelated to aggressive dominance. Consequently, female rats (usually low in the aggressive dominance hierarchy) often are the most dominant animals in feeding.

Three male–female pairs of Sprague-Dawley-strain rats, identified by tail and back dyes, were allowed to roam freely in a 5- × 10-ft. room that was illuminated 14 hr each day. The rats had been housed communally in same-sex groupings from weaning until 90 days, when they were segregated into male–female pairs. After weaning of their first litters, the three pairs of rats were placed in the room. Tables, cages, and other objects were scattered about the room. Food was placed in an open hopper once each day for 30 min. Water was continuously available from drinking tubes placed within a metal enclosure with just their spouts protruding. The rats were undisturbed except for daily food delivery of Purina lab chow to one of the hoppers and exchanging of empty for full drinking tubes and semiweekly cleaning of the room. Food was always delivered during the light portion of the illumination cycle, but was equally likely to occur at any time within the middle 12 hr of that period. A video camera provided a view of the area around the food hoppers. After 1-week adaptation to the environment, video tapes of the rats' feeding behavior were made. As reported by Lore and Flannely (1977), I found that one male–female pair consistently spent more time at the filled hopper than the other rats and were most likely to be the first to feed. Similarly, the dominant pair were more likely to push other rats aside at the hopper than the other rats, although I never observed behaviors that would casually be described as aggressive (e.g., biting, boxing) during food presentation.

Next, a conditioning procedure was begun. Presentation of a moderately loud pulsed white noise preceded food delivery for 2 min each day. All rats quickly learned to approach the food hopper when the noise was presented. The dominance hierarchy observed earlier during feeding itself was also observed during the cue for food delivery: The same two rats were most likely to be first to reach the hopper and spend the greatest amount of time in the vicinity of the hopper. Nondominant rats, however, were more likely to attempt to crowd out the dominant rats during the CS than during food presentation itself. Similarly, a fair amount of aggressive behavior, usually one of the dominant pair biting or pouncing at another rat that attempted to push the dominant rat away from the hopper, was seen during the CS presentations, but not during food presentations. One might entertain a frustration–aggression notion or speculate that it is the presence of food that suppresses aggressive dominance tendencies and sets the occasion for a different set of dominance behaviors. For instance, one might suspect that during CSs a compromise or blend between aggressive and feeding dominances might arise. Only feeding times had been videotaped, however, and casual observations at other times of the day showed no evidence for aggressive behavior in the colony.

I then changed the nature of the CS. A flashing light located above the food hopper was presented for 2 min prior to food delivery. Although initially some of the rats oriented and reared toward the visual CS, by the seventh day of training the rats showed conditioned behaviors indistinguishable from those evoked by the auditory CS previously. In fact, the rats seemed to ignore the light after its onset. Next, I introduced a discrimination procedure in which the flashing light predicted the delivery of food to a new hopper located 2 ft. from the original hopper, but the pulsed noise predicted nonoccurrence of food. The original hopper was left in the room. The rats gradually learned to approach the new hopper during the light and show little initiation of social prefeeding behavior during the noise. Interestingly, the dominant rats were the first to learn the new contingency, often leaving the other rats jostling at the inappropriate hopper.

Further experiments along these lines could potentially examine relations between a variety of preorganized behavior patterns that show common elements and help clarify the role of conditioning in their display. For example, we attempted to examine the response of colony members to a novel intruder rat that predicted the delivery of food. Intruders into established colonies are frequently met with bouts of aggressive grooming, sometimes followed by obvious fighting and biting. On the other hand, Timberlake's "intruders" paired with food were contacted in a more positive manner, apparently more resembling social feeding activities. Timberlake (1983) noted that integration of early and terminal behaviors from different behavior systems might be difficult, and thus it would be of interest to determine what aspects of these two behavior systems the CR to the intruder might comprise. Unfortunately, the experiment was too crude to be of use: The colony rats interacted little with the intruder rat prior to food delivery. Opening the door to release the intruder rat was a well-established signal for food delivery and may well have blocked conditioning to the intruder. Furthermore, since the intruders were always new to the experimental room and food hoppers, they seldom approached the food hoppers, where interaction with the colony members would be maximized.

The point of these experiments basically is to note that the determinants of conditioned behavior lie both in the experimental context and in the subject's natural biological and ecological makeup. A greater appreciation of the role of naturally occurring behavior systems in learned behavior would both make the results of many conditioning experiments more interpretable and further understanding of those behavior systems themselves.

A behavior systems approach suggests another important but often neglected type of study, the comparative study. Different species presumably possess different behavioral modules and thus would show very different types of conditioned behaviors in response to various conditioned stimuli. Of course, there is nothing novel about the idea that different species might perform different URs, and hence learn different CRs, but it is interesting to note how minor differences in species' interactions with reinforcers might result in drastic differences in the form of learned responses. For instance, Timberlake (1983) repeated his social module conditioning experiments in hamsters, a nonsocial rodent. As anticipated, presentation of another hamster as a food signal had no greater facilitating effect on social contact than random presentations of food and signal. Although perfectly reasonable from a behavior systems perspective, that finding might not be as predictable from a conditioned value approach, for instance.

Additionally, an appreciation of the ontogeny of both conditioned and unconditioned behavior patterns seems essential within a behavior systems view. Are the behavior patterns engaged by CSs resembling "natural signals" for the US truly preorganized, or was that organization the result of specific conditioning experience with event sequences early in life? Or, are other types of experience sufficient? For example, is some adult social feeding experience necessary for the normal display of conditioned social feeding modules, or is early social feeding, which may exhibit very different patterns and preferences, adequate? Or is no social feeding experience necessary?

In summary, the behavior systems approach suggests that our guide for understanding the origins of conditioned behavior is the study of naturally occurring behavior patterns, following the normal strategies of the evolutionary biologist. Many traditional laboratory experiments may be tapping into only one module of a behavior system or in fact only a portion of one, a "truncated" system. Experiments like mine involving flashing lights and tones may be providing cues that are so distantly related to naturally related cues that the observed behavior patterns may represent aberrations more than natural integration of anticipatory behavior systems.

For instance, the orienting behavior that I observed may not represent a conditioning enhanced processing of the CS in general, but simply a small component of a sequence of appetitive behaviors, only one of which was supportable by the conditions at hand. For example, the protruding illuminated lens CS used in one of my experiments (above; Holland, 1980b) might have engendered nosing and investigatory behaviors because of its size and shape resemblance to a rat's head, but smaller contactable CSs (e.g., Peterson et al., 1972; Timberlake et al., 1982) would generate biting and chewing. On the other hand, perhaps orientation is a basic property of general behavioral adaptation, separate from any particular behavior system, or is a module contained within many such systems (see Hollis, 1982).

Similarly, perhaps the presumably truncated, unnatural behavior patterns observed in such experiments may be profitably viewed and better understood in the context of more integrated behavior systems. Consider the head jerk behavior observed in the presence of auditory cues for food in my experiments (above). The origins of that behavior were somewhat puzzling because it did not occur either as part of the unconditioned response to auditory stimuli or as part of the response to food delivery. Furthermore, its sensitivity to manipulations like omission, CS–US interval changes, and US devaluation procedures was between that of obviously CS-determined behaviors like startle responding and US-determined behaviors like magazine behavior. Initially (Holland, 1977) I suggested that head jerk behavior might be simply the consequence of the peripheral interaction of startle and magazine behavior. In support of that claim, I cited correlational analyses that showed that startle and head jerk behaviors covaried on a trial by trial basis and noted that manipulations that eliminated startle behavior generally eliminated head jerk behavior as well (Holland, 1980a).

That view is no longer tenable, however. First, as noted above, signaling auditory CSs prevents the acquisition of startle behavior but has little effect on head jerk behavior. Second, Holland (1981) noted that the joint presentation of a conditioned visual cue that evoked magazine behavior with a novel auditory cue that evoked startle responding did not result in the display of head jerk behavior.

But head jerk behavior might be profitably viewed as a conditioning enhanced version of a natural searching behavior termed *headsweeping* (MacFarlane, Pedersen, Cornell, & Blass, 1983); that search behavior might represent either search for the CS or search for the US. Or it may be atavistic, harkening back to the extreme paw extension and head movement responses shown by infant rats in response to auditory cues paired with food (Rudy & Hyson, 1982) and often in our laboratory seen in response to forced detachment from the nipple.

It is interesting to note that experiments that investigate the independence of various components of conditioned behavior, like those I have reported (above; Holland, 1979a,b, 1980a,b; Holland & Straub, 1979) and those of Timberlake (Timberlake, 1983; Timberlake *et al.*, 1982) have an analog in ethologists' attempts to determine if a particular releasing stimulus controls a single action pattern or multiple, separately elicitable action patterns. Thus, it seems reasonable to suggest that investigation of the independence of components of conditioned behavior patterns should be accompanied by parallel investigations of unconditioned behavior sequences which are believed by the behavior systems view to be tapped by conditioning.

IV. Conclusion

The behavior systems and learning abilities of organisms are products of their species' evolutionary history. It is my view that the study of Pavlovian conditioning reveals an adaptive mechanism by which organisms adjust to relatively short-term variations in their environment, specifically relations among events.

That adaptive value may be described at two levels. At a more general level, some investigators (e.g., Anokhin, 1974) have pointed out that there are certain universal or invariant relations among events in the environment (e.g., temporal order, causal relations) that constrain the life of all organisms. A plastic ability to deal with these relations among any set of events, for example, the ability to predict upcoming events, would in general surely be of value to a species, assuming of course that individual behavior systems (which after all are what are making contact with the environment) make profitable use of that information (presumably, behavior systems in which the cost of learning was greater than the benefits would not make use of this predictive ability.)

At a more local level, however, it seems reasonable to suspect that individual CRs themselves provide selective advantage for organisms in their natural environments. Unlike many advocates of functional (e.g., Johnston, 1982; Plotkin & Odling-Smee, 1979) and learning theoretic (see Miller, Greco, Vigorito, & Marlin, 1983, for a discussion) approaches alike, I suspect that most, if not all, of the Pavlovian CRs studied in our laboratories reflect at least portions of adaptive behavior complexes and thus represent valid behavioral investigative tools. Certainly the consequences of learning food preferences, locations of food sources, probabilities of finding foods in various patches, fear, correlations among events, timing, and so forth studied in the laboratory could potentially make contact with selection pressures. Hollis (1982), for example, has argued persuasively for the adaptive value of a wide spectrum of laboratory CRs ranging from digestive and cardiac system responses through flavor aversions and sign tracking to defensive/aggressive behaviors and courtship behaviors. Further, in many cases she cites evidence that the occurrence of CRs does in fact increase fitness of an individual and/or its kin. For instance, rats consume signaled food more quickly and efficiently than they consume unsignaled food (Zamble, 1973). Similarly, Hollis (1984) has shown that signals for territorial intrusion permit blue gourami fish to more aggressively and successfully defend their territories. Presumably, feeding efficiency, territorial security, and so forth would eventually be translated into reproductive advantage. Thus, it is conceivable that even the more obviously artificial laboratory environments involve the measurement of ecologically valid behaviors and hence may be profitably used as simplified versions of natural environments. Of course, the adaptive role of CRs is most likely to be obvious in those Pavlovian situations that bear the greatest resemblance to ecologically valid tasks.

Clearly our theories of learned behavior should be consistent with ecological and ethological considerations. We need not only knowledge of the mechanisms of learning processes but also of "response rules," the mechanisms by which a variety of behavior systems make use of learning processes. Understanding the nature of learned changes in particular behavior systems will require understanding of the function of those systems. Although the study of the proximal causes of variations in CR form (e.g., as a consequence of various manipulations of CS type) is a valid approach to understanding behavior mechanisms, it is likely that the most efficient statements of response rules will make use of knowledge of the normal function of behavior systems engaged by various CSs, the natural, unlearned organization within those systems, and the ontogeny of those systems. Thus, like other authors (e.g., Domjan & Galef, 1983; Johnston, 1982), I suggest that a purely conceptual or "cognitive" approach to conditioning may contribute proportionately less to an understanding of learned behavior systems than will a more functional analysis.

I suggest, however, that our attempts to understand the origins of learned behavior patterns must also take notice of a distinction between the operating characteristics of an association mechanism and of individual behavior systems' use of information provided by that mechanism. More specifically, we must determine if developmental variations, behavior systems variations, and so forth in the "rules" of learning are those of underlying learning or of a particular behavior system's use of that learning. Suppose an organism fails to exhibit a conditioned response when a particular pair of events is presented. Is the organism incapable of learning a relation between the two stimuli, or is it simply unable to use that relational knowledge in a particular behavior system?

Interestingly, that question is not particularly meaningful within either the associationist or the functionalist tradition alone. The functionalist claims that only the endpoint, behavior, makes contact with selection pressures, and the associationist often has little to say about why learned behavior is not manifest. But within a synthetic view, the question is not only meaningful, but may provide use with important insights into the generation and organization of behavior. From a functional perspective, we suspect that the particular behavioral expression is not an adaptive one, that is, it is more costly than the benefits it provides. But selection often disregards mechanism: Both the inability to learn a relation and the inability to translate that relation into behavior would have similar consequences for selection. Neither possibility is intrinsically "more important" than the other, but the answer to such questions would certainly provide us with more complete conceptions of the organization of behavior.

How should the study of learned behavior proceed? Continued study of the operating characteristics of conceptual learning systems seems essential. In the past few years, conditioning theorists have noted a variety of important phenomena such as blocking, overshadowing, interference, correlational effects, and within-compound associations that have changed drastically our concepts of learning. To end that study would be to severely limit our specification of the operating characteristics of learning.

However, it is important to note that an understanding of the nature of behavior systems is essential for the use of conditioned responses as measures of underlying cognitive processes. Many learning theorists have championed the use of particular response measures as "true" conditioned responses which tap directly the operating characteristics of associative processes. We have often favored truncated or limited responses like single muscle twitches because we hoped they removed as much of the specialized as possible. But it is unlikely that a "pure" measure of association exists. We must engage some behavior system to observe our hypothetical learning process. Without an understanding of the workings of that behavior system we may make erroneous conclusions about the workings of our underlying process. The problem is that apparently quantitative variations in a particular measured response as a function of some independent variable may be partially a consequence of that manipulation's engaging other behavior systems not measured by the experimenter. From this point of view, investigations involving associations among CSs, that is, events that do not normally engage extensive behavior systems (e.g., Rescorla, 1980) are especially promising, since those studies may go farthest in providing a direct tap on the operating characteristics of associative mechanisms. Research from a more functional perspective should also be encouraged. Clearly, we need to do more than simply speculate about the adaptiveness of various learned behavior systems. Experimental evidence that Pavlovian conditioned behavior *can* provide more effective adaptation to the environment, at least in terms of some reasonable currency, certainly seems worthwhile. Unfortunately, despite the frequent use of this strategy in ascertaining the possible adaptive value of various unconditioned behavior patterns, there has been little investigation of this type with learned behavior patterns (but see Hollis, 1984, in press).

Similarly, comparative studies involving closely related species that show differences in learned behavior would be valuable. Those investigations would first have to identify differences in selection pressures that may have acted on those species by examining their natural behavioral ecologies and then convincingly relate those differences to differences in learned performance. Furthermore, those investigations should determine whether the differences in performance reflect differences in ability to learn relations between events or in the mechanism of translation of learning to performance. For instance, Garcia and his associates (e.g., Brett, Hankins, & Garcia, 1976) describe investigations comparing the types of cues that come to control food aversions in two closely related hawks. Prior to eating, one species carried its prey in its beak whereas the other carried its prey in its talons. A reasonable hypothesis is that beak-carrying hawks would be more likely to use flavor cues in food selection. Since the learning of flavor aversions probably forms a module of feeding behaviors, one would expect flavor aversions generated by cue–toxin pairings to be formed more rapidly in the beak-carrying species. That outcome was indeed found by Brett *et al.* (1976). Additionally, they found that the talon-carrying species formed visual aversions more readily than did the beak-carrying species. Thus, the outcome was not attributable to some general inability to learn aversions in the one species, but rather to the display of flavor aversions. The next step in such an analysis would be to determine if the species differences in learning the flavor aversions were the result of differences in their abilities to learn the flavor–illness relation or in the translation of that knowledge into behavior. For example, perhaps a third cue could be discovered to which both species learn equivalent aversions. The ability of a conditioned flavor cue to interfere with the acquisition of an aversion to that third cue might then serve as an alternative measure of conditioning to the flavor.

A third valuable type of investigation would be the more detailed study of learned behavior systems. Typically, students of Pavlovian conditioning in the laboratory have restricted their attention to a single, often rather restricted measure of learning. Observation of a variety of behavior systems, the activation of which is encouraged by the choice of less constrained conditioning contexts and stimuli, would permit us to ascertain any general rules for interactions among behavior modules. Especially valuable would be information concerning when certain modules are or are not integrated into the conditioned response and the independence of various modules.

Fourth, equally valuable would be a study of so-called "unlearned" behavior systems. Within a behavior systems approach it is these patterns that reappear in various forms as learned behaviors. Obviously, it is important then to understand *their* origins and determinants, both proximal and functional, if we are to understand the determinants of CRs. This information would provide background information for a fifth strategy, the comparison of the effects of various manipulations on learned and unlearned behavior patterns. How plastic are the various portions of learned behavior patterns? Are the properties and sensitivities of learned behavior patterns different from those of their unlearned counterparts?

Finally, the origins of many learning abilities and behavior patterns may be more easily understood if we examine their ontogeny. Questions of developmental fixity or sensitivity are frequently examined in the literature of animal behavior: What early experiences influence the occurrence of particular behavior patterns in later life? Are the behavior patterns engaged by CSs resembling natural signals for the US truly preorganized, or was that organization itself the result of specific conditioning experience with event sequences early in life? Or, is somewhat more general experience sufficient? And once again, care must be taken to separate the ontogeny of particular behavior systems from that of more general learning functions.

I believe that a model of animal behavior must address these concerns. They are of special interest to those of us who believe Pavlovian conditioning plays an important part in the life and adaptation of organisms because our current theories of conditioning say little about the involvement of conditioning in behavior and make little contact with the methods, attitudes, and concepts of other students of animal behavior.

ACKNOWLEDGMENT

I am indebted to R. A. Rescorla for his helpful advice and comments over the past 12 years. Some of the ideas contained in this article were described briefly by us in the *Annual Review of Psychology,* 1982.

REFERENCES

Anokhin, P. K. *Biology and neurophysiology of the conditional reflex and its role in adaptive behavior.* Oxford: Pergamon, 1974.

Bayroff, A. G., & Lard, K. E. Experimental social behavior of animals: III. Imitational learning of white rats. *Journal of Comparative Psychology,* 1944, **37,** 165–171.

Black, A. H., Carlson, N. J., & Solomon, R. L. Exploratory studies of the conditioning of autonomic responses in curarized dogs. *Psychological Monographs,* 1962, **76.**

Blanchard, R. J., & Blanchard, D. C. Crouching as an index of fear. *Journal of Comparative and Physiological Psychology,* 1969, **67,** 370–375. (a)

Blanchard, R. J., & Blanchard, D. C. Passive and active reactions to fear-eliciting stimuli. *Journal of Comparative and Physiological Psychology,* 1969, **68,** 129–135. (b)

Blanchard, R., & Honig, W. K. Surprise value of food determines its effectiveness as a reinforcer. *Journal of Experimental Psychology: Animal Behavior Processes,* 1976, **2,** 67–74.

Boakes, R. A., Poli, M., Lockwood, M. J., & Goodall, G. A study of misbehavior: Token reinforcement in the rat. *Journal of the Experimental Analysis of Behavior,* 1978, **29,** 115–134.

Bolles, R. C., & Collier, A. C. Effects of predictive cues on freezing in rats. *Animal Learning & Behavior,* 1976, **4,** 6–8.

Breland, K., & Breland, M. *Animal behavior.* New York: Macmillan, 1966.

Brett, L. P., Hankins, W. G., & Garcia, J. Prey-lithium aversions. III. Buteo hawks. *Behavioral Biology,* 1976, **17,** 87–98.

Cleland, G. G., & Davey, G. C. L. The effects of satiation and reinforcer devaluation on signal-centered behavior in the rat. *Learning and Motivation,* 1982, **13,** 343–360.

Cohen, D. Effect of conditioned stimulus intensity on visually conditioned heart rate change in the pigeon: A sensitization mechanism. *Journal of Comparative and Physiological Psychology,* 1974, **87,** 495–499.

Culler, E. A. Recent advances in some concepts of conditioning. *Psychological Review,* 1938, **45,** 134–153.

Davey, G. C. L., Oakley, D. A., & Cleland, G. G. Autoshaping in the rat: Effects of omission on the form of the response. *Journal of the Experimental Analysis of Behavior,* 1981, **36,** 75–91.

Debold, R. C., Miller, N. E., & Jensen, D. O. Effect of strength of drive determined by a new technique for appetitive classical conditioning of rats. *Journal of Comparative and Physiological Psychology,* 1965, **59,** 102–108.

DeToledo, L. Changes in heart rate during conditioned suppression in rats as a function of

US intensity and type of CS. *Journal of Comparative and Physiological Psychology*, 1971, **77**, 528–538.

Detoledo, L., & Black, A. H. Heart rate: Changes during conditioned suppression in rats. *Science*, 1966, **152**, 1404–1406.

Dickinson, A., & Mackintosh, N. J. Reinforcer specificity in the enhancement of conditioning by posttrial surprise. *Journal of Experimental Psychology: Animal Behavior Processes*, 1979, **5**, 162–177.

Domjan, M., & Galef, B. G. Biological constraints on instrumental and classical conditioning: Retrospect and prospect. *Animal Learning & Behavior*, 1983, **11**, 151–161.

Domjan, M., & Gillan, D. G. Aftereffects of lithium-conditioned stimuli on consummatory behavior. *Journal of Experimental Psychology: Animal Behavior Processes*, 1977, **3**, 322–334.

Domjan, M., Gillan, D. J., & Gemberling, G. A. Aftereffects of lithium-conditioned stimuli on consummatory behavior in the presence or absence of the drug. *Journal of Experimental Psychology: Animal Behavior Processes*, 1980, **6**, 49–64.

Dykman, R. A. Toward a theory of classical conditioning: Cognitive, emotional, and motor components of the conditioned response. In B. Maher (Ed.), *Experimental approaches to personality* (Vol. II). New York: Academic Press, 1965.

Estes, W. K. New perspectives on some old issues in association theory. In N. J. Mackintosh & W. K. Honig (Eds.), *Fundamental issues in associative learning*. Halifax, Nova Scotia: Dalhousie Univ. Press, 1969.

Ewer, R. F. The biology and behavior of a free-living population of black rats (Rattus rattus). *Animal Behaviour Monographs*, 1971, **4**(3).

Fowler, H. Cognitive associations as evident in the blocking effects of response-contingent CSs. In S. H. Hulse, H. Fowler, & W. K. Honig (Eds.), *Cognitive processes in animal behavior*. Hillsdale, NJ: Erlbaum, 1978. Pp. 109–153.

Galef, B. G., Jr., & Clark, M. M. Mother's milk and adult presence: Two factors determining initial dietary selection by weanling rats. *Journal of Comparative and Physiological Psychology*, 1972, **78**, 220–225.

Garcia, J., Kovner, R., & Green, K. S. Cue properties versus palatability of flavors in avoidance learning. *Psychonomic Science*, 1970, **20**, 313–314.

Gormezano, I. Investigations of defense and reward conditioning in the rabbit. In A. H. Black & W. H. Prokasy (Eds.), *Classical conditioning* (Vol. 2). New York: Appleton, 1972. Pp. 151–181.

Grill, H. J. Sucrose as an aversive stimulus. *Neuroscience Abstracts*, 1975, **1**, 525.

Guthrie, E. R. Association and the law of effect. *Psychological Review*, 1940, **47**, 127–148.

Hearst, E. Pavlovian conditioning and directed movements. In G. Bower (Ed.), *The psychology of learning and motivation* (Vol. 9). New York: Academic Press, 1975.

Hearst, E., & Jenkins, H. M. Sign tracking: the stimulus-reinforcer relation and directed action. *Psychonomic society monograph*. Austin, Texas: Psychonomic Society, 1974.

Hendersen, R. W. Conditioned and unconditioned fear inhibition in rats. *Journal of Comparative and Physiological Psychology*, 1973, **84**, 554–561.

Heth, C. D. Simultaneous and backward fear conditioning as a function of number of CS–UCS pairings. *Journal of Experimental Psychology: Animal Behavior Processes*, 1976, **2**, 117–129.

Heth, C. D., & Rescorla, R. A. Simultaneous and backward fear conditioning in the rat. *Journal of Comparative and Physiological Psychology*, 1973, **82**, 434–443.

Hilgard, E. R., & Marquis, D. G. *Conditioning and learning*. New York: Appleton, 1940.

Hogan, J. A. Conditioned responses in Pavlovian conditioning situations. *Science*, 1974, **186**, 156–157.

Holland, P. C. Conditioned stimulus as a determinant of the form of the Pavlovian conditioned response. *Journal of Experimental Psychology: Animal Behavior Processes,* 1977, 3, 77–104.

Holland, P. C. Differential effects of omission contingencies on various components of Pavlovian appetitive conditioned behavior in rats. *Journal of Experimental Psychology: Animal Behavior Processes,* 1979, 5, 178–193. (a)

Holland, P. C. The effects of qualitative and quantitative variation in the US on individual components of Pavlovian appetitive conditioned behavior in rats. *Animal Learning & Behavior,* 1979, 7, 424–432. (b)

Holland, P. C. CS–US interval as a determinant of the form of Pavlovian appetitive conditioned responses. *Journal of Experimental Psychology: Animal Behavior Processes,* 1980, 6, 155–174. (a)

Holland, P. C. Influence of visual conditioned stimulus characteristics on the form of Pavlovian appetitive conditioned responding in rats. *Journal of Experimental Psychology: Animal Behavior Processes,* 1980, 6, 81–97. (b)

Holland, P. C. The effects of satiation after first- and second-order appetitive conditioning. *Pavlovian Journal of Biological Science,* 1981, 16, 18–24.

Holland, P. C. Unblocking in Pavlovian appetitive conditioning. *Journal of Experimental Psychology: Animal Behavior Processes,* 1984, in press.

Holland, P. C., & Rescorla, R. A. The effect of two ways of devaluing the unconditioned stimulus after first- and second-order appetitive conditioning. *Journal of Experimental Psychology: Animal Behavior Processes,* 1973, 1, 355–363.

Holland, P. C., & Rescorla, R. A. Second-order conditioning with food unconditioned stimulus. *Journal of Comparative and Physiological Psychology,* 1975, 88, 459–467.

Holland, P. C., & Ross, R. T. Within-compound associations in serial compound conditioning. *Journal of Experimental Psychology: Animal Behavior Processes,* 1981, 7, 228–241.

Holland, P. C., & Straub, J. J. Differential effects of two ways of devaluing the unconditioned stimulus after Pavlovian appetitive conditioning. *Journal of Experimental Psychology: Animal Behavior Processes,* 1979, 5, 65–78.

Hollis, K. L. Pavlovian conditioning of signal-centered action patterns and autonomic behavior: A biological analysis of function. In J. S. Rosenblatt, R. A. Hinde, C. Beer, & M. C. Busnel (Eds.), *Advances in the study of behavior* (Vol. 12). New York: Academic Press, 1982. Pp. 1–64.

Hollis, K. L. The biological function of Pavlovian conditioning: The best defense is a good offense. *Journal of Experimental Psychology: Animal Behavior Processes,* 1984, in press.

James, J. H., & Wagner, A. R. One-trial overshadowing: Evidence for distributive processing. *Journal of Experimental Psychology: Animal Behavior Processes,* 1980, 6, 188–205.

Jenkins, H. M., Barrera, F. J., Ireland, C., & Woodside, B. Signal-centered action patterns in dogs in appetitive classical conditioning. *Learning and Motivation,* 1978, 9, 272–296.

Johnston, T. D. Selective costs and benefits in the evolution of learning. In J. S. Rosenblatt, R. A. Hinde, C. Beer, & M. C. Busnell (Eds.), *Advances in the study of behavior* (Vol. 12). New York: Academic Press, 1982. Pp. 65–106.

Johnston, T. D., & Turvey, M. T. A sketch of an ethological metatheory for theories of learning. In G. H. Bower (Ed.), *The psychology of learning and motivation* (Vol. 14). New York: Academic Press, 1980. Pp. 147–205.

Kamin, L. J. Attention-like processes in classical conditioning. In M. R. Jones (Ed.), *Miami Symposium on the prediction of behavior: Aversive stimulation.* Coral Gables, Florida: Univ. of Miami Press, 1968. Pp. 9–32.

Kaye, H., & Pearce, J. M. The strength of the orienting response during Pavlovian conditioning. *Journal of Experimental Psychology: Animal Behavior Processes,* 1984, 10, 90–109.

Keith-Lucas, T., & Guttman, N. Robust single-trial delayed backward conditioning. *Journal of Comparative and Physiological Psychology*, 1975, **88**, 468–476.

Kierylowicz, H., Soltysik, S., & Divac, I. Conditioned reflexes reinforced by direct and indirect food presentation. *Acta Biologica Experimentalis*, 1968, **28**, 1–10.

Kimmel, H. D. Amount of conditioning and intensity of conditioned stimulus. *Journal of Experimental Psychology*, 1959, **58**, 283–288.

Konorski, J. *Integrative activity of the brain*. Chicago, Illinois: Univ. of Chicago Press, 1967.

LeClerc, R., & Reberg, D. Sign-tracking in aversive conditioning. *Learning and Motivation*, 1980, **11**, 302–317.

Liddell, H. S. The conditioned reflex. In F. A. Moss (Ed.), *Comparative psychology*. New York: Prentice-Hall, 1934. Pp. 247–296.

Lieberman, D. A., McIntosh, D. C., & Thomas, G. V. Learning when reward is delayed: A marking hypothesis. *Journal of Experimental Psychology: Animal Behavior Processes*, 1979, **5**, 224–242.

Locurto, C. M. Contributions of autoshaping to the partitioning of conditioned behavior. In C. M. Locurto, H. S. Terrace, & J. Gibbon (Eds.), *Autoshaping and conditioning theory*. New York: Academic Press, 1981. Pp. 101–135.

Lore, R., & Flannelly, K. Rat societies. *Scientific American*, 1977, **236**, 106–116.

Lorenz, K. Z. Innate bases of learning. In K. H. Pribram (Ed.), *On the biology of learning*. New York: Harcourt, 1969. Pp. 13–93.

MacFarlane, D. A. The role of kinesthesis in maze learning. *University of California Publications in Psychology*, 1930, **4**, 277–305.

MacFarlane, B. A., Pedersen, P. E., Cornell, C. E., & Blass, E. M. *Animal Behaviour*, 1983, **31**, 462–471.

Mackintosh, N. J. *The psychology of animal learning*. New York: Academic Press, 1974.

Mackintosh, N. J. A theory of attention: Variations in the associability of stimuli with reinforcement. *Psychological Review*, 1975, **82**, 276–298.

Maltzman, I. Orienting in classical conditioning and generalization of the galvanic skin response to words: An overview. *Journal of Experimental Psychology: General*, 1977, **106**, 111–119.

Miller, R. R., Greco, C., Vigorito, M., & Marlin, N. A. Signaled tailshock is perceived as similar to a stronger unsignaled tailshock: Implications for a functional analysis of classical conditioning. *Journal of Experimental Psychology: Animal Behavior Processes*, 1983, **9**, 105–131.

Moore, J. W., & Stickney, K. J. Formation of attentional-associative networks in real-time-role of the hippocampus and implications for conditioning. *Psychological Psychology*, 1980, **8**, 207–217.

Mowrer, O. H. On the dual nature of learning—a reinterpretation of conditioning and problem solving. *Harvard Educational Review*, 1947, **17**, 102–148.

Mowrer, O. H. *Learning theory and behavior*. New York: Wiley, 1960.

Mowrer, O. H., & Aiken, E. G. Contiguity vs. drive-reduction in conditioned fear: Temporal variations in conditioned and unconditioned stimulus. *American Journal of Psychology*, 1954, **67**, 26–38.

Nairne, J. S., & Rescorla, R. A. Second-order conditioning with diffuse auditory reinforcers in the pigeon. *Learning and Motivation*, 1981, **12**, 65–91.

Patten, R. L., & Rudy, J. W. Orienting during classical conditioning: Acquired versus unconditioned responding. *Psychonomic Science*, 1967, **7**, 27–28.

Pearce, J. M., & Hall, G. A model for Pavlovian learning: Variations in the effectiveness of conditioned but not of unconditioned stimuli. *Psychological Review*, 1980, **106**, 532–552.

Perkins, C. C. An analysis of the concept of reinforcement. *Psychological Review*, 1968, **75**, 155–172.

Peterson, G. B., Ackil, J. E., Frommer, G. P., & Hearst, E. Conditioned approach and contact behavior towards signals for food or brain-stimulation reinforcements. *Science,* 1972, **177**, 1009–1011.

Pinel, J. P. J., Treit, D., & Wilkie, D. M. Stimulus control of defensive burying in the rat. *Learning and Motivation,* 1980, **11**, 150–163.

Plotkin, H. C., & Odling-Smee, F. J. Learning, change, and evolution: An enquiry into the teleonomy of learning. In J. S. Rosenblatt, R. A. Hinde, C. G. Beer, & M.-C. Busnel (Eds.), *Advances in the study of behavior* (Vol. 10). New York: Academic Press, 1979. Pp. 1–41.

Prokasy, W. K. Classical eyelid conditioning: Experimenter operations, task demands, and response shaping. In W. F. Prokasy (Ed.), *Classical conditioning.* New York: Appleton, 1965. Pp. 208–225.

Rashotte, M. E., Griffin, R. W., & Sisk, C. L. Second-order conditioning of the pigeon's key-peck. *Animal Learning & Behavior,* 1977, **5**, 25–38.

Rescorla, R. L. *Second-order conditioning.* Hillsdale, New Jersey: Erlbaum, 1980.

Rescorla, R. A., & Holland, P. C. Associations in Pavlovian conditioned inhibition. *Learning and Motivation,* 1977, **8**, 429–447.

Rescorla, R. A., & Solomon, R. L. Two process learning theory: Relationships between classical conditioning and instrumental learning. *Psychological Review,* 1967, **74**, 151–182.

Rescorla, R. A., & Wagner, A. R. A theory of Pavlovian conditioning: Variations in the effectiveness of reinforcement and nonreinforcement. In A. H. Black & W. F. Prokasy (Eds.), *Classical conditioning* (Vol. 2). New York: Appleton, 1972. Pp. 64–99.

Ross, R. T., & Holland, P. C. Conditioning of simultaneous and serial feature-positive discriminations. *Animal Learning & Behavior,* 1981, **9**, 293–303.

Ross, R. T., & Holland, P. C. Serial positive patterning: Implications for "occasion-setting". *Bulletin of the Psychonomic Society,* 1982, **19**, 159–162.

Rozin, P., & Kalat, J. W. Specific hungers and poison avoidance as adaptive specializations of learning. *Psychological Review,* 1971, **78**, 459–486.

Rudy, J. W., & Hyson, R. L. Consummatory response conditioning to an auditory stimulus in neonatal rats. *Behavioral and neurobiology,* 1982, **34**, 209–214.

Schull, J. A conditioned opponent theory of Pavlovian conditioning and habituation. In G. H. Bower (Ed.), *The psychology of learning and motivation* (Vol. 13). New York: Academic Press, 1979. Pp. 57–90.

Schwartz, B. The role of positive conditioned reinforcement in the maintenance of key pecking which prevents delivery of primary reinforcement. *Psychonomic Science,* 1972, **28**, 277–278.

Schwartz, B. Maintenance of key-pecking by response-independent food presentation: The role of the modality of the signal for food. *Journal of the Experimental Analysis of Behavior,* 1973, **20**, 17–23.

Sheffield, F. D. Relation between classical conditioning and instrumental learning. In W. F. Prokasy (Ed.), *Classical conditioning.* New York: Appleton, 1965. Pp. 302–322.

Shettleworth, S. J. Reinforcement and the organization of behavior in Golden Hamsters: Pavlovian conditioning with food and shock USs. *Journal of Experimental Psychology: Animal Behavior Processes,* 1978, **4**, 152–169.

Siegel, S. Morphine tolerance acquisition as an associative process. *Journal of Experimental Psychology: Animal Behavior Processes,* 1977, **3**, 1–13.

Siegel, S. The role of conditioning in drug tolerance and addiction. In J. D. Keehn (Ed.), *Psychopathology in animals.* New York: Academic Press, 1979. Pp. 143–168.

Skinner, B. F. *The behavior of organisms.* New York: Appleton, 1938.

Smith, M. C. CS–US interval and US intensity in classical conditioning of the rabbit's nictitating membrane response. *Journal of Comparative and Physiological Psychology,* 1968, **66**, 679–687.

Sokolov, Y. N. *Perception and the conditioned reflex.* Oxford: Pergamon, 1963.

Solomon, R. L., & Corbit, J. D. An opponent-process theory of motivation. I. Temporal dynamics of effect. *Psychological Review,* 1974, **81**, 119–145.

Stiers, M., & Silberberg, A. Lever-contact responses in rats: Automaintenance with and without a negative response-reinforcer dependency. *Journal of the Experimental Analysis of Behavior,* 1974, **22**, 497–506.

Sutherland, N. S., & Mackintosh, N. J. *Mechanisms of animal discrimination learning.* New York: Academic Press, 1971.

Terlecki, L. J., Pinel, J. P. J., & Treit, D. Conditioned and unconditioned defensive burying in the rat. *Learning and Motivation,* 1979, **10**, 337–350.

Teyler, T. Effects of restraint on heart-rate conditioning in rats as a function of US location. *Journal of Comparative and Physiological Psychology,* 1971, **77**, 31–37.

Thompson, R. F., Berger, T. W., Berry, S. D., Clark, G. A., & Kettner, R. E. Neuronal substrates of learning and memory: Hippocampus and other structures. In C. D. Woody (Ed.), *Representation of involved neural functions.* New York: Plenum, 1982.

Timberlake, W. The functional organization of appetitive behavior: Behavior systems and learning. In M. D. Zeiler & P. Harzem (Eds.), *Advances in the analysis of behavior* (Vol. 3). *Biological factors in learning.* New York: Wiley, 1984.

Timberlake, W., & Grant, D. L. Autoshaping in rats to the presentation of another rat predicting food. *Science,* 1975, **190**, 690–692.

Timberlake, W., Wahl, G., & King, D. Stimulus and response contingencies in the misbehavior of rats. *Journal of Experimental Psychology: Animal Behavior Processes,* 1982, **8**, 62–85.

Tolman, E. C. *Purposive behavior in animals and men.* New York: Appleton, 1932.

Tomie, A. Effect of unpredictable food on the subsequent acquisition of autoshaping: Analysis of the context-blocking hypothesis. In C. M. Locurto, H. S. Terrace, & J. Gibbon (Eds.), *Autoshaping and conditioning theory.* New York: Academic Press, 1981. Pp. 181–215.

Wagner, A. R. Expectancies and the priming of STM. In S. H. Hulse, H. Fowler, & W. K. Honig (Eds.), *Cognitive processes in animal behavior.* Hillsdale, New Jersey: Erlbaum, 1978. Pp. 177–209.

Wagner, A. R. SOP: A model of automatic memory processing in animal behavior. In N. S. Spear & R. R. Miller (Eds.), *Information processing in animals: Memory mechanisms.* Hillsdale, New Jersey: Erlbaum, 1981.

Walker, E. G. Eyelid conditioning as a function of the intensity of conditioned and unconditioned stimuli. *Journal of Experimental Psychology,* 1960, **59**, 303–311.

Wasserman, E. A. The effect of redundant contextual stimuli on autoshaping the pigeon's key peck. *Animal Learning & Behavior,* 1973, **1**, 198–201. (a)

Wasserman, E. A. Pavlovian conditioning with heat reinforcement produces stimulus-directed pecking in chicks. *Science,* 1973, **181**, 875–877. (b)

Wasserman, E. A., Franklin, S., & Hearst, E. Pavlovian appetitive contingencies and approach vs. withdrawal to conditioned stimuli in pigeons. *Journal of Comparative and Physiological Psychology,* 1974, **86**, 616–627.

Wasserman, E. A., Hunter, N. B., Gutowski, K. A., & Bader, S. A. Autoshaping chicks with heat reinforcement: The role of stimulus-reinforcer and response-reinforcer relations. *Journal of Experimental Psychology: Animal Behavior Processes,* 1975, **1**, 158–169.

Wickens, D. D., Nield, A. F., Tuber, D. S., & Wickens, C. D. Strength, latency, and form of conditioned skeletal and autonomic responses as a function of CS-UCS intervals. *Journal of Experimental Psychology,* 1969, **80**, 165–170.

Wikler, A. Conditioning of successive adaptive responses to the initial effects of drugs. *Conditional Reflex,* 1973, **8**, 193–210.

Williams, D. R. *The relation of autoshaping to superstition and ethological observations of learned behavior.* Paper read at the annual meeting of the South Eastern Psychological Association, 1972.

Williams, D. R. Biconditional behavior: Conditioning without constraint. In C. M. Locurto, H. S. Terrace, & J. Gibbon (Eds.), *Autoshaping and conditioning theory.* New York: Academic Press, 1981. Pp. 55–99.

Wilson, R. S. Autonomic changes produced by noxious and innocuous stimulation. *Journal of Comparative and Physiological Psychology,* 1964, **58**, 290–295.

Wilson, R. S. Cardiac response: Determinants of conditioning. *Journal of Comparative and Physiological Psychology,* 1969, **68**, 1–23.

Woodruff, G., & Williams, D. R. The associative relation underlying autoshaping in the pigeon. *Journal of the Experimental Analysis of Behavior,* 1976, **26**, 1–14.

Zamble, E. Classical conditioning of excitement anticipatory of food reward: Partial reinforcement. *Psychonomic Science,* 1968, **10**, 115–116.

Zamble, E. Augmentation of eating following a signal for feeding in rats. *Learning and Motivation,* 1973, **4**, 138–147.

Zener, K. The significance of behavior accompanying conditioned salivary secretion for theories of the conditioned response. *American Journal of Psychology,* 1937, **50**, 384–403.

DIRECTED FORGETTING IN CONTEXT

Mark Rilling

MICHIGAN STATE UNIVERSITY
EAST LANSING, MICHIGAN

Donald F. Kendrick

MIDDLE TENNESSEE STATE UNIVERSITY
MURFREESBORO, TENNESSEE

Thomas B. Stonebraker

GREENVILLE COLLEGE
GREENVILLE, ILLINOIS

I. Introduction

In research on human information processing, the stimulus control of short-term forgetting has been investigated with a paradigm called directed forgetting (for a review see Bjork, 1972). In the typical directed-forgetting procedure some items are followed by a remember cue (R-cue), while other items are followed by a forget cue (F-cue). The subjects are instructed to rehearse the items followed by the R-cue in preparation for a test of retention, and they are instructed to forget the items followed by the F-cue. Actually, the subjects are tested on all of the items. Directed forgetting is the phenomenon obtained when retention of the R-cued items is superior to the memory of the F-cued items.

THE PSYCHOLOGY OF LEARNING
AND MOTIVATION, VOL. 18

The standard procedure for studying short-term memory in animals is the delayed matching-to-sample paradigm. At the beginning of a trial in the delayed matching-to-sample paradigm, one of two to-be-remembered or sample stimuli is presented for a period of time. Termination of the sample stimulus is followed by a delay interval during which no discriminative stimuli are present. After a delay interval, a test for retention consists of the presentation of the comparison stimulus or stimuli. An indicator response to the comparison stimulus that matches the sample stimulus is reinforced. Otherwise the indicator response is nonreinforced. For example, in the choice procedure the comparison stimuli are presented on the side keys. Choice of the comparison stimulus that matches the sample stimulus is reinforced whereas choice of the nonmatching stimulus is nonreinforced.

Short-term forgetting is defined as the failure of an encoded sample stimulus to control the choice response to the comparison stimuli. Encoding is the process of transforming the sample stimulus while it is present. Stimulus control of forgetting in animals, an analog to directed forgetting in humans, is carried out by introducing instructional stimuli within the delayed matching-to-sample paradigm. These cues are a class of discriminative stimuli selected from a dimension orthogonal to the sample and comparison stimuli. These instructional stimuli indicate whether the test for retention will occur. An R-cue indicates that the comparison stimuli are presented as usual, whereas an F-cue signals cancellation of the comparison stimuli. The F-cue always signals cancellation of the comparison stimuli during training.

During testing for directed forgetting the comparison stimuli are presented following the F-cue on rare probe trials in violation of previous training. Directed forgetting is a decrement in accuracy of matching on F-cued probe trials as compared with R-cued trials. The R- and F-cues are presented during the delay interval as post sample stimuli to assure that the animal has encoded the sample stimulus.

The purpose of this article is to present a theory of directed forgetting which emphasizes the role of attention in the delayed matching-to-sample paradigm and the context at the time of the test for retention. First consider the basic phenomenon. Stonebraker and Rilling (1981) employed a successive delayed matching-to-sample procedure developed by Wasserman (1976). The sample and comparison stimuli were presented on the same key separated by a delay interval. At the beginning of each trial, a red or green color was randomly presented on the key as the sample stimulus. Following the delay interval of 4 sec, the key was again randomly illuminated red or green as the comparison stimulus. Responses to the comparison stimulus were reinforced on a fixed-interval, 5-sec schedule on matching trials (red–red or green–green). The comparison stimulus terminated automatically without reinforcement after 5 sec on nonmatching trials (red–green or green–red).

The discriminative stimuli predicting the occurrence (R-cue) or cancellation (F-cue) of the comparison stimuli were introduced immediately following the sample stimulus. A vertical line presented on the key served as an R-cue, and a white horizontal line served as the F-cue. Since the birds often turned away from the key following an F-cue, a tone was introduced prior to the onset of the comparison stimulus as an additional indicator for that stimulus.

The dependent variable was a discrimination ratio based on the rate of responding during the comparison stimulus on matching (reinforced) and nonmatching (nonreinforced) trials: 100% indicates a perfect discrimination with no responding on nonmatching trials and 50% indicates no discrimination with equal response rates on matching and nonmatching trials.

In the test for directed forgetting, probe trials were introduced in which the F-cue (horizontal lines) was followed by the comparison stimulus. The contingencies on these F-cued probe trials were identical to the contingencies on R-cued trials. That is, on probe trials, responses terminating comparison stimuli on matching trials were reinforced, whereas nonmatching comparison stimuli terminated automatically after 5 sec without reinforcement. On probe trials in which the F-cue was presented immediately after the sample stimulus, the matching accuracy across sessions for the four birds was 52, 44, 50, and 60% as compared with matching accuracies of 85, 82, 81, and 81% on R-cued trials. Clearly, directed forgetting is a powerful phenomenon strong enough to effectively eliminate stimulus control by a sample stimulus that occurred only 4 sec earlier.

Figure 1 illustrates the phenomenon of directed forgetting for one of the birds in the Stonebraker and Rilling (1981) experiment. On probe session trials with the R-cue, discriminative responding during the test stimuli is maintained by the high response rates on matching trials (R–R and G–G) and the low response rates on nonmatching trials (R–G and G–R). Directed forgetting was observed on those probe trials in which the comparison stimuli were presented following the F-cue. In the successive procedure directed forgetting is observed as an increase in the rate of responding on the nonmatching trials (R–G and G–R), whereas the procedure has little effect on responding on matching trials (R–R and G–G). Thus the effect of the F-cue for this pigeon was to effectively eliminate control by the sample stimulus by reducing accurate matching from above 80% to near chance.

Investigators have observed directed forgetting in pigeons across many variations of the basic procedure (Grant, 1981; Kendrick, Rilling, & Stonebraker, 1981; Maki & Hegvik, 1980; Maki, Olson, & Rego, 1981; Stonebraker & Rilling, 1981). The finding of directed forgetting in rats by Grant (1982) demonstrates the across-species generality of the phenomenon. The articles on the basic empirical work by Grant (1981) and Maki (1981) demonstrate that relatively trivial explanations do not account for the basic phe-

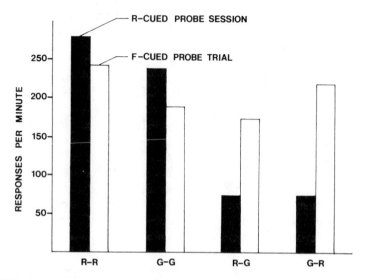

Fig. 1. Rate of responding to the comparison stimuli on baseline and probe sessions for the two matching (R–R and G–G) and the two nonmatching (R–G and G–R) trials. Directed forgetting is measured by the difference between the R-cued trials and the F-cued trials and is observed as approximately equal levels of responding on the F-cued probe trials.

nomenon. The robust size of the directed-forgetting phenomenon suggests the operation of potent psychological processes. The data are ripe for theoretical interpretation. First, consider the theoretical question of whether rehearsal is the cognitive process brought under stimulus control in these experiments on directed forgetting.

II. Stimulus Control of Rehearsal

Honig and Thompson (1982), Riley, Cook, and Lamb (1981), and Roitblat (1982) assume that a representation is encoded during the presentation of the sample stimulus in the delayed matching-to-sample task. A representation (Roitblat, 1982) is a cognitive transformation that allows the sample stimulus to control subsequent behavior. Theorists differ in their assumptions about the type of representation encoded by the pigeon. The representation could be a copy of the sample stimulus, a copy of the matching comparison stimulus, or an intermediate representation different from the sample or comparison stimulus. The type of representation does not concern us here because our analysis is applicable to all types of representations. The question of interest here is whether during the delay in the delayed matching-to-sample task the representation is maintained by a process of rehearsal.

Rehearsal is the active maintenance of a representation after the termination of the stimulus that produced the representation. Since rehearsal is a well-documented phenomenon in human information processing (Johnson, 1980), evidence for rehearsal in pigeons would demonstrate that this process is not unique to humans. In fact the data (Grant, 1984a; Maki, 1981) demonstrate similarities in rehearsal between people and pigeons.

In humans rehearsal is a controlled process (Shiffrin & Schneider, 1977), that is, a process that can be manipulated by providing instructions. If rehearsal in pigeons is a controlled process, then it should be possible to bring rehearsal under stimulus control. The most convincing evidence for stimulus control of rehearsal in pigeons comes from experiments on directed forgetting in which the temporal location of the cues was manipulated within the delay interval.

An experiment by Stonebraker and Rilling (1981) varied the temporal location of the F-cue from the beginning to the end of the delay interval in order to determine if the F-cue controlled termination of a process similar to rehearsal in humans. If directed forgetting is a controlled process, then the F-cue should be maximally effective when presented immediately after the termination of the sample stimulus under the assumption that the F-cue blocks or terminates a process of rehearsal or active maintenance.

The temporal locations of the R- and F-cues within the 4-sec retention interval was varied at three times within the delay: immediately after the sample, 0 sec; in the middle of the delay, 2 sec; and at the end of the delay, 3.5 sec. If the F-cue controls rehearsal, then presenting the F-cue at 0 sec should prevent rehearsal, but delaying the F-cue for 2 and 3.5 sec should provide progressively more opportunity for rehearsal. A successive procedure using either red or green sample stimuli was employed. During training half of the trials contained F-cues and half contained R-cues. On probe trials during testing the horizontal line (F-cue) was followed by presentation of comparison stimuli and the contingencies were identical to those of R-cued trials so that responding to the test stimulus was reinforced on matching trials and extinguished on nonmatching trials.

The results of this experiment are presented in Fig. 2. Presenting the F-cue at 0 sec reduced matching accuracy from 90% on R-cued trials to 59% on F-cued trials. When the sample-cue interval was 2 sec, matching accuracy on F-cued trials increased to 71%, whereas at 3.5 sec accuracy on F-cued trials was 88% or about equal to the R-cue percentage of 92.3. These results suggest that the F-cue terminates rehearsal.

In an experiment similar to Stonebraker and Rilling, Grant (1981a) varied

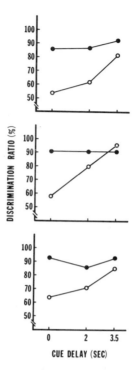

Fig. 2. Mean discrimination ratios as a function of the delay between the sample and the instructional stimulus within the 4-sec delay interval. The F-cued results (O—O) were calculated from the responses to comparison stimuli on F-cued probe trials during the five probe sessions. The R-cued results (●—●) were calculated from the responses to comparison stimuli on all of the R-cued trials during the five probe sessions. A discrimination ratio of 1.00 indicates perfect matching with responding exclusively on matching trials, and a ratio of .50 indicates chance performance with equal rates of responding on matching and nonmatching trials.

the point of interpolation of the F-cue at the beginning, middle, and end of the delay interval. The F-cue was most effective in producing forgetting when placed at the beginning of the interval.

In a further experiment, Grant (1981a) varied the length of the retention interval from 3 to 6 sec and placed the forget cue at the beginning of the delay interval. If the F-cue terminates processing of the sample stimulus, while the R-cue maintains a rehearsal process, there should be a greater decrement in retention at the longer delay for the F-cue than the R-cue. The results of Grant's experiment showed that the rate of forgetting was faster on F-cued trials than on R-cued trials especially at the longer retention interval. The faster rate of forgetting on F-cued probe trials than on R-cued probe trials suggests that these cues acquire control of a process of re-hearsal. An F-cue reduces processing of the representation, whereas an R-cue maintains it. Furthermore, these data parallel the human findings in which Bjork (1970) found that an F-cue is most effective when presented immediately after the to-be-forgotten item, but has little if any effect when presented at the time of recall.

III. Surprising versus Expected Sample Stimuli

One of the major results of rehearsal in human information processing is that it increases the amount of time an event remains active in short-term memory (Atkinson & Shiffrin, 1968). The first use of the concept of re-hearsal in animal learning was in a series of experiments in classical con-ditioning by Wagner and his students (Wagner, Rudy, & Whitlow, 1973; Terry & Wagner, 1975). Wagner's strategy was to compare memory for the same unconditioned stimulus (US) made "surprising" or "expected" by its relationship to a conditioned stimulus (CS). Surprise was operationally de-fined by the pairing of a previously conditioned CS− with the US; expected trials were defined by the pairing of a previously conditioned CS+ with the US. The results of these experiments supported Wagner's interpretation that a surprising US is rehearsed and therefore remembered better than an expected US. These experiments suggest that rehearsal in animals also in-creases the amount of time that an event remains active in short-term mem-ory.

Maki (1979) extended Wagner's concepts from classical conditioning to the matching-to-sample paradigm by asking whether a surprising sample stimulus is remembered better than an expected sample stimulus. The sam-ple stimulus was food or no food (2 sec of darkness), and the comparison stimuli were green and red disks. When the sample stimulus was food, the choice of red was reinforced. When the sample stimulus was no food, the choice of green was reinforced. Separately the birds were trained to dis-criminate between vertical and horizontal lines: vertical (S+) was paired with food whereas horizontal (S−) signaled no food. A surprising sample stimulus was defined by pairing S− with food and S+ with no food. An expected sample stimulus was defined by pairing S+ with food and S− with no food. Maki found that matching accuracy on surprising trials was better than matching accuracy on expected trials. This suggests that a sur-prising sample was rehearsed more than an expected sample.

In an extension of the research on surprising versus expected sample stim-uli, Grant, Brewster, and Stierhoff (1983) varied the retention interval be-tween the sample and the test while controlling for the similarity of expected and surprising probe trials to the trials of training. Grant found that at a retention interval of 10 sec matching performance dropped to chance for the expected sample stimulus. For the surprising sample stimulus, however, there was no decrement in performance at 10 sec since matching accuracy remained constant as a function of the retention interval. The demonstration that the rate of forgetting for surprising sample stimuli was slower than the rate of forgetting for expected sample stimuli suggests that surprising events produce more rehearsal than expected events.

IV. Primacy and Recency in Animal Memory

Further evidence for rehearsal in animals comes from the serial probe recognition task, in which the subject is presented with a sequence of stimuli, one at a time, followed by a test of recognition memory. On the recognition test, a single test item, the probe, is presented. The task of the subject is to determine whether the probe was one of the items presented on the list. In research on human information processing, the primacy effect refers to the finding that early items in the list are recognized better than later items, whereas the recency effect refers to the finding that the last items are recognized better than the earlier items. When both primacy and recency effects are obtained in the same experiment, the result is the familiar U-shaped serial position curve.

In order to determine if primacy and recency effects are obtained in pigeons and monkeys, Sands and Wright (1980) and Wright, Santiago, Sands, and Urcuioli (1984) modified the serial probe recognition procedure for use with animals. The items were colored slides projected on the top half of a screen by a carousel slide projector. The test for recognition consisted of the presentation of a probe item on the bottom half of the screen. If the probe item matched one of the items on the list, the "same" response was reinforced. On different trials the probe was not contained in any list for that session and a "different" response was reinforced.

The parameter that controlled the primacy or recency effect was the delay between the presentation of the final item in the list and the presentation of the probe. With no delay a recency effect was obtained with the highest percentage correct for the last item on the list. At a delay of 10 sec a primacy effect was obtained with the highest percentage correct for the first item on the list. At intermediate delays a U-shaped serial position curve was obtained. Primacy and recency effects have been obtained for many years in studies of human memory. The discovery of primacy effects in particular for pigeons and monkeys demonstrates an additional similarity between the human and infrahuman memory systems.

While several theoretical interpretations of these effects are entertained by Wright, Santiago, Sands, and Urcuioli (1984), a rehearsal interpretation is the first explanation that comes to mind. First, consider the case in which there is a long delay between the end of the list and the probe test. The presentation of the first item on the list commands attention from the animal, with successive items rapidly filling up the limited capacity of short-term memory. Rehearsal of the items occurs during the delay. Each successive item is rehearsed less during the delay so that the earlier items have a stronger associative representation at the time of the test. The primacy effect reflects the differential rehearsal of the items on the list.

Second, consider the case in which there is no delay between the end of the list and the probe test. With no delay there is no opportunity for rehearsal. The last items on the list remain in active memory. Therefore, recognition of the last items on the list is good. Recall of the first items on the list suffers from the absence of rehearsal. Whether this standard interpretation of the primacy and recency effects turns out to be correct is less important than the prospect of developing unified theories for human and animal memory.

V. The Updating of Animal Memory

An earlier article in this series (Bjork, 1978) was devoted to the updating of human memory. Attention to the task at hand is facilitated by forgetting previous tasks. Persuasive evidence for updating in humans is an experiment by Bjork, Bjork, and Glenberg (see Bjork, 1978), in which a forget instruction between sublists eliminated the proactive interference from the first sublist. The research on updating demonstrates that the forgetting of information that is no longer current is an active process which can be controlled by the subject.

An experiment on updating in pigeons which confirms the work of Bjork has been carried out by Grant (1984a). Proactive interference is produced in the delayed matching-to-sample paradigm by presenting an alternative presample stimulus immediately before the regular sample stimulus. For example, if the regular sample stimuli are red and green, proactive interference is obtained on trials when a red presample stimulus precedes a green sample stimulus. Grant's strategy was to present an F-cue between the presample and the sample stimulus to see if the F-cue attenuated proactive interference.

The birds were trained with red and green sample stimuli. A horizontal line was the F-cue and a vertical line was the R-cue. First the birds were trained in the conventional directed-forgetting paradigm with only a single sample stimulus. On half of the trials the presentation of the horizontal line

following the sample terminated the trial, and on the other half of the trials
the vertical line signaled a test of memory by the presentation of the comparison stimuli. After a demonstration that the F-cue was effective in producing directed forgetting for a single sample stimulus, the proactive
interference trials were introduced by presenting the two samples, red and
green, successively. On R–R trials the interfering sample was followed by
an R-cue; on F–R trials the interfering sample was followed by an F-cue.
The second or to-be-remembered sample was always followed by an R-cue.
Proactive interference was obtained on R–R trials. Proactive interference
was reduced on F–R trials as the accuracy of matching was 10% higher
when the F-cue separated the interfering stimuli. In other words, an F-cue
produces updating in pigeons as well as people because an F-cue selectively
reduces processing of the preceding stimulus.

Grant's results provide support for the construct of rehearsal in pigeons.
On F–R trials the presentation of an F-cue terminates rehearsal of the interfering sample stimulus, whereas the R-cue maintains rehearsal of the second sample stimulus during the retention interval. Proactive interference is
attenuated and updating is thereby obtained by blocking rehearsal of the
to-be-forgotten stimuli. A final experiment by Grant provides a direct test
of the rehearsal interpretation of directed forgetting by varying the interval
between the first interfering sample and the onset of the second sample.
The R- and F-cues were presented immediately after the interfering sample.
The results of this experiment demonstrated that the F-cue was most effective in eliminating proactive interference at the longest values between
the interfering and sample stimuli, exactly the outcome predicted by the
rehearsal interpretation. Thus the same cognitive process appears to underlie updating in people and pigeons.

A converging set of operations is required to invoke an explanation of
behavior in terms of a theoretical process that cannot be observed directly.
The research on directed forgetting, memory for surprising versus expected
samples, the primacy effect in serial probe recognition tasks, and the updating of animal memory each point to rehearsal as a theoretical process
in pigeon short-term memory. There are similarities in the process of rehearsal between people and animals.

VI.   An Attentional Theory of Directed Forgetting

Theories of short-term animal memory (e.g., Roberts & Grant, 1976) have
rarely mentioned the concept of attention. Yet by incorporating a concept
of attention, a wide range of disparate phenomena fall into place. Kendrick
and Rilling (1984) have developed a theory called AIM, a theory of active

and inactive memory, the major construct of which is attention. The metatheoretical assumption of our approach to the memory system of the pigeon is that of evolutionary continuity (Wasserman, 1981), that is, that the information-processing system of pigeons is quantitatively similar, but simpler than the human information-processing system.

Most theories of memory (Shiffrin & Schneider, 1977; Wagner, 1981) assume that a memory representation can be in one of two states, active or inactive. A memory in the active state has the potential to control behavior, but a memory in the inactive state does not. Similar terms for these states are the short-term store and the long-term store. The inactive memory is associative and contains the "rules" acquired by the organism in learning the delayed matching-to-sample task.

The most important characteristic of active memory is its limited capacity (Shiffrin, 1976). This limited capacity is called attention, which means that some stimuli receive more processing than other stimuli. Attention is not a single process but a set of cognitive processes requiring experimental analysis. A constraint upon the active memory system is that very little information is maintained in active memory.

Two characteristics of active memory which are relevant for directed forgetting are selective attention and limitations on the capacity for rehearsal. While these capacity limitations are well documented for the human information-processing system (Shiffrin, 1976), much less is known about capacity limitations on the pigeon's information-processing system. Research by Riley (1984) with compound stimuli in the delayed matching-to-sample task demonstrates that the pigeon can process one element more easily than two. Such data suggest that the pigeon has a limited capacity system controlled by a process of selective attention. The data reviewed in the preceding section provide evidence for a process of rehearsal. Thus two of the prime characteristics of the active memory for the human information-processing system—selective attention and rehearsal—are also found in the information-processing system of the pigeon.

In order to understand the role of selective attention in the delayed matching-to-sample task, consider the cognitive processes which occur during the three stages of the procedure: presentation of the sample stimulus, presentation of the delay interval, and presentation of the test for retention. Attention is conceived to operate in parallel with the cognitive processes controlled by the environmental events of the procedure.

Presentation of the sample stimulus activates a representation of the relevant features of the sample stimulus which have been stored in long-term memory. This process of encoding the representation is automatic because of the extensive training that has been given in the matching-to-sample task. Presentation of the sample stimulus also activates associative information from inactive memory. For example, if the task is symbolic matching and the sample stimulus is food and the correct test stimulus is a green keylight, the sample may activate associative information about the green test stimulus. Presentation of the sample stimulus directs the pigeon's attention to the representation produced by the sample and to representations of stimuli associated with the sample.

By definition, the rehearsal process begins with the termination of the sample stimulus during the delay interval. Attention to the representation during the delay is necessary for the maintenance of rehearsal. In directed forgetting the R-cue controls attention to the representation, which is necessary for the maintenance of rehearsal. Presumably any event during the delay correlated with the presentation of the test, even food or a schedule of reinforcement interpolated within the delay interval, could function as an R-cue. As long as the animal focuses attention on the representation throughout the entire delay interval, the representation will remain active and control the generation of the correct response at the presentation of the test stimuli.

The heart of the attentional interpretation of directed forgetting is that the F-cue functions as a switch controlling shifts in attention. When the F-cue is correlated with the termination of the matching procedure, the F-cue acquires control of whatever events the bird attends to during the intertrial interval. These intertrial stimuli generate new representations in active memory which displace the representation generated by the sample stimulus from active memory. In this case, the F-cue terminates the process of rehearsal and the active representation becomes less accessible. Control over the correct response by the correct test stimulus is weakened because the representation encoded by the sample stimulus is less active.

The control of attention resolves the major inconsistency in directed forgetting. When the F-cue is associated with a sample—independent discrimination instead of extinction, Grant (1981a) obtained directed forgetting while Kendrick *et al.* (1981) and Maki and Hegvik (1981) obtained remembering. There are three differences between Grant's procedure and ours. First, Grant used a successive matching procedure, whereas we used two-choice matching. Second, Grant's procedure resulted in 50% response-independent reinforcement associated with F-cue trials. Our procedure resulted in 100% response-dependent reinforcement. Third, Grant's procedure merely presented a single "dot" stimulus after F-cues, whereas ours was a two-choice sample-independent discrimination.

The notion of attention controlled by the F-cue explains the discrepant findings as follows. The F-cue simply failed to switch attention away from sample stimulus information in our procedure, but did produce inattention to sample information in Grant's procedure. Why should this be so? And how can we test this assertion? In Grant's procedure, the F-cues are associated with response-independent reinforcement. The bird's behavior and external stimuli are irrelevant following F-cues. Attention to sample information (i.e, rehearsal) is unnecessary, as is attention to stimuli following the F-cue. In our procedure, however, the F-cue is associated with response-dependent, sample-independent discriminative stimuli. External stimuli and behavior both control the probability of reinforcement. Inattention to sample information is still unnecessary, but inattention to stimuli following the F-cue would reduce the probability of reinforcement from nearly 100 to 50%. It is our contention that attention to events and stimuli following the F-cue is crucial for accurate matching performance on F-cued test trials.

Kendrick (1984) has recently completed a test of the attention hypothesis by replicating and modifying Grant's procedure. First, an exact replication of Grant's "dot test" was carried out and, consistent with previous findings, directed forgetting was obtained. Next, the birds were trained with a sample-independent, successive discrimination following the F-cues. Probability of reinforcement was 50% in both conditions. The discrimination task was response independent; 100% reinforcement was correlated with a small white triangle and 0% reinforcement was correlated with a small white square. Three birds pecked at high rates during the triangle and rarely pecked during the square. Test trials were infrequently presented; the color test stimuli, red or green, were presented in place of the triangle or square following the F-cue. Performance on these test trials did not differ from baseline, indicating that the birds retained sample information in this condition. These results confirm previous findings and demonstrate that one crucial factor in directed forgetting is the presence or absence of discriminative stimuli following the F-cues. Why should discriminative stimuli determine whether pigeons forget or remember? Because discriminative stimuli force the birds to attend to stimuli after the F-cue, thus promoting the successful retrieval of sample stimulus information at the time of a test. Directed forgetting is only obtained when the F-cue switches attention away from the matching procedure.

VII. Retrieval in Short-Term Memory

In a review of long-delay learning Lett (1979) points out that logically there are two ways that a representation can control behavior. One possibility is that the representation of the to-be-remembered stimulus remains active throughout the delay interval so that the memory is still active when the test for retention occurs. This is the rehearsal theory of memory, which is quite plausible for the cases in which the retention interval is short.

The other possibility is that the memory of the stimulus becomes inactive at some point during the retention interval, but that the stimuli of the retention test reactivate a representation of the to-be-remembered stimulus. Reactivation has been favored for many years as a theory of long-term memory, but not as a theory of short-term memory. In this section we propose that rehearsal is only part of the story of how the pigeons solve the delayed matching-to-sample task. Retrieval is the process that completes the story. Consider the case in which an F-cue converts a representation of a sample stimulus from the active to the inactive state. Does this mean that the sample stimulus has irrevocably lost control of the test response? If the test stimulus reactivates a representation of the sample stimulus, then this reactivated representation could control accurate matching performance.

Animals have two mechanisms for remembering events: rehearsal and retrieval. Both mechanisms are necessary for a complete explanation of the behavioral phenomena obtained in the delayed matching-to-sample paradigm.

Accounts of animal memory that rely upon retrieval are well documented (D'Amato, 1973; Medin, 1975; Spear, 1973, 1978, 1981). These theories typically rely on context-dependent retrieval processes. Following Spear (1978), a contextual stimulus is any stimulus that has acquired control over the indicator response excluding the target discriminative stimuli. Most theories of human memory (Shiffrin & Schneider, 1977; Tulving & Thompson, 1973) and animal memory (Medin, 1975; Spear, 1978; Wagner, 1978, 1979) assume that the presence of the contextual stimuli present during training is necessary for retrieval of the target memory. Therefore, changes in the contextual stimuli between training and testing is a major determinant of forgetting. Spear (1978) assumes that contextual stimuli acquire a capacity to function as retrieval cues because contextual stimuli are incorporated with the discriminative stimuli of the learning task as an attribute of memory for an episode. The contextual viewpoint converts memory into a problem of stimulus control in which the task of an experimental analysis is to determine if a particular event is a contextual stimulus controlling retrieval. Context-dependent retrieval has been investigated extensively in the retention of learning in long-term memory (see Spear, 1978).

As an illustration of research on the role of context in the delayed matching-to-sample paradigm, the context in which the sample stimulus is presented should be considered. The sample stimulus is often preceded by a presample or "preparatory" stimulus such as a white light on the key or a flashing houselight. A presample stimulus could be viewed as an instruction to attend to or remember the next event. If the animal encodes the presample stimulus as an attribute of the sample stimulus, then presenting the sample stimulus on a probe trial without the presample stimulus should produce a retention decrement. Similarly, if the sample stimuli are always presented during training in an unsignaled fashion without a presample stimulus on the key, then preceding the sample stimulus with a presample stimulus on a probe trial should produce a decrement in retention.

Colwill and Dickinson (1980a,b) have evaluated the role of the context of the sample stimulus in delayed matching-to-sample performance. They varied the similarity of the conditions between training and testing and found a generalization decrement in retention when there was a change in the signaling conditions for the sample stimulus between training and testing. These experiments demonstrate that the context of the sample stimulus is an important variable determining the level of accuracy in delayed matching-to-sample experiments.

VIII. The Behavioral Context Hypothesis

Rehearsal is part of the explanation for the phenomenon of directed forgetting, but it is not the whole story. In research on directed forgetting with people, researchers hunted for several years for a missing mechanism to account for data on directed forgetting not explicable in terms of rehearsal. An experiment by Geiselman, Bjork, and Fishman (1983) demonstrated that an F-cue may produce forgetting by disrupting retrieval. The F-cue blocks retrieval at the time of recall when the retrieval processes are weak. Disrupted retrieval, our behavioral context hypothesis, also explains some data on directed forgetting in pigeons that does not mesh with the rehearsal interpretation.

Our research on directed forgetting has also investigated the role of contextual stimuli in the performance of short-term memory discriminations, but we have focused on the context during the retention test, rather than the context at encoding. As Spear (1978) points out, stimuli produced by behavior may be part of the context necessary for retrieval. Rilling (1967) demonstrated that the choice responses of pigeons are sensitive to control by preceding behavior. This suggests that forgetting may occur if the behavior preceding the indicator response fails to occur at the time of the retention test. Accordingly, comparison stimuli effect retrieval of a representation of the most recent sample stimulus only when the comparison stimuli are presented in the context in which they were presented during learning or baseline maintenance or both.

We have observed that one salient difference between an R-cue and an F-cue is the difference in the birds' behavior following each stimulus. Following the R-cue, all birds consistently remained oriented toward the key and most pecked at the dark key throughout the delay interval until the onset of the comparison stimuli. Following the F-cue, the delay-interval pecking was immediately terminated, and the typical pigeon moved away from the stimulus panel. These behaviors were not sample-specific since the same pattern of behaviors was observed after each sample stimulus.

These considerations led Kendrick *et al.* (1981) to develop the behavioral context hypothesis. This theory states that the comparison stimuli effect retrieval of the representation controlled by the sample stimulus only when the comparison stimuli are presented in the behavioral context established during original learning. The directed-forgetting effect is thus in part a retrieval failure resulting from the presentation of the comparison stimuli in the behavioral context established by the F-cue. In original learning, the comparison stimuli are only presented in the context established by the R-cue.

IX. The F-Cue Function in Context

The F-cue always signals cancellation or substitution of the comparison stimuli during training. A variety of different events are defined as F-cues, but the most common is comparison omission or termination of the trial. Certain comparison substitution procedures, for example, a sample independent discrimination in which one stimulus is always reinforced and another stimulus is always extinguished, produce remembering rather than forgetting on probe trials when the comparison stimuli are presented following the F-cue. A major problem for theories of directed forgetting is to explain why certain types of F-cues produce forgetting whereas others produce remembering.

Kendrick *et al.* (1981) carried out an experimental analysis of the function of the F-cue in directed forgetting. They found that when F-cues and R-cues controlled different behaviors at the end of the delay, matching on probe trials was poor and directed forgetting was obtained. When both R- and F-cues controlled the same behavior at the end of the delay, matching on probe trials was good and remembering was obtained.

In the Kendrick *et al.* study, the basic procedure was a two-choice, delayed matching-to-sample with red and green key lights as sample and comparison stimuli. Two experimental conditions were compared in an ABA design. In the A condition, the F-cue signaled cancellation of the comparison stimulus and substitution of an unconditional discrimination. When the F-cue was followed by the sample-independent discrimination, one side key was illuminated by a white horizontal bar and the other side key was illuminated by a white vertical bar. A peck to the vertical bar produced reinforcement, whereas a peck to the horizontal bar initiated the intertrial interval. These outcomes occurred independently of the preceding sample stimulus. In the B condition, the F-cue signaled extinction and the cancellation of the comparison stimuli as in the basic directed-forgetting paradigm. After reaching a criterion of 80% correct choice performance for 5 days in a row, a test session was carried out in which the comparison stimuli were presented on probe trials following the F-cue.

Figure 3 shows the percentage of correct choice responses in baseline and probe test conditions as a function of the R- and F-cue conditions. When the F-cue was followed by a sample-independent discrimination (the left and right panels of the figure), all four pigeons maintained a high accuracy

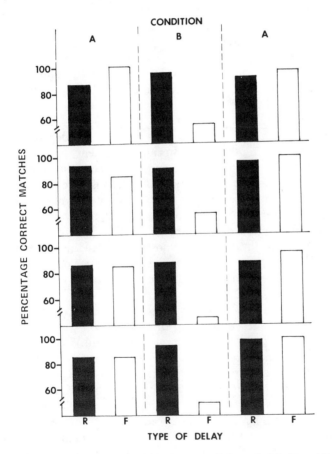

Fig. 3. Percentage correct matching choice responses on R-cued trials (R) and F-cued probe trials (F) when the F-cue was followed by sample-independent discriminative stimuli (Condition A) and when the stimuli were omitted (Condition B).

of choice responses. In fact, on probe trials performance averaged 97.5% correct, slightly better than the 93.7% obtained following the R-cue during testing. The middle panel shows that the F-cue EXT condition effectively reduced matching accuracy on F-cued trials. The F-cue test probe mean for all birds dropped to 53.3%, near chance, as compared to the 92.4% for the test data obtained following the R-cue. The data of Fig. 3 clearly demonstrate that when the F-cue is followed by extinction and cancellation of the comparison stimulus, matching accuracy is reduced to near chance on probe trials. When the F-cue is followed by an unconditional discrimination, however, there is no loss of matching accuracy when a conditional discrimination is substituted for the unconditional discrimination.

On the F-cued trials, memory of the sample stimulus was not required to gain reinforcement since a single peck to the S+, the vertical bar, produced reinforcement independently of whether the sample stimulus was red or green. Yet on F-cued probe trials, when the comparison stimuli were presented in place of the unconditional discriminative stimuli, matching performance was accurate. The basic findings of this experiment have also been obtained by Maki and Hegvik (1980).

Kendrick *et al.* (1981) also demonstrated that the directed-forgetting effect is dependent on delay-interval behavior and not dependent on nonreinforcement following the F-cue. In this experiment, reinforcement after the F-cue was response-independent and the pigeons maintained accurate probe matching. In a second condition, the pigeons were required to orient away from the response keys (insert their heads into the magazine opening) on F-cued trials in order to receive reinforcement, and inaccurate matching performance was obtained on probe trials. These results were viewed as support for the behavioral context hypothesis. When the R-cues and F-cues controlled similar behavior, remembering was obtained on the F-cued probe trials, and when they controlled different behaviors, forgetting was obtained.

The behavioral context hypothesis, as a retrieval account, requires that behavior during the presentations of the comparison stimuli is critical and that behavior during the delay interval is irrelevant. In experiments with pigeons, the R-cue acquires control over pecking or orienting to the key so directed forgetting should occur whenever the F-cue controls a response that is incompatible with the behavior controlled by the R-cue. In terms of context-dependent retrieval, the context is not the behavior during the delay interval per se, but the response-produced stimuli from the baseline behavior, occurring during the time of the comparison stimuli presentation.

The purpose of a final experiment was to determine if behavior at the end of the delay interval was the primary factor determining whether the F-cue produced forgetting or remembering. At the beginning of the F-cued delay interval, the birds were trained to insert their heads into the food magazine. In the first condition, presentation of the unconditional stimuli on the side keys was contingent upon the presence of the pigeon's head in the magazine, defined as the interruption of a photobeam, after the 4-sec delay interval following the sample stimulus. In this condition, the F-cue controlled the behavior of inserting the head into the magazine and then orienting and accurately pecking the reinforced side key. Thus, the behaviors at the end of the R-cued and F-cued delays were similar, whereas the behaviors during the delays differed. According to the behavioral context hypothesis, the contexts in which the probe trials' comparison stimuli are presented (after the F-cue) are similar to the context in which they occur in baseline R-cued trials. Therefore matching accuracy should not be reduced on probe trials.

This was supported by the finding that when the pigeons had been trained to produce food by discriminatively pecking the side keys following the insertion of their head into the food hopper, delayed matching-to-sample performance was not disrupted. The results of this experiment confirm the prediction of the behavioral context interpretation. When the F-cue controlled orienting to the food hopper during the delay and orienting to the response keys at the end of the delay interval, accurate matching performance was obtained. In other words, when the comparison stimuli were presented in the behavioral context established during original learning, that is, orienting to the response keys, accurate remembering resulted.

The behavioral context hypothesis explains directed forgetting as follows. When the representation generated by the sample stimulus is inactive following the F-cue, the comparison stimuli retrieve the representation generation by the sample stimulus only when the test stimuli are presented in the presence of the behavior controlled by the R-cue. When the end-of-delay behavior controlled by the F-cue is similar to the end-of-delay behavior controlled by the R-cue, the "behavior context" is appropriate to support retrieval and probe matching is good. Whenever the end-of-delay behavior controlled by the F-cue differs from the behavior controlled by the R-cue, however, the "behavioral context" is inappropriate and the comparison stimuli fail to reactivate the representation generated by the sample stimulus, and probe matching is poor.

X. Conclusions

Two sets of theoretical processes—one controlled by the sample stimulus and the other controlled by the test stimulus—are necessary to encompass the phenomenon of animal memory observed in the delayed matching-to-sample paradigm. The sample stimulus commands attention. After the termination of the sample, the representation is maintained by a process of rehearsal which requires attention from the organism. If the rehearsal process maintains the representation in an active state throughout the delay interval, a correct response is generated when the test stimulus is presented. The R-cue maintains the active representation throughout the delay by controlling the attention and rehearsal processes. Once the representation controlled by the R-cue becomes inactive, the R-cue cannot function as a retrieval cue and cannot reactivate an inactive representation.

When the F-cue signals omission of the test for retention, the F-cue terminates the process of rehearsal and the representation generated by the sample stimulus goes from an active to an inactive state. Attention to the representation during the delay is necessary for maintenance rehearsal. The heart of the attentional interpretation of directed forgetting is that the F-cue functions as a switch controlling shifts in attention. When attention shifts from the representation controlled by the sample stimulus to other stimuli, control over the indicator response by the representation is weakened and directed forgetting occurs. A distractor interpolated during the delay interval in a paradigm of retroactive interference produces forgetting by the same mechanism as the F-cue, by shifting attention from the representation generated by the sample to the distractor.

Retrieval is the process controlled by the test stimuli. Retrieval is a second process of remembering which comes into play when the representation controlled by the sample stimulus has become inactive during the delay. Although retrieval is usually only considered in connection with long-term memories, the theory proposed here extends the retrieval process to the delayed matching-to-sample task. Retrieval is a process that may operate when the rehearsal process is interrupted.

Retrieval is optimal when the context during the test for retrieval is identical to the context during training. Forgetting may be obtained by manipulating the context in which the sample stimulus is presented, by changing the context during the delay, or changing the context in which the comparison stimuli are presented.

During training the correct choice response is preceded by a stream of behavior which, in the pigeon's case, is pecking the key on which the sample was presented. This delay-interval behavior is not to be confused with the sample-specific mediating behavior that may also occur in the delayed matching-to-sample task. The behavioral context hypothesis states that the comparison stimuli effect retrieval of the representation controlled by the sample stimulus only when the comparison stimuli are presented in the behavioral context established during original learning. In particular the behavior at the end of the delay immediately preceding the test for retrieval must be similar to the behavior of training in order for remembering to occur. When the R- and F-cues acquire control over different end-of-delay behaviors, directed forgetting occurs, but remembering is obtained when the R- and F-cues control the same end-of-delay behavior. In other words, the behavioral context of the test for retrieval must be similar to the behavioral context of training in order for remembering to occur.

As recently as 1978 it was possible to publish an article stressing the qualitative differences between information processing in people and pigeons (Premack, 1978). In comparison with people and other primates, Premack leaves the reader with the notion that the pigeon's memory system "lacks flexibility" and is quite inferior. The data that have emerged within the past few years produce a different picture. Rehearsal or active processing is a hallmark of the human memory. Four sets of converging operations: directed forgetting, surprising versus expected sample stimuli, a primacy effect, and updating all point to a model of pigeon short-term memory in which rehearsal is a viable theoretical construct. What is surprising about these data is the qualitative similarity in rehearsal between people and animals. The pigeon has not become more intelligent in this short period of time, but the experimenters have.

ACKNOWLEDGMENT

Preparation of this article was supported by Grant BNS-8110966 from the National Science Foundation.

REFERENCES

Atkinson, R. C., & Shiffrin, R. M. Human memory: A proposed system and its control processes. In K. W. Spence (Ed.), *The psychology of learning and motivation* (Vol. 2). New York: Academic Press, 1968.

Bjork, R. A. Positive forgetting: The noninterference of items intentionally forgotten. *Journal of Verbal Learning and Verbal Behavior,* 1970, **9**, 255–268.

Bjork, R. A. Theoretical implications of directed forgetting. In A. W. Melton & E. Martin (Eds.), *Coding processes in human memory.* New York: Holt, 1972.

Bjork, R. A. The updating of human memory. In G. H. Bower (Ed.), *The psychology of learning and motivation* (Vol. 12). New York: Academic Press, 1978.

Colwill, R. M., & Dickinson, A. Short-term retention of "surprising" events by pigeons. *Quarterly Journal of Experimental Psychology,* 1983, in press.

Colwill, R. M., & Dickinson, A. Short-term retention of "surprising" events following differential training conditions. *Animal Learning & Behavior,* 1980, **8,** 561-566.

D'Amato, M. R. Delayed matching and short-term memory in monkeys. In G. H. Bower (Ed.), *The psychology of learning and motivation* (Vol. 7). New York: Academic Press, 1973.

Geiselman, R. E., Bjork, R. A., & Fishman, D. L. Disrupted retrieval in directed forgetting: A link with posthypnotic amnesia. *Journal of Experimental Psychology: General,* 1983, **112,** 58-72.

Grant, D. S. Stimulus control of information processing in pigeon short-term memory. *Learning and Motivation,* 1981, **12,** 19-39. (a)

Grant, D. S. Short-term memory in the pigeon. In N. E. Spear & R. R. Miller (Eds.), *Information processing in animals: Memory mechanisms.* Hillsdale, New Jersey:. Erlbaum, 1981. (b)

Grant, D. S. Stimulus control of information processing in rat short-term memory. *Journal of Experimental Psychology: Animal Behavior Processes,* 1982, **8,** 154-164.

Grant, D. S. Rehearsal in pigeon short-term memory. In H. L. Roitblat, T. G. Bever, & H. S. Terrace (Eds.), *Animal cognition.* Hillsdale, New Jersey: Erlbaum, 1984, in press. (a)

Grant, D. S. Directed forgetting and intertrial interference in pigeon delayed matching. *Canadian Journal of Psychology,* 1984, in press. (b)

Grant, D. S., Brewster, R. G., & Stierhoff, K. A. "Surprisingness" and short-term retention in pigeons. *Journal of Experimental Psychology: Animal Behavior Processes,* 1983, **9,** 63-79.

Grant, D. S., & Roberts, W. A. Sources of retroactive inhibition in pigeon short-term memory. *Journal of Experimental Psychology: Animal Behavioral Processes,* 1976, **2,** 1-16.

Honig, W. K., & Thompson, R. K. Retrospective and prospective processing in animal working memory. In G. H. Bower (Ed.), *The psychology of learning and motivation* (Vol. 16). New York: Academic Press, 1982.

Johnson, R. E. Memory-cased rehearsal. In G. H. Bower (Ed.), *The psychology of learning and motivation* (Vol. 14). New York: Academic Press, 1980.

Kendrick, D. F. *Directed forgetting in pigeons is mediated by expectancies for test stimuli.* In preparation, 1984.

Kendrick, D. F., & Rilling, M. AIM: A theory of active and inactive memory. In D. F. Kendrick, M. Rilling, & M. R. Denny (Eds.), *Animal memory.* Hillsdale, New Jersey: Erlbaum, 1984, in press.

Kendrick, D. F., Rilling, M., & Stonebraker, T. B. Stimulus control of delayed matching in pigeons: Directed forgetting. *Journal of the Experimental Analysis of Behavior,* 1981, **36,** 241-251.

Lett, B. T. Long delay learning: Implications for learning and memory theory. In W. S. Sutherland (Ed.), *Tutorial essays in psychology: A guide to recent advances* (Vol. 2). Hillsdale, New Jersey: Erlbaum, 1979.

Maki, W. S. Pigeons' short-term memories for surprising vs. expected reinforcement and non-reinforcement. *Animal Learning & Behavior,* 1979, **7,** 31-37.

Maki, W. S. Directed forgetting in pigeons. In N. E. Spear & R. R. Miller (Eds.), *Information processing in animals: Memory mechanisms.* Hillsdale, New Jersey: Erlbaum, 1981.

Maki, W. S. Prospects for a theory of working memory. In H. L. Roitblat, T. G. Bever, & H. S. Terrace (Eds.), *Animal cognition.* Hillsdale, New Jersey: Erlbaum, 1984, in press.

Maki, W. S., & Hegvik, D. K. Directed forgetting in pigeons. *Animal Learning & Behavior,* 1980, **8,** 567-574.

Maki, W. S., Olson, D., & Rego, S. Directed forgetting in pigeons: Analysis of cue functions. *Animal Learning & Behavior,* 1981, **9,** 189-195.

Medin, D. L. A theory of context in discrimination learning. In G. H. Bower (Ed.), *The psychology of learning and motivation* (Vol. 9). New York: Academic Press, 1975.

Premack, D., On the abstractness of human concepts: Why it would be difficult to talk to a pigeon. In S. H. Hulse, H. Fowler, & W. K. Honig (Eds.), *Cognitive processes in animal behavior.* Hillsdale, New Jersey: Erlbaum, 1978.

Riley, D. A. Do pigeons decompose stimulus compounds? In H. L. Roitblat, T. G. Bever, & H. S. Terrace (Eds.), *Animal cognition,* Hillsdale, New Jersey: Erlbaum, 1984.

Riley, D. A., Cook, R. G., & Lamb, M. R. A classification and analysis of short-term retention codes in pigeons. In G. H. Bower (Ed.), *The psychology of learning and motivation* (Vol. 15). New York: Academic Press, 1981.

Rilling, M. Number of responses as a stimulus in fixed-interval and fixed-ratio schedules. *Journal of Comparative and Physiological Psychology,* 1967, **63**, 60-65.

Roberts, W. A., & Grant, D. S. Studies of short-term memory in the pigeon using the delayed matching-to-sample procedure. In D. L. Medin, W. A. Roberts, & R. T. Davis (Eds.), *Processes in animal memory.* Hillsdale, New Jersey: Erlbaum, 1976, 79-112.

Roberts, W. A., Mazmanian, D. S., & Kraemer, P. J. Directed forgetting in monkeys. *Animal Learning & Behavior,* 1984, **12**, 29-40.

Roitblat, H. L. The meaning of representation in animal memory. *The Behavioral and Brain Sciences,* 1982, **5**, 353-406.

Sands, S. F., & Wright, A. A. Primate memory: Retention of serial list items by a rhesus monkey. *Science,* 1980, **209**, 938-940.

Shiffrin, R. M. Capacity limitations in information processing, attention, and memory. In W. K. Estes (Ed.), *Handbook of learning and cognitive processes* (Vol. 4). Hillsdale, New Jersey: Erlbaum, 1976.

Shiffrin, R. M., & Schneider, W. Controlled and automatic human information processing: II. Perceptual learning, automatic attending, and a general theory. *Psychological Review,* 1977, **84**, 127-190.

Spear, N. E. Retrieval of memory in animals. *Psychological Review,* 1973, **80**, 163-194.

Spear, N. E. Retrieval of memories: A psychobiological approach. In W. K. Estes (Ed.), *Handbook of learning and cognitive processes* (Vol. 4). Hillsdale, New Jersey: Erlbaum, 1978.

Spear, N. E. Extending the domain of memory retrieval. In N. E. Spear & R. R. Miller (Eds.), *Information processing in animals: Memory mechanisms.* Hillsdale, New Jersey: Erlbaum, 1981.

Stonebraker, T. B., & Rilling, M. Control of delayed matching-to-sample performance using directed forgetting techniques. *Animal Learning & Behavior,* 1981, **9**, 196-201.

Terry, W. S., & Wagner, A. R. Short-term memory for "surprising" vs. "expected" unconditioned stimuli in Pavlovian conditioning. *Journal of Experimental Psychology: Animal Behavior Processes,* 1975, **1**, 122-133.

Tulving, E., & Thompson, D. M. Encoding specificity and retrieval processes in episodic memory. *Psychological Review,* 1973, **80**, 352-373.

Wagner, A. R. Expectancies and the priming of STM. In S. H. Hulse, H. Fowler, & W. K. Honig (Eds.), *Cognitive processes in animal behavior.* Hillsdale, New Jersey: Erlbaum, 1978.

Wagner, A. R. Habituation and memory. In A. Dickinson & R. A. Boakes (Eds.), *Mechanisms of learning and motivation: A memorial volume to Jerzy Konorski.* Hillsdale, New Jersey: Erlbaum, 1979.

Wagner, A. R. SOP: A model of automatic processing in animal behavior. In N. E. Spear & R. R. Miller (Eds.), *Information processing in animals: Memory mechanisms.* Hillsdale, New Jersey: Erlbaum, 1981.

Wagner, A. R., Rudy, J. W., & Whitlow, J. W., Jr. Rehearsal in animal conditioning. *Journal of Experimental Psychology,* 1973, **97,** 407–426.

Wasserman, E. A. Successive matching-to-sample in the pigeon: Variations on a theme by Konorski. *Behavior Research Methods and Instrumentation,* 1976, **8,** 278–282.

Wright, A. A., Santiago, H. C., Sands, S. F., & Urcuiolo, P. J. Monkey and pigeon serial probe recognition performance: Effects of item pool size on proactive interference and item specific associations. In H. L. Roitblat, T. G. Bever, & H. S. Terrace (Eds.), *Animal cognition.* Hillsdale, New Jersey: Erlbaum, 1984, in press.

EFFECTS OF ISOLATION REARING ON LEARNING BY MAMMALS

Robert Holson and Gene P. Sackett

UNIVERSITY OF WASHINGTON
SEATTLE, WASHINGTON

I. Introduction

Throughout history people have been fascinated by tales of children raised in isolation from human intercourse. Herodotus told of the earliest known

THE PSYCHOLOGY OF LEARNING
AND MOTIVATION, VOL. 18

isolation experiment, conducted on human infants by an Egyptian monarch (Rawlinson, 1947). Hundreds of reports concern children supposedly reared by animals ranging from wolves to pigs, sheep, and even bears (Favazza, 1977). These mostly apocryphal tales concern the impact of early experience on development and later behavior. Understanding such relationships underlies contemporary controversies about causes of class, race, and cultural differences in learning and other behavioral activities (Jensen, 1973; Kamin, 1974). The importance of early experience is also central to issues concerning developmental continuities (Sackett, Sameroff, Cairns, & Suomi, 1981). Clear findings about the effects of early experience could have a profound impact on social policy, education, and child-rearing techniques.

Early experience involving isolation rearing is a major technique for studying aspects of normal and deviant development. Trends in current isolation research were begun by Hebb (1949), who studied the effects of isolation on the learning abilities of rodents. Subsequent research has focused on various degrees and types of early experience, followed by tests to assess response acquisition, memory, and concept formation. This article reviews these experiments, describing performance of isolation-reared mammals on learning tasks.

TERMINOLOGY

With respect to isolation as an independent variable, conditions involving explicit sensory deprivation or distortion are excluded. In the isolation conditions reviewed, all senses received stimulation but the situation lacked one or more intermodal or response-contingent experiences found in more typical rearing environments. In this sense, "isolation" is used synonomously with "experiential deprivation." As deprivation represents a continuum, isolation is also used in a relative sense. For example, if rats caged alone are compared with littermates reared in pairs, the solitary pups are the isolates. If rats reared in pairs are compared with others reared in large groups, however, the more experientially deprived paired rats are the isolates.

Certain terms are used widely in isolation studies. Primates are raised alone in visually enclosed chambers ("total social isolation") or standard laboratory wire cages ("partial social isolation"). Control conditions involve a variety of less socially restricted laboratory settings, or even rearing in the wild. In contrast, many rodent studies compare rearing in large, highly stimulating "playground" environments (EC rearing) with socially housing several rats in a wire cage (SC) or isolating a single rat in a wire cage (IC). Although the rodent IC setting resembles primate partial isolation, both sets of terms are used here.

With respect to the dependent variable, learning is traditionally defined as change over time in response to cues, objects, or symbols correlated with rewards or punishments. Thus, learning is used as a strictly behavioral measure, derived from a variety of tasks confronting subjects with novel or altered cues to reward or punishment. These include maze performance, discrimination, concept formation, extinction, reversal, delayed feedback, passive and active avoidance, and operant bar pressing.

Many of these tasks are studied because they resemble problem types on human IQ tests. They are thought to measure aspects of animal conceptual, cognitive, or intellectual ability. Because few if any behaviors are unidimensional, however, performance on these tasks involves more than learning or cognition. Performance also involves other factors such as affect and motivation. Therefore, performance is emphasized in preference to more inclusive terms such as learning or even problem solving. This emphasis avoids the implication that performance differences are necessarily due to specific intellectual defects, or that the learning problem presented by the experimenter is the same problem perceived by the subject. In this context, identification of specific causes underlying isolate-control differences in performance is the major goal of this article.

Although there is reasonable agreement about the existence of isolate performance differences on specific tasks, a variety of theories have been advanced to explain them. The article begins by examining these theories. The empirical studies are then described and the results related to theoretical explanations. The article concludes with recommendations for future research, identifying unsolved problems, and possible improvements in experimental design.

II. Theoretical Issues

A. CONCEPTUAL DEFICITS

Hebb (1949) was the first theorist to predict that specific and distinctive learning deficits would follow isolation rearing. He explained isolate behavior in cognitive terms, anchored to what was known or speculated about neural functions. Early experience was supposed to build up concepts of external reality; subsequent learning occurred in conjunction with these higher order concepts, called phase sequences in terms of corresponding neural activity. These were assumed to develop from repeated successful firing across a synapse, facilitating subsequent transmission within that set of synapses. These neural assemblages were proposed to be in secondary association cortical areas, not in primary sensory cortex. Thus, in this view cognitive activity is derived from networks of phase sequences in the higher sensory processing areas which develop through experience with varied environmental stimulation. It was proposed that concepts are acquired slowly in early development because of dependence on repeated experience. In contrast, adult concept acquisition was supposed to be more rapid because it uses the higher order concepts already developed in childhood. Consequently, lack of diverse early experience should result in higher order conceptual deficits but not in sensory deficiencies.

Hebb's theories lead to the following predictions:

1. Isolation rearing will produce conceptual, not sensory, deficits.
2. These deficits will be localized in association cortex.
3. The deleterious effects of early isolation will be slow to reverse in adulthood, if they reverse at all.

B. STIMULUS HYPERREACTIVITY

Melzack (1965, 1968) proposed an attentional theory linking isolate performance deficits to hyperreactivity. Repeated experience was assumed to produce neural inhibition of familiar sensory input, with this filtering occurring in sensory brain regions. Because isolates lack varied experiences, they are flooded with novel input when placed in new test situations. Much of this novel input is not pertinent to task performance and also causes excessive arousal. This novelty enhancement effect (Konrad & Melzack, 1975), caused by poor inhibition of sensory intake with consequent hyperarousal, was also supposed to lower inhibition of prepotent responses. The effects of these mechanisms on isolate performance were predicted to be hyperreactivity, distractability, and response perseveration. This syndrome, however, was not assumed to be pathological. It should occur in any animal exposed to very high novelty, and these effects should diminish with repeated exposures to a test situation.

Fuller (1967) also emphasized the affective component of response to novelty. His concept of emergence trauma generated by the initial removal from an isolation environment, however, assumed a subsequently permanent pathological response to novelty. This response was expected to result in performance deficits due to enhanced timidity when faced with new test situations. Others have interpreted the isolation syndrome in similar terms (Riesen, 1961; Riesen & Zilbert, 1975; Mason, Davenport, & Menzel, 1968).

In contrast to Hebb's theory, the stimulus hyperreactivity position makes the following predictions:

1. Isolate learning will be impaired by affective or attentional, but not conceptual, deficiencies.
2. Severe deficits after release from isolation will diminish with increased test environment familiarity.

3. Learning tests employing a familiar apparatus inside the isolation environment, or those begun only after prolonged adaptation to a test situation, should reveal no isolate disadvantage.

C. INHIBITION DEFICIT

Melzack's theory proposes that isolate deficits in inhibiting sensory intake or motor responses are a secondary product of novelty enhancement. Others suggest that inhibition difficulties are the primary isolate deficit (Ough, Beatty, & Khalili, 1972; Morgan, Einon, & Nicholas, 1975). Because isolates do not have contingent probabilistic experiences as infants, Sackett (1970) proposed that they do not learn to inhibit responses. Consequently, they repeatedly perform inappropriate or maladaptive behaviors when faced with changing contingencies in postisolation environments.

Although there is overlap between the primary inhibition deficit position and hyperreactivity theory, the models differ in several ways. In the inhibition model, isolation effects arise from lack of specific response inhibition experience. The hyperreactivity view attributes isolate effects to a general lack of varied sensory experience. Hyperreactivity thus predicts a broad range of deficits on almost any performance measure. Inhibition theory predicts isolate deficits only on tasks that specifically require inhibition. These would include tests involving adaptation to novel test settings, reinforcement of low response rates, reversal, and extinction, but exclude maze learning and discrimination. Neither model predicts the concept learning deficits called for by Hebb's theory.

D. ATROPHY

All of the aforementioned theories assume that isolate behavioral capacities fail to develop owing to lack of necessary early experiences. In contrast, atrophy theories assume that isolation causes behavioral systems that mature at or shortly after birth to regress, thereby being unavailable to support subsequent development (Lessac & Solomon, 1969). Regression is assumed to be caused by anatomical–physiological degeneration (Riesen, 1960; Gyllensten, Malmfors, & Norrlin, 1965), failure to develop synapses, or loss of synaptic connections owing to lack of input or disuse (Floeter & Greenough, 1979).

Although it is not clear exactly which abilities or anatomical systems will atrophy during isolation, these theories make two important predictions: (1) atrophic isolation effects will be permanent because they eliminate physiological substrates required for subsequent development; and (2) atrophic processes are not limited to early life. Unlike the other theories, atrophy theories predict that isolation effects can occur in juveniles and adults for systems that require input and use to maintain anatomical–physiological integrity (e.g., Riege, 1971).

E. SPECIFIC LEARNING AND TRANSFER

All of the theories described so far posit specific disorder(s) caused by isolation rearing. A contrasting position explains isolation effects on the basis of early learning (Suomi, Harlow, & Novack, 1974; Rosenzweig, 1971). Isolates differ from controls in opportunity to learn about the external world. If specific early learning is required for later performance on specific tasks, isolates will be at a disadvantage relative to experienced individuals. Considering the limited specific experience of isolates, this theory also predicts isolate-control differences in response to novelty. Of major importance, isolates are not expected to have permanent learning disabilities or pathological novelty responses. Effects should disappear as normal but inexperienced isolates learn what experienced animals already know.

This theory has an important implication about the temporal locus of isolation effects. Once specific learning has occurred, forgetting should be slow and reestablishment of forgotten material should be prompt. Therefore, owing to a primacy effect, only very early isolation should have large effects on subsequent performance. Early learning is important because it is first learning, not because of developmentally critical or sensitive periods for such learning. Thus, early experience will have later effects only because a great deal of specific learning ordinarily occurs in early postnatal life. In addition, isolates do develop a number of habitual behaviors during rearing, presumably based on feedback from their own responses. Isolation may therefore involve "wrong" learning in addition to not learning a number of specific behaviors. The long-term effects of inappropriate learning should be more difficult to reverse than simple ignorance. Thus, both interference and inappropriate transfer from specific learning during isolation may affect postisolation performance adversely. Failure to develop response inhibition could also be considered inappropriate learning. If so, the concept of a primary inhibition deficit would be a special case of the more general "specific learning" view.

Specific learning deficit theory makes the following predictions:

1. Isolate performance deficits will occur only on tasks that require prior specific learning opportunities not present during isolation.
2. Isolate performance deficiencies are not due to permanent pathological, conceptual, emotional, or inhibitory deficits.
3. Isolate responses to novelty will differ from those of experienced individuals only when isolates are less familiar with the class of stimuli presented.

4. Isolates will learn as rapidly as controls on tasks that do not require prior learning and do not conflict with inappropriate learning.

5. Isolate deficits due to lack or inappropriateness of specific prior learning will be reversed by postisolation learning experiences.

6. Isolation will have marked effects only when it occurs before normal completion of specific learning under nonisolation conditions. Isolation during or after late infancy will therefore have few or no detrimental effects, except for those caused by forgetting preisolation specific learning.

Table I summarizes the various theoretical assumptions about processes affected by isolation and consequent effects on postrearing performance. Although these theories share some features, the overall pattern of predicted effects varies from model to model. This differential pattern will be used to evaluate the models with respect to the experimental literature.

III. Dependent Variables: Isolate Performance on Learning Tasks

A. OVERVIEW

This review is organized by type of task and by species tested on each task. Findings are classified by degree of certainty. For performance to be "established" requires two successful replications within a single species and task. Findings with only one successful task–species replication are called "probable." Single unreplicated findings are considered to be "indicated." Contradictory findings are classified as "uncertain."

The isolate literature will be introduced with respect to its modern history. Systematic research was begun in the late 1940s by Hebb at McGill University. Hebb argued that early experiential deprivation should produce intellectual deficits. Rats reared at home as pets performed better than isolates on a rat "intelligence" test. This finding initiated a series of studies on isolation and enrichment in rats and dogs. Following this early work, research on rodents was begun at Berkeley in the late 1950s. Rosenzweig, Bennett, and colleagues began the still active investigation of behavioral and neural consequences following isolation and enrichment. These studies emphasized effects on brain mechanisms more than learning and behavior. Even their studies using brain weight as a single measure are important to this review, however, as they involve important questions about sensitive periods and recovery from experiential deprivation.

Two groups were responsible for extending isolation research to primates. In the mid 1950s, Davenport, Menzel, and colleagues at the Yerkes Primate Center began a 14-year experiment with chimpanzees involving total social isolation from birth. Harlow and colleagues at the University of Wisconsin initiated the most intensive investigation of primate isolation us-

TABLE I

Isolation Effects Predicted by the Principal Theoretical Models

Theory	Performance on learning tasks		Conceptual deficits?	Sensitive periods?	Isolation duration-severity effects?	Deficits reversible?
	Cause of problem	Performance deficit				
Concept formation	Lack of higher order sensory concepts	Normal on simple tasks, deficient on complex tasks	Yes	Yes	No	Slow, but possible
Novelty enhancement	Affective hyper-reactivity to test situations	Greatest at training onset, wanes with familiarity	No	Yes	Yes	Fully on specific tasks, possible permanent problem with novelty
Inhibition	Inability to inhibit prepotent responses	On tasks eliciting responses that compete with successful performance	No	Yes	Yes	Full compensation not possible after prolonged early isolation
Atrophy	Loss of ability due to disuse or lack of input	On tasks requiring abilities that develop during isolation period	Possible	No	Yes	Inversely proportional to isolation severity and duration
Specific learning and transfer	Ignorance and inappropriate learning	Only after isolation from birth on tasks facilitated by prior learning	Yes	Yes	No	Fully and rapidly

ing rhesus macaques. They studied social behavior and learning by hundreds of isolate monkeys from the late 1950s to the end of the 1970s.

While other laboratories and investigators have made important contributions, these four pioneering efforts generated the majority of findings underlying our current understanding of mammalian isolation rearing effects.

B. NONSPECIFIC EFFECTS OF ISOLATION
    ON PERFORMANCE

Performance on learning tasks is affected by motivational, attentional, and emotional differences between subjects. Yet the purpose of this article, and the majority of experiments in it, is to assess "intellectual" abilities of isolates relative to controls, independent of such factors. To this end, it must be shown that these factors have no effects or have been controlled. This section reviews data suggesting that isolates are motivationally and emotionally different from experienced animals.

Isolates are hyperreactive to novelty. On emergence from isolation, rats, dogs and primates exhibit neophobia—unwillingness to approach novel objects. Disturbance to novelty is even seen in the isolation cage (Melzack, 1954; Davenport & Rogers, 1968; Misslin, 1982).

Neophobia probably underlies findings that isolates require prolonged adaptation to new stimuli and apparatus, independent of task content, before formal testing can begin. For example, chimpanzees were tested on delayed response in their home cages 6 years after emergence from isolation. Two of eight isolates balked completely (refused to respond to test stimuli) and were dropped from the study. The remainder balked more frequently than social controls and had longer response latencies early in the test series (Davenport & Rogers, 1968). Two-year-old rhesus macaques that had been reared in total isolation for 9 months after birth required 29 consecutive weeks of adaptation before being testable on discrimination learning problems (Harlow, Schiltz, & Harlow, 1969). Socially raised controls require only 2 to 5 days for adaptation.

Isolate rodents also react with fear to novel stimuli, and care must be taken to avoid being bitten when handling isolate rats (Ader, 1965; Moyer & Korn, 1965) and mice (Weltman, Sackler, Schwartz, & Owens, 1968). Isolate rodents also have long latencies to emerge from a small box into an open field (Einon & Morgan, 1977; Hahn, 1965). Because experimenters typically do not interact with rodents as intimately as with primates, little attention has been paid to their test adaptation. They are often put directly into test situations on emergence from isolation. Many rodent learning tests require picking up and handling of subjects at the end of every trial, a procedure that may maintain isolate fearfulness.

Pretest adaption procedures do not necessarily protect against neophobia. Adaptation procedures generally involve a simplified version of the learning task, which is run to a predetermined criterion. Then the actual task is introduced. This introduction could retrigger isolate fear and consequent performance deficits, thereby posing a major problem in distinguishing true learning deficits from deficits induced by novelty.

One solution to this problem is to predict how hyperreactive animals will differ from subjects with true intellectual deficits. Hyperreactive subjects should do poorly on simple tasks that change frequently, when under low drive, and on tests outside of the home cage which involve handling. Conversely, purely intellectual deficits should be pronounced only on difficult tasks, not on simple ones, and intellectually deficient subjects should be no more impaired than normal subjects when tests involve repeated introduction of novel stimuli. Furthermore, hyperreactivity should produce identifiable error patterns. Impaired performance should occur at task outset, moderating over time. Such impairment might involve balking, freezing, and higher response latencies on early test sessions, and may include withdrawal from test stimuli and increased defecation. Most important, timid animals should eventually habituate, in time attaining control group performance levels. In contrast, animals with actual intellectual impairment tested on a series of simple to complex tasks should not differ initially from controls, but should show increasing deficits as task difficulty increases. Such subjects should plateau at difficulty levels significantly below those of controls.

Fearfulness and withdrawal are not the only form of isolate response to novelty. Early stimulus deprivation may result in subsequent stimulus hunger, yielding enhanced exploration and a concomitant reduction in task-related behavior. This effect was found in a T-maze study of colony-caged adult rats that had been totally isolated for 90 days after weaning (Sackett, Keith-Lee, & Treat, 1963). Unlike socially reared controls, hungry isolates preferred stimulation over food on their initial trials. Ehrlich (1961) also reported enhanced lever pressing for light onset in isolate rats.

In addition to showing emotional effects, isolates may differ motivationally from controls. For example, prolonged isolation of monkeys has produced hyperphagia and polydipsia (Miller, Mirsky, Caul, & Sakata, 1969; Miller, Caul, & Mirsky, 1971; Fittinghoff, Lindburg, & Mitchell, 1971), with excessive drinking accompanied by excessive eating due to increased meal size. Hyperphagia can also occur in isolate rats, which often weigh more than nonisolated littermates (Morgan, 1973; Morgan & Einon, 1975). Although this may be partially due to activity differences, Shelley (1965) found that isolate rats ate more than group-caged subjects, even after the grouped rats were placed in isolation. Others have found that isolates eat more than group-caged rats during the day but not at night (Morgan & Einon, 1975; Morinan & Leonard, 1980), and still others have found that isolate mice eat more than controls throughout the 24-hour day (Giacalone, Tarsella, Valzelli, & Garattini, 1968; Weltman, Sackler, & Sparber, 1966; Miller, Pachter, & Valzelli, 1979).

Such heightened isolate food motivation can certainly influence test performance. Thus, Gluck (1971) found that isolate rhesus macaques pressed a lever more than controls for food under continuous reinforcement conditions. Morgan and Einon (1975) found that isolate rats shuttled across an open field for food more than did controls.

Responses to pain also appear to differ between isolates and controls. Melzack and Scott (1957) found that when isolate dogs were introduced to a novel environment they did not respond to pain with avoidance behavior. Lore (1969) also found that isolate rats had 60% more nose-to-candle flame contacts than controls when tested in a novel cage, but showed not such difference when tested in the familiar home cage. Increased emotionality in novel environments thus appears to alter isolate perception of, or reaction to, pain.

Although novelty can mask pain in isolate rats and dogs, under familiar test conditions isolate rhesus macaques may overreact to pain. Angermeier and Phelps (1971) found that isolate monkeys require lower levels of shock than controls to motivate match-to-sample performance. Isolate monkeys also displayed excessive withdrawal reactions to electric shock on their home cage water tubes (Lichstein & Sackett, 1971). However, these same monkeys tolerated much higher shock levels than controls when required to make a 2-sec shocked tube contact for access to water. Similarly, Seitz (1959) found that isolate cats, unlike controls, displaced an electrified wire cage to gain access to food put underneath the cage.

C. SPATIAL LEARNING IN MAZES

The only traditional learning task with a sizable isolate literature is maze performance. There are over 50 reports of rodent performance and a smaller number of carnivore studies. Since 62% of these studies used the Hebb–Williams maze, this task will be described next.

1. The Hebb–Williams "Intelligence" Test

The Hebb–Williams procedure (Hebb & Williams, 1946; Rabinovitch & Rosvold, 1951) was intended to be a rodent intelligence test. The apparatus is a large box with entrance and goal in opposite corners. Barriers can be placed in a variety of configurations between the entrance and the goal.

Subjects are usually deprived of food for 23 hours. The standard test series begins with 6 adaptation problems, followed by 8 trials on each 12 test problems. A subject's score is the number of dead end and repeat error zone entries summed for all 96 test trials.

Several features of the procedure merit comment. The 12 problems are extremely simple. The positions of start and goal are invariant, most dead ends are visible before a choice is made, and no problem involves more than 5 choice points. This yields a maximum of only eight possible error zones on the most complex barrier pattern. Because rats can learn mazes with 25 choice points (Cameron, 1928), and enrichment-reared (EC) rats average less than one error per trial, the test relates more to goal-directedness than to spatial learning ability. This is also suggested by the adaptation procedure. Criterion requires nine consecutive runs within 60 sec. This is essentially a reaction-time measure and may have little to do with subsequent behavior at barrier choice points. The test also requires handling before and after every trial, so emotionality may influence performance. As a new problem is given on each test day, novelty reactions could also affect performance independent of spatial learning ability.

Studies of factors influencing performance on the Hebb–Williams maze show that the test is reliable (Rabinovitch & Rosvold, 1951; Rajalaskshmi & Jeeves, 1968) and sensitive to many interventions. These include hypothyroidism (Davenport, Gonzalez, Carey, Bishop, & Hagquist, 1976), brain lesions (Ain, Lubar, Moon, & Kulig, 1969; Hughes, 1965; Rabinovitch & Rosvold, 1951, Schwartz, 1964; Smith, 1959; Will & Rosenzweig, 1976; Will, Rosenzweig, & Bennett, 1976; Will, Rosenzweig, Bennett, Hebert, & Morimoto, 1977), malnutrition (Tanabe, 1972; Wells, Geist, & Zimmermann, 1972), electroconvulsive shock (Greenough, Fulcher, Yuwiler, & Geller, 1970), and strain differences (Cooper & Zubek, 1958). This sensitivity to seemingly disparate variables suggests that performance is determined by many response and ability factors. For example, Rajalakshmi and Jeeves (1968) found that test scores correlated with visual discrimination and reversal performance. Pollard (1963) found very slow running times on Trial 1 of each new problem, even after prolonged adaptation. This was attributed to renewed situational reactivity after each 24-hour period between tests. Similarly, Barry (1957) found that when rats were not habituated to handling they avoided the goal area. Clearly, performance on this "intelligence" test involves more than spatial learning.

2. Carnivores

Early work at McGill University studied isolation-reared Scotch terriers (Clarke, Heron, Featherstonehaugh, Forgays, & Hebb, 1951; Thompson & Heron, 1954). Postrearing tests involved running around a wire barrier to reach food and an "orientation" task in which food was switched from one corner to another after every 10 trials. Isolates had long latencies, made many errors, and showed high response perseveration compared with socially raised controls. Isolates also made more errors on the Hebb–Williams maze, although their learning curves were identical to those of controls but offset by a constant amount over the 12 problems. Barrier test error and perseveration effects were also found by Lessac and Solomon (1969) for isolate beagles. These studies isolated subjects for most of the first postnatal year. A barrier task deficit was also found in puppies after only 1 week of isolation, however, from postnatal Day 28 to 35 (Fox & Stelzner, 1966).

Cats also appear to be affected on barrier problems (Wilson, Warren, & Abbott, 1965). All kittens were reared in the presence of mother and siblings. From postnatal Day 45 to 90 an "enriched" group received daily playroom experience, another group received daily handling, and an "isolate" group lived together in enclosed boxes. On the Hebb–Williams maze the enriched kittens made fewer errors than the other two groups.

These findings are important as they suggest that for carnivores either (1) maze performance is adversely affected by even nonsevere, short-duration deprivation, or (2) a brief period of daily enrichment is sufficient to improve performance. It is also likely that barrier task performance differences were a consequence of hyperemotionality. This characteristic was reported for isolates in each of the studies reviewed here.

3. Rodents

Table II lists all available rodent maze studies by type of isolated and control rearing, maze type, and outcome. Articles reporting significant effects in some experiments but not in others are listed in both columns. In 44 studies, isolated subjects performed more poorly than less isolated or enriched controls. Twelve experiments failed to find significant rearing differences. Three of these ran only a few trials on exceptionally simple tests (Greenough, Yuwiler, & Dollinger, 1973; LeBouf & Peeke, 1969; Peeke, LeBoeuf, & Herz, 1971). Another studied differences between two enrichment conditions, EC versus the same number of rats reared in glass boxes inside the EC environment (Forgus, 1955b). Six others employed importance departures from standard test procedures to be described below. Only two failures to detect isolation effects are without apparent explanation (Hughes, 1965; Woods, Fiske, & Ruckelshaus, 1961), although the Hughes study reported a deficit for brain-damaged but not sham-operated isolates. This analysis establishes a relation between isolation rearing and increased maze errors. The specific nature of the isolate deficits is less certain, however.

Increased isolate errors are accompanied by greater time to reach goal

TABLE II

MAZE PERFORMANCE OF ISOLATE RODENTS

Rearing conditions	Studies finding significant isolate deficits	Studies not finding isolate deficits
	Hebb–Williams Maze	
EC–IC[a]	Cummins *et al.* (1973); Dennenberg and Morton (1962); Eingold (1956); Forgays and Forgays (1952); Forgays and Read (1962); Hebb (1947); Hymovitch (1957); Smith (1959, 1972); Sturgeon and Reid (1971); Tanabe (1972); Wells *et al.* (1972); Will and Rosenzweig (1976); Will *et al.* (1976, 1977)	Reid *et al.* (1968); Will and Rosenzweig (1976); Will *et al.* (1977); Hughes (1965)
EC–SC	Brown (1968); Cooper and Zubek (1958); Dawson and Hoffman (1958); Dennenberg *et al.* (1968); Nyman (1967); Rabinovitch and Rosvold (1951); Schwartz (1964); Schweikert and Collins (1966); Woods *et al.* (1960, 1961)	
IC–IC	Ravizza and Herschberger (1966)	
	Other maze tasks	
EC–EC	Forgus (1955a,b); Walk (1958)	Forgus (1955b)
EC–IC	Bingham and Griffiths (1952); Einon (1980); Einon and Morgan (1980); Greenough *et al.* (1972a[b],b); Riege (1971); Rosenzweig (1971); West and Greenough (1972)	Davenport (1976); Greenough *et al.* (1973); Hoffman (1959)
EC–SC	Forgus (1954); Freeman and Ray, (1972); Greenough *et al.* (1972b); Henderson (1970a,[b] 1976,[b] 1977[b]); Hoffman (1959); Luchins and Forgus (1955); Ray and Hochhauser (1969); Rosenzweig (1971)	LeBoeuf and Peeke (1969); Peeke *et al.* (1971)
SC–IC		Meyers and Fox (1963); Rosenzweig (1971)

[a] EC, Enriched "playground"; SC, standard laboratory social cages; IC, isolation cage; IC–IC, isolation with and without climbing; EC–EC, enriched with and without restricted movement.

[b] Studies on mice; all others used rats.

areas (Will *et al.*, 1976, 1977; Greenough, Madden, & Fleischmann, 1972; Schweikert & Collins, 1966; Riege, 1971; Wells *et al.*, 1972). This slowing could be caused by excessive exploration, which would increase errors, or by enhanced timidity and "freezing," which might not affect errors. Distinguishing between these possibilities could identify one cause of isolate deficits.

The hypothesis that errors can arise from enhanced exploration was suggested by Woods (1959), who found that hungry rats often enter and then leave a goal box without eating. Isolate rats were found to be hyperactive in an open field, and the same isolates compared with SC controls made more Hebb–Williams maze errors (Woods, Ruckelshaus, & Bowling, 1960). When Smith (1972) repeated this experiment, however, within-group correlations between open field activity and maze errors were not significant for either isolates or controls. Even the hypothesis of increased isolate activity is questionable. Some studies did report this outcome (Smith, 1972; Woods *et al.*, 1960; Sackett, 1967; Morgan, 1973; Zimbardo & Montgomery, 1957), some reported no isolate-control activity difference (Brown, 1968; Hoffman, 1959; Forgays & Read, 1962; Freeman & Ray, 1972), and some even found that isolates were less active than controls (Denenberg & Morton, 1964; Duke & Seaman, 1964; Ferchmin, Bennett, & Rosenzweig, 1975; Manosevitz, 1970; Gill, Reid, & Porter, 1966).

Unfortunately, there are few reports of quantified activity levels during actual maze trials. Meyers and Fox (1963) noted anecdotally that isolate rats showed frequent fear-freezing reactions in both blind alleys and correct pathways of a five-choice point maze. Isolates were hypoexploratory in three studies using a four-arm maze with each arm baited, entering fewer arms than controls (Forgus, 1954; Luchins & Forgus, 1955; Hoffman, 1959). One study directly measured activity during tests on a complex maze (Holson, 1983). Isolates made fewer floor grid crossings than EC controls on the first of 3 test days. Taken together, these studies suggest that slow maze running by isolates is caused by timidity rather than curiosity.

Isolate timidity caused by neophobia should result in longer time to reach pretest adaptation criteria. Despite the routine use of adaptation in the Hebb–Williams paradigm, only two studies reported data on isolate behavior during adaptation (Reid, Gill, & Porter, 1968; Sturgeon & Reid, 1971). In both, isolates were slower to adapt than controls and made more test trial errors. When unusually rigorous adaptation was coupled with reduction to 80% of baseline body weight, however, there was no increase in isolate errors (Reid *et al.*, 1968). This finding suggests that prolonged adaptation coupled with high hunger motivation may eliminate isolate performance problems.

Total errors summarize the outcomes in most of these studies. Only three reports presented learning curves. Each showed errors declining over trials within a problem at an identical rate for isolate and control rats (Woods, 1959; Woods et al., 1960; Meyers & Fox, 1963). In two of these studies, isolates did make more errors. Relative to controls, however, their learning curves were simply offset by a constant amount, much like those reported for isolate dogs (Thompson & Heron, 1954). Furthermore, given prolonged practice, isolates eventually attain the same asymptotic performance levels as controls (Schweikert & Collins, 1966; Greenough et al., 1972a; Sturgeon & Reid, 1971). These learning curve data suggest that isolate rodent maze errors may have little to do with their actual spatial learning ability.

Types of maze errors were studied by Brown (1968), who analyzed trials where dead ends could and could not be seen before entry. Isolates had more errors than controls on both types of trials. On a different task, the radial eight-arm maze, both young and adult isolate rats made more errors than EC controls (Einon, 1980; Einon & Morgan, 1980). The young isolates used the strategy of going to the adjacent arm less frequently than the controls, but adults from either background did not. Furthermore, isolates could use extramaze strategies to locate the correct arm as well as the EC rats (Einon, 1980).

Another series of five experiments measured initial and repetitive incorrect arm entries and errors on first versus subsequent trials of each barrier problem (Will & Rosenzweig, 1976; Will et al., 1976, 1977). The only consistent finding was that isolates with sham lesions and controls did not differ on first-trial error rate. In two of the above experiments, isolates had a higher overall error rate. In two others, isolates made more repetitive, but not initial, errors. A final experiment found no group differences in either initial or repetitive errors. Clearly, no conclusions can be made from these studies concerning type of isolate errors.

While there are almost no observational analyses of isolate behavior in mazes, some investigators have manipulated aspects of the standard test situations. An important finding is that nonisolate rats depend on extramaze cues more than do isolates. Forgays and Forgays (1952) and Hymovitch (1952) ran the standard Hebb–Williams test, then retested after rotating the maze 90 degrees. Following rotation, EC rats made more errors than isolates. Brown (1968) compared the standard Hebb–Williams procedure with one involving 45° maze rotation after every trial. Isolates made more errors than EC controls in the stationary condition. Isolate performance did not differ between conditions, but EC rats made more errors with rotation. When tested with familiar versus novel observers standing outside an open field, EC rats showed more effect on motor activity than did isolates (McCall, Lester, & Dolan, 1969). This increased dependence on extramaze cues suggests that nonisolates have greater sensitivity than isolates to external events and a wider range of response to situational stimuli.

It is tempting to conclude that lack of prior learning to use external land-marks accounts for increased isolate maze errors. Yet isolates did more poorly than controls even when all extramaze cues were removed and the maze was rotated 180° after every trial (Ravizza & Herschberger, 1966). In addition, blinded EC rats performed better on the Hebb–Williams maze than blinded isolates (Hymovitch, 1952). Thus, although experienced rats may be more impaired than isolates when extramaze cues are invalidated, increased use of extramaze cues must not be the only source of EC supe-riority under standard test conditions.

A number of motivation studies suggest that under high drive isolates perform as well as controls. Rats were tested on the Hebb–Williams maze under food-deprivation or shock-avoidance conditions. All subjects did bet-ter on shock escape, with isolate-control differences occurring only under food deprivation (Woods et al., 1961). Isolate deficits, however, may di-minish with severe hunger. While most studies employed 23-hour depri-vation, some involved reduction of body weight to 80% of normal. Among 6 studies using such severe weight reduction (Riege, 1971; Will & Rosen-zweig, 1976; Will et al., 1976, 1977; Meyers & Fox, 1963; Reid et al., 1968), 4 failed to find isolate-control differences. Among 37 studies using less se-vere deprivation, only 6 failed to find an isolate deficit. These results yield a significant difference between outcomes of studies using reduced weight versus those using deprivation ($p < .02$, Fishers Exact test), suggesting that high hunger drive ameliorates isolate deficits.

Handling is thought to reduce fear and test reactivity in rats (Denenberg, 1975). Handled rats did not perform better than nonhandled rats, however, whether reared in IC (Denenberg & Morton, 1962; Bernstein, 1972; Green-ough et al., 1972a; Schaefer, 1957) or EC (Denenberg & Morton, 1962) environments. When handled IC and EC rats were compared directly, an isolate deficit was still found (Woods, 1959; Ravizza & Herschberger, 1966). Thus, effects of isolation seem to be independent of handling per se and, by implication, independent of fear and test reactivity.

A single study (Greenough, Wood, & Madden, 1972b) assessed effects of spacing trials rather than the massed trials used in all of the other studies reviewed here. IC, SC, and EC mice were tested on the Lashley III four-choice point alternation maze. Only SC performance was improved by spac-ing, so there seems to be no direct relation between spacing and degree of deprived rearing.

Overall these studies suggest two alternative explanations for isolate def-icits: (1) isolates have a conceptual difficulty learning spatial relationships, or (2) isolate maze difficulties result from neophobia. Neophobia seems to be ruled out for Hebb–Williams maze deficits because pretest adaptation is employed and handling does not reduce isolate errors. The failure of isolates to use extramaze cues and the superior performance of EC subjects even when extramaze cues are removed provides direct evidence for impairment of isolate spatial learning abilities. A cognitive explanation is also supported by anatomical evidence. Decreased cortical volume results from IC rearing, an effect most pronounced in the parietal region (Diamond, 1967; Diamond, Johnson, & Ingham, 1971). This area is involved in processing visual information and lesions in it produce deficits in rat maze performance (Will & Rosenzweig, 1976; Will et al., 1976, 1977).

Evidence for neophobia includes higher overall isolate errors without slower learning rates, eventual attainment of control asymptotic levels, no deficit under high motivation, and slow pretest adaptation. Along with isolate hypoactivity found in some studies, this outcome pattern suggests that some type of fear may conflict with error-free isolate performance. One study specifically addresses this neophobia issue.

IC and EC rats were run on three daily sessions in a complex alternation maze (Holson, 1983). Even on Day 1, both groups made errors at a rate significantly below chance. On Day 2 isolates began to shuttle between the goal and start box, making few errors in either direction but not eating the food rewards. After the same amount of testing, EC rats did not retrace, but went directly to the goal and ate. This suggests that isolates may have a food neophobia, an idea supported by several lines of evidence. In this experiment, IC and EC subjects often took food from the goal and transported it to a more remote area before eating. This behavior suggests a reluctance to eat in the goal area. Such enhanced food neophobia among isolates was also found in other studies (Morgan et al., 1975; Einon, 1980), and retreating from a goal without eating was reported by both Woods (1959) and Hebb (1949).

Fear of eating in the goal area may be enhanced by experimenter behavior. In standard maze procedures, each time the rat eats in the goal it is picked up and removed from the maze. This procedure could reinforce isolate fear, thereby prolonging adaptation to eating in the goal area. Lack of experimenter influence may explain the divergent result found using an automated Hebb–Williams maze (Davenport, Hagquist, & Rankin, 1970). Trials within each problem used the same barrier pattern, with goal and start area alternating direction from one trial to the next. Performance was observed over closed-circuit TV, so any association between eating and handling was removed. Using this procedure, Davenport (1976) found no isolate-control differences in five studies involving over 100 subjects.

In summary, the literature supports both cognitive and emotional interpretations of isolation deficits. The evidence is largely indirect, however, as no single study used procedures comparing predictions from both hypotheses. Furthermore, the test mazes used may be too simple to tax the excellent spatial learning abilities of rats. What seems needed are more complex spatial learning tests, observational data on both goal-directed and off-task behaviors, and procedures eliminating contact between experimenter and subject.

D. VISUAL DISCRIMINATION

Rearing kittens (Blakemore & Mitchell, 1973) or rat pups (Corrigan & Carpenter, 1979) with visual input limited to vertical stripes results in deficits on tasks involving horizontal stripe discrimination. This is caused by altered activity of orientation- sensitive visual cortex neurons (Hirsch & Spinelli, 1970). Such findings suggest that defects should also occur following deprivation of visual form, shape, color, or texture stimulation. It is therefore disappointing that (1) most discrimination studies involve isolates reared in wire cages with full visual access to laboratory or vivarium stimulation, and (2) all rodent studies comparing EC and IC rearing have used only simple light/dark discrimination problems.

1. Rodents

Table III summarizes the outcome of rodent discrimination studies by type of rearing condition and discrimination test. The effects of EC versus IC rearing (Table III, top section) are uncertain. No differences were found in four studies, while some isolate decrement was demonstrated in five studies. In other studies, the type of social environment was varied (Table III, upper middle sections). When tested on light/dark problems, SC subjects showed no disadvantage over EC subjects. On more complex problems, only a difficult discrimination between triangles and U-shapes versus circles (Forgus, 1954) yielded an SC deficit relative to EC performance. Little can be concluded because the discrimination tasks were generally simple, emotional reactivity or test adaptation problems were not reported, error analyses were not performed, and nontask behaviors were not observed. This is unfortunate because specific transfer studies provide evidence that prior experience affects later discrimination performance (Table III, lower middle sections).

Specific transfer studies typically house subjects together in settings that are identical except for specific stimuli, usually triangles and circles, attached to cage walls. Subsequently, exposed and nonexposed groups are tested on discrimination between these, or similar, stimuli. In most experiments rats with rearing exposure discriminated better than nonexposed animals. This finding is probably due to specific learning, since (1) rearing exposure effects do not usually generalize beyond the class of stimuli experienced (Gibson, Walk, Pick, & Tighe, 1958; Kawachi, 1965; Bennett,

TABLE III

Visual Discrimination (VD) Performance after Differential Rearing Experience[a]

Nonsocial stimulation	Test condition	Differential rearing has effects on discrimination	Differential rearing has no effects
		Social–isolation rearing conditions	
Standard EC–IC[b]	Black/white Light/dark	Greenough et al. (1972[c]); Greenough et al. (1973); Bernstein (1972, 1973); Edwards et al. (1969)	Bingham and Griffiths (1952); Gill et al. (1966); Krech et al. (1962); Bennett et al. (1970)
		Social–social rearing conditions	
Standard EC–SC	Black/white Light/dark Form discrimination	Forgus, 1954	Henderson (1972[c]); Dawson and Hoffman (1959) Henderson (1972[c])
Standard EC–SC Same stimuli in reading cage and on VD task	Form discrimination (usually triangle and circle)	Gibson and Walk (1956); Gibson et al. (1958); Kerpelman (1965); Bennett and Ellis (1968); Kawachi (1965); Meier and McGee, (1959); Bennett et al. (1970, 1971); Bateson and	Walk et al. (1958); Gibson et al. (1959); Walk et al. (1959); Oswalt (1972); Levitt and Bennett (1975)

Different stimuli in rearing cage and on VD task	Form discrimination	Chantrey (1972[d]); Bennett and Anton (1972); Bennett et al. (1972); Oswalt (1972); Levitt and Bennett (1975); Hall (1979)	Gibson et al. (1958); Kawachi (1965); Bennett et al. (1971)
		Gibson et al. (1958); Meier and McGee (1959); Bennett et al. (1971); Brown (1971); Brown and King (1971); Bateson and Chantrey (1972[d]); Bell and Livesey (1977, 1981)	
Isolation–isolation rearing conditions			
Same stimuli	Form discrimination	Forgus (1958a,b); Franken and Bray (1973); Ernst et al. (1976); Corrigan and Carpenter (1979)	Baird and Becknell (1962); Yeterian and Wilson (1976); Corrigan and Carpenter (1979)
Different stimuli	Form discrimination	Forgus (1958a,b); McCall and Lester (1969)	

[a] All studies on rats unless specifically noted.
[b] EC, Enriched "playground"; SC, standard laboratory social cages; IC, isolation cage.
[c] Studies on mice.
[d] Studies on monkeys.

Anton, & Levitt, 1971), (2) prior exposure at any age has comparable effects (Bennet & Anton, 1972; Hall, 1979), and (3) effects are seen with a variety of caging conditions (see Table III). Of special importance, exposed and nonexposed rats show similarly poor performance on early trials; group differences emerge only later (Walk, Gibson, Pick, & Tighe, 1958; Bennett & Ellis, 1968; Kawachi, 1965; Bennett et al., 1971; Oswalt, 1972; Ernst, Yee, & Dericco, 1976).

The nature of this specific transfer effect may reside in the relative novelty or familiarity of the test stimuli. Facilitation by prior exposure was most evident when testing occurred in a novel setting (Bell & Livesey, 1981), even though learning tests in a novel apparatus generally yield poor rodent performance. A novelty interpretation is also suggested by findings that prior exposure effects do not occur when rats are tested in a familiar apparatus (Walk et al., 1958; Bell & Livesey, 1977, 1981).

Effects of apparatus familiarity and prior exposure to specific stimuli may involve food neophobia. Kerpelman (1965) gave rats 2 or 22 hours of daily home cage exposure to circles and triangles in their home cages. Half of each group were fed with the stimuli present, the others with the stimuli absent. On later circle–triangle discrimination, exposed subjects performed better than inexperienced animals—but only when they had eaten in the presence of the cues. This effect was replicated by Bennett and Ellis (1968). As with reluctance to eat from a novel container (Mitchell, Scott, & Williams, 1973), rats may avoid novel stimuli serving as cues to food when such cues are presented in novel, but not in familiar, environments.

Specific transfer is also affected by novelty when exposure occurs to only one of two stimuli used on subsequent discrimination tests. Preexposed rats do better when the novel rather than familiar cue is rewarded (Walk et al., 1958; Bennett, Levitt, & Anton, 1972; Franken & Bray, 1973). Unlike the delayed effect of preexposing both positive and negative cues, this novelty preference occurs early in testing and disappears later. In monkeys such novelty effects are more general and pronounced: Preexposure to two test stimuli impairs, rather than enhances, monkey visual discrimination compared with the results of tests using novel positive and negative stimuli (Bateson & Chantrey, 1972).

These rodent studies clearly show that prior exposure to learning cues does transfer to discrimination performance. Relative familiarity of preexposed cues may be the stimulus attribute that is transferred, however, not specific form discrimination per se. Thus, for rats the presence of familiar cues appears to facilitate performance, perhaps by decreasing food neophobia in novel environments. As in maze performance, it seems likely that isolate rodents' deficits on simple discrimination problems result from novelty, not perceptual deficiencies.

2. Carnivores and Primates

Visual discrimination has also been assessed in carnivore and primate isolates. Neither isolate dogs (Fuller, 1967) nor cats (Wilson et al., 1965) had difficulty on black/white tests, which is not surprising as even visual cortex ablation does not abolish visual intensity discrimination (Bauer & Cooper, 1964).

Visual discrimination has been studied in rhesus macaques reared in total or partial social isolation from birth to 3, 6, 9, or 15 months. Two-object discrimination tasks in the Wisconsin General Test Apparatus (WGTA; Harlow, 1949) were used in several studies from the Wisconsin laboratory (Harlow, Rowland, & Griffin, 1964; Harlow et al., 1969; Harlow, Harlow, Schiltz, & Mohr, 1971; Rowland, 1964; Griffin & Harlow, 1966; Mason & FitzGerald, 1962; Gluck, Harlow, & Schiltz, 1973). No isolate deficits were found for either simple object discrimination or formation of object quality learning set. Isolates, however, required 4 to 50 times longer for WGTA adaptation than the typical 2–5 days for controls before actual learning trials could begin (Harlow et al., 1969). Two other studies tested rhesus macaque isolates on a match-to-sample task (Angermeier, Phelps, & Reynolds, 1967; Angermeier & Phelps, 1968). No isolate deficits were found using either shock escape or avoidance motivation. Thus, isolate macaques, like carnivores and rodents, apparently have no difficulty learning simple visual discriminations. Even when discrimination tests require concept formation, as in learning set and match to sample, monkey isolates perform as well as controls. Because no study conducted an error analysis, however, nothing can be said concerning qualitative differences in the way isolate and control monkeys actually solve complex problems.

A fine-grain analysis was made for isolate chimpanzee discrimination behavior (Davenport, Rogers, & Menzel, 1969; Davenport, Rogers, & Rumbaugh, 1973; Nissen, Chow, & Semmes, 1951). Isolates had no overall discrimination deficit, but their error patterns differed from those of controls (Davenport et al., 1969). Following extensive delayed response testing, subjects were given 78 six-trial, two-object learning set problems in their home cages. Despite slower adaptation, high distractability, and longer response latencies by isolates, over all problems they did not differ from controls in between-problem learning rates. Isolates responded differently, however, on the second trial of a problem. When the first choice was correct, isolates and controls continued to respond to that object. When the first choice was wrong, isolates had a significantly lower probability of switching to the initially nonchosen object on Trial 2. This suggests that isolate chimpanzees have a problem with reversal or response perseveration, but not with perceptual discrimination.

In summary, no mammalian species has difficulty learning simple two-choice visual discriminations following isolation rearing. The few deficits found probably result from effects related to novelty or reward patterns. Other than learning set and match to sample, however, few studies have involved difficult discriminations and none have involved a graded series of task difficulty tested to failure. Thus it is uncertain whether isolation does affect quantitative or qualitative aspects of higher order conceptual processes.

E. ODDITY LEARNING

One intellectually demanding test for primates is oddity discrimination, choosing the one stimulus that is unlike all others. Even adult monkeys and chimpanzees have difficulty mastering such problems (Harlow, 1959). Rogers and Davenport (1971) presented chimpanzees with four plaques covered with wallpaper designs. Three had the same design and one, which hid food, had a different design. The designs were switched on each of 50 daily trials presented over 34 days. The six isolates had an overall learning deficit, as did one of seven controls. Isolates and this single control also showed more perseveration, displaying strong position preferences regardless of oddity relationships.

Twelve rhesus macaques reared in wire cages as partial isolates were compared with 12 group-reared controls on 256 six-trial oddity problems (Gluck *et al.*, 1973). Testing began at 2 years of age, after the animals had been studied on visual discrimination and learning set. Despite no evidence of isolate-control differences on the earlier tasks, isolates were impaired on oddity. They had a lower overall probability of correct responses, but no difference in learning rate.

These primate isolate deficits occurred after extensive prior test experience. Thus, lack of adaptation is not likely to have been the cause. Since oddity is a difficult task for primates, these findings suggest that, given a sufficient challenge, isolates may have a true concept-learning deficiency.

F. MEMORY TASKS

Delayed response and retention of passive avoidance training are two tasks used to assess animal memory. A number of experimenters have exposed isolates to such problems, studying delayed response in primates and carnivores, passive avoidance in rodents.

1. *Primates and Carnivores*

Rhesus macaques that had been completely isolated for 9 months showed a small deficit on the first 400 trials of a 5-sec delayed response, but then improved rapidly to control levels (Harlow *et al.*, 1969). Later studies, however, failed to replicate this effect (Harlow *et al.*, 1971; Gluck *et al.*, 1973; Yeaton, O'Connell, & Strobel, 1978). Isolate chimpanzees were given tests with five stimulus objects. Indirect cueing was provided by a plaque placed over the object that concealed a reward (Davenport & Rogers, 1968). Twelve days of 100 daily trials included delay intervals of 0, 5, and 10 sec. Two isolates were dropped from the study for prolonged balking. The remaining five isolates were initially inferior to controls at all delays, but eventually were inferior only at the longest delay. Isolates also made more errors to stimuli at the ends of the linear array and at the outset of testing had longer latencies and balked more than controls. These effects appeared to be caused by heightened distractability.

In one carnivore study, Scotch terriers were tested on delays from 0 to 300 sec, but six of seven isolates did not even master the zero delay (Thompson & Heron, 1954). This result was attributed to inattention to the test stimuli. Since delayed response is probably more a test of attention than memory (Fletcher, 1965), these findings may only provide evidence for isolate hyperactivity or emotionality interfering with correct performance.

2. Rodents

Conflicting results have been found in studies of 24-hour passive avoidance retention in rodents. In one study, isolation facilitated retention: SC rats took longer to reenter a shock compartment than EC rats (Freeman & Ray, 1972). In three studies, no differences occurred between IC and EC rats (Kirkby, 1970; Davenport, 1976; Davenport *et al.*, 1976). In three other studies, isolate rats (Gardner, Bolfano, Mancino, D'Amico, & Gardner, 1975) and mice (Essman, 1970; Greenough *et al.*, 1970) showed retention deficits. These disparate results occurred despite similar rearing and test conditions. Although subtle rearing or testing differences may have produced these varied outcomes, taken together these studies provide no evidence for a primary isolate memory deficit, at least where 24-hour retention is concerned.

Spontaneous alternation and the Olton radial eight-arm maze may be sensitive to short-term, interference-generated memory problems, at least in hippocampal rats. Isolates have difficulties on the eight-arm maze (Einon, 1980; Einon & Morgan, 1980), but not necessarily with spontaneous alternation; Kirkby and Kirkby (1968) reported such deficits but that finding was not supported by Einon and Morgan (1978). Since eight-arm maze performance, like passive avoidance, is doubtless sensitive to emotional and attentional factors as well as memory factors, isolate rearing effects on memory have yet to be adequately tested. What seems needed are more careful assessments of both short- and long-term memory abilities of isolates.

G. Operant Responding

Operant studies suggest that isolating rats for 21–36 days starting at 5–7 weeks of age may have little effect on food motivation. After this rearing period, bar pressing on a continuous reinforcement (CRF) schedule did not differ between food-deprived isolates and IC controls (Ough *et al.*, 1972; Davenport *et al.*, 1976), nor were differences found for variable (Gibson, Gill, & Porter, 1968) or fixed interval schedules (Morgan & Einon, 1975). Longer isolation however (from Day 14 to 170), produced greater CRF pressing in isolates (Hitt & Gerall, 1966). Since nondeprived isolate rats press more for sucrose pellets than group-caged controls (Morgan *et al.*, 1975), this increased responding for food may involve accentuated hunger. Increased food motivation could also explain why isolates overresponded on a delayed response schedule rewarding low response rates (Ough *et al.*, 1972; Morgan & Einon, 1975). Increased CRF pressing for food was also reported for total isolate monkeys (Gluck, 1971; Gluck & Sackett, 1976).

In summary, isolates have no difficulty mastering simple reinforcement schedules. They may even have a food fixation leading to increased CRF responding. These findings are not established, however, owing to lack of replication, and no studies have addressed the causes of increased food motivation. This issue is important because increased isolate hunger could have effects on performance in many learning tasks.

H. Learning Paradigms Involving Inhibition

Good performance on a number of learning tasks depends on inhibition of unlearned or previously acquired behaviors. Foremost among these tasks are extinction and reversal. Studies using such tasks provide one test of the hypothesis that isolation rearing affects inhibition of high-probability responses.

1. Operant and Aversive Responding

Isolation can affect extinction in rats, dogs, and monkeys. After prolonged training on a VI schedule, isolates bar-pressed more than did SC controls during extinction (Gluck & Pearce, 1977). Similarly, rats learned to pull a ball out of a tunnel leading to food (Morgan *et al.*, 1975). IC subjects did this more frequently than SC controls when satiated and when food was no longer put in the goal. After IC and EC hypothyroid and normal rats learned to bar press for food, they were given a single 15-min extinction session. Hypothyroid, but not normal, isolates extinguished more slowly than their EC controls (Davenport *et al.*, 1976). Isolate mice responded longer than controls during extinction of a two-way shuttle shock avoidance response (Yen, Katz, & Krop, 1971). In another study, rats were trained with a warning buzzer followed by electric shock (Gibson *et al.,* 1968). Then the buzzer was presented without shock, interfering with bar pressing for food. Bar pressing was depressed longer by the buzzer in isolates than in controls. Slower extinction of response to an aversive stimulus was partially replicated using a unique situation (Angermeier, Philhour, & Higgins, 1965). Rats were trained individually to escape shock by running to one end of a straight alley. Isolates extinguished running more slowly than controls when tested in groups of three or four but not with one or two others.

In one study in rhesus macaques, total isolates and controls were food deprived and trained to press a lever for food, and then the food delivery was disconnected (Gluck & Sackett, 1976). Isolates pressed more than controls during the first of 3 extinction days. Melzack (1965) also found an extinction deficit in beagles. Following 9 months in isolation, subjects learned to press on a window to obtain food. The isolates pressed more than controls on six subsequent daily 20-min extinction trials.

These results suggest that isolates are slower to extinguish both appetitive and aversive responses. The cause could be enhanced isolate hunger and pain motivation or failure to attend to changes in reinforcement contingencies. In the latter case, isolates should also be unreactive to novelty. Since isolates are affected by novelty, their slower extinction is more likely caused by motivational factors.

2. Reversal

Isolate deficits are also seen in reversal learning. In extensive rat studies at Berkeley, the age at onset of isolation, and also the duration of isolation, were varied. Effects on reversal were measured by light/dark choices at each of four maze choice points leading to food. Isolates learned an initial light-positive discrimination as well as controls, and reversed to dark-positive at control levels. On a second reversal from dark back to light, however, a clear isolate deficit was seen if isolation had begun in the first 30 postnatal days (Krech, Rosenzweig, & Bennett, 1962; Bennett, Rosenzweig, & Diamond, 1970). Dawson and Hoffman (1958) also found no isolate rat deficit in learning a light-positive discrimination and reversing to dark-positive, but they did not present a second dark/light reversal.

Although light aversion could explain the Berkeley dark-to-light effect, isolate reversal deficits are found on other tasks. Isolate rats were slower than controls to reverse between two levers for food (Hitt & Gerall, 1966); to push rather than pull, or pull rather than push, a ball blocking access to food (Morgan, 1973; Einon, Morgan, & Kibbler, 1978); and to reverse maze pathways leading to food (Nyman, 1967). Similarly, on an aversive task, isolates took longer to reverse a conditioned avoidance response involving either light-to-dark or dark-to-light cue changes (Doty, 1972).

These studies provide evidence for a reversal deficit independent of type of motivation and response. Only one study failed to obtain this effect. Using a Lashley apparatus, Gill *et al.* (1966) trained rats to jump at a black or white card blocking entrance to a food compartment. Errors were punished by a fall into a safety net. Training proceeded to a criterion (39 of 40 correct responses), with balks punished by electric shock. When the positive stimulus was reversed, subjects fixated on the original stimulus for 180 trials. Another 320 trials were required for full reversal. No differences were found between isolates and controls, probably because of a ceiling effect as this task elicits extreme emotional reactions in rats (Maier, 1949).

Reversal deficits are also reported for isolate dogs but not for cats. Fuller (1966) trained beagles on a two-choice spatial discrimination, which was then reversed 12 times. Isolates were impaired on the first 3 reversals. In a subsequent experiment, isolates did poorly on reversal at a level not quite reaching statistical significance (Fuller, 1967). A single study of cats used a similar problem but found no group difference (Wilson *et al.,* 1965). This result may not be meaningful, however, as the isolate cats had been reared with mother and siblings, whereas the dogs were total social isolates.

Although reversal has not been tested in isolate monkeys, research in chimpanzees suggests that a deficit also occurs in primates. Subjects received a series of 40 visual discrimination problems, each followed by 10 reversal trials. By the time these tests were conducted, the 13-year-old isolates had been living in groups with socially reared controls for 11 years and had undergone thousands of trials involving delayed response, discrimination, and oddity learning. Despite their experience, the isolates showed poorer overall reversal performance and slower learning rates than controls (Davenport *et al.,* 1973).

In summary, the literature reveals an isolate reversal deficit across paradigms and species. This is especially interesting in view of contentions by Bitterman (1965) and Rumbaugh (1969) that reversal is the best single indicator of phylogenetic differences in intelligence. Thus, the isolate reversal deficit may identify a true effect on intellectual ability. Impaired reversal, however, can result from many problems, including excessive emotionality, and no studies have been designed to determine specific causes of the isolate reversal deficit.

3. Response Perseveration

A variety of other reports, many already reviewed, point to response perseveration as a basic cause of isolate performance deficits. This effect is robust, occurring across different tasks, motivation conditions, and species. For example, in a four-arm maze with all arms baited, isolate rats returned to the same arm more frequently than controls and were slower to adopt a novel route to a goal (Forgus, 1954; Luchins & Forgus, 1955; Hoffman, 1959). Perseveration has also been found in a nonreward situation, with isolate rats repeating, rather than changing, responses when tested for spontaneous alternation (Kirkby & Kirkby, 1968). A second study, however, could not replicate this result (Einon & Morgan, 1980).

Isolate perseveration is not limited to situations that elicit fear of novelty. Morgan and Einon (1975) used a delayed response task that involved lever pressing in one chamber, shuttling to an adjoining chamber, waiting a set time, then pressing a second lever. Isolate rats made perseverative errors involving several consecutive presses in the same chamber and anticipatory errors involving changing chambers before pressing. On a two-level win-stay, lose-shift task, isolates had a stronger tendency than controls to re-press a lever following nonreward rather than switching to the other level (Morgan et al., 1975).

Perseveration is also found in dogs and chimpanzees. Studies of simple spatial behavior showed that isolate dogs respond repetitiously to previously, but not currently, rewarded areas in an open field (Clarke et al., 1951; Thompson & Heron, 1954; Melzack, 1965). Isolate chimpanzees were slower to reverse an incorrect first response on visual discrimination tests (Davenport et al., 1969) and showed more perseverative responses in oddity learning (Rogers & Davenport, 1971).

Few studies have specifically addressed causes of isolate perseveration. Among the possibilities, fear can produce response fixation, low exploration, and decreased probability of reversing a response from familiar to novel stimuli. Enhanced fear, however, does not explain perseveration by well-adapted isolate chimpanzees in oddity learning, or lever perseveration of isolate rats on win-stay, lose-shift problems. Enhanced hunger could explain isolate perseveration during extinction of food-rewarded responses. An equivalent amount of reward under higher isolate motivation should result in a strong "habit," given the same number of learning trials as controls. This would produce perseveration of newly acquired behaviors under changed reward conditions such as extinction or reversal. But hunger motivation would not explain deficits in avoidance responding or increased suppression of food-rewarded responses by a warning stimulus. To incorporate these findings, a variety of motives, and perhaps emotional reactions, would have to be enhanced in isolates. Perseveration in off-task behavior, leading to prolonged isolate test adaptation, can be viewed more cognitively as resulting from lack of specific prior experience with response alternation. Thus, isolates may overlearn self-directed behaviors during rearing, which compete or interfere with the object-directed behaviors required for later successful learning performances.

In conclusion, it is not surprising that animals raised in temporally and spatially unchanging environments adapt poorly to change. Although mechanisms of such behavior remain to be elucidated, attempts to do so should prove rewarding. Perseverative responding also occurs after certain brain lesions (Brutkowski, 1965; Douglas, 1967), early malnutrition (Zimmermann, Geist, & Wise, 1974), and degenerative diseases of aging (Goodrick, 1968; Bartus, Dean, & Fleming, 1979). Identifying the causes of isolate perseveration may be important for explaining the general syndrome in addition to understanding isolate deficits.

I. AVOIDANCE LEARNING

Avoidance learning is the most contradictory aspect of the isolation-learning literature. Avoidance tasks have been especially popular in mouse studies. An isolate deficit in two-way avoidance, initially reported for several strains of mice (Valzelli, Bernasconi, & Gomba, 1974; Valzelli, Bernasconi, & Cusumano, 1977), was not replicated (Valzelli & Pawlowski, 1979). Another study using some of the same strains and similar rearing and test procedures also did not find an isolate deficit (Goldberg, Insulaco, Hefner, & Salama, 1973). In an earlier study, however, isolate mice learned a shock avoidance shuttle response more rapidly than group-caged controls and extinguished more slowly (Yen et al., 1971). A small avoidance deficit was reported for SC compared with EC rats (Ray & Hochhauser, 1969). Four other rat studies, however, failed to find poorer isolate performance (Ader, 1965; Parsons & Spear, 1972; Freeman & Ray, 1972; Eclancher & Karli, 1981). Using a different procedure, Reynolds (1963) tested isolates and controls for 30 days on shock escape, with five trials per day. Isolates showed higher escape latencies than controls and lost more weight. This finding is consonant with previously discussed work showing greater isolate reactivity to actual shock or anticipation of shock.

Three experiments studied avoidance learning in carnivores. In one, cats reared in isolation boxes with mother and siblings showed no difference compared with EC controls (Wilson et al., 1965). The other two studies demonstrated an isolation effect in dogs. Training prior to isolation protected against this deficit (Lessac & Solomon, 1969), which was probably caused by increased isolate freezing (Melzack & Scott, 1957). Increased freezing was also found in avoidance testing of rhesus macaque isolates (Rowland, 1964; Harlow et al., 1964). Freezing, however, did not prevent these monkey isolates from making as many correct shuttle responses as controls. Adult rhesus macaques that had been reared in total isolation from birth to 12 months were tested on a Sidman avoidance task, which required them to press a level to avoid shock when a light appeared on a TV screen. They learned the proper response as rapidly as adult wild-born controls (Miller, Caul, & Mirsky, 1967).

In summary, results of isolate studies using active or passive shock avoidance range from large deficits to actual improvement in learning rates. These conflicting results may not be accidental. They may be due to differences in isolate responses to shock and threat of shock. As reviewed earlier, isolates may be overreactive to pain. This would explain the enhanced isolate freezing found in some studies, and the finding that a warning CS suppressed bar pressing longer in isolates than in controls (Gibson *et al.,* 1968). Such hyperreactivity could result in better active avoidance performance or enhanced freezing, depending on the degree of fear evoked by a particular situation. In consequence, isolate avoidance might be either facilitated or impaired. Clearly, more must be understood about pain and fear responses in isolates before appropriate procedures for studying aversively motivated isolate learning can be designed.

This concludes the review of dependent measures. Table IV summarizes the overall results in terms of degree of certainty of reported effects in each species for each type of learning problem. These results will be discussed following a review of the effects of rearing condition variations on selected learning variables.

IV. Independent Variables

The isolation literature has focused on identifying deficits more than manipulating circumstances giving rise to deficits. Consequently, it is difficult to find evidence for differential effects of specific rearing variables on learning. The available studies involve variations in type and duration of isolation, issues concerning sensitive periods, and genetic factors.

A. ISOLATION TYPE

One aspect of isolation environments that may affect learning is transfer of specific rearing experiences to test situations. Some maze studies have been criticized for including maze experience as part of control enriched conditions, thereby producing a potential effect of specific prior experience rather than EC per se (Gluck & Harlow, 1971; Harlow *et al.,*1971). Thus the question arises whether isolation can influence learning irrespective of specific prior experiences.

Many studies that demonstrate isolate deficits did include rearing with simple mazes (Hymovitch, 1952; Woods, 1959; Woods *et al.,* 1960, 1961; Forgays & Read, 1962) or specific training on maze tasks in EC but not IC conditions (e.g., Bingham & Griffiths, 1952; Nyman, 1967). Other experiments did not include direct exposure to mazes, yet also found isolate deficits (Cooper & Zubek, 1958; Denenberg, Woodcock, & Rosenberg, 1968;

TABLE IV

EFFECTS OF ISOLATION DURING REARING ON LEARNING TASK PERFORMANCE

Isolation Effect	Rat	Mouse	Dog	Cat	Monkey	Chimpanzee
Slow adaptation	P[a]	P	In		Est	P
Maze deficits	Est	P	Est	In		
Isolate performance less disturbed by maze rotation	Est					
Slower to reach goal area	Est					
Isolate performance normal under high motivation	P					
Prior handling does not improve isolate performance	Est					
Hypoexploratory in simple mazes	In					
Spontaneous alternation deficit	Un					
Visual discrimination						
No deficit on simple tasks	Un	Un	P		Est	P
Specific transfer of some learning during isolation	Est				In	
No learning set deficit					Est	In
Delayed response deficit			In		Un	
Oddity learning deficit					In	In
Operant responding						
CRF differences	Un				In	
Slower extinction	Est		In		In	
DRL deficits	P					
Shock avoidance						
Deficits	Un	Un	P			
No deficits					P	
Passive avoidance deficit	Un					
Reversal task deficit	Est		In	No		In
Response perseveration	Est		Est			P
Motivation						
Hyperphagia	P	Est			Un	
Abnormal pain response	In		In		P	
Tend to approach on approach/avoid tasks					In	In
Deficits increase with severity of isolation	Est		P			
Early life sensitive periods	Est					
Specific deficits disappear with practice	Est	P			In	

[a] Est, Established finding (three or more confirming reports); P, probable (two independent reports); In, indicated (one unreplicated report); Un, uncertain (conflicting reports); No, effect tested for but not found.

Smith, 1972; Cummins, Walsh, Budtz-Olsen, Konstantinas, & Horsfall, 1973; Brown, 1968; Schweikert & Collins, 1966). Thus, specific maze experience does not appear to be a necessary condition for EC–IC effects.

On the other hand, specific early experience does improve maze performance. Forgays and Forgays (1952) compared isolates with socially caged rats that had been reared with barriers or in identical caging without barriers. The barrier group did best on the Hebb–Williams maze, but both social groups performed better than isolates. Brown (1968) reared rats in groups of 25 in boxes the same size as the Hebb–Williams apparatus. One social condition had no objects in the box, a second had "junk" objects in the box, and a third had actual Hebb–Williams barrier patterns. These subjects were all compared with rats that had been reared in triplets in much smaller cages. On later Hebb–Williams tests, rats reared in the actual maze did not differ from rats reared with junk objects. Both performed better than rats reared socially in the empty box. Most important, each 25-rat group had fewer errors than the 3-rat groups reared in the small cages. Similarly, Schweikert and Collins (1966) reared groups of 7 rats in a standard EC environment, a maze, or an empty box with a very low roof. On later Hebb–Williams trials, maze-reared rats ran as quickly as EC subjects, but required as many trials to reach criterion as the group raised in the empty box. The EC rats were superior to the empty box subjects on all measures. Finally, Bingham and Griffiths (1952) used a response alternation learning test to draw comparisons between EC rats reared with and without specific maze experience and IC subjects. The two EC groups did not differ from each other, and both performed better than isolates.

These studies established transfer of specific maze experience to later testing, a finding consonant with the effects of prior exposure on later visual discrimination. These findings also showed that specific transfer is not necessary for poorer isolate performance. Other studies also indicated that restricted physical activity of isolates is not responsible for deficits. Neither access to a running wheel (Hymovitch, 1952; Bernstein, 1973) nor reduced cage size (Morgan, 1973; Henderson, 1977; Bingham & Griffiths, 1952) influenced postisolation maze performance.

If specific learning and reduced activity do not fully account for isolate deficits, then what does? One possibility is that the degree of deficit is proportional to the severity, but not actual type, of experiential deprivation. Thus, when the number of rats was held constant across housing conditions in a number of studies, greater degrees of sensory deprivation produced greater deficits in maze performance (Sturgeon & Reid, 1971; Henderson, 1977; Forgus, 1954, 1955a,b; Luchins & Forgus, 1955; Walk, 1958; Schweikert & Collins, 1966; Brown, 1968; Cooper & Zubek, 1958; Hoffman, 1959; Nyman, 1967). This relation extends to rats reared in social isolation. Those with greater nonsocial stimulation do better on mazes (Hymovitch, 1952; Ravizza & Herschberger, 1966) and passive avoidance retention (Gardner et al., 1975) than those deprived of varied nonsocial input. Brain studies also show a positive relation between cortical weight and degree of nonsocial sensory stimulation in IC rats (Rosenzweig, Bennett, Herbert, & Morimoto, 1978). On the other hand, controlling for nonsocial stimulation, investigators have found that group-caged rats and mice outperform isolates on mazes (Forgays & Forgays, 1952; Meyers & Fox, 1963), reversal (Morgan, 1973; Hitt & Gerall, 1966), extinction (Morgan, Einon, & Moris, 1977), other inhibitory tasks (Morgan & Einon, 1975; Morgan et al., 1975), passive avoidance (Gardner et al., 1975), active avoidance (Valzelli et al., 1974, 1977), and shock escape (Reynolds, 1963).

These studies establish a quantitative relation between amount of rearing stimulation and performance on later learning tasks. It is not clear, however, whether this relation is caused by lack of specific learning or by more general changes in affect, inhibition, or arousal. For example, any rearing experience involving location of self and others in the larger environment could result in positive transfer on maze tasks. It is not obvious, however, how social experience can produce specific positive transfer on reversal tasks, where isolate deficits are more likely due to emotional reactivity.

B. ISOLATION DURATION

If isolation effects result from lack of specific learning, then relatively brief exposure to appropriate experience should protect against deficits. Results obtained by manipulating duration of exposure to enriched stimulation indicate that prolonged exposure is not necessary for good performance. Eingold (1956) found that continuous exposure of IC rats to enrichment from Day 50 to 60 produced as much improvement in maze performance at 120 days as exposure from Day 50 to 70. Similarly, Nyman (1967) found that maze deficits in SC rats were reduced by 1 hour of daily EC exposure for 10 days starting at Day 30, 50, or 70. The reduction was even greater if exposure occurred for 10 hours each day. Furthermore, no difference in maze performance was found following 2 versus 24 hours of daily EC given between Day 36 and 99 (Will et al., 1977). Even more impressive was Henderson's (1976) finding in mice, that one 12-hour exposure to EC had as much effect on maze performance as 6 weeks of continuous exposure.

Other experiments using brief periods of enrichment yielded similar results. Hymovitch (1952) gave IC rats 2.5 hours of daily EC exposure from Day 24 to 77, whereas Denenberg and Morton (1964) used the same procedure but for only 25 days. Both studies showed large positive enrichment effects, as did Tanabe (1972) , who gave IC rats 5 hours of enrichment daily from Day 25 to 60. These effects of brief enrichment are apparently not restricted to species with very short infancies. Exposure to a playroom for 5 hours daily from Day 45 to 90 was sufficient to produce significant differences on the Hebb–Williams maze at 120 days in otherwise socially reared kittens (Wilson *et al.,* 1965). On the other hand, Fox and Stelzner (1966) studied brief isolation rather than enrichment. They found that maternally reared dogs given a single week in isolation from Day 28 to 35 had deficits on simple barrier tasks begun at Day 40.

Stimulation-induced brain changes show lability comparable to behavioral effects. Differences in cortical depth and RNA were found after weanling rats received only 4 days of EC or IC exposure (Diamond, Ingham, Johnson, Bennett, & Rosensweig, 1976; Ferchmin, Eterovic, & Caputto, 1970; Zolman & Morimoto, 1965). Most significant, after a lifetime in isolation, 509-day-old rats tested for 21 daily sessions in the Hebb–Williams maze subsequently showed a significant increase in cortical weight (Cummins *et al.,* 1973).

In summary, brief periods of isolation or enrichment produce detectable effects on both brain and behavior. The finding that short periods of enrichment improve later learning in isolates supports the specific learning and transfer view of isolate deficits. The less well-established finding that brief isolation produces behavioral decrements in enriched animals does not support this position, however, unless EC subjects given isolation forget their previous learning as rapidly as IC animals learn from interpolated enrichment. Such symmetry in brief enrichment and isolation effects, if true, suggests some form of IC atrophy and EC activation as causal factors rather than functional mechanisms affecting learning or cognitive abilities.

C. SENSITIVE PERIODS

Attempts to demonstrate sensitive periods for isolation effects are subject to methodological problems common to long-term research (Schaie, 1965). Suppose that one group is isolated from birth through Month 3, and a comparison group lives in some control condition prior to later isolation from Month 4 to 6. If testing is done immediately after isolation, the age at test is not comparable and the preisolation experience may benefit the late isolates. If the early isolates are given control housing from Month 4 to 6 followed by testing, time between end of isolation and start of testing will be confounded. Furthermore, the control experience may have a different effect if it occurs after rather than before isolation. Thus, in any of these designs group differences cannot be unequivocably attributed to age at isolation. Resolution of these problems involves complex experiments in which some groups get equal exposure to the same experiences at different ages, while other groups have longer exposures that overlap those of the short exposure conditions (Nyman, 1967; Solomon & Lessac, 1968). Unfortunately, few studies actually meet these design requirements.

A more conceptual issue concerns demonstrations that enrichment and isolation produce effects late in life. Of itself, this finding would not exclude earlier sensitive periods. The earlier period must simply produce greater effects rather than being the sole temporal locus of effects as with critical periods. Studies of enrichment and isolation at different periods in the life cycle have addressed this issue.

Rats were isolated after being reared with mother and siblings in an EC environment or in a nest box without EC experience (Forgays & Read, 1962). The preweaning EC isolates had better maze performance. Superior maze performance was also found for rats that received EC versus nest box preweaning experience, even when all animals subsequently lived in small groups for a year prior to testing (Denenberg et al., 1968). This finding is impressive because there are only about 10 days between eye opening and weaning. The only negative report concerning preweaning EC (Smith, 1972) may have occurred because the pups were unable to locomote into the EC area through a door in their nest box lid.

Enrichment late in life also has established effects. Riege (1971) kept weanling rats in an SC situation for 310 days, then in IC or EC for 90 days. The late isolates had poorer maze performance than the EC rats. Will and Rosenzweig (1976) also found a late isolate maze deficit after group-caged 120-day-old rats were put in IC or EC for 60 days. These studies, however, did not determine whether the differences were caused by isolation, enrichment, or both. The results of a study by Doty (1972) are clearer. Rats were caged in pairs for 300 postweaning days, then tested before and after a subsequent year of EC or SC caging. The enrichment year improved reversal and passive avoidance performance. The group caging year had the opposite effect. Similar results were found for brain effects. Late IC and EC after as much as a year of group caging produced corresponding decrements or increments in brain weight and chemical activity (Rosenzweig & Bennett, 1978; Riege, 1971; Rosenzweig, Bennett, & Krech, 1964; Cummins et al., 1973; Cummins & Livesey, 1979).

These findings suggest that both brain and behavior respond to differential experience throughout life. As already noted, symmetrical effects occur for both IC and EC experience, not just improved performance following enrichment. These results argue against critical periods for isolation effects, but do not address the question of sensitive periods.

Several rodent studies using brief EC exposure provided evidence for a sensitive period centered around postnatal Day 50 (Forgays & Read, 1962; Nyman, 1967; Eingold, 1956). Enrichment at this age improved maze performance more than exposure earlier or later. These studies tested all subjects at the same post-EC age. The findings are especially impressive as the superior 50-day animals had a longer group-caged pretest waiting period than those given EC later in life. A similar effect was found for reversing visual discriminations. An IC deficit occurred when EC versus IC exposure was begun at 25 days, but not at 60 days (Bennett *et al.*, 1970). The single failure to replicate this effect had a design fault (Brown, 1968). Rats received EC exposure at 20–60, 20–100, or 60–100 days. The 60 to 100-day group, however, lived in a supplier's colony under unspecified conditions prior to entering the experiment.

In other studies of sensitive periods, experimenters have attempted to reverse effects of early IC and EC by changing to the opposite condition. These studies met with little success. Hymovitch (1952) reared IC and EC rats from Day 21 to 130 and compared their maze performance with that of rats reared in IC from Day 21 to 85 followed by 25 days of EC, or in EC from Day 21 to 85 followed by 25 days of IC. Late isolation did not reduce performance below that of rats exposed to long-term enrichment. Similarly, late enrichment did not improve performance above that of long-term isolates. Nyman (1967) exposed rats to EC for 1 or 8 hours per day at 30–40, 50–60, or 70–80 days of age and then exposed all subjects to 240 hours of EC during Days 100–110. The late EC exposure did not alter the original maze error differences among the early EC groups. Woods (1959) also reared rats in IC and EC for 130 days after weaning and compared them with subjects that had received IC from Day 23 to 65 followed by EC until 150 days. Hebb–Williams tests at 95 and 154 days showed that 30 days of EC were sufficient for early isolates to perform better than long-term isolates at 95 days. The performance of these enriched early isolates, however, was still significantly inferior to that of the long-term enriched rats when scores at both ages were combined. Bernstein (1972) conducted a similar study using an automated dark/light visual discrimination test. Rats isolated from Day 21 to 66 followed by 45 days of EC learned more slowly than rats that received early EC followed by IC. When 45 early IC days were followed by 90 EC days, however, subjects performed as well as those receiving 90 EC days followed by 45 IC days.

These remedial treatment results are not easily interpreted. Prolonged testing, without any change in housing conditions, also eradicates initial differences between isolates and controls (Bingham & Griffiths, 1952; Woods, 1959; Sturgeon & Reid, 1971; Dawson & Hofman, 1958; Bennett *et al.*, 1970). These prolonged testing studies do show rapid recovery from isolation effects. The results, however, could be test-specific; in none of these studies were the tests that demonstrated recovery followed by tests of different learning tasks.

Taken together, these studies offer evidence that there is a sensitive period in mid to late infancy during which the effects of early isolation or enrichment are demonstrated on learning test performance. The results show both stronger effect of rearing manipulations at specific early life periods and less reversibility of early versus later experience. These effects, however, have been reported only for rodents, many of the studies have not been replicated, and specific variables causing sensitive period and reversibility effects have not been identified. Future studies of these phenomena would be especially important for life-span development theories.

D. GENETIC DIFFERENCES IN ISOLATION EFFECTS

Genetic factors influence effects of isolation on learning measures. These are especially prominent for strains within a species and between closely related species. Henderson (1970, 1972) found large differences in the effect of isolation on maze performance in six inbred mouse strains. Differences between IC and SC mouse strains were also found for two-way avoidance performance (Valzelli et al., 1974, 1977; Valzelli & Pawlowski, 1979). Cooper and Zubek (1958) also found that Hebb–Williams maze performance differed between IC-reared "bright" and "dull" rat strains. Considering tests not specifically designed to study learning, isolate differences in social, emotional, and exploratory behavior have been found between breeds of dogs (Fuller, 1967) and closely related species of macaque monkeys (Sackett, Ruppenthal, Fahrenbruch, Holm, & Greenough, 1981). Large individual differences have also been reported between isolates of the same strain or species. Fuller (1967) found that some isolate beagles were normal on postrearing tests, whereas others, including littermates of the "normal" animals, displayed a full range of isolate characteristics. Large individual variability has also been found in isolate chimpanzees (Davenport & Rogers, 1970) and rhesus macaques (Clark, 1968).

Most isolation studies have ignored individual differences, considering them as "error" variance. This is unfortunate for at least two reasons. Marked genetic differences may reflect temperament or emotionality effects on learning performance (e.g., Fuller, 1967; Sackett, 1970; Valzelli & Pawlowski, 1979). If true, this would argue against interpreting isolate deficits as conceptual or specific learning problems. Furthermore, large genetic effects demand experimental designs controlling or manipulating heritable characteristics related to risk for isolation-rearing deficits. Such designs could facilitate identification of both genetic and nongenetic mechanisms that produce isolation effects and are required to generalize from animal studies to the human condition.

V. Conclusions

A. EMPIRICAL FINDINGS

Table IV summarizes all findings concerning isolation effects on learning task performance. Here we present the most important conclusions from those findings.

1. Isolation Rearing Affects Performance on a Wide Range of Learning Tasks

Nearly every type of traditional learning task is affected by isolation rearing. This is particularly true of mazes, where isolation deficits are found in all species studied. Isolation also produces a broad pattern of deficits involving inhibition of prior learning, but it is unclear whether these are caused by learning or performance factors.

2. Isolation Produces Similar Effects across a Wide Range of Mammals

The agreement found across species leads to reasonable confidence in conclusions drawn from this literature. Isolation impairs maze performance, reversal, and extinction of operant responses in every species tested so far. Moreover, all isolate mammals appear to be neophobic, and in many species isolates exhibit increased food and water consumption. Given this agreement, the prior conclusion of an increasing phylogenetic trend for the severity of isolation effects seems incorrect with respect to learning (Bronfenbrenner, 1968).

3. The Nature and Causes of Isolate Performance Differences Are Not Understood

This conclusion is the most important in this article. It was stressed in the discussion of maze performance and transfer of learning, and the reasons for reversal and extinction deficits are not any clearer.

4. Isolation Has a Greater Impact on Affect than on
Simple Learning Abilities

The historic hypothesis of a strong relation between early experience and cognitive-learning abilities seems implicit in the approach of Western science to education and personality. Twentieth century educational practices reflect a belief in the plasticity of conceptual ability; conversely, motivation and emotion are usually relegated to the sphere of personality variables assumed to be under strong genetic control. Results of isolation studies, however, point in the opposite direction. Although isolates differ from normally reared individuals in emotion, social behavior, and probably motivation, they have no difficulty in learning simple problems involving discrimination and may not even have difficulty solving more demanding problems such as learning set formation. Even if isolates are shown in future work to have true conceptual disabilities, these are likely to account for less performance variance than the emotional and social consequences of isolation.

5. Early Isolation Is More Damaging than Late Isolation

There appears to be a sensitive period for isolation effects in infant mammals that is not due simply to greater ignorance of the outside world. Increased susceptibility to isolation and benefit from enrichment seem to exist in developing as opposed to mature organisms. This is a conclusion with important practical implications and one which we propose with no little skepticism. Even equating for total exposure to specific experiences, early isolation has a more pronounced effect than late isolation. The evidence is often poorly reported, however, and the mechanisms are not well studied. Consequently, we know little about the true strength of this effect and nothing of its causes. Older animals may learn more slowly, and thus not benefit as much as younger animals from short enrichment exposure. On the other hand, young animals may actually be selectively and permanently impaired by experiential deprivation. These potentially critical findings are yet of little consequence without a more thorough experimental analysis.

6. Considerable Recovery from Deficits Occurs Shortly
after Leaving Isolation

Since recovery occurs even after severe brain damage, this finding is important only relative to prior conclusions that early isolation has devastating permanent consequences on social and emotional behavior of primates. Other important questions, however, remain unresolved. It is not known whether early isolation produces permanent asymptotic impairment of any single learning task. Little is known about the nature of recovery processes or effective therapeutic environments for reversing isolate learning deficits. All we can say is that with prolonged testing, isolates achieve criterion levels of performance.

7. Deficits Are Proportional to the Duration and Severity of Isolation

While this finding seems well established, it is difficult to interpret. It could imply that greater experience with stimulus change, novelty, and probabilistic contingencies yields greater general ability to solve novel learning tasks. It could also result from specific problems of isolates, still largely unidentified, affecting performance on specific types of tasks.

8. Genetic Differences Affect Susceptibility to Isolation Effects

This conclusion is almost a tautology; it would be remarkable if no genetic-environmental interactions affected isolate behavior. The point is not that such effects exist, but that they have hardly been studied. This is important because even if there were no overall isolation effects on specific abilities, subsections of a population might be prone to such effects. Designing genetic predisposition studies is a formidable task, however, especially when we know so little about the nature and permanence of isolation effects.

B. THEORETICAL IMPLICATIONS

With respect to Hebb's prediction of cognitive effects, we can conclude at the least that established isolate performance deficits are not due exclusively to cognitive problems. In fact, research since 1950 suggests that the principal effects of isolation are not conceptual at all. Hebb's thesis, however, has been poorly tested with respect to higher order conceptual abilities. The only direct positive evidence is the poor performance of isolate monkeys and chimpanzees on oddity learning. These data do fit Hebb's predicted isolate pattern of mastering simple tasks but having difficulty on conceptually more demanding problems. Even for this evidence, however, task analysis suggests that the isolate deficit is caused by response perseveration rather than inability to learn the oddity concept.

Melzack's proposal of isolate hyperreactivity to novelty does appear to explain at least some isolate effects. From mice to apes, isolate performance is characterized by prolonged test adaptation, avoidance of novel test stimuli, and high levels of balking. The finding that deficits are proportional to isolation severity also favors this interpretation. Hyperreactivity, however, does not explain all isolation effects. Isolate hyperphagia, response perseveration, transfer of specific prior learning, and performance failures after initial success seem to require other explanations.

The inhibition hypothesis, isolate unwillingness or inability to stop making appropriate high-probability responses, descriptively fits many findings. With the possible exception of extinction, however, most of these "inhibitory" deficits have equally attractive or overlapping alternative explanations. Problems with reversal learning may indicate an actual cognitive deficiency. Heightened fear and frustration can produce response perseveration. So, rather than an inhibition problem, perseveration may be due to hyperreactivity caused by neophobia. Finally, failure to inhibit may be a special case of a specific prior learning deficit, albeit one that seems to persist in the isolate's postrearing behavioral repertoire.

The atrophy hypothesis is the least well framed and consequently has been poorly tested. Reduced brain size following both early and late isolation does suggest a reversible atrophy mechanism. Atrophy, however, should produce permanent negative consequences, yet the data suggest that most, or all, initial isolate performance problems can be reversed by subsequent testing or enriched housing experiences.

All of these theories are alike in predicting that isolation will have a disruptive, possibly pathologial, impact on behavior. In contrast, lack of specific prior learning may account for many isolation effects. Rapidity of recovery as measured by attainment of criterion performance and the ameliorating effect of even brief postisolation enrichment support this view. Positive transfer of specific rearing experiences to later maze learning and visual discrimination also supports this position. Transfer effects may involve adaptation to novelty in the rearing environment, however, rather than specific prior learning about shapes, forms, or localizing stimuli in space. Thus, novelty enhancement may be the actual attribute that facilitates later learning. Sensitive periods for early enrichment or isolation are also difficult to explain in terms of specific learning. This theory would be weakened even further if future work provides definitive evidence for irreversible learning deficits. Unfortunately, the specific learning and transfer view, like the other theories, is supported mainly by circumstantial evidence, not by controlled analytical studies involving test-specific predictions from alternative hypotheses.

The assumption of sensitive periods in infancy for differential effects of experience is itself a theoretical proposition. The literature lends some support to this position, but the reversibility of sensitive period effects remains an important issue. If effects of severe early isolation on learning prove to be fully reversible, experimental interest in sensitive periods, and even in isolation effects in general, should disappear.

To summarize, only Melzack's novelty enhancement theory and the inhibition deficit hypothesis have been demonstrated in purposely designed experiments, and neither view, either alone or together, adequately explains many known effects of isolation on learning. Full evaluation of all these theories is hampered by lack of information about specific rearing and organismic variables producing isolate performance deficiencies. This poses difficulty for distinguishing between these alternatives and proposing other explanations.

C. IMPLICATIONS FOR EXPERIMENTAL DESIGN

Much of the research involving isolation effects on learning is weak in experimental design. In their discussion of work on early experience almost 30 years ago, Beach and Jaynes (1954) concluded that "much if not most of the presently available evidence . . . is equivocal and of undetermined reliability." Regrettably, intervening research has done little to alter this conclusion. Few investigators fully record, analyze, and report off-task behavior of their isolate subjects. Few systematic multiple-treatment or multiple-test analyses have been attempted. As pointed out by Rosenzweig (1971), few investigators have even attempted to replicate their own findings. Undoubtedly methodology can be improved, and toward this end we propose six recommendations.

1. Specific Test Deficits Must Be Analyzed More Thoroughly

Although a rearing variation may produce effects on a learning task, any of a large number of factors may be responsible. Studies are needed to determine which among these possibilities actually cause observed differences. In part this involves more careful behavioral observation and study of errors. On maze tasks, motor activity, behavior at choice points, and path retracing can be recorded. Similarly, reasons for errors such as side or stimulus preferences, responding to specific cues rather than relational dimensions, or responding on the basis of past reward rather than current stimuli can be uncovered by error analyses. While more thorough measurement and analysis are important, it is also necessary to design experiments to assess specific hypothesized isolate problems. For example, the hypothesis that isolate maze deficits are caused by food neophobia can be tested by providing novel or familiar rewards in novel or familiar containers.

2. Long-Term, Systematic Research Programs
Must Be Established

A single experiment is not likely to resolve any question of importance in this field. Yet the majority of published studies are by researchers who produced one, or at most two, articles before moving on to other problems. Among 50 articles on maze performance, 48% of the authors published only once on this topic, another 28% published twice. Untangling early experience effects requires complex long-term experiments to test specific hypotheses systematically. It seems unlikely that many profound advances will occur with the often hit-or-miss forays forming much of the work to date.

3. Genetic Factors Should Be Studied as a Source
of Variance

Interindividual variability in response to experiential deprivation is great. Measuring the extent of this variance and understanding its sources is not only necessary for controlling nonexperiential factors, but may reveal important causes of isolation effects on learning. Genetic background can be studied in most experiments, particularly those using inbred rodents. Matched-sibling control groups allow analysis of familiar or litter variance. In fact, most effects of isolation and enrichment on brain parameters are identifiable only when litter variance is controlled. Even in primate studies, paternal half siblings are easily produced. Since many of these primate studies take several years, using full siblings in experimental and control groups is not impossible. Thus, sex, strain, species, and kinship can all be studied as potential sources of genetic variance.

4. Experiments Should Invoke Testing to Failure on
Learning Batteries Graded in Difficulty

A primary issue is whether early isolation produces irreversible effects, or even any effect at all, on higher conceptual abilities. To resolve this issue, isolates and controls must be challenged by difficult problems after they achieve criterion on simpler tasks. This strategy can guard against type II statistical error. It can also determine whether early isolation is followed by full recovery or only partial compensation.

5. Learning Test Procedures Must Control for Effects
of Hyperreactivity

Failure to adapt to novelty can cause poor performance on any learning task. Experimental procedures must either minimize or measure novelty effects. This can be done by extensive adaptation and by purposely testing for effects of novelty. A little-used technique is to present learning problems in an automated home cage unit with which the subject is completely familiar.

6. Total Duration of Rearing Experiences Must Be Equated in Testing for Developmental Effects

Simply showing that early isolates with no prior nonisolation experience are different from late isolates with intervening experience does not demonstrate sensitive periods. A critical design requirement is that all primary groups have the same duration of isolation and nonisolation. For example, two groups of rodents might receive 90 days of isolation followed by 90 days of enrichment, or vice versa, while controls would receive 180 days of enrichment or isolation. Subsequent tests would reveal a sensitive period if one or both experimental groups differed from their control.

D. A MAJOR UNANSWERED QUESTION: ISOLATION FROM WHAT?

This article raises a number of methodological, factual, and theoretical issues concerning effects on performance caused by depriving mammals of varied experiences during rearing. Future research may well resolve important issues on the dependent variable side relating to learning. Such studies using standard total isolation treatments, however, will not tell us much about another fundamental developmental issue in this research area, namely, what rearing conditions are necessary for maximizing an individual's later cognitive abilities and attainments? For example, primate studies on behaviors other than learning suggest that social stimulation has greater quantitative and qualitative impact on development than does nonsocial stimulation. Similarly, it has been suggested that permanent hyperactivity in isolate rats is a result of lack of social play in early life (Einon & Morgan, 1977; Einon et al., 1978). A major question for human and nonhuman primate behavior is whether this will also hold for learning. If it does, a critical task will be to identify the specific features of social interaction that facilitate later learning and cognitive performance. Such ability maximization studies will undoubtedly require an interdisciplinary effort, including a systematic variation of social and nonsocial experience and manipulation of neuroanatomy and chemistry during and after rearing.

ACKNOWLEDGMENT

Work on this article was supported by NIH grants HD08633 and HD02274 from the NICHD Mental Retardation Branch and RR00166 from the Animal Resources Branch.

REFERENCES

Ader, R. Effects of early experience and differential housing on behavior and susceptibility to gastric erosions in the rat. *Journal of Comparative and Physiological Psychology,* 1965, **60**, 233–238.

Ain, B. R., Lubar, J. F., Moon, R. D., & Kulig, B. M. Effect of septal and neocortical damage on complex maze learning. *Physiology and Behavior,* 1969, **4**, 235–238.

Angermeier, W. F., & Phelps, J. B. Early experience and levels of noxious stimulation in monkeys. *Psychologische Forschung,* 1971, **34**, 246–252.

Angermeier, W. F., Phelps, J. B., & Reynolds, H. H. The effects of differential early rearing upon discrimination learning in monkeys. *Psychonomic Science,* 1967, **8**, 379–380.

Angermeier, W. F., Philhour, P., & Higgins, J. Early experience and social groups in fear extinction of rats. *Psychological Reports,* 1965, **16**, 1005–1010.

Baird, J. C., & Becknell, J. C., Jr. Discrimination learning as a function of early form exposure. *The Psychological Record,* 1962, **12**, 309–313.

Barry, H. Habituation to handling as a factor in retention of maze performance in rats. *Journal of Comparative and Physiological Psychology,* 1957, **50**, 366–367.

Bartus, R. T., Dean, R. L., & Fleming, D. L. Aging in the rhesus monkey: Effects on visual discrimination learning and reversal learning. *Journal of Gerontology,* 1979, **34**, 209–219.

Bateson, P. P. G., & Chantrey, D. F. Retardation of discrimination learning in monkeys and chicks previously exposed to both stimuli. *Nature (London),* 1972, **237**, 173–174.

Bauer, J. H., & Cooper, R. M. Effects of posterior cortical lesions on performance of a brightness discrimination task. *Journal of Comparative and Physiological Psychology,* 1964, **58**, 84–92.

Beach, F. A., & Jaynes, J. Effects of early experience upon the behavior of animals. *Psychological Bulletin,* 1954, **51**, 239–263.

Bell, J. A., & Livesey, P. J. The effect of prior experience with visual shapes under differing conditions of reinforcement on subsequent discrimination learning in the rat. *The Psychological Record,* 1977, **27**, 683–691.

Bell, J. A., & Livesey, P. J. Cue significance learning from differentially reinforced prior exposure to shape stimuli in albino and brown rats. *The Psychology Record,* 1981, **31**, 195–220.

Bennett, E. L., Rosenzweig, M. R., & Diamond, M. C. Time course of effects of differential experience on brain measures and behavior of rats. In W. L. Byrne (Ed.), *Molecular approaches to learning and memory.* New York: Academic Press, 1970. Pp. 55–88.

Bennett, T. L., & Anton, B. S. Critical periods for early experience in transfer of perceptual learning. *Perceptual and Motor Skills,* 1972, **35**, 743–746.

Bennett, T. L., Anton, B. S., & Levitt, L. Stimulus relevancy and transfer of perceptual learning. *Psychonomic Science,* 1971, **25**, 159–160.

Bennett, T. L., & Ellis, H. C. Tactual-kinesthetic feedback from manipulation of visual forms and nondifferential reinforcement in transfer of perceptual learning. *Journal of Experimental Psychology,* 1968, **77**, 495–500.

Bennett, T. L., Levitt, L., & Anton, B. S. Effect on exposure to a single stimulus on transfer of perceptual learning. *Perceptual and Motor Skills,* 1972, **34**, 559–562.

Bennett, T. L., Rickert, E. J., & McAllister, L. E. Role of tactual-kinesthetic feedback in transfer of perceptual learning for rats with pigmented irises. *Perceptual and Motor Skills,* 1970, **30**, 916–918.

Bernstein, L. The reversibility of learning deficits in early environmentally restricted rats as a function of amount of experience in later life. *Journal of Psychosomatic Research,* 1972, **16**, 71–73.

Bernstein, L. A study of some enriching variables in a free environment for rats. *Journal of Psychosomatic Research,* 1973, **17,** 85–88.

Bingham, W. E., & Griffiths, W. J., Jr. The effect of different environments during infancy on adult behavior in the rat. *Journal of Comparative and Physiological Psychology,* 1952, **45,** 307–312.

Bitterman, M. E. The evolution of intelligence. *Scientific American,* 1965, **212,** 92–100.

Blakemore, C., & Mitchell, D. E. Environmental modification of the visual cortex and the neural basis of learning and memory. *Nature (London),* 1973, **241,** 467–468.

Bronfenbrenner, U. Early deprivation in mammals: A cross-species analysis. In G. Newton & S. Levine (Eds.), *Early experience and behavior.* Springfield, Illinois: Thomas, 1968. Pp. 727–757.

Brown, C. P. Cholinergic activity in rats following enriched stimulation and training. *Journal of Comparative and Physiological Psychology,* 1971, **75,** 408–416.

Brown, C. P., & King, M. G. Developmental environment: Variables important for later learning and changes in cholinergic activity. *Developmental Psychobiology,* 1971, **4,** 275–286.

Brown, R. T. Early experience and problem-solving ability. *Journal of Comparative and Physiological Psychology,* 1968, **65,** 433–440.

Brutkowski, S. Functions of prefrontal cortex in animals. *Psychological Review,* 1965, **45,** 721–746.

Cameron, N. Cerebral destruction in its relation to maze learning. *Psychological Monographs,* 1928, **39,** (1), 1–68.

Clarke, D. L. *Immediate and delayed effects of early, intermediate, and late social isolation in the rhesus monkey.* Unpublished doctoral dissertation, University of Wisconsin, 1968.

Clarke, R. S., Heron, W., Featherstonehaugh, M. L., Forgays, D. G., & Hebb, D. O. Individual differences in dogs: Preliminary reports on the effects of early experience. *Canadian Journal of Psychology,* 1951, **5,** 150–156.

Cooper, R. M., & Zubek, J. P. Effects of enriched and restricted early environments on the learning ability of bright and dull rats. *Canadian Journal of Psychology,* 1958, **12,** 159–164.

Corrigan, J. G., & Carpenter, D. L. Early selective visual experience and pattern discrimination in hooded rats. *Developmental Psychobiology,* 1979, **12,** 67–72.

Cummins, R. A., & Livesey, P. J. Enrichment-isolation, cortex length and the rank order effect. *Brain Research,* 1979, **178,** 89–98.

Cummins, R. A., Walsh, R. N., Budtz-Olsen, O. E., Konstantinas, T., & Horsfall, C. R. Environmentally induced changes in the brains of elderly rats. *Nature (London),* 1973, **243,** 516–518.

Davenport, J. W. Environmental therapy in hypothyroid and other disadvantaged animal populations. In R. N. Walsh & W. T. Greenough (Eds.), *Environments as therapy for brain dysfunction.* New York: Plenum, 1976. Pp. 71–114.

Davenport, J. W., Gonzalez, L. M., Carey, J. C., Bishop, S. B., & Hagquist, W. W. Environmental stimulation reduces learning deficits in experimental cretinism. *Science,* 1976, **191,** 578–579.

Davenport, J. W., Hagquist, W. W., & Rankin, G. R. The symmetrical maze: An automated closed-field test series for rats. *Behavioral Research Methods and Instrumentation,* 1970, **2,** 112–118.

Davenport, R. K., & Rogers, C. M. Intellectual performance by differentially reared chimpanzees. I. Delayed response. *American Journal of Mental Deficiency,* 1968, **72,** 674–680.

Davenport, R. K., & Rogers, C. M. Differential rearing of the chimpanzee: A project survey. *The Chimpanzee,* 1970, **3,** 337–360.

Davenport, R. K., Rogers, C. M., & Menzel, E. W. Intellectual performance of differentially reared chimpanzees: II. Discrimination-learning set. *American Journal of Mental Deficiency*, 1969, **73**, 963–969.

Davenport, R. K., Rogers, C. M., & Rumbaugh, D. M. Long-term cognitive deficits in chimpanzees associated with early impoverished rearing. *Developmental Psychology*, 1973, **9**, 343–347.

Dawson, W. W., & Hoffman, C. S. The effects of early differential environments on certain behavior patterns in the albino rat. *The Psychological Record*, 1958, **8**, 87–92.

Denenberg, V. H. Effects of exposure to stressors in early life upon later behavioral and biological processes. In L. Levi (Ed.), *Society, stress and disease: Childhood and adolescence* (Vol. 2.). London and New York: Oxford Univ. Press, 1975. Pp. 269–281.

Denenberg, V. H., & Morton, J. R. C. Effects of preweaning and postweaning manipulations upon problem-solving behavior. *Journal of Comparative and Physiological Psychology*, 1962, **55**, 1096–1098.

Denenberg, V. H., & Morton, J. R. C. Infantile stimulation, prepubertal sexual-social interaction, and emotionality. *Animal Behaviour*, 1964, **12**, 11–13.

Denenberg, V. H., Woodcock, J. M., & Rosenberg, K. M. Long-term effects of preweaning and postweaning free-environment experience on rats' problem-solving behavior. *Journal of Comparative and Physiological Psychology*, 1968, **66**, 533–535.

Diamond, M. C. Extensive cortical depth measurements and neuron size increases in the cortex of environmentally enriched rats. *Journal of Comparative Neurology*, 1967, **131**, 357–364.

Diamond, M. C., Ingham, C. H., Johnson, R. E., Bennett, E. L., & Rosenzweig, M. R. Effects of environment on morphology of rat cerebral cortex and hippocampus. *Journal of Neurobiology*, 1976, **7**, 75–85.

Diamond, M. C., Johnson, R. E., & Ingham, C. Brain plasticity induced by environment and pregnancy. *International Journal of Neuroscience*, 1971, **42**, 171–178.

Doty, B. A. The effects of cage environment upon avoidance responding of aged rats. *Journal of Gerontology*, 1972, **27**, 358–360.

Douglas, R. J. The hippocampus and behavior. *Psychological Bulletin*, 1967, **67**, 416–442.

Duke, J. O., & Seaman, J. L. Postweaning experiences and emotional responsiveness. *Psychological Reports*, 1964, **14**, 543–546.

Eclancher, F., & Karli, P., Influence of rearing conditions on the acquisition of the two-way active avoidance responses by rats septalectomized at an early age. *Behavioural Brain Research*, 1981, **3**, 83–98.

Edwards, H. P., Barry, W. F., & Wyspianski, J. O. Effect of differential rearing on photic evoked potentials and brightness discrimination in the albino rat. *Developmental Psychology*, 1969, **2**, 133–138.

Ehrlich, A. The effects of past experience on the rat's responses to novelty. *Canadian Journal of Psychology*, 1961, **15**, 15–19.

Eingold, B. *Problem-solving by mature rats as conditioned by the length, and age at imposition, of earlier free-environment experience.* Doctoral disseration, University of Florida, 1956.

Einon, D. F. Spatial memory and response strategies in rats: Age, sex and rearing differences in performance. *Quarterly Journal of Experimental Psychology*, 1980, **32**, 473–489.

Einon, D. F., & Morgan, M. J. A critical period for social isolation in the rat. *Developmental Psychobiology*, 1977, **10**, 123–132.

Einon, D. F., & Morgan, M. J. Early isolation produces enduring hyperactivity in the rat, but no effect upon spontaneous alternation. *Quarterly Journal of Experimental Psychology*, 1978, **30**, 151–156.

Einon, D. F., & Morgan, M. J. Effects of postoperative environment on recovery from dorsal hippocampal lesions in young rats: Tests of spatial memory and motor transfer. *Quarterly Journal of Experimental Psychology,* 1980, **32,** 137–148.

Einon, D. F., Morgan, M. J., & Kibbler, C. C. Brief periods of socialization and later behavior in the rat. *Developmental Psychobiology,* 1978, **11,** 213–225.

Ernst, A. J., Yee, R., & Dericco, D. Effect of angle stimulation during development on adult discrimination ability in rats. *Animal Learning and Behavior,* 1976, **4,** 241–246.

Essman, W. B. Some neurochemical correlates of altered memory consolidation. *Transactions of the New York Academy of Science,* 1970, **32,** 948–973.

Favazza, A. R. Feral and isolated children. *British Journal of Medical Psychology,* 1977, **50,** 105–111.

Ferchmin, P. A., Bennett, E. L., & Rosenzweig, M. R. Direct contact with enriched environment is required to alter cerebral weight in rats. *Journal of Comparative and Physiological Psychology,* 1975, **88,** 360–367.

Ferchmin, P. A., Eterovic, E. A., & Caputto, R. Studies of brain weight and RNA content after short periods of exposure to environmental complexity. *Brain Research,* 1970, **20,** 49–57.

Fittinghoff, N. A., Lindburg, D. G., & Mitchell, G. Failure to find polydipsia in isolation-reared monkeys. *Psychonomic Science,* 1971, **22,** 277–278.

Fletcher, H. J. The delayed-response problem. In A. M. Schrier, H. F. Harlow, & F. Stollnitz (Eds.), *Behavior of nonhuman primates* (Vol. 1). New York: Academic Press, 1965. Pp. 129–165.

Floeter, M. K., & Greenough, W. T. Cerebellar plasticity: Modification of Purkinje cell structure by differential rearing in monkeys. *Science,* 1979, **206,** 227–229.

Forgays, D. G., & Forgays, J. W. The nature of the effect of free-environmental experience in the rat. *Journal of Comparative and Physiological Psychology,* 1952, **45,** 322–328.

Forgays, D. G., & Read, J. M. Crucial periods for free-environmental experience in the rat. *Journal of Comparative and Physiological Psychology,* 1962, **55,** 816–818.

Forgus, R. H. The effect of early perceptual learning on the behavioral organization of adult rats. *Journal of Comparative and Physiological Psychology,* 1954, **47,** 331–336.

Forgus, R. H. Influence of early experience on maze-learning with and without visual cues. *Canadian Journal of Psychology,* 1955, **9,** 207–214. (a)

Forgus, R. H. Early visual and motor experience as determiners of complex maze learning ability under rich and reduced stimulation. *Journal of Comparative and Physiological Psychology,* 1955, **48,** 215–220. (b)

Forgus, R. H. The effect of different kinds of form preexposure on form discrimination. *Journal of Comparative and Physiological Psychology,* 1958, **51,** 75–78. (a)

Forgus, R. H. The interaction between form preexposure and test requirements in determining form discrimination. *Journal of Comparative and Physiological Psychology,* 1958, **51,** 588–591. (b)

Fox, M. W., & Stelzner, D. Behavioral effects of differential early experience in the dog. *Animal Behavior,* 1966, **14,** 273–281.

Franken, R. E., & Bray, G. P. Prolonged duration of the "novelty effect" following prolonged exposure to a single discrimination. *Animal Learning and Behavior,* 1973, **1,** 233–236.

Freeman, B. J., & Ray, O. S. Strain, sex, and environment effects on appetitively and aversively motivated learning tasks. *Developmental Psychobiology,* 1972, **5,** 101–109.

Fuller, J. L. Transitory effects of experiential deprivation upon reversal learning in dogs. *Psychonomic Science,* 1966, **4,** 273–274.

Fuller, J. L. Experiential deprivation and later behavior. *Science,* 1967, **158,** 1645–1652.

Gardner, E. B., Boitano, J. J., Mancino, N. S., D'Amico, D. P., & Gardner, E. L. Environmental enrichment and deprivation: Effects on learning, memory and exploration. *Physiology and Behavior,* 1975, **14,** 321–328.

Giacolone, E., Tarsella, M., Valzelli, L., & Garattini, S. Brain serotonin metabolism in isolated aggressive mice. *Biochemical Pharmacology,* 1968, **17,** 1315–1327.

Gibson, E., & Walk, R. The effect of prolonged exposure to visually presented patterns on learning to discriminate them. *Journal of Comparative and Physiological Psychology,* 1956, **49,** 239–242.

Gibson, E. J., Walk, R. D., Pick, H. L., & Tighe, T. J. The effect of prolonged exposure to visual patterns on learning to discriminate similar and different patterns. *Journal of Comparative and Physiological Psychology,* 1958, **51,** 584–587.

Gibson, W. E., Gill, J. H., & Porter, P. B. Effects of differential rearing and levels of motivation. *Psychological Reports,* 1968, **23,** 771–774.

Gibson, W. E., Walk, R. D., & Tighe, T. J. Enhancement and deprivation of visual stimulation during rearing as factors in visual discrimination learning. *Journal of Comparative and Physiological Psychology,* 1959, **52,** 74–81.

Gill, J. H., Reid, L. D., & Porter, P. B. Effects of restricted rearing on Lashley stand performance. *Psychological Reports,* 1966, **19,** 239–242.

Gluck, J. P. *An operant analysis of the effects of differential rearing experiences in rhesus monkeys.* Unpublished doctoral dissertation, University of Wisconsin, 1971.

Gluck, J. P., & Harlow, H. F. The effects of deprived and enriched rearing conditions on later learning: A review. In L. E. Jarrard (Ed.), *Cognitive processes of nonhuman primates.* New York: Academic Press, 1971. Pp. 285–319.

Gluck, J. P., Harlow, H. F., & Schiltz, K. A. Differential effect of early enrichment and deprivation on learning in the rhesus monkey *(Macaca mulatta). Journal of Comparative and Physiological Psychology,* 1973, **84,** 598–604.

Gluck, J. P., & Pearce, H. E. Acquisition and extinction of an operant response in differentially reared rats. *Developmental Psychobiology,* 1977, **10,** 143–149.

Gluck, J. P., & Sackett, G. P. Extinction deficits in socially isolated rhesus monkeys *(Macaca mulatta). Developmental Psychology,* 1976, **12,** 173–174.

Goldberg, M. E., Insulaco, J. R., Hefner, M. A., & Salama, A. I. Effect of prolonged isolation on learning, biogenic amine turnover and aggressive behavior in three strains of mice. *Neuropharmacology,* 1973, **12,** 1049–1058.

Goodrick, C. L. Learning, retention, and extinction of a complex maze habit for matureyoung and senescent Wistar albino rats. *Journal of Gerontology,* 1968, **23,** 298–304.

Greenough, W. T., Fulcher, J. K., Yuwiler, A., & Geller, E. Enriched rearing and chronic electroshock: Effects on brain and behavior in mice. *Physiology and Behavior,* 1970, **5,** 371–373.

Greenough, W. T., Madden, T. C., & Fleischmann, T. B. Effects of isolation, daily handling and enriched rearing on maze learning. *Psychonomic Science,* 1972, **27,** 279–280. (a)

Greenough, W. T., Wood, W. E., & Madden, T. C. Possible memory storage differences among mice reared in environments varying in complexity. *Behavioral Biology,* 1972, **7,** 717–722. (b)

Greenough, W. T., Yuwiler, A., & Dollinger, M. Effects of posttrial eserine administration on learning in "enriched"- and "impoverished"-reared rats. *Behavioral Biology,* 1973, **8,** 261–272.

Griffin, G. A., & Harlow, H. F. Effects of three months of total social deprivation on social adjustment and learning in the rhesus monkey. *Child Development,* 1966, **37,** 534–547.

Gyllensten, L., Malmfors, T., & Norrlin, M. L. Effect of visual deprivation on optic centers of growing and adult mice. *Journal of Comparative Neurology,* 1965, **124,** 149–160.

Hahn, W. W. Some effects of group size on behavior and physiology of the rat. *Journal of Psychosomatic Research,* 1965, **8,** 455–465.

Hall, G. Exposure learning in young and adult laboratory rats. *Animal Behaviour,* 1979, **27,** 586–591.

Harlow, H. F. The formation of learning sets. *Psychological Review,* 1949, **56,** 51–65.

Harlow, H. F. The development of learning in the rhesus monkey. *American Scientist,* 1959, **47,** 479–485.

Harlow, H. F., Harlow, M. K., Schiltz, K. A., & Mohr, D. J. The effect of early adverse and enriched environments on the learning ability of rhesus monkeys. In L. E. Jarrard (Ed.), *Cognitive processes of nonhuman primates.* New York: Academic Press, 1971. Pp. 121–148.

Harlow, H. F., Rowland, G. L., & Griffin, G. A. The effect of total social deprivation on the development of monkey behavior. *Psychiatric Research Reports,* 1964, **19,** 116–135.

Harlow, H. F., Schiltz, K. A., & Harlow, M. K. Effects of social isolation on the learning performance of rhesus monkeys. *Proceedings of the 2nd International Congress Primatology,* 1969, **1,** 178–185.

Hebb, D. O. The effects of early experience on problem-solving ability at maturity. *American Psychologist,* 1947, **2,** 306–307.

Hebb, D. O. *The organization of behavior: A neuropsychological theory.* New York: Wiley, 1949.

Hebb, D. O., & Williams, K. A method of rating animal intelligence. *Journal of General Psychology,* 1946, **34,** 59–65.

Henderson, N. D. Genetic influences on the behavior of mice can be obscured by laboratory rearing. *Journal of Comparative and Physiological Psychology,* 1970, **72,** 505–511.

Henderson, N. D. Relative effects of early rearing environment and genotype on discrimination learning in house mice. *Journal of Comparative and Physiological Psychology,* 1972, **79,** 243–253.

Henderson, N. D. Short exposures to enriched environments can increase genetic variability of behavior in mice. *Developmental Psychobiology,* 1976, **9,** 549–554.

Henderson, N. D. The role of motor learning and cage size in the early enrichment effect in mice. *Developmental Psychobiology,* 1977, **10,** 481–487.

Hirsch, H. V., & Spinelli, D. N. Visual experience modifies distribution of horizontal and vertically oriented receptive fields in cats. *Science,* 1970, **168,** 869–871.

Hitt, J. C., & Gerall, H. D. Simple and complex learning in rats reared socially or in isolation. *Psychonomic Science,* 1966, **4,** 179–180.

Hoffman, C. S. Effects of early environmental restriction on subsequent behavior in the rat. *Psychological Record,* 1959, **9,** 171–177.

Holson, R. *The maze deficit in isolation-reared rats: A result of food neophobia?* In preparation, 1984.

Hughes, K. R. Dorsal and ventral hippocampus lesions and maze learning: Influence of preoperative environment. *Canadian Journal of Psychology,* 1965, **19,** 325–332.

Hymovitch, B. The effects of experimental variations of problem solving in the rat. *Journal of Comparative and Physiological Psychology,* 1952, **45,** 313–321.

Jensen, A. R. *Educability and group differences.* New York: Harper, 1973.

Kamin, L. J. *The science and politics of IQ,* New York: Halsted, 1974.

Kawachi, J. Effect of previous perceptual experience of specific three-dimensional objects on later visual discrimination behavior in rats. *Japanese Psychological Research,* 1965, **7,** 20–27.

Kerpelman, L. C. Preexposure to visually presented forms and nondifferential reinforcement in perceptual learning. *Journal of Experimental Psychology,* 1965, **69,** 257–262.

Kirkby, R. J. Early environment experience and avoidance learning in the rat. *Psychonomic Science*, 1970, **19**, 30–31.

Kirkby, R. J., & Kirkby, J. E. Note: Early environmental experience and spontaneous alternation. *Psychological Reports*, 1968, **23**, 1278.

Konrad, K., & Melzack, R. Novelty-enhancement effects associated with early sensory-social isolation. *Psychological Bulletin*, 1975, **82**, 986–995.

Krech, D., Rosenzweig, M. R., & Bennett, E. L. Relations between brain chemistry and problem solving among rats raised in enriched and impoverished environments. *Journal of Comparative and Physiological Psychology*, 1962, **55**, 801–807.

LeBoeuf, B. J., & Peeke, H. V. S. The effect of strychnine administration during development on adult maze learning in the rat. *Psychopharmacologia*, 1969, **16**, 49–53.

Lessac, M. S., & Solomon, R. L. Effects of early isolation on the later adaptive behavior of beagles: A methodological demonstration. *Developmental Psychology*, 1969, **1**, 14–25.

Levitt, L., & Bennett, E. L. The effects of crowding under different rearing conditions on emotionality and transfer of perceptual learning. *Behavioral Biology*, 1975, **15**, 65–72.

Lichstein, L., & Sackett, G. P. Reactions by differentially raised rhesus monkeys to noxious stimulation. *Developmental Psychobiology*, 1971, **4**, 339–352.

Lore, R. K. Pain avoidance behavior of rats in restricted and enriched environments. *Developmental Psychology*, 1969, **1**, 482–484.

Luchins, A. S., & Forgus, R. H. The effect of differential postweaning environment on the rigidity of animals' behavior. *Journal of Genetic Psychology*, 1955, **86**, 51–58.

Maier, N. R. F. *Frustration: The study of behavior without a goal.* New York: McGraw-Hill, 1949.

Manosevitz, M. Early environment enrichment and mouse behavior. *Journal of Comparative and Physiological Psychology*, 1970, **71**, 459–466.

Mason, W. A., Davenport, R. K., & Menzel, E. W. Early experience and the social development of rhesus monkeys and chimpanzees. In G. Newton & S. Levine (Eds.), *Early experience and behavior*. Springfield, Illinois: Thomas, 1968. Pp. 440–480.

Mason, W. A., & FitzGerald, F. L. Intellectual performance of an isolation-reared rhesus monkey. *Perceptual and Motor Skills*, 1962, **15**, 594.

McCall, R. B., & Lester, M. L. Differential enrichment potential of visual experience with angles versus curves. *Journal of Comparative and Physiological Psychology*, 1969, **69**, 644–648.

McCall, R. B., Lester, M. L., & Dolan, C. G. Differential rearing and the exploration of stimuli in the open field. *Developmental Psychology*, 1969, **1**, 750–762.

Meier, G. W., & McGee, R. K. A reevaluation of the effect of early perceptual experience on discrimination performance during adulthood. *Journal of Comparative and Physiological Psychology*, 1959, **52**, 390–395.

Melzack, R. The genesis of emotional behavior: An experimental study of the dog. *Journal of Comparative and Physiological Psychology*, 1954, **47**, 166–168.

Melzack, R. Effects of early experience on behavior: Experimental and conceptual considerations. In P. H. Hoch & J. Zubin (Eds.), *Psychopathology of perception*. New York: Grune & Stratton, 1965. Pp. 271–300.

Melzack, R. Early experience: A neuropsychological approach to heredity–environment interactions. In G. Newton & S. Levine (Eds.), *Early experience and behavior*. Springfield, Illinois: Thomas, 1968. Pp. 65–82.

Melzack, R., & Scott, T. H. The effects of early experience on the response to pain. *Journal of Comparative and Physiological Psychology*, 1957, **50**, 155–161.

Meyers, R. D., & Fox, J. Differences in maze performance of group versus isolation reared rats. *Psychological Report*, 1963, **12**, 199–202.

Miller, B. L., Pachter, J. S., & Valzelli, L. Brain tryptophan in isolated aggressive mice. *Neuropsychobiology,* 1979, **5**, 11–15.

Miller, R. E., Caul, W. F., & Mirsky, I. A. Community of affects between feral and socially isolated monkeys. *Journal of Personality and Social Psychology,* 1967, **7**, 231–239.

Miller, R. E., Caul, W. F., & Mirsky, I. A. Patterns of eating and drinking in socially isolated rhesus monkeys. *Physiology and Behavior,* 1971, **7**, 127–134.

Miller, R. E., Mirsky, I. A., Caul, W. F., & Sakata, T. Hyperphagia and polydipsia in socially isolated rhesus monkeys. *Science,* 1969, **165**, 1027–1028.

Misslin, R. Some determinants of the new object reaction of mouse. *Biology of Behavior,* 1982, **3**, 209–214.

Mitchell, D., Scott, D. W., & Williams, K. D. Container neophobia and the rat's preference for earned food. *Behavioral Biology,* 1973, **9**, 613–624.

Morgan, M. J. Effects of postweaning environment on learning in the rat. *Animal Behaviour,* 1973, **21**, 429–442.

Morgan, M. J., & Einon, D. F. Incentive motivation and behavioral inhibition in socially isolated rats. *Physiology and Behavior,* 1975, **15**, 405–409.

Morgan, M. J., Einon, D., & Moris, R. G. M. Inhibition and isolation rearing in the rat: Extinction and satiation. *Physiology and Behavior,* 1977, **18**, 1–5.

Morgan, M. J., Einon, D. F., & Nicholas, D. Effects of isolation rearing on behavioral inhibition in the rat. *Journal of Quarterly Experimental Psychology,* 1975, **27**, 615–634.

Morinan, A., & Leonard, B. E. Some anatomical and physiological correlates of social isolation in the young rat. *Physiology and Behavior,* 1980, **24**, 637–640.

Moyer, K. R., & Korin, K. H. Behavioral effects on isolation in the rat. *Psychonomic Science,* 1965, **3**, 503–504.

Munn, N. L. *Handbook of psychological research on the rat: An introduction to psychology.* Boston, Massachusetts: Houghton-Mifflin, 1950.

Nissen, H. W., Chow, K. L., & Semmes, J. Effects of restricted opportunity for tactual, kinesthetic, and manipulative experience on the behavior of a chimpanzee. *American Journal of Psychology,* 1951, **64**, 485–507.

Nyman, A. J. Problem solving in rats as a function of experience at different ages. *Journal of Genetic Psychology,* 1967, **110**, 31–39.

Oswalt, R. M. Relationship between level of visual pattern difficulty during rearing and subsequent discrimination in rats. *Journal of Comparative and Physiological Psychology,* 1972, **81**, 122–125.

Ough, B. R., Beatty, W. W., & Khalili, J. Effects of isolated and enriched rearing on response inhibition. *Psychonomic Science,* 1972, **27**, 293–294.

Parsons, P. J., & Spear, N. E. Long-term retention of avoidance learning by immature and adult rats as a function of environmental enrichment. *Journal of Comparative and Physiological Psychology,* 1972, **80**, 297–303.

Peeke, H. V. S., LeBoeuf, B. J., & Herz, M. J. The effect of strychnine administration during development on adult maze learning in the rat. II. Drug administration from day 51 to 70. *Psychopharmacology,* 1971, **19**, 262–265.

Pollard, J. S. More rats and cats in the closed field test. *Australian Journal of Psychology,* 1963, **15**, 52–56.

Rabinovitch, M. S., & Rosvold, H. E. A closed field intelligence test for rats. *Canadian Journal of Psychology.* 1951, **5**, 122–128.

Rajalakshmi, R., & Jeeves, M. A. Performance on the Hebb–Williams maze as related to discrimination reversal learning in rats. *Animal Behaviour,* 1968, **16**, 114–116.

Ravizza, R. J., & Herschberger, A. C. The effect of prolonged motor restriction upon later behavior of the rat. *Psychological Record,* 1966, **16**, 73–80.

Rawlinson, G. (Translator). *The History of Herodotus. Book II.* New York: Tudor, 1947.

Ray, O. S., & Hochhauser, S. Growth hormone and environmental complexity effects on behavior in the rat. *Developmental Psychology,* 1969, **1,** 311-317.

Reid, L. D., Gill, J. H., & Porter, P. B. Isolated rearing and Hebb-Williams maze performance. *Psychological Reports,* 1968, **22,** 1073-1077.

Reynolds, H. H. Effects of rearing and habituation in social isolation on performance of an escape task. *Journal of Comparative and Physiological Psychology,* 1963, **56,** 520-525.

Riege, W. H. Environmental influences on brain and behavior of year-old rats. *Developmental Psychobiology,* 1971, **4,** 157-167.

Riesen, A. H. Effects of stimulus deprivation on the development and atrophy of the visual sensory system. *American Journal of Orthopsychiatry,* 1960, **30,** 23-36.

Riesen, A. H. Excessive arousal effects of stimulation after early sensory deprivation. In P. Solomon, P. Kubzansky, P. Liderman, J. Mendelson, R. Trumbull, & D. Wexler (Eds.), *Sensory deprivation.* Cambridge, Massachusetts: Harvard Univ. Press, 1961. Pp. 34-40.

Riesen, A. H., & Zilbert, D. E. Behavioral consequences of variations in early sensory environments. In A. H. Riesen (Ed.), *The developmental neuropsychology of sensory deprivation.* New York: Academic Press, 1975. Pp. 211-252.

Rogers, C. M., & Davenport, R. K. Intellectual performance of differentially reared chimpanzees: III. Oddity. *American Journal of Mental Deficiency,* 1971, **75,** 526-530.

Rosenzweig, M. R. Effects of environment on development of brain and of behavior. In E. Tobach, L. R. Aronson, & E. Shaw (Eds.), *The biopsychology of development.* New York: Academic Press, 1971. Pp. 303-342.

Rosenzweig, M. R., & Bennett, E. L. Experimental influences on brain anatomy and brain chemistry in rodents. In G. Gottlieb (Ed.), *Studies on the development of behavior and the nervous system* (Vol. 4), *Early influences.* New York: Academic Press, 1978. Pp. 289-327.

Rosenzweig, M. R., Bennett, E. L., Hebert, M., & Morimoto, H. Social grouping cannot account for cerebral effects of enriched environment. *Brain Research,* 1978, **153,** 563-576.

Rosenzweig, M. R., Bennett, E. L., & Krech, D. Cerebral effects of environmental complexity and training among adult rats. *Journal of Comparative and Physiological Psychology,* 1964, **57,** 438-439.

Rowland, G. L. *The effects of total social isolation upon learning and social behavior in rhesus monkeys.* Unpublished doctoral dissertation, University of Wisconsin, 1964.

Rumbaugh, D. M. The transfer index. In C. R. Carpenter (Ed.), *Proceedings of the Second International Congress of Primatology* (Vol. 1). Basel: Karger, 1969. Pp. 267-273.

Sackett, G. P. Response to stimulus novelty and complexity as a function of rats' early rearing experiences. *Journal of Comparative and Physiological Psychology,* 1967, **63,** 369-375.

Sackett, G. P. Innate mechanisms, rearing conditions, and a theory of early experience effects in primates. In M. R. Jones (Ed.), *Miami Symposium on the Prediction of Behavior: Early Experience.* Coral Gables, Florida: Univ. of Miami Press, 1970. Pp. 11-60.

Sackett, G. P., Keith-Lee, P., & Treat, R. Food versus perceptual complexity as rewards for rats previously subjected to sensory deprivation. *Science,* 1963, **141,** 518-520.

Sackett, G. P., Ruppenthal, G. C., Fahrenbuch, C. E., Holm, R. A., & Greenough, W. T. Social isolation rearing effects in monkeys vary with genotype. *Developmental Psychology,* 1981, **17,** 313-318.

Sackett, G. P., Sameroff, A. J., Cairns, R. B., & Suomi, S. J. Continuity in behavioral development: Theoretical and empirical issues. In K. Immelmann, G. B. Barlow, M. Main, & L. Petrinovitch (Eds.), *Behavioral development: The Bielefeld interdisciplinary project.* London and New York: Cambridge Univ. Press, 1981. Pp. 23-67.

Schaefer, T. *The effects of early experience: Infant fondling and later behavior in the white rat.* Unpublished doctoral dissertation, University of Chicago, 1957.

Schaie, K. W. A general model for the study of developmental problems. *Psychological Bulletin*, 1965, **64**, 92–107.

Schwartz, S. Effect of neonatal cortical lesions and early environmental factors on adult rat behavior. *Journal of Comparative and Physiological Psychology*, 1964, **57**, 72–77.

Schweikert, G. E., & Collins, G. The effects of differential postweaning environments on later behavior in the rat. *Journal of Genetic Psychology*, 1966, **109**, 255–263.

Seitz, P. F. D. Infantile experience and adult behavior in animal subjects. II. Age of separation from the mother and adult behavior in the cat. *Psychosomatic Medicine*, 1959, **21**, 353–378.

Shelley, H. P. Eating behavior: Social facilitation or social inhibition? *Psychonomic Science*, 1965, **3**, 521–522.

Smith, C. J. Mass action and early environment in the rat. *Journal of Comparative and Physiological Psychology*, 1959, **52**, 154–156.

Smith, H. V. Effects of environmental enrichment on open-field activity and Hebb–Williams problem solving in rats. *Journal of Comparative and Physiological Psychology*, 1972, **80**, 163–168.

Solomon, R. L., & Lessac, M. S. Control group design for experimental studies of developmental processes. *Psychological Bulletin*, 1968, **70**, 145–150.

Sturgeon, R. D., & Reid, L. D. Rearing variations and Hebb–Williams maze performance. *Psychological Report*, 1971, **29**, 571–580.

Suomi, S. J., Harlow, H. F., & Novak, M. A. Reversal of social deficits produced by isolation rearing in monkeys. *Journal of Human Evolution*, 1974, **3**, 527–534.

Tanabe, G. Remediating maze deficiencies by the use of environmental enrichment. *Developmental Psychology*, 1972, **7**, 224.

Thompson, W. R., & Heron, W. The effects of restricting early experience on the problem-solving capacity in dogs. *Canadian Journal of Psychology*, 1954, **8**, 17–31.

Valzelli, L., Bernasconi, S., & Cusumano, G. Prolonged isolation and alcohol effect on avoidance learning in two strains of mice. *Neuropsychobiology*, 1977, **3**, 135–143.

Valzelli, L., Bernasconi, S., & Gomba, P. Effect of isolation on some behavioral characteristics in three strains of mice. *Biological Psychiatry*, 1974, **9**, 329–334.

Valzelli, L., & Pawlowski, L. Effect of *p*-chlorophenylalanine on avoidance learning of two differentially housed mouse strains. *Neuropsychobiology*, 1979, **5**, 121–128.

Walk, R. D. "Visual" and "visual–motor" experience: A replication. *Journal of Comparative and Physiological Psychology*, 1958, **51**, 785–787.

Walk, R. D., Gibson, E. J., Pick, H. L., & Tighe, T. J. Further experiments on prolonged exposure to visual forms: The effect of single stimuli and prior reinforcement. *Journal of Comparative and Physiological Psychology*, 1958, **51**, 483–487.

Walk, R. D., Gibson, E. J., Pick, H. L., & Tighe, T. J. The effectiveness of prolonged exposure to cutouts versus painted patterns for facilitation of discrimination. *Journal of Comparative and Physiological Psychology*, 1959, **52**, 519–521.

Wells, A. M., Geist, C. R., & Zimmermann, R. R. Influence of environmental and nutritional factors on problem solving in the rat. *Perceptual and Motor Skills*, 1972, **35**, 235–244.

Weltman, A. S., Sackler, A. M., Schwartz, R., & Owens, H. Effects of isolation stress on female albino mice. *Laboratory Animal Care*, 1968, **18**, 426–435.

Weltman, A. S., Sackler, A. M., & Sparber, S. B. Endocrine metabolic and behavioral aspects of isolation stress in female albino mice. *Aerospace Medicine*, 1966, **37**, 804–810.

Will, B. E., & Rosenzweig, M. R. Effêts de l'environnement sur la récuperation fonctionnelle après lésions cerebrales chez des rats adultes. *Biology of Behavior*, 1976, **1**, 5–16.

Will, B. E., Rosenzweig, M. R., & Bennett, E. L. Effects of differential environments on recovery from neonatal brain lesions, measured by problem-solving scores. *Physiology and Behavior*, 1976, **16**, 603–611.

Will, B. E., Rosenzweig, M. R., Bennett, E. L., Hebert, M., & Morimoto, H. Relatively brief environmental enrichment aids recovery of learning capacity and alters brain measures after postweaning brain lesions in rats. *Journal of Comparative and Physiological Psychology,* 1977, **91**, 33–50.

Wilson, M., Warren, J. M., & Abbott, L. Infantile stimulation, activity and learning by cats. *Child Development,* 1965, **36**, 843–853.

Woods, P. J. The effects of free and restricted environmental experience on problem-solving behavior in the rat. *Journal of Comparative and Physiological Psychology,* 1959, **52**, 399–402.

Woods, P. J., Ruckelshaus, S. I., & Bowling, D. M. Some effects of "free" and "restricted" environmental rearing conditions upon adult behavior in the rat. *Psychological Reports,* 1960, **6**, 191–200.

Woods, P. J., Fiske, A. S., & Ruckelshaus, S. I. The effects of drives conflicting with exploration on the problem-solving behavior of rats reared in free and restricted environments. *Journal of Comparative and Physiological Psychology,* 1961, **54**, 167–169.

Yeaton, S. P., O'Connell, M. F., & Strobel, D. A. Malnutrition and social isolation: Learning in the developing rhesus monkey. *Physiology and Behavior,* 1978, **20**, 125–128.

Yen, H. C., Katz, M. H., & Krop, S. Effects of some psychoactive drugs on conditioned avoidance response in aggressive mice. *Archives Internationales de Pharmacodynamie et de Therapie,* 1971, **190**, 103–109.

Yeterian, E. H., & Wilson, W. A. Cross-modal transfer in rats following different early environments. *Bulletin of the Psychonomic Society,* 1976, **7**, 551–553.

Zimbardo, P. G., & Montgomery, K. C. Effects of "free-environment" rearing upon exploratory behavior. *Psychological Reports,* 1957, **3**, 589–594.

Zimmermann, R. R., Geist, C. R., & Wise, L. A. Behavioral development, environmental deprivation, and malnutriton. In G. Newton & A. H. Riesen (Eds.), *Advances in psychobiology.* New York: Wiley, 1974. Pp. 133–192.

Zolman, J. F., & Morimoto, H. Cerebral changes related to duration of environmental complexity and locomotor activity. *Journal of Comparative and Physiological Psychology,* 1965, **60**, 382–387.

ARISTOTLE'S LOGIC

Marilyn Jager Adams

BOLT BERANEK AND NEWMAN INC.
CAMBRIDGE, MASSACHUSETTS

I. Introduction

Experiences are but the seeds of our knowledge. What we "know" or "understand" is the product of interpreting those experiences—of interrelating, interpolating, extrapolating, or, more generally, of constructing inferences on those experiences. It follows that, to the extent that we revere reality, we would like our inferences to be rational, or at least to have some means of recognizing when they are irrational. Herein lies the cultural importance of systems of logic. Systems of logic provide axiomatic, content-independent bases for assessing the validity of our inferences.

For reasons of both its history and its apparent simplicity, it has been the Aristotelian syllogistic logic, more than any other, to which we have turned to evaluate human reasoning. The verdict, upheld over thousands

THE PSYCHOLOGY OF LEARNING
AND MOTIVATION, VOL. 18

of years, is that for the untrained mind the inclination to follow the logic is at best slight. In Erickson's words, "For *most* syllogisms, the modal response is incorrect" (p. 41, 1978). Moreover, as all of us who have taught or taken courses in logic can attest, it is often only with considerable difficulty that the untrained mind can be trained to follow the logic of the syllogism.

From such observations, one might conclude that people are fundamentally irrational. Indeed, it has been argued that from a psychological perspective, the logic is artificial and irrelevant, that thought responds not to such formalities but to knowledge-based pragmatic constraints. More recently, however, psychologists have tended to endorse a different position. People's errors, they have argued, stem not from any difficulties with the logic per se, but from other processes that are necessarily involved in interpreting and solving the syllogisms. It is, for example, well documented that people suffer interpretive biases due to mismatches between the formal and everyday significance of the logic's language. Moreover, it has been argued that the operations required for encoding and interrelating the premise information are sufficiently complex that they may critically tax the reasoner's processing capacity such that would-be-sound deductions are distorted or aborted.

Neither of these classes of excuses is very satisfying. The logic does, after all, delineate the conclusions that may and may not be legitimately drawn from an argument. If reason were truly impervious to the laws of logic, then no one could have proper justification to say so. Similarly, it is of little comfort to assert that our thought processes are fundamentally obedient to the laws of logic while qualifying that, for reasons of confusion or capacity, our thoughts are not.

The latter tack is all the more unsettling when we consider that Aristotle intended the syllogisms to represent the most elementary of possible arguments. The basic propositions of the logic correspond to the simplest dyadic relations: They assert nothing more than that all or some of one class is or is not related to all or some of another. Furthermore, as the syllogisms consist of but three such propositions, two premises and a conclusion, they correspond to the simplest implicative chains. If, as Aristotle argued [*Analytica Priora (AP)* I,23, I,25],[1] every valid argument consists, at core, of nothing more than a chain of these simple syllogisms, and if we do not possess the interpretive wherewithal to follow the syllogisms when

---

[1]Reference to Aristotle's work will include the title of the treatise followed by the number of the relevant chapter or, in the case of the *Analytica Priora*, the relevant book and chapter. For direct quotes, page and column citations are also included. The titles of the treatises are abbreviated in subsequent mention.

presented one by one, what are we to expect of our capacity for more natural complex arguments?

Moreover, confusion about Aristotelian logic is not the sole prerogative of the casual reasoner. Consider the very basic question of how many of the pairs of simple propositions yield valid conclusions. According to Wason and Johnson-Laird (1972), the answer is 27; according to Erickson (1974), Langer (1953), and Lemmon (1965), it is 24; according to Guyote and Sternberg (1981), Mates (1972), Prior (1973), and Revlis (1975a), it is 19; and according to the *McGraw-Hill Encyclopedia of Science and Technology* (1960), it is 15. Could it be that after thousands of years of trying to train ourselves to analyze the arguments validly, we still don't know how many valid forms there are? If we don't know how many, we can't possibly know which.

The fact of these discrepancies raises the possibility that the apparent irreconcilability of logic and thought may derive in part from some fault with the logic or at least its presentation. It is to this possibility that the present article is addressed.

The body of the article is divided into three major sections. Section II presents a review of the logic with the purpose of establishing the sources and significance of the differences over its interpretation. The purpose of Section III is to review prominent theories of the psychology of syllogistic reasoning and to extract from them the major classes of difficulty that beset the human reasoner. Finally, in Section IV, these difficulties will be examined against our clarified understanding of the essentials of the logic. The goal will be to discern which of the difficulties must indeed reflect weaknesses in our logical dispositions and which might be alleviated through changes in the presentation of the logic.

II. How Many Syllogisms Are Valid?

A. A REVIEW OF THE LOGIC

The building blocks of the logic are simple propositions. Not all sentences are propositions, Aristotle explained, "only such are propositions as have in them either truth or falsity" [*De Interpretatione* (*DI*) 4,17a]. Moreover, of propositions there are only two kinds: simple and composite. A simple proposition is "that which asserts or denies something [a predicate] of something [a subject]" (*DI* 5,17a). A composite proposition is nothing more than a compounding of simple propositions.

Aristotle further recognized that, besides being either positive or negative, the character of simple propositions may differ in quantity, as the intended scope of the predicate may be either *universal*, applying to all instances subtended by the subject, or *particular*, applying to but some subset of those. There thus result just four basic propositional frames, as shown in Table I. Through tradition, the universal and particular affirmative frames are labeled *A* and *I*, respectively, from the mnemonic *AFFIRMO*, and expressed as "All (subject) are (predicate)" and "Some (subject) are (predicate)." Analogously, the two negative frames are designated *E* and *O*, from the mnemonic N*E*G*O*, and expressed as "No (subject) are (predicate)" and "Some (subject) are not (predicate)."

A syllogism was introduced by Aristotle as "discourse in which, certain things being stated, something other than what is stated follows of necessity from their being so" (*AP* I,1,24b). So described, "syllogism" would seem to be a synonym for "valid argument." As Aristotle had it, however, most valid arguments are more complex than syllogisms. More precisely, most valid arguments consist of *chains* of syllogisms. Syllogisms include only those minimal arguments that logically establish a new relationship between just two terms by means of a relationship that each is known to hold with some third or intermediate term (*AP* I,23).

Formally, then, a syllogism must consist of two premises: one connecting each of the terms in question to the intermediate term (*AP* I,25). Inasmuch as the intermediate term must occur as either the subject or the predicate of each premise, a syllogism may be configured in any of four ways, as shown in Table II. Notably, Aristotle recognized only the first three of these syllogistic figures. Whether he omitted the fourth from his system through insight or oversight has been a matter of much controversy.

Accepting all four figures for the time being and allowing that each of their premises can be filled out with any of the four propositional frames, the syllogism is seen to admit just 64 different pairs of premises. The force of the theory derives from the claim that to specify which of these few pairs of premises yield valid conclusions would be to establish an axiomatic system that was sufficient for evaluating the validity of any argument.

1. The Principal Problem

But why has it been so difficult to establish which of the 64 pairs of premises yield valid conclusions? The principal reason is that, whereas the

TABLE I

THE FOUR TYPES OF CATEGORICAL PROPOSITIONS

A	(Universal affirmative):	All (subject) are (predicate)
I	(Particular affirmative):	Some (subject) are (predicate)
O	(Particular negative):	Some (subject) are not (predicate)
E	(Universal negative):	No (subject) are (predicate)

TABLE II

THE FOUR POSSIBLE COMBINATIONS OF SUBJECT–PREDICATE
ARRANGEMENTS OF TWO END TERMS (A AND C) AND A MIDDLE TERM (B)
ACROSS THE TWO PREMISES OF A SYLLOGISTIC ARGUMENT

	Figure 1	Figure 2	Figure 3	Figure 4
Premise 1:	B–A	A–B	B–A	A–B
Premise 2:	C–B	C–B	B–C	B–C
	(Conclusion)	(Conclusion)	(Conclusion)	(Conclusion)

conclusions that follow necessarily from a pair of premises depend on the
minimal relationships that can be established between its terms, those relationships bear an ambiguous correspondence to the premises. For example, whether the premise "All A are B" is seen to entail that "All B are
A" depends on whether A is understood to be equivalent or subordinate
to B. Similarly, "Some A are B" may or may not be seen to entail that
"Some A are not B" or that "Some B are not A."

Euler, while conducting a correspondence course with a German princess,
recognized this problem and invented a set of five diagrams to help her out
(Woodworth, 1938). (This is believed to be the earliest documented evidence
that it is not only the "common man" who had had difficulty with the
logic.) These five diagrams represent all possible relationships that may obtain between two sets. They are shown, together with their consistent propositions, in Table III. A glance at this table reveals the source of the
confusion. Only one of the propositions, "No A are B," is uniquely as-

TABLE III

THE CORRESPONDENCE BETWEEN THE FOUR CATEGORICAL PROPOSITIONS
AND THE FIVE RELATIONS THAT MAY OBTAIN BETWEEN TWO SETS

Propositions	Euler Diagrams				
A: All A are B	+	+			
I: Some A are B	+	+	+	+	
O: Some A are not B			+	+	+
E: No A are B					+

sociated with just one of the five set relations, and none of the five set relations is uniquely associated with just one of the propositions.

Not surprisingly, a failure to consider the complete range of set relations that is consistent with a given premise has been found to be a common source of error in syllogistic reasoning (Ceraso & Provitera, 1971; Erickson, 1974, 1978; Neimark & Chapman, 1975). Having done so, however, an even less tractable problem arises in the requirement that, in order to deduce the conclusion of a syllogism, the reasoner must consider all combinations of set relations that are consistent with its *combined* premises. To gain some insight into the difficulty of this task, you are challenged to deduce the conclusion to the premises "Some *B* are *A* and no *C* are *B*." To help you out, I have depicted the set relations corresponding to the combined premises in Fig. 1. All you have to do is study the diagrams and determine whether a valid conclusion about the relation between *A* and *C* exists and, if so, what it is.

It is apparently this problem of generating combined interpretations of the premises that, above all others, has plagued students of the syllogism. It has proved to be a potent factor in psychological studies of syllogistic reasoning (Erickson, 1974; Johnson-Laird & Steedman, 1978; Guyote & Sternberg, 1981), and it seems that even Aristotle fell victim to it as he explicitly denied the validity of several syllogisms only to resurrect them in a (possibly postdated) addendum to his text. In this vein, Johnson-Laird (1982) has noted,

> Whenever I have presented a reasoning problem informally, I have noticed the difficulties that people get themselves into if they use Euler circles. The problem is that there is no simple algorithm for using them that one can learn like one learns, say, the algorithm for long multiplication. Merely drawing circles does not guarantee that all their

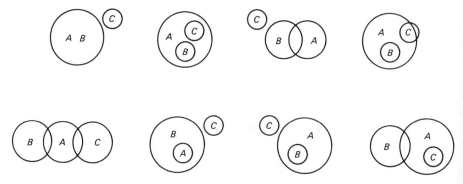

Fig. 1. Set relations corresponding to the premises "Some *B* are *A* and no *C* are *B*." By studying these diagrams, can you determine the conclusion?

possible combinations will be considered exhaustively. The same problem applies to the notation that I have invented for depicting the structure of mental models; if there were a simple algorithm, then doubtless most of us would have mastered it when we first learned to reason. (p. 26)

2. A Solution to the Problem

But a straightforward solution to this problem can be invented. Indeed, it follows directly from the Euler diagrams. Specifically, instead of searching directly for the conclusions that may follow each pair of premises, we may begin instead by enumerating those that follow from each pair of Euler's set relations.

Table IV shows all such combinations for the first figure of the syllogism. The first two columns of the table are headed by the Euler diagrams corresponding to the premise "All B are A," whereas the first two rows are headed by the diagrams corresponding to the premise "All C are B." Similarly, the first four columns and rows correspond respectively to the premises "Some B are A" and "Some C are B"; the last three columns and rows correspond respectively to the premises "Some B are not A" and "Some C are not B"; and finally, the premises "No B are A" and "No C are B" are represented respectively by the last column and row.

The conclusions that follow from each pair of diagrams are given in that cell of the table that represents their intersection. Particular conclusions that follow only as subalterns or, effectively, understatements of universals, are shown in parentheses. All other conclusions represent the strongest necessary statements that can be made about the relationship of C to A and, conversely, A to C. Where a cell contains only a dashed line, no necessary conclusion exists; more specifically, each such cell admits all eight possible conclusions, that is, A, E, I, and O propositions about the relationship of A to C as well as that of C to A.

The conclusions to these pairs of set relations should be relatively transparent. For safety's sake, however, the rationale for each is presented below:

J,P. *All C are A*—This is necessarily true because C is a proper subset of B and B is a proper subset of A.
(*Some C are A*)—This is the subaltern of "All C are A": If "*All C are A*," it is necessarily true that "Some C are A."
Some A are C—Because C is a subset of A, some A are necessarily C.
Some A are not C—Because C is a *proper* subset, that is, is not coextensional with A, there must be some A that are *not C*

J,Q. *All C are A*—C is equivalent to B, and all of B are included in A.
(*Some C are A*)—This is the subaltern of "All C are A."
Some A are C—Because B and C are equivalent, those A which are B must also be C.

TABLE IV

Complete Euler Matrix for the First Syllogistic Figure

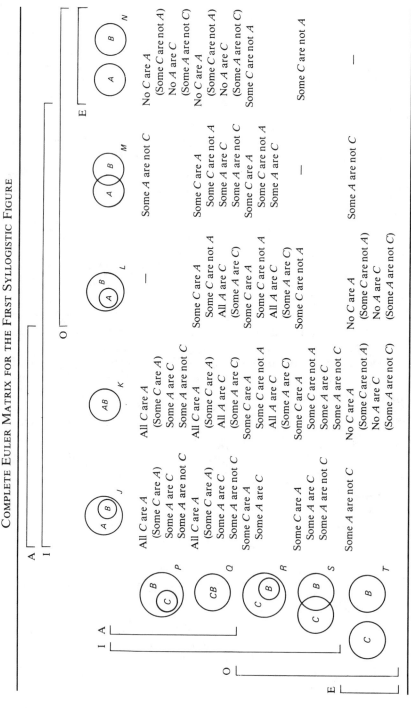

Some A are not C—Because *B* is a proper subset of *A*, some *A* are not *B*. Because *B* and *C* are equivalent, those *A* which are not *B* cannot be *C*.

J,R.   *Some C are A*—Because all *B* are contained in *A*, those *C* which are *B* must be contained in *A*.

Some A are C—Because all *B* are contained in *C*, those *A* which are *B* must be contained in *C*.

J,S.   *Some C are A*—Because all *B* are contained in *A*, those *C* which overlap with *B* must be contained in *A*.

Some A are C—Because all *B* are *A*, those *A* which are *B* must overlap with *C*.

Some A are not C—Because all *B* are *A*, those *B* that do not overlap with *C* must correspond to *A* that are not *C*.

J,T.   *Some A are not C*—Because *B* and *C* are disjoint, those *A* that are *B* cannot be *C*.

K,P.   *All C are A*—Because all *C* are *B* and *B* is equivalent to *A*, it follows that all *C* must be *A*.

(*Some C are A*)—This is the subaltern of "All *C* are *A*."

Some A are C—*A* and *B* are equivalent. Therefore, if *C* is a subset of *B*, it must also be a subset of *A*.

Some A are not C—Because *C* is a *proper* subset of *B*, there must be some *B* or, equivalently, some *A*, that are not *C*.

K,Q.   *All C are A*—Both *A* and *C* are equivalent to *B* and therefore to each other.

(*Some C are A*)—This is the subaltern of "All *C* are *A*."

All A are C—Both *A* and *C* are equivalent to *B* and, therefore, to each other.

(*Some A are C*)—This is the subaltern of "All *A* are *C*."

K,R.   *Some C are A*—Because *B* is a subset of *C*, some *C* must be *B*. Because *A* and *B* are equivalent, those *C* that are *B* must also be *A*.

Some C are not A—Because *B* is a proper subset of *C*, there must be some *C* that extend beyond *B* and, therefore, beyond *B*'s equivalent, *A*.

All A are C—*A* is equivalent to *B*, and *B* is a proper subset of *C*.

(*Some A are C*)—This is the subaltern of "All *A* are *C*."

K,S.   *Some C are A*— Because *A* and *B* are equivalent, *A* must overlap with *C* to the same extent as *B* does.

Some C are not A—Because *A* and *B* are equivalent, *A* must fail to overlap with *C* to the same extent as *B* does.

Some A are C—Because *A* and *B* are equivalent, *A* must overlap with *C* to the same extent as *B* does.

Some A are not C—Because *A* and *B* are equivalent, *A* must fail to overlap with *C* to the same extent as *B* does.

K,T.   *No C are A*— Because *A* and *B* are equivalent, *A* must be disjoint with *C* just as *B* is.

(*Some C are not A*)—This is the subaltern of "No *C* are *A*."

No A are C—Because *A* and *B* are equivalent, *A* must be disjoint with *C* just as *B* is.

(*Some A are not C*)—This is the subaltern of "No *A* are *C*."

L,P.   *No valid conclusion*—*A* and *C* might be related by any of the eight possible conclusions.

L,Q.   *Some C are A*—Because *B* and *C* are equivalent and *B* contains *A*, *C* must also contain *A*.

Some C are not A—Because *A* is a proper subset of *B*, it must also be of *C*.

All A are C—Because *B* and *C* are equivalent and all *A* are *B*, all *A* must be *C*.

(*Some A are C*)—This is the subaltern of "All *A* are *C*."

L,R.   *Some C are A*—If *A* is a subset of *B* and *B* is a subset of *C*, then *A* must be a subset of *C*.
       Some C are not A—*A* must be a proper subset of *C*.
       All A are C—*A* must be a subset of *C*.
       (*Some A are C*)—This is the subaltern of "All *A* are *C*."

L,S.   *Some C are not A*—Because all *A* are contained within *B* but some *C* is distinct from *B*, at least some *C* must not be *A*.

L,T.   *No C are A*—Because all *A* are contained within *B* and *B* and *C* are disjoint, no *C* can be *A*.
       (*Some C are not A*)—This is the subaltern of "No *C* are *A*."
       No A are C—Because all *A* are contained within *B* and *B* and *C* are disjoint, no *A* can be *C*.
       (*Some A are not C*)—This is the subaltern of "No *A* are *C*."

M,P.   *Some A are not C*—Because all *C* are contained within *B* but some *A* are distinct from *B*, at least some *A* must not be *C*.

M,Q.   *Some C are A*—Because *B* and *C* are equivalent, *C* must overlap with *A* to the same extent that *B* does.
       Some C are not A—Because *B* and *C* are equivalent, *C* must fail to overlap with *A* to the same extent that *B* does.
       Some A are C—Because *B* and *C* are equivalent, *A* must overlap with *C* just as with *B*.
       Some A are not C—Because *B* and *C* are equivalent, *A* must fail to overlap with *C* just as with *B*.

M,R.   *Some C are A*—Because *C* includes *B*, *C* must overlap with *A* at least to the extent that *B* does.
       Some C are not A—Because all *B* are *C*, those *B* that are not *A* must correspond to *C* that are not *A*.
       Some A are C—At least those *A* that overlap with *B* must be *C*.

M,S.   *No valid conclusion*—*A* and *C* might be related by any of the eight possible conclusions.

M,T.   *Some A are not C*—At least those *A* that are *B* must not be *C*.

N,P.   *No C are A*—Because all *C* are contained in *B* and *B* is disjoint from *A*, no *C* can be *A*.
       (*Some C are not A*)—This is the subaltern of "No *C* are *A*."
       No A are C—*A* is disjoint from *B* and must therefore be disjoint from *B*'s subset, *C*.
       (*Some A are not C*)—This is the subaltern of "No *A* are *C*."

N,Q.   *No C are A*—If *B* and *C* are equivalent, then *C* must be disjoint from *A* just as *B* is.
       (*Some C are not A*)—This is the subaltern of "No *C* are *A*."
       No A are C—If *B* and *C* are equivalent, then *C* must be disjoint from *A* just as *B* is.
       (*Some A are not C*)—This is the subaltern of "No *A* are *C*."

N,R.   *Some C are not A*—At least those *C* that are *B* cannot be *A*.

N,S.   *Some C are not A*—At least those *C* that are *B* cannot be *A*.

N,T.   *No valid conclusion*—*A* and *C* might be related by any of the eight possible conclusions.

Returning to the syllogisms, a conclusion will follow necessarily from a pair of premises if and only if it follows necessarily from every pair of set relations entailed by those premises. Thus, to determine which of the premise pairs of the first syllogistic figure do indeed yield valid conclusions, one need only collapse across corresponding pairs of Euler diagrams and identify the common conclusions.

The 16 premise pairs of the first syllogistic figure are shown in Table V. Again, premises relating the A and B terms are listed across the top of the table, and those relating B and C are listed down the side. At least one valid conclusion is shown to follow from 6 of the premise pairs: AA, AI, AE, IE, EA, and EI. For each of these pairs of premises, the conclusions cited in Table V can be seen to occur in every one of the pertinent cells of Table IV. (Ignore the superscripts on these conclusions for now; their significance will be explained in the following section.) As an example, consider the premise pair AI: "All B are A" and "Some C are B." The first of these premises is represented by the Euler diagrams heading the first two columns (J and K) of Table IV; the second premise is represented by the first four rows (P, Q, R, and S) of Table IV. An examination of the eight cells comprising the intersection of these columns and rows reveals that only two conclusions appear in every one. These, then, are the conclusions to the AI argument cited in Table V: "Some C are A" and "Some A are C."

The 10 remaining cells of Table V are empty, indicating that no valid conclusion follows from the corresponding pairs of premises. An examination of Table IV confirms that for none of these pairs of premises do the underlying set relations yield any consistent conclusion. Moreover, for 9 of these 10 premise pairs, the related portion of Table IV contains at least one empty or inconclusive cell: If a pair of premises proves inconclusive under any of its interpretations, no valid conclusion can be said to exist. The tenth pair of inconclusive premise is AO. Looking back at Table IV, we see that each of the six set combinations underlying this premise pair does yield some necessary conclusion. Looking across these six cells, however, we see that the conclusions in one cell are, in general, contradicted by the conclusions in another; for example, "Some C are A" is contradicted by "No A are C" and "All A are C" by "Some A are not C." The only conclusion that is not explicitly contradicted is "Some C are not A"; however, the necessity of this conclusion is nullified by the fact that both it and its contradictory, "All C are A," are possible but unnecessary conclusions for cell J,R.

The combined set relations for the second through fourth syllogistic figures are presented in Tables VI, VII, and VIII. For each of these tables, the first two columns and rows correspond to the A premises, the first four to the I premises, the last three to the O premises, and the last alone to the E premises. The justification for the conclusions in these tables is not presented as it was for the first figure, but readers are invited to verify them

TABLE V

First Figure Premise Pairs and Conclusions as Derived from the Corresponding Euler Matrix (Table IV)

Second premise	First premise			
	A: All B are A	I: Some B are A	O: Some B are not A	E: No B are A
A: All C are B	All C are A[A1, P1, P2, C, B] (Some C are A)[C] Some A are C[A3, P1]	—	—	No C are A[A1, P1, P2, C, B] (Some C are not A)[C] No A are C[A3, P1]
I: Some C are B	Some C are A[A1, P1, P2, C, B] Some A are C[A3, P1]	—	—	(Some A are not C) Some C are not A[A1, P1, P2, C, B]
O: Some C are not B	—	—	—	—
E: No C are B	Some A are not C[A2, P1]	Some A are not C[A2, P1]	—	—

[a] Superscripts denote sources endorsing conclusions as follows: A1, *Analytica Priora* I,4–6; A2, *Analytica Priora* I,7; A3, *Analytica Priora* II,1; P1, first mnemonic poem; P2, second mnemonic poem; C, contemporary authorities; B, Boolean authorities.

on their own. When experiencing difficulty in affirming or denying any given conclusion, a good strategy is that of testing its contradictory. For example, uncertainty about whether "All A must be C" can be removed by asking whether it is possible or impossible that "Some A are not C." If any proposition and its contradictory are both possible, neither is necessary. In general, A and O premises with matching subject and predicate contradict each other, as do I and E premises.

It is the compellingness of the individual conclusions in these tables that provides the primary test of their composite accuracy. Two checks on this accuracy, however, can be had from the inherent structure of the tables. The first check derives from the fact that all of the Euler tables (Tables IV, VI, VII, and VIII) should be identical except that their rows and columns have been permuted. To facilitate this check, the labels for the Euler diagrams in Tables VI–VIII have been carried over from Table IV, for example, the same diagram heads column J in all four tables.

The second check derives from the fact that the diagrams heading the rows of the tables are essentially identical to those heading the columns except that the set C has replaced the set A. Because of this, solutions must be reflected in literal converse, that is, with the subject and predicate terms interchanged across corresponding cells of the table. This reflection is most easily seen in the second and third figures (Tables VI and VII) because comparable diagrams occur in the same order across the rows and columns. For each of the second and third figures, the conclusions in the second column of the first row are precisely the converse of those in the second row of the first column, those in the third column of the first row are the converse of those in the third row of the first column, and so on, such that the only unique cells in the matrix are those which fall along the diagonal or, equivalently, those for which comparable diagrams are mapped against each other. Although, because of differences in the horizontal and vertical orderings of the diagrams, this reciprocity is less obvious for the first and fourth figures (Tables IV and VIII), it is nonetheless present. The tables for the first and fourth figures, moreover, permit a check on *each other*: They are essentially identical tables except that the rows of one correspond to the columns of the other, and vice versa, but with the subject and predicate terms interchanged.

In Tables IX–XI, the set relations for the second, third, and fourth figures have been collapsed into syllogisms through the same procedure as was explained for the first figure: A conclusion is cited as valid for a given premise pair if and only if it follows necessarily from all relevant pairs of Euler relations.

Across all four figures (Tables V, IX–XI), there are 27 pairs of premises that yield valid conclusions. Counting the different conclusions that these

TABLE VI

Complete Euler Matrix for the Second Syllogistic Figure

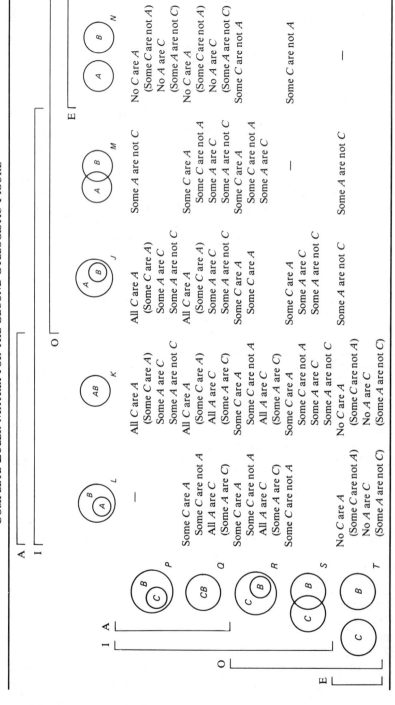

TABLE VII

COMPLETE EULER MATRIX FOR THE THIRD SYLLOGISTIC FIGURE

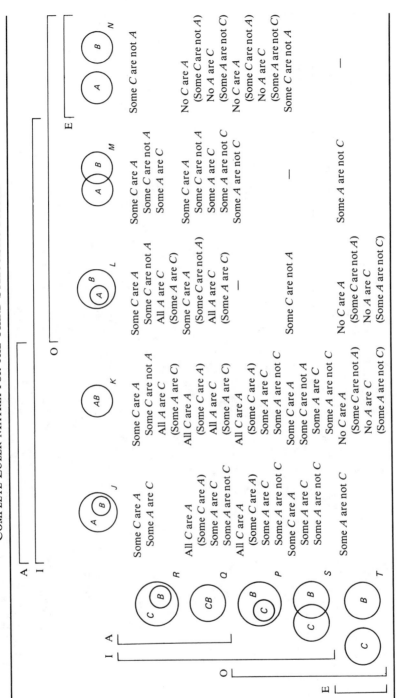

TABLE VIII

COMPLETE EULER MATRIX FOR THE FOURTH SYLLOGISTIC FIGURE

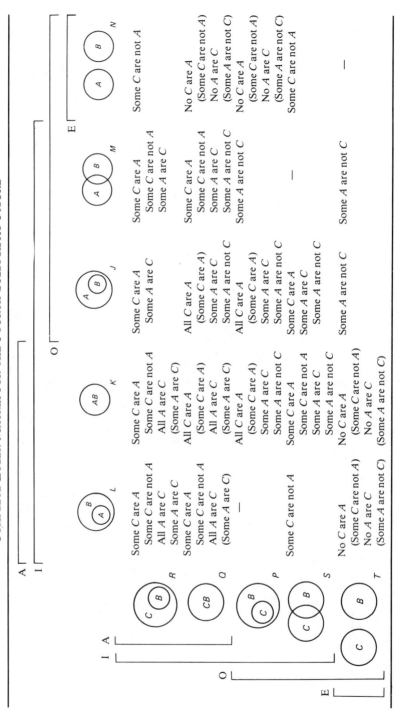

TABLE IX

SECOND FIGURE PREMISE PAIRS AND CONCLUSIONS AS DERIVED FROM THE CORRESPONDING EULER MATRIX (TABLE VI)

Second premise	First premise[a]			
	A: All A are B	I: Some A are B	O: Some A are not B	E: No A are B
A: All C are B	—	—	Some A are not C	No C are A[A1, P1, P2, C, B] (Some C are not A)[C] No A are C[A3] (Some A are not C)
I: Some C are B	—	—	—	Some C are not A[A1, P1, P2, C, B]
O: Some C are not B	Some C are not A[A1, P1, P2, C, B]	—	—	—
E: No C are B	No C are A[A1, P1, P2, C, B] (Some C are not A)[C] No A are C[A3] (Some A are not C)	Some A are not C[A2]	—	—

[a]Superscripts denote sources endorsing conclusions as follows: A1, *Analytica Priora* I,4–6; A2, *Analytica Priora* I,7; A3, *Analytica Priora* II,1; P1, first mnemonic poem; P2, second mnemonic poem; C, contemporary authorities; B, Boolean authorities.

271

TABLE X

THIRD FIGURE PREMISE PAIRS AND CONCLUSIONS AS DERIVED FROM THE CORRESPONDING EULER MATRIX (TABLE VII)

Second premise	First premise[a]			
	A: All B are A	I: Some B are A	O: Some B are not A	E: No B are A
A: All B are C	Some C are A [A1, P1, P2, C, B] Some A are C [A3]	Some C are A [A1, P1, P2, C, B] Some A are C [A3]	Some C are not A [A1, P1, P2, C, B]	Some C are not A [A1, P1, P2, C, B]
I: Some B are C	Some C are A [A1, P1, P2, C, B] Some A are C [A3]	—	—	Some C are not A [A1, P1, P2, C, B]
O: Some B are not C	Some A are not C	—	—	—
E: No B are C	Some A are not C [A2]	Some A are not C [A2]	—	—

[a] Superscripts denote sources endorsing conclusions as follows: A1, *Analytica Priora* I,4–6; A2, *Analytica Priora* I,7; A3, *Analytica Priora* II,1; P1, first mnemonic poem; P2, second mnemonic poem; C, contemporary authorities; B, Boolean authorities.

TABLE XI

FOURTH FIGURE PREMISE PAIRS AND CONCLUSIONS AS DERIVED FROM THE CORRESPONDING EULER MATRIX (TABLE VIII)

Second premise	First premise[a]			
	A: All A are B	I: Some A are B	O: Some A are not B	E: No A are B
A: All B are C	Some C are $A^{P2,C}$ All A are C (Some A are C)	Some C are $A^{P2,C,B}$ Some A are C	—	Some C are not $A^{P2,C}$
I: Some B are C	—	—	—	Some C are not $A^{P2,C,B}$
O: Some B are not C	—	—	—	—
E: No B are C	No C are $A^{P2,C,B}$ (Some C are not A^C) No A are C (Some A are not C)	Some A are not C	—	—

[a] Superscripts denote sources endorsing conclusions as follows: P2, second mnemonic poem; C, contemporary authorities; B, Boolean authorities.

premises yield, there are a total of 48 valid syllogisms, or 12 in each figure. It is also worth noting at this point that like the Euler matrices from which they are derived, each of the second and third figures (Tables IX and X) exhibits a diagonal symmetry but with terms interchanged. The first and fourth figures (Tables V and XI) do not exhibit such internal symmetry but bear an analogous relation to each other. If the *A* and *C* terms of its premises and conclusions are interchanged, the fourth figure is precisely a diagonal reflection of the first.

The Euler matrices developed in this section are thus worthwhile in several ways. First, they provide a relatively transparent and manageable method for evaluating the validity of the arguments. Second, the redundancy among the matrices provides both means for checking their accuracy and, perhaps more importantly, insight into the logical relationship among the four syllogistic figures. Finally, the matrices clearly reveal the underlying simplicity of the logic. Note that if the redundancies that exist within and between tables are factored out, the entire logic of the syllogism—the whole interpretive morass with which we began—reduces to the diagonal half of just one of the matrices, that is, to just 15 pairs of Euler diagrams.

B.   Aristotle's Solution

Aristotle, you will recall, recognized only three of the four traditional syllogistic figures. In the beginning of the *Analytica Priora,* he introduces each of these figures in separate chapters, enumerating their valid moods. These moods are presented in Aristotle's (translated) words below. For ease of reference, I have prefixed each with the number of its figure and the letters designating the types of propositions corresponding to its first premise, second premise, and conclusion, in that order.

1-AAA: If *A* is predicated of all *B*, and *B* of all *C*, *A* must be predicated by all *C*. (*AP* I,4,25b)

1-EAE: If *A* is predicated of no *B*, and *B* of all *C*, it is necessary that no *C* will be *A*. (*AP* I,4,26a)

1-AII: Let all *B* be *A* and some *C* be *B*. Then "if predicated of all" means what was said above, it is necessary that some *C* is *A*. (*AP* I,4,26a)

1-EIO:.   And if no *B* is *A* but some *C* is *B*, it is necessary that some *C* is not *A*. (*AP* I,4,26a)

2-EAE: Let *M* be predicated of no *N*, but of all *O* since, then the negative relation is convertible, *N* will belong to no *M*: but *M* was assumed to belong to all *O*: consequently *N* will belong to no *O*. (*AP* I,5,27a)

2-AEE: Again, if *M* belongs to all *N* but to no *O*, then *N* will belong to no *O*. For if *M* belongs to no *O*, *O* belongs to no *M*: but *M* (as was said) belongs to all *N*; *O* then will belong to no *N*: for the first figure has again been formed. But since the negative relation is convertible, *N* will belong to no *O*. (*AP* I,5,27a)

2-EIO: For if M belongs to no N, but to some O, it is necessary that N does not belong to some O. For since the negative statement is convertible, N will belong to no M: but M was admitted to belong to some O: therefore N will not belong to some O for the result is reached by means of the first figure. (AP I,5,27a)

2-AOO: Again, if M belongs to all N but not to some O, it is necessary that N does not belong to some O: for if N belongs to all O and M is predicated also of all N, it is necessary for M to belong to all O. But we assumed not to belong to some O. And if M belongs to all N but not to all O, we shall conclude that N does not belong to all O: the proofs the same as the above. (AP I,5,27a)

3-AAI: If [the terms] are universal, whenever both P and R belong to all S, it follows that P will necessarily belong to some R. For since the affirmative statement is convertible, S will belong to some R: consequently so that since P belongs to all S, and S to some R, P must belong to some R: for a syllogism in the first figure is produced. It is possible to demonstrate this also *per impossible* and by exposition. For if both P and R belong to all S, should one of the S's, e.g., N, be taken, both P and R will belong to this, and thus P will belong to some R. (AP I,6,28a)

3-EAO: If R belongs to all S, but P to no S, there will be a syllogism to prove that P will not belong to some R. This may be demonstrated in the same way as before by converting the premise RS. It might be proved also *per impossible*, as in the former cases. (AP I,6,28a)

3-IAI: For if R belongs to all S, P to some S, P must belong to some R. For since the affirmative statement is convertible S will belong to some P: consequently since R belongs to all S, and S to some P, R must also belong to some P: therefore P must belong to some R. (AP I,6,28b)

3-AII: Again if R belongs to some S, and P to all S, P must belong to some R. This may be demonstrated in the same way as the preceding. And it is possible to demonstrate also *per impossible* and by exposition, as in the former cases. (AP I,6,28b)

3-OAO: But if one term is affirmative, the other negative, and if the affirmative is universal, a syllogism will be possible whenever the minor term is affirmative. For if R belongs to all S, but P does not belong to some S, it is necessary that P does not belong to some R. For if P belongs to all R, and R belongs to all S, then P will belong to all S: but we assumed that it did not. Proof is possible also without reduction *ad impossible*, if one of the Ss be taken to which P does not belong. (AP I,6,28b)

3-EIO: But if the negative term is universal, whenever the major is negative and the minor affirmative there will be a syllogism. For if P belongs to no S, and R belongs to some S, P will not belong to some R: for we shall have the first figure again, if the premise RS is converted. (AP I,6,28b)

The above stand as the sum total of valid syllogisms offered in Aristotle's initial exposition of the syllogism. Surely for this reason, Aristotle is very often cited as having recognized but 14 valid moods.

If we map Aristotle's list against Tables V, IX, and X, we find he missed out on two or three conclusive premise pairs per figure. The missing premise pairs were not overlooked by Aristotle in these chapters: They were explicitly rejected. His argument against each is presented below:

1-AEX: But if the first term [A] belongs to all the middle [B], but the middle to none
          of the last term [C], there will be no syllogism in respect of the extremes; for
          nothing necessary follows from the terms being so related; for it is possible
          that the first should belong either to all or to none of the last so that neither
          a particular nor a universal conclusion is necessary. But if there is no nec-
          essary consequence, there cannot be a syllogism by means of these premises.
          As an example of a universal affirmative relation between the extremes we
          may take the terms animal, man, horse; of a universal negative relation, the
          terms animal, man, stone. (AP I,4,26a)

1-IEX: Again, if no C is B, but some B is or is not A, or not every B is A, there
          cannot be a syllogism. Take the terms white, horse, swan: white, horse, raven.
          (AP I,4,26a)

2-OAX: But if M is predicated of all O, but not of all N, there will be no syllogism.
          Take the terms animal, substance, raven; animal, white, raven. (AP I,5,27b)

2-IEX: Nor will there be a conclusion when M is predicated of no O, but of some
          N. Terms to illustrate a positive relation between the extremes are animal,
          substance, unit; a negative relation, animal, substance, science. (AP I,5,27b)

3-AEX: But if R belongs to no S, P to all S, there will be no syllogism. Terms for
          the positive relation are animal, horse, man: for the negative relation animal,
          inanimate, man. (AP I,6,28a)

3-AOX: But whenever the major is affirmative, no syllogism will be possible, e.g., if
          P belongs to all S, and R does not belong to some S. Terms for the universal
          affirmative relation are animate, man, animal. For the universal negative
          relation it is not possible to get terms, if R belongs to some S, and does not
          belong to some S. For if P belongs to all S, and R to some S, then P will
          belong to some R: but we assumed that it belongs to no R. We must put the
          matter as before. Since the expression "it does not belong to some" is in-
          definite, it may be used truly of that also which belongs to none. But if R
          belongs to no S, no syllogism is possible, as has been shown. Clearly then
          no syllogism will be possible here. (AP I,6,28b)

3-IEX: But if the negative term is universal, whenever the major is a negative and
          the minor affirmative there will be a syllogism. For if P belongs to no S, and
          R belongs to some S, P will not belong to some R: for we shall have the first
          figure again, if the premise RS is converted. But when the minor is negative,
          there will be no syllogism. Terms for the positive relation are animal, man,
          wild: for the negative relation, animal, science, wild—the middle in both being
          the term wild. (AP I,6,28b)

Aristotle achieves most of these refutations by setting up contrary arguments with triads of concrete terms. To follow this part of the discourse,
each triad of the terms must be substituted, in the order presented, for the
syllogistic variables in alphabetical order. Using the refutation of the first
figure premises AE as an example, the terms "animal, man, and horse"
and "animal, man, and stone" should be substituted, in turn, for the terms
A, B, and C, respectively. The first triad yields the premise pair, "All men

are animals, and no horses are men," thus admitting the conclusion, "All horses are animals." In contrast, the second triad yields the premises "All men are animals, and no stones are men," inviting the conclusion that "No stones are animals." Having thus demonstrated that both A and E propositions *may* follow from the premises, Aristotle concludes that *no* proposition *must* follow from the premises.

If you find this method of disproof somewhat unclear or unsatisfying, be comforted: Authorities on Aristotle have agreed on neither the specifics of its implementation nor its logical acceptability. Patzig (1968), having summarized these points of dispute, argues that although the method may be lacking in formal aesthetics, it is perfectly correct. In its behalf, he quotes Philoponus, an early (sixth century AD) and much admired interpreter of Aristotle: "Ten thousand examples cannot prove a universal proposition, but *one* example is enough to refute it" (p. 183).

Philoponus aside, Aristotle's disproofs do suffer one very serious shortcoming. Although adequate for the task of contrasting conclusions in which the C term serves as the subject and the A term as the predicate, the procedure, under Aristotle's implementation, is moot with respect to conclusiveness of arguments involving the converse subject-predicate arrangement. If one's purpose is solely that of enumerating concludent premise pairs, without regard to their various conclusions, then this distinction generally makes little difference since, to most of the categorical propositions, there corresponds another with converted subject and predicate terms: "All C are A" entails "Some A are C"; "Some C are A" entails "Some A are C"; "No C are A" entails "No A are C." But this is not true for O propositions: From "Some C are not A" one may infer with equal uncertainty that all, some, not some, or no A are C. It follows that where the only necessary conclusion of a premise pair is "Some A are not C," its concludence cannot be discovered by examining predications of C by A. Consistent with this point, the concludent premise pairs that Aristotle rejects in chapters 4-6 are precisely those that yield "Some A are not C" as their sole conclusion.

At some point Aristotle recognized this problem. In the beginning of I,7 of the *Analytica Priora,* in a section purportedly written sometime later than the text that surrounds it (see Lukasiewicz, 1957; Patzig, 1968), Aristotle asserts:

It is evident also that in all the figures, whenever a proper syllogism does not result, if both the terms are affirmative or negative nothing necessary follows at all, but if one is affirmative, the other negative, and if the negative is stated universally, a syllogism always results relating the minor [as predicate] to the major term, e.g., if A belongs to all or some B, and B belongs to no C; for if the premises are converted it is necessary that C does not belong to some A. Similarly, also in the other figures: a syllogism always results by means of conversion." (*AP* I,7,29a)

Through this paragraph, he reinstates the previously rejected AE and IE premise pairs for each of the three figures. Through the phrase "a syllogism always results relating the minor to the major term," he is simply pointing out that the conclusion will read "Some A are not C" instead of the standard "Some C are not A." He still ignores the AO pairs of the second and third figures. Perhaps this was an oversight. Alternatively, Patzig (1968) argues that he omitted their mention for the same reason that he forewent explicit statement of the AE and IE arguments in figures 2 and 3: Through valid conversions, each of the arguments can be shown to be redundant with some other, previously proved mood of the same figure.

Later in the *Analytica Priora*, Aristotle additionally notes that any premise pair that yields an A, I, or E conclusion must also yield some conclusion with converted subject and predicate terms:

Since some syllogisms are universal, others particular, all the universal syllogisms give more than one result, and of particular syllogisms the affirmative yield more than one, the negative yield only the stated conclusion. For all propositions are convertible save only the particular negative: and the conclusion states one definite thing about another definite thing. Consequently all syllogisms have the particular negative yield more than one conclusion, e.g. If A has been proved to belong to all or to some B, then B must belong to some A: and if A has been proved to belong to no B, then B belongs to no A. This is a different conclusion from the former. But if A does not belong to some B, it is not necessary that B should not belong to some A: for it may possibly belong to all A. (*AP* II,1,53a)

In the final analysis, then, Aristotle's count of valid syllogisms for the first three figures is very close to that developed in Section II,A. Of the 19 premise pairs that were found valid herein, Aristotle acknowledged 17, and, as previously mentioned, his omission of the last 2 can be explained on grounds of efficiency. Of the various conclusions to those premises adduced herein, Aristotle explicitly defended all but the subalterns. His neglect of the subalterns can also be explained on grounds of efficiency: Having concluded, for example, that a pair of premises necessarily implies that "All C are A," is there any need or even advantage in separately listing the fact that it also implies "Some C are A"? The greatest discrepancy between the present list of valid syllogisms and Aristotle's lies in his total omission of the fourth figure.

To understand better the relation between the various counts of valid syllogisms, the conclusions in Tables V, IX, X, and XI have been annotated with respect to the sources by which they have been endorsed. The scripts A1, A2, and A3 are owed to Aristotle: A1 marks those 14 syllogisms he defended in his initial exposition of the syllogism (*AP* I,4-6); A2 marks those syllogisms he added on first considering the possibility of conclusions with *A*-*C* subject-predicate arrangements (*AP* I,7); and A3 marks those syllogisms he acknowledged on considering the valid converses of previously proved conclusions (*AP* II,1).

C. OTHER COUNTS

The centuries that have passed since Aristotle have afforded a lot of opportunity for scholars to clarify Aristotle's's intentions, and some of these clarifications appear, in retrospect, to reflect outstanding misunderstandings. It has, for example, been authoritatively asserted that only the first figure syllogisms can be valid (Kant, 1762); that only two of the fourth figure syllogisms can be valid (Maier, 1900); that none of the fourth figure syllogisms can be valid (Prantl, 1925); that none of the syllogisms Aristotle raised in I,7 can be valid (Maier, 1900); and that any valid syllogism will be rendered invalid if the order of its two premises is exchanged (Lemmon, 1965; Maier, 1900; Prantl, 1925; Waitz, 1846). At the outset of this section, let me note that I will only consider positions that still enjoy some critical degree of acclaim.

1. Medieval and Renaissance Counts

It may be more to the Medieval and Renaissance philosophers than to Aristotle himself that our present view of the logic is owed. The Medieval logician very obligingly invented a mnemonic poem to help us remember the valid moods of the syllogism. Many of us were admonished at some point in our lives to memorize this poem. Many of us at least can recognize it. Or can we? The poem, as it turns out, shows up in several different versions. Across some of these versions, the differences are only superficial. Across others, however, they are significant. Here are two representative versions:

Barbara Celarent Darii Ferio Baralipton Celantes Dabitis Fapesmo Frisesomorum; Cesare Campestres Festino Baroco; Darapti Felapton Disamis Datisi Bocardo Ferison. (From Mates, 1972)

Barbara, Celarent, Darii, Ferio-*que prioris* Cesare, Camestres, Festino, Baroco *secundae* *Tertia* Darapti, Disamis, Datisi, Felapton Bocardo, Ferison *habet, Quarta insuper addit* Bramantip, Camenes, Dimaris, Fesapo, Fresison. (From Prior, 1973).

Each of the proper names in these poems corresponds to a valid mood; the first three vowels of each give the type of proposition serving, respectively, as the first premise, second premise, and conclusion of the syllogism.

For example, *Barbara* refers to the syllogism *AAA* and *Celarent* to the syllogism *EAE*. For the second, third, and fourth figures, the consonants are
significant, too, as they provide instructions as to how the moods can be
transformed to valid moods of the first figure. The figures are separated
by semicolons in the first poem and by appropriate words in the second.
Both of the poems name 19 valid syllogisms, or 5 in excess of Aristotle's
original 14. The major difference between them is that, in the first poem,
the 5 new moods have been added to the first figure, whereas in the second,
they have been added to the fourth figure. In our tables, the moods named
by the first and second poem are denoted by P1 and P2, respectively.

The genesis of the five new moods of the first poem is quite easy to un-
cover. Two of them, *Fapesmo* and *Frisesomorum*, correspond to the once
rejected syllogisms of the first figure that Aristotle reinstated in Chapter 7,
Book I, of the *Analytica Priora* (A2 in Table V). The other three correspond
to the permissible conversions of first figure premises that he raises in Chapter 1, Book II, of the *Analytica Priora* (A3 in Table V).

What is hard to understand about the first poem is why like additions
were not made to the second and third figures. Was it because the validity
of the AE and IE premises was only explicitly drawn out for the first figure?
But Aristotle did follow their proof with "similarly also in the other figures:
a syllogism always results by means of conversion" (*AP* I,7,29a). Was it
because all of his examples of valid conversions used the letters *A* and *B*
as variables? True, in the definitions of the syllogisms, only the first figure
moods are expressed with the variables *A* and *B*. But the conclusions of
those moods involved only the variables *A* and *C*. Besides, variables are
variables and, more than that, Aristotle very clearly states that "*all* [italics
mine] syllogisms save the particular negative yield more than one
conclusion." In all my reading on the logic, I have never run across an
attempt to justify the unbalanced nature of this particular list of moods.

In the second poem, the five additional moods are accorded to the fourth
figure. Historians do not agree as to exactly who was responsible for the
eventual formalization of the fourth figure. Its inspiration, however, is quite
commonly traced to that same section of the *Analytica Priora* in which
Aristotle acknowledges the validity of AEO and IEO arguments. Again,
the wording of the relevant section is:

> It is evident also that in all the figures, whenever a proper syllogism does not result, if
> both the terms are affirmative or negative nothing necessary follows at all, but if one is
> affirmative, the other negative, and if the negative is stated universally, a syllogism al-
> ways results relating the minor [as predicated] to the major term, e.g., if *A* belongs to
> all or some *B*, and *B* belongs to no *C*; for if the premises are converted it is necessary
> that *C* does not belong to some *A*. Similarly, also in the other figures: a syllogism always
> results by means of conversion. (*AP* I,7,29a)

Thus, through valid conversions, the premises "All (some) B are A" and "No C are B" can be transformed to "Some A are B" and "No B are C." If the order of the two new premises is reversed (which is permissible because they are linked only by a logical conjunction), the resulting pair is very similar to the previously validated pair, EI (*Ferio*). Indeed, the only difference is that there is an A where the C should be and vice versa. To accommodate this difference, the conclusion of the premises must also be converted: It must read "Some A are not C" instead of "Some C are not A." But Aristotle warned us of this in asserting that the resulting syllogism would relate the "minor term to the major."

On the other hand, as A and C are nothing more than the names of variables, the logic of the argument is truly indifferent to which of them occurs in which position. If we switch them, calling A by C and C by A, then our transformed argument conforms precisely to *Ferio*, conclusion and all. To maintain consistency with our original premise pair, the A and C variables must be switched in them as well. Thus transposed, the original premise pair becomes "All (some) B are C" and "No A are B" and yields the conclusion "Some C are not A."

The only problem now is that the original but now reconfigured premises no longer fit the mold of the first figure. On the other hand, if they are reordered to read, "No A are B" and "All (some) B are C," they are perfectly suited to the fourth figure. Thus we have *Fesapo* and *Fresison*. By beginning with Aristotle's discussion of validly converted conclusions (*AP* II,1) and applying essentially the same logic as was laid out above, the fourth figure syllogisms *Bramantip, Camenes,* and *Dimaris* are similarly had from *Barbara, Celarent,* and *Darii* of the first figure.

Note that any implications of Aristotle's appended section with respect to the second and third figures are effectively ignored in this second poem as they were in the first. I would argue further that the fourth figure moods of this poem are had only through a relatively tortured overinterpretation of what Aristotle actually said. On the other hand, the second poem can be defended over the first in that there is at least a system to its bias: It names all and only all of the premise pairs that produce conclusions having the C term as subject and the A term as predicate.

2. The Dominant Contemporary Count

The number of valid moods most often cited by contemporary authorities on the logic is 24 (e.g., Langer, 1953; Lemmon, 1965; Lukasiewicz, 1957; Prior, 1973). These moods are denoted with a C (for contemporary) in Tables V, IX, X, and XI. They consist precisely of the 19 moods named by our second mnemonic poem plus those 5 that are had by substituting each of the pertinent universal conclusions (e.g., All C are A) with its subaltern (e.g., Some C are A).

In contemporary works, the need to justify the exclusion of syllogisms whose conclusions involve the A term as subject and the C term as predicate is finessed through definition. Prior's (1973) example is typical:

> This [a categorical syllogism] is an inference involving three categorical propositions—two as premises and one as conclusion—and with three terms . . . distributed as follows: the predicate of the conclusion, called the "major term" appears in one of the premises, called in consequence the "major premiss" . . . the subject of the conclusion, called the "minor term," appears in the other premiss, called in consequence the "minor premiss"; and the third term, called the "middle term," appears in both premises, but is not in the conclusion at all. These characteristics suffice to define "categorical syllogism." (pp. 110-111)

To be sure, there is much material in the *Analytica Priora* to support this constraint, not the least of which is that, in his initial exposition of the syllogism, Aristotle examines the validity of C-A conclusions only. But there is also much to suggest that his initial preoccupation with C-A conclusions was fostered by a combination of rhetorical consistency and logical oversight rather than knowing conviction. Patzig (1968), having combed through *Analytica Priora* quite thoroughly, marshals a very convincing collection of evidence that the order of the terms in a conclusion was irrelevant to Aristotle's concept of a syllogism.

3. The Boolean Count

There is one other number that is cited with sufficient prominence to deserve note: 15. As this number arises in Boolean treatments of the logic, the pertinent moods are marked with a B in Tables V, IX, X, and XI. The rationale for 15 valid moods derives from the observation that a particular proposition, by virtue of the definition of "some," implicitly asserts that there exists at least one entity corresponding to its subject term. Particular propositions will therefore be false whenever no such entity exists. In contrast, universal propositions may be true regardless of whether their terms are empty. By implication, given true universal premises, the logic can never in itself guarantee the necessity of a particular conclusion. Such modes can be valid only if appropriate assumptions about the existence of their terms are added.

Because the existence of the terms generally *is* assumed in psychological studies of the logic, the so-called existential fallacy is of little concern in the present context. It is, however, of interest that the count of 15 valid syllogisms is had by deleting those 9 moods with universal premises and particular conclusions from the 24 moods so often cited by other contemporary logicians (C in Tables V, IX, X, and XI). Thus, the Booleans, too, admit the fourth figure, but restrict consideration to those syllogisms whose conclusions involve C-A subject–predicate arrangements.

D. ASSESSING THE ALTERNATIVES

The 24 moods that are generally recognized as valid by contemporary logicians stand as exactly half of the 48 that were shown to be valid earlier in this article. More specifically, they are exactly that half of the syllogisms for which the C term serves as subject of the conclusion and the A term as predicate.

The issue of whether the order of the terms in the conclusion should be part of the definition of syllogism is not merely one of formal meticulousness. It relates to the very purpose of the theory. Under the dominant contemporary interpretation, the theory amounts to a specification of which all possible pairs of the categorical premises or, equivalently, all possible pairs of minimally qualified and quantified dyadic relations between A and B and C and B will allow one to infer whether A can be attributed to C. In contrast, with *no* requirements as to the order of the terms in the conclusion, the theory becomes a specification of which of all possible pairs of minimally qualified and quantified dyadic relations between A and B and C and B will permit *any* valid inference to be drawn about the relationship between A and C. I submit that it is people's appreciation of the latter that has been of primary interest to psychologists. Moreover, I strongly suspect that the latter was the closer to Aristotle's primary interest, and this may also relate to the status of the controversial fourth figure.

The traditional fourth figure was essentially ignored by Aristotle. Why? In I,23 of the *Analytica Priora*, he asserts that in order to relate A to B syllogistically,

we must take something in relation to both and this is possible in three ways (either by predicating A of C and C of B, or C of both, or both of C) and these are the figures of which we have spoken, it is clear that every syllogism must be made in one or the other of these figures. (*AP* I,23,41a)

Thus, Aristotle was not only very definite in his insistence that the logic be based on exactly three figures, but expressed it in a way that makes the absence of the fourth glaringly obvious. On the other hand, as we have seen, the validity of all five of the traditionally endorsed premise pairs of the fourth figure are defended, at least indirectly, by Aristotle in I,7 and II,1.

How are we to reconcile these passages? If Aristotle recognized the individual moods of the fourth figure, why did he reject the figure as a whole? The argument endorsed by Lukasiewicz (1957) is that Aristotle only came to recognize the fourth figure some time after most of the *Analytica Priora* had been written. To correct for his error, Aristotle then inserted the relevant passages of I,7 and II,1. To be sure, the fourth figure is developed with less rigor than the other three. But, Lukasiewicz continues, "Aristotle did not have time to draw up systematically all the new discoveries he had made, and left the continuation of his work to his pupil Theophrastus" (p. 27). (In view of this argument, it is worth noting that Theophrastus accorded the new moods of I,7 and II,1 to the first figure, not the fourth.)

In contrast with Lukasiewicz, Patzig (1968) argues that Aristotle appended the relevant passages of I,7 and II,1 to the text to correct, not for an overlooked fourth figure, but for the overlooked possibility of *A–C* conclusions. It is Patzig's belief that Aristotle purposefully ignored the fourth figure because, within the definitional system that he had set up, there was no graceful way to distinguish it clearly from the first. "The price of this course," Patzig reflects, "is that his three figures do not contain all of the syllogisms which he admits to be valid—thus confuting the assertion of [the above passage] that all valid syllogisms belong to one of the three figures" (p. 109).

I am inclined to agree with the essence but not the tone of Patzig's argument. I believe Aristotle excluded the fourth figure, not because he found it difficult to articulate a definition for it that was both clear and distinct from that of the first, but because he found it to be *logically* indistinguishable from the first.

A glance back at Tables V and XI proves the logical equivalence of these two figures. The two tables are identical except that the rows of one appear as the columns of the other. There are also two apparent differences between them that result from the exchange of their rows and columns. First, where there are Cs in one of the tables, there are As in the other. But, again, A and C are only labels for variables; whether A is called by C and vice versa is of no substantive difference in itself. Second, for equivalent syllogisms, the order of the premises is reversed across figures such that EAE of the first figure corresponds to AEE of the second EIO of the first to IEO of the fourth, and so on. But, as discussed previously, the order of the premises of a syllogism is immaterial to its logic.

If their variables are replaced with real-world terms, the equivalence of the two figures becomes even more obvious. As examples, consider the following pairs:

(1) Figure 1   All mammals are animals
     AAA   All horses are mammals
                   _____
                   All horses are animals

     Figure 4   All horses are mammals
     AAA   All mammals are animals
                   _____
                   All horses are animals

(2) Figure 1   No mammals are insects
     EAE   All horses are mammals
                   _____
                   No horses are insects

     Figure 4   All horses are mammals
     AEE   No mammals are insects
                   _____
                   No horses are insects

The point is that, except for the order of the premises, the two syllogisms of each pair are identical.

It might be objected that I contrived the similarity of the above pairs of syllogisms in that what I substituted for the A term in one, I substituted for the C term in the other. This construal of the terms is necessary, however, in order that the premises of each argument be true—the sin qua non of the syllogism. Moreover, the way in which Aristotle originally distinguished between the terms depended on neither the letters by which they were called, nor the premises in which they occurred, nor their order in the conclusion. Rather, it depended on the relative status of the sets to which the terms referred: "I call that the major in which the middle is contained and that term minor which comes under the middle" (AP I,4,26a). By this functional definition, the substitutions in the above arguments are for matched terms; for example, "horse" consistently serves as the term which, by formal or syntactic constraints, must be the minor term in each of the syllogisms.

The notion that Aristotle would have taken this sort of equivalence between the first and fourth figure as sufficient grounds for admitting but one of them to the system finds support in the thematic structure of his text. In I,4-6, Aristotle does indeed delineate all possible arguments in each of the three figures. But the valid syllogisms of the first figure are treated differently from those of the second and third. Specifically, the four moods of the first figure that are presented as valid in I,4, are presented as such without justification. Instead of proving their validity, Aristotle asserts that they are "perfect" where a "perfect" syllogism has been defined as one "which needs nothing other than what has been stated to make plain what necessarily follows" (AP I,2,24b). Each of the valid moods of the second and third figure are, in contrast, proved to be such. In particular, their proofs consist in demonstrations that each of them can, through some series of valid conversions, be derived from one of the valid moods of the first figure. In keeping with this, Aristotle asserted over and over again that the valid second and third figure syllogisms are *not* perfect—they can be *made* perfect only by means of the first figure and certain supplementary statements or operations.

The suggestion is that Aristotle's purpose in these chapters is only incidentally one of enumerating concludent combinations of categorical premises. His primary purpose seems instead to be one of reducing valid argumentation to the minimal necessary system. This goal seems even more apparent in I,7. As discussed previously, the chapter begins with the reinstatement of the previously rejected AE and IE premise pairs. Again, each of these premise pairs is defended by relating it, through conversion, to some previously validated mood. Next, Aristotle reminds us that it is only by reduction to the first figure that syllogisms of the second and third figures are proved valid. He then demonstrates that the particular moods of the first figure, *Darii* and *Ferio*, can be reduced to the universal moods, *Barbara* and *Celarent*. The conclusion that follows, and that Aristotle spends the rest of the chapter emphasizing, is that *"all* syllogisms may be reduced to the universal syllogisms in the first figure" (*AP* I,7,29b).

The remainder of Book I of the *Analytica Priora* is essentially addressed to the issues of how to recognize syllogisms of the different figures in any of the various costumes they may take on; how to discriminate true syllogisms from their various fraudulent cousins; and how to analyze or construct extended arguments through syllogistic chains. Again, Aristotle is firm throughout in his reference to exactly three figures. Moreover, he treats the three in a way that is consistent with the hypothesis that he perceived the fourth figure as logically equivalent with the first. For example:

> If then the middle term is a predicate and subject of predication, or if it is a predicate, and something else is denied of it, we shall have the first figure: if it both is a predicate and is denied of something, the middle figure: if other things are predicated of it, or one is denied, the other predicated, the last figure . . . we shall recognize the figure by the position of the middle term. (*AP* I,32,47b).

If it was indeed Aristotle's intention to exclude the fourth figure from the formal logic, then the additional moods cited in I,7 and II,1 of the *Analytica Priora* must have been meant for the first three figures. By implication, it must not have been Aristotle's intention to exclude arguments with A–C subject–predicate structures from the logic. We are thus back to the position that Aristotle's reckoning of the valid moods of the first three figures was very close to that adduced herein (see Section II,B).

At a more general level, the foregoing discussion suggests that to criticize Aristotle for failing to articulate as many syllogisms as the system would admit is misdirected. His intention would seem to have been, instead, to collapse the system to as few syllogisms as it would demand. Across Book I of the *Analytica Priora*, Aristotle argued (1) that any valid argument can be reduced to a chain of syllogisms; (2) that any syllogism can be reduced to one of the "perfect" syllogisms of the first figure; and (3) that any first figure syllogism can, in turn, be reduced to one of the two universal, first figure syllogisms. In context, the syllogistic system seems little more than an intermediate step in the effort to isolate the essential logic of argumentation.

III. Theories of the Psychology of Syllogistic Reasoning

In the section to follow, we will examine theories of the psychology of syllogistic reasoning. The goal will be to extract from them some common set of factors that might explain people's difficulty with the arguments. Afterward, we will return to the logic as Aristotle developed it and reconsider the issue of whether the logic was poorly designed for humans or humans were poorly designed for logic.

A. THE PERFECT SYLLOGISMS

Aristotle suggested that people should, in general, be naturally competent with the four "perfect," first figure syllogisms, *Barbara, Celarent, Darii,* and *Ferio.* In Philoponus's words:

> A perfect syllogism is one the conclusion of which everybody is able to draw; as if someone said "the just is beautiful; the beautiful is good" for here anyone can understand "therefore the just is good." An imperfect syllogism is one the conclusion of which a logician can draw, e.g., "every man is substance; every man is animal." The conclusion of this is: "Therefore some substance is animal". . . . For perfect syllogisms both have necessity and evidently have it; imperfect syllogisms, such as all those of the second and third figures, have necessity but do not have it evidently: they need a logician to take the necessity which comes from the premises but is not evident, and lead it into the light by means of conversions. (Cited in Patzig, 1968, p. 73)

The careful reader may have noticed that the "perfect" example provided by Philoponus corresponds to a syllogism of the traditional fourth figure, not the first. This is consistent with Aristotle's text. In formal presentations of the syllogisms, Aristotle generally expressed the relations between terms, not with the simple copula, but with such phrases as "belongs to" and "is predicated of." For example, his formal description of *Barbara* was "If *A* is predicated of all *B* and *B* of all *C*, *A* must be predicated of all *C*" (*AP* I,4,25b). When Aristotle did connect the terms of first figure syllogisms with the simple copula, he very often transposed the order of their premises as well, so that, like Philoponus's example, they fit the mold of the fourth figure, for example, "If planets do not twinkle and what does not twinkle is near, then the planets must be near" (*Analytica Posteriora* 78a).

Aside from adding support to our hypothesis that Aristotle perceived the first and fourth figures as logically indistinguishable, such examples provide an explanation for his contention that the logic of the first figure syllogisms should be especially natural or apparent. Specifically, in Aristotle's renditions of first figure syllogisms, the "middle" or repeated term generally occurs in the middle of the two premises, sandwiched between the two outer terms. In this way, the order of the terms in these syllogisms directly supports notice and coordination of any transitive relations between them. [See Kneale & Kneale (1965) and Patzig (1968) for a defense of this argument.]

Psychological studies have invariably been based on the traditional rather than the Aristotelian syllogistic. In traditional presentations of the logic, the terms are linked with the copula but the premises are not transposed. Within the traditional framework, therefore, it is not the first figure but the fourth that exhibits the "perfect" syntactic chaining of terms. In particular, it is those traditional fourth figure moods with nontraditional *A*–*C* conclusions that should be most accessible to the naive reasoner.

In keeping with this, in a study in which subjects were asked to generate conclusions for all 64 pairs of premises, Johnson-Laird and Steedman (1978) found that concludent premises of the fourth figure evoked valid responses slightly more often than did concludent premises of the other figures, including the first (see also Johnson-Laird, 1982, for replications of this effect). And, as would be predicted, the fourth figure conclusions given were strongly biased toward *A*–*C* subject–predicate structures.

On the other hand, as compared with all valid moods, the four "perfect" fourth figure moods (AAA, IAI, AEE, and IEO) did not, by any means, stand out as being especially easy. Furthermore, Johnson-Laird and Steedman's subjects were significantly more prone to generate conclusions even to *inconcludent* premise pairs of the fourth figure than to inconcludent pairs of the others. It thus seems that although the chaining of the terms in the fourth figure may indeed boost the availability of a conclusion, there is no evidence that it does the same for its underlying logic. Together these findings imply that, with respect to the psychological transparency of an argument, there must be other factors that are at least as important as the order of the terms.

B. THE ATMOSPHERE HYPOTHESIS

Proper interpretation of a syllogism depends upon precise analysis of the interrelations that may hold between its terms, but this, Woodworth (1938) pointed out, sometimes involves more work than the reasoner is willing or able to invest. In such cases, Woodworth and Sells (1935) hypothesized, reasoners frequently base their responses on the "atmosphere" of quantity and quality set by the premises. Specifically, when both premises are affirmative, reasoners will tend toward an affirmative response. When both premises are universal, reasoners will tend toward a universal response. When either premise is particular or negative, a particular or negative response will be more likely. Woodworth (1938) suggested that the mechanism governing the atmosphere effect is one and the same as that which prompts us toward such grammatical errors as "The laboratory equipment in these situations *were* in many instances . . ." (p. 817). That is to say that the effect was intended, as it sounds, to reflect nothing more profound than linguistic gloss.

At least part of the reason that the atmosphere hypothesis has received so much attention in the psychological literature is that many would like so much to disprove it. Not surprisingly, many perceive the hypothesis as a dismaying attack on human rationality (c.f. Ceraso & Provitera, 1971; Wason & Johnson-Laird, 1972). But, regardless of the authors' positions, the data and the hypothesis have, on balance, persisted in agreeing with each other quite well (e.g., Begg & Denny, 1969; Ceraso & Provitera, 1971; Chapman & Chapman, 1959; Revlis, 1975b; Simpson & Johnson, 1966; Guyote & Sternberg, 1981). Could this be pure coincidence? Or is it the case, as the effect suggests, that human argumentation is driven as much by rhyme as by reason?

An escape from this dilemma can be found through the Euler tables (Tables IV, VI, VII, and VIII). An examination of these tables reveals that for every pair of premises except EE, regardless of the figure, there is at least one legitimate interpretation that leads necessarily to a conclusion predicted by the atmosphere hypothesis. More precisely, as shown in the last column of Table XII, for every pair of premises except EE, the *majority* of legitimate interpretations—82% on average—lead necessarily to either the A–C or the C–A conclusion that is favored by their atmosphere. What this means is that the now well-documented atmosphere effect may not be the product of linguistic whimsy at all: it may instead be the product of solid deductive reasoning, albeit on but a fraction of the appropriate representations of the premise information. At the very least, Table XII makes clear that, once having been raised through whatever process, the probability with which an invalid conclusion that is consistent with the atmosphere hypothesis can be properly rejected will depend on the completeness with which the reasoner has encoded the premises of the argument.

But neither is the complete encoding of a pair of premises enough to guarantee the demise of such a conclusion. The right-most column of Table XIII shows that for every legitimate interpretation of every pair of premises, at least one of the two conclusions favored by the atmosphere effect is *possible* or *may* follow. The other tabulations in Table XIII show that either atmosphere conclusion by itself may follow from every interpretation of the majority of pertinent premise pairs as well as from the majority of interpretations of every pertinent premise pair. The significance of these counts is that, even if all interpretations of a pair of premises have been recognized, the probability of dismissing an invalid atmosphere conclusion will depend additionally on the rigor of the reasoner's hypothesis-testing procedure. In particular, people are known to have a strong tendency toward examining available information only for support and not for falsification of their working hypotheses (for a review, see Wason & Johnson-Laird, 1972). To the extent that this tendency is operative in syllogistic reasoning tasks, Table XIII shows that it would generally support any bias toward conclusions predicted by the atmosphere hypothesis.

Taken together, Tables XII and XIII suggest that the atmosphere effect may stem, not from syntactic set as originally hypothesized, but from the process involved in the interpretation of the ambiguous quantifiers and the verification of candidate conclusions. If reasoners concentrate on just one of the possible interpretations of a pair of premises for purposes of deducing and ascertaining the necessity of a trial conclusion, Table XII shows that they may well end up with a proposition that is consistent with the atmosphere hypothesis. If, before committing themselves to such a trial solution, reasoners proceed to check its compatibility, but not its necessity, against other interpretations of the premises, Table XIII shows that they may well fail to reject the conclusion even if it is invalid. Furthermore, in multiple-choice or true–false tasks, as have been used in most psychological studies of the logic, the process of deciding upon a response might consist only in the second of these steps. That is, instead of going to the bother of independently generating trial conclusions from the premises, the reasoner might simply work from the alternatives provided, checking the compatibility or possibility of each against the various interpretations of the premises. Such a shortcut would render conclusions predicted by the atmosphere hypothesis all the more likely.

On the other hand, syntactic explanations of the atmosphere effect have been resuscitated of late. Specifically, it is argued that such syntactic bias is a consequence of the fact that the syllogisms are presented, and therefore

TABLE XII

NECESSARY CONCLUSIONS THAT ARE CONSISTENT WITH THE ATMOSPHERE HYPOTHESIS

Premises	Conclusion favored by atmosphere	Total number of relevant interpretations	Figure 1 A-C	Figure 1 C-A	Figure 2 A-C	Figure 2 C-A	Figure 3 A-C	Figure 3 C-A	Figure 4 A-C	Figure 4 C-A	Percentage all figures A-C	Percentage all figures C-A	Percentage all figures A-C or C-A
AA	A	4	1	4[a]	2	2	2	2	4[a]	1	56	56	88
AI	I	8	8[a]	8[a]	6	6	8[a]	8[a]	6	6	88	88	88
AO	O	6	4	3	3	6[a]	6[a]	2	4	4	71	63	92
AE	E	2	1	1	2[a]	2[a]	1	1	2[a]	2[a]	75	75	75
IA	I	8	6	6	6	6	8[a]	8[a]	8[a]	8[a]	88	88	88
II	I	16	12	12	12	12	12	12	12	12	75	75	75
IO	O	12	6	7	6	7	9	4	9	4	63	46	83
IE	O	4	4[a]	2	4[a]	2	4[a]	2	4[a]	2	100	50	100
OA	O	6	4	4	6[a]	3	2	6[a]	3	4	63	71	92
OI	O	12	4	9	7	6	4	9	7	6	46	63	83
OO	O	9	2	6	3	3	4	4	6	2	42	42	72
OE	O	3	2	1	2	0	2	1	2	0	67	17	67
EA	E	2	2[a]	2[a]	2[a]	2[a]	1	1	1	1	75	75	75
EI	O	4	2	4[a]	2	4[a]	2	4[a]	2	4[a]	50	100	100
EO	O	3	0	2	0	2	1	2	1	2	17	67	67
EE	E	1	0	0	0	0	0	0	0	0	0	0	0
		100	58	71	63	63	66	66	71	58	64.5	64.5	82

Note header: *Number of relevant interpretations for which favored conclusion is necessary*

[a] Valid conclusions.

TABLE XIII

Possible Conclusions That Are Consistent with the Atmosphere Hypothesis

Premises	Conclusion favored by atmosphere	Total number of relevant interpretations	Figure 1 A-C	Figure 1 C-A	Figure 2 A-C	Figure 2 C-A	Figure 3 A-C	Figure 3 C-A	Figure 4 A-C	Figure 4 C-A	Percentage all figures A-C	Percentage all figures C-A	Percentage all figures A-C or C-A
			Number of relevant interpretations for which favored conclusions is possible										
AA	A	4	1	4	3	3	3	3	4	1	69	69	100
AI	I	8	8	8	8	8	8	8	8	8	100	100	100
AO	O	6	5	6	4	6	6	4	6	5	88	88	100
AE	E	2	2	2	2	2	2	2	2	2	100	100	100
IA	I	8	8	8	8	8	8	8	8	8	100	100	100
II	I	16	16	16	16	16	16	16	16	16	100	100	100
IO	O	12	10	12	10	12	12	10	12	10	92	92	100
IE	O	4	4	4	4	4	4	4	4	4	100	100	100
OA	O	6	5	6	6	4	4	6	6	5	88	88	100
OI	O	12	10	12	12	10	10	12	12	10	92	92	100
OO	O	9	8	9	9	9	9	9	9	8	97	97	100
OE	O	3	3	3	3	3	3	3	3	3	100	100	100
EA	E	2	2	2	2	2	2	2	2	2	100	100	100
EI	O	4	4	4	4	4	4	4	4	4	100	100	100
EO	O	3	3	3	3	3	3	3	3	3	100	100	100
EE	E	1	1	1	1	1	1	1	1	1	100	100	100
		100	90	100	95	95	95	95	100	90	95	95	100

tend to be treated, as linguistic information rather than logical formalisms. In treating the syllogisms as efforts after linguistic communication, the reasoner tends to ascribe a certain degree of rhetorical coherence to them which, as logical formalisms, they do not warrant.

In particular, Begg and Harris (1982) have found that people strive to establish some consistency amid the relationships expressed within the arguments. In their experiment, subjects were given pairs of inconcludent premises and asked to fill in or instantiate their terms so that they would be true in the real world. Instead of interpreting the two premises independently, subjects were found to treat them as a package, imposing the same relationship on each. Thus, the likelihood was that if one premise was instantiated so as to express intersection, so too, if possible, would be the other; if one premise was instantiated so as to express subordination, so too, if possible, would be the other; and so on. Inasmuch as greater ambiguity is equivalent to greater interpretive freedom, it is not surprising that this tendency was especially evident for particular premises. Furthermore, although the subjects were not asked to express conclusions to the pairs of premises, their instantiations were such that the implicit relationship between the A and C terms was highly likely to match the relationship imposed on at least one of the two premises.

In short, Begg and Harris's (1982) subjects behaved in close compliance with the atmosphere hypothesis. Given the choice, people evidently prefer to instantiate the terms of a syllogism such that the argument as a whole does not merely consist of a series of disjointed propositions, but instead, within the available degrees of freedom, attains a coherent, interarticulated rhetorical structure. Given the strength of their own disposition toward this end, it should not be surprising for them to suppose the same of others and, in particular, of the syllogism's producer. Thus, within Begg and Harris's framework, the atmosphere effect is seen as the *result* of efforts after consistent syntactic structure rather than vice versa.

To summarize, although the atmosphere hypothesis, as originally presented, might easily be seen to impute a distasteful degree of irrationality to the reasoner, the effect it predicts might alternatively result through certain categories of entirely rational, if imperfect, reasoning strategies. The first of these categories may be seen as a response to the inherent ambiguity of the categorical propositions: by choice or default the reasoner may focus attention on the implications of but some subset of the permissible interpretations of the premises. The second of these categories reflects a common weakness of the human reasoner but may be aggravated by the heavy processing load that is required for syllogistic reasoning and by the format of the typical experimental task: The reasoner may attempt to verify the generality of a tentative conclusion by checking only its compatibility but not its necessity against alternate interpretations of the premises. The third category of strategy through which the atmosphere effect might be produced consists in treating the syllogisms as efforts after linguistic communication rather than logical formalisms. Within this category, the reasoner will be prone toward overinterpreting the premises such that the information they are seen to offer approximates the completeness and coherence that is to be expected of cooperative discourse.

C. THE CONVERSION HYPOTHESIS

Woodworth (1938) reported a very simple experiment of Eidens (1929) in which subjects were asked to answer questions of the form. "What can you say about P, given that all S are P?" The questions were varied so as to probe all four types of categorical propositions. The important result, Woodworth summarized, was that most of the eleven subjects, all of them highly educated adults, answered with the converse for all of the propositions, including A and O.

Woodworth took this result in stride, pointing out that the atmosphere phenomenon should make it easy to accept illicit converses. Later, however, Chapman and Chapman (1959) suggested that the tendency toward illicit conversion was inspired in and of itself and was better viewed as a cause than a consequence of the atmosphere effect.

Most recently, Revlin (Revlin & Leirer, 1978; Revlis, 1975a,b) has adopted Chapman and Chapman's conversion hypothesis as a central assumption of his theory of the psychology of syllogistic reasoning. According to Revlin, in the course of interpreting quantified relations between two categories, there exists an operation that treats the relation as symmetric. Through this operation, the reasoner automatically encodes both the given relation and its converse. If the original proposition was meaningful, but the converse is silly (e.g., "all ducks are birds" versus "All birds are ducks"), then the converse is dropped. Otherwise, it becomes the priority representation in the reasoner's meaning stack. Combining this version of the conversion hypothesis with the assumption that, at least in multiple-choice tasks, people are biased against responding that no valid conclusion exists, Revlin has succeeded in predicting his subjects' performance quite well.

Despite the successes of Revlin's model, the assumption that the encoding of a categorical premise obligatorily includes its conversion is suspect. First, when the variables of the syllogistic formulae are replaced with meaningful terms, errors of conversion become rare. As mentioned above, Revlin holds that this is not evidence that conversion has not occurred, but only that an additional semantic evaluation process also occurs. In contrast, Chapman and Chapman (1959) suggested that, at least for A propositions, it might be the very presence of the variable terms that provokes conversion. Specifically, they suggested that, with letters for terms, the syllogisms take on a mathematics-like formality, and that the subjects, accordingly, interpret the copula, "are," as meaning "equal to" and, therefore, as being convertible.

Detracting further from Revlin's thesis is the fact that when adults have been asked to interpret the categorical propositions in terms of the Euler diagrams, blatant conversion errors have been nonexistent (Begg & Harris, 1982; Neimark & Chapman, 1975). That is, propositions of the form "All A are B" were never construed to mean that B was a subset of A (diagram J of our Euler tables); similarly, "Some A are not B" was never construed to mean that A was a subset of B (diagram L). Both of these errors might be expected if Revlin's strong version of the conversion hypothesis were taken at face value. Notably, Neimark and Chapman (1975) found that, very occasionally, their youngest subjects (12 year olds) did commit these errors, and under the load of solving complete syllogisms, it is entirely possible that adults would too. Still, it seems clear that people do not automatically convert the premises in the course of encoding them.

The observation that led Chapman and Chapman (1959) to suggest the conversion hypotheses was that those invalid moods which were most consistently misjudged as valid would in fact have been valid had they been presented in a different figure. Inasmuch as it is precisely the order of the terms within premises that distinguishes one figure from another, such errors could be fully reconciled by the conversion of one or both of the arguments' premises. The difficulty with this explanation is, of course, that willy-nilly conversion of the premises will not work. Transforming a particular mood from invalid to valid by changing its figure depends on converting the exact right combination of premises. Within Revlin's theory, reasoners are driven toward this combination by force of their bias against responding "no valid conclusion": Through a systematic process, they discard the converted version of the first and then the second premise until a concludent combination is found.

An alternative and more plausible explanation for apparent conversion errors was suggested (but not pursued) by both Chapman and Chapman (1959) and Revlin (1978; Revlis, 1975a). Specifically, such errors would be expected if, instead of recognizing all possible interpretations of the premises, people tended to encode only the symmetrical version of each type. Thus, A propositions would be represented by identity relation (diagram K or Q in the Euler tables), I and O propositions by intersecting sets (diagram M or S), and E propositions by nonintersecting sets (diagram N or T). An examination of Tables IV, VI, VII, and VIII proves that, if people did so, the apparent concludence of any given argument would be wholly dependent on its mood and independent of its figure—for example, AAA arguments would always involve cell K,Q and, therefore, would always seem as solid in the second figure as they would in any other. Furthermore, unlike the automatic conversion hypothesis, the notion that people may selectively attend to the symmetrical representations of the categorical propositions has, as will be discussed in the next section, received relatively strong empirical support.

D. THE SET ANALYSIS THEORY

Virtually no article on the psychology of the syllogism has failed to note that at least part of the reasoner's difficulty with the arguments may derive from the ambiguity of the categorical propositions. Ceraso and Provitera (1971) suggested that this might indeed be the principle source of difficulty. To test their hypothesis, they compared people's performance on two different sets of syllogisms. The premises for the first set of syllogisms consisted of the traditional categorical propositions. For the second set, each premise consisted of an unambiguous description of exactly one of the Euler relations, for example, the subset–superset relation was expressed as "Whenever I have a yellow block, it is striped, but there are some striped blocks which are not yellow" (p. 403). As predicted, the subjects' performance was considerably better with the modified syllogisms. Moreover, they responded to the traditional syllogisms as though they had been presented with the modified syllogisms. The only other major category of error in Ceraso and Provitera's data was directly related to the number of distinct ways in which the two premise relations could be combined.

Following Ceraso and Provitera's lead, Erickson (1974) theorized that people might generally interpret the categorical propositions in terms of just one of their underlying relations. His assumptions about the probabilities with which any one of these relations would be chosen are given in Table XIV. Using these values, Erickson tested the predictions of his theory against the performance of subjects with valid syllogisms in a conclusion-production task. The fit proved to be excellent. Interestingly, it was even better under the assumption that subjects examine but one of the possible combinations of their chosen Euler relations ($r = .97$) than under the assumption that they examine all possible combinations of the pair of relations ($r = .84$). Through subsequent experiments, Erickson has developed estimates of the probabilities with which, for given pairs of Euler relations, each of the various combined interpretations will be chosen. With these estimates, the theory has also proved to be a good predictor of people's performance on invalid syllogisms.

TABLE XIV

ERICKSON'S (1974) ESTIMATES OF THE PROBABILITIES
WITH WHICH EACH OF THE SET RELATIONS WILL BE USED
TO REPRESENT EACH OF THE CATEGORICAL PROPOSITIONS

Propositions	A in B	AB	B in A	$A \cap B$	A, B disjoint
All A are B	.25	.75	0	0	0
Some A are B	0	0	.25	.75	0
Some A are not B	0	0	0	1	0
No A are B	0	0	0	0	1

Implicit in the values in Table XIV are the suggestions, first, that people are indeed somewhat biased toward the symmetrical representation of each of the propositions and, second, that there are indeed certain legitimate interpretations of the particular propositions which people are biased against. According to Erickson, these values were based on nothing more than a rough retrofit from his conclusion-production data. Nevertheless, they are quite consistent with results from studies in which subjects were directly requested to map the propositions onto the Euler diagrams (Begg & Harris, 1982; Neimark & Chapman, 1975). The only significant exception is that the latter investigators found that, like affirmative particular propositions, negative particulars readily admit the appropriate subset–superset relation as well as the intersection relation.

Begg and Harris (1982) have argued that the motive behind people's incomplete mappings of the particular propositions is, once again, the tendency to treat the syllogisms as instances of normal linguistic offerings. Applying Grice's (1967) conversational maxims, the reasoner can expect that the information to be conveyed has been expressed as succinctly but completely and unambiguously as possible given his or her own known interpretative needs and biases. In particular, the reasoner may expect that "some" is intended to mean "some but not all." If the communicator meant for the possibility of "all" to be understood, it should have been specified; if the communicator meant to be vague, the quantifier should have been omitted all together.

Finally, reasoners' willingness to make do with the first joint interpretation of the premises that they generate, may be taken as another instance of their reluctance or inability to recognize bona fide challenges to their working hypotheses.

E. THE ANALOGICAL THEORY

Recently, Johnson-Laird and Steedman (1978) proposed a very appealing model of human syllogistic reasoning. Within their model, people represent the classes corresponding to the terms of the arguments by imagining some arbitrary number of their exemplars. The relations between classes are then encoded as positive or negative pointers from the exemplars corresponding to the subject of a proposition to the exemplars corresponding to the predicate. To capture the multiple meanings of the propositions, the representations may include optional exemplars that are accordingly connected or not. For example, the proposition "All A are B" would be represented by a set of as which point, one-to-one, to a set of bs; the possibility that not all B are A would be recognized by including some optional bs that are not connected to as. Similarly, "Some A are B" would be represented by some number of as pointing, one-to-one, to some number of bs and an optional set of unconnected as and bs. The negative relations are not as gracefully configured, but the idea is the same. The second premise is then represented by relating some set of cs to the same set of bs. In this way, the process of combining the two premises is merely a concomitant of encoding them.

A conclusion to the syllogism is formulated by examining the paths that can be constructed from the as to the cs via the bs. If the as and cs can only be connected via positive pointers, the reasoner is expected to conclude that some A are C. If all of the as can be thus connected, the reasoner is expected to conclude that all A are C. The conditions for the negative relations are similar.

Because the terms of the arguments are represented as sets of discrete elements, there is rarely but one way in which the paths between the as and the cs might be configured. As an example, consider the premises "All A are B" and "All C are B." If all of the as and the cs point to the *same* subset of bs, the evident conclusion will be "All A are C"; if all of the as point to *different* bs from any of the cs, the evident conclusion will be "No A are C"; if the linked bs overlap, the evident conclusion will be "Some A are C." To ascertain the validity of their conclusions, therefore, reasoners must test them to see whether there is any alternate arrangement or reading of the pointers that would render them false.

The very nice aspect of Johnson-Laird and Steedman's model is that, within it, the dominant categories of reasoning errors are the products of very plausible hazards of the representational process. Failures to recognize all possible interpretations of the premises are produced by failures to register or properly interconnect all conceivable optional elements. The atmosphere effect will be produced by a bias toward linking the as and the cs to the same subset of bs. The common reluctance to seek falsifying evidence for one's working conclusion would be equivalent to a reluctance or difficulty in radically altering one's established representation of the premise information.

The model also handles and even elaborates the effect of the order of the terms that was anticipated by Aristotle in his distinction between perfect and imperfect syllogisms. Recall that, within the model, the links between the terms of a proposition are unidirectional—they are schematized by pointers extending from the exemplars of its subject to the exemplars of its predicate. The underlying assumption is that the relation should be far more difficult to access in the reverse direction.

From this assumption, the general advantage of the first and fourth figure syllogisms follows readily. In the representations for both of these figures, one end term should point *to* the middle term while the other should point *from* the middle term. Thus, a natural path is set up from one end to the other. The assumption also leads to the prediction that the concludence of those first figure syllogisms that were initially overlooked by Aristotle and disallowed within the traditional framework should be especially difficult to establish. The reason is that the conclusion can only be established by traversing the paths through the terms in the unnatural direction, from predicates to subjects. For the same reason, the converse syllogisms of the fourth figure should be equally elusive. These effects are in fact strongly expressed in the performance of Johnson-Laird and Steedman's subjects.

The explanation for this subject-to-predicate effect is to be found, once again, in the linguistic predispositions evoked by the arguments. In normal language, the subject of a sentence, or more generally, the information presented earlier in a discourse, sets the topic or context within which later information is to be interpreted. To the extent that reasoners treat the syllogisms as normal language, they will carry certain expectations about the coherence or relations in topic or emphasis that ought to hold among the premises and the conclusion they beg. As a consequence, reasoners are likely to display a certain deference toward using whichever of the end terms has served as a subject in the premises, as the subject or topic of their conclusions. According to Sanford and Garrod (1981), this bias is not merely a question of linguistic cooperation, but a product of the way in which the information is processed in memory. Under this view, the reasoner is virtually obliged to maintain the topic of the argument.

F.   THE TRANSITIVE CHAIN MODEL

The transitive chain model was recently proposed by Guyote and Sternberg (1981) and is mentioned here primarily for the sake of completeness. At the level of premise representation, the model resembles Erickson's

(1974, 1978) in that it is assumed that what people understand from the categorical premises is exactly that information that is schematized in the Euler diagrams. Instead of representing the information with the Euler diagrams as Erickson has, however, Guyote and Sternberg restate it in a propositional form of their own invention. As an example, the Euler diagram showing that B is a proper set of A would, within Guyote and Sternberg's model, be represented as:

$$B \rightarrow A \qquad \left| \begin{array}{l} a_1 \rightarrow B \\ a_2 \rightarrow -B \end{array} \right.$$

Letting upper-case letters refer to whole classes and lower-case letters to parts of classes, this representation is to mean that all of class B belongs to A whereas at least one member of class A belongs to B and at least one does not. Again, that is exactly what is conveyed by the corresponding Euler diagram. Inasmuch as both Erickson and Guyote and Sternberg assert that the representations they use in explicating their respective theories should correspond to reasoners' mental representations, not literally, but only by analogy, the difference in their representational schemes is, in itself, of no theoretical significance.

Guyote and Sternberg's premise combination process resembles that of Johnson-Laird and Steedman's (1978) in that it consists in building paths from representations of one of the end terms to the representations of the other via their common associations with the middle term. It is in this process, however, that Guyote and Sternberg's choice of representational scheme makes a difference. First, within Johnson-Laird and Steedman's model, A–C versus C–A conclusions are had by traversing the same representation of the premises in opposite directions. In contrast, within Guyote and Sternberg's model, the availability of both A–C and C–A conclusions depends upon constructing and processing two separate interpretive chains: $ABBC$ and $CBBA$. Oddly enough, although Guyote and Sternberg assume that people generally do process the relations between premises in both directions, the multiple-choice task through which their model is tested includes only A–C responses. Second, within Johnson-Laird and Steedman's model, the classes are consistently represented by collections of tokens, such that alternate interpretations of the individual premises can be captured within the same representation and alternate interpretations of the combined premises are had by varying the paths from one end of the representation to the other. As an explanatory device, Johnson-Laird and Steedman's model has the additional asset that the various relations that can be constructed between the A and C terms are open to concrete manipulation and visual inspection by the reader. In contrast, within Guyote and Sternberg's model, each interpretation of each premise gets its own, separate mental representation, and complete representation of the combined premises requires the construction of a separate *ABBC* and *CBBA* chain for every different pair of interpretations of the individual premises. Furthermore, because the representational scheme only admits symbols for whole classes or their exceptional elements, the relations that may hold between the two end terms of a chain are generally not transparent; their specification is instead supposed to depend upon the application of the appropriate interpretive rules. Unfortunately, in order to respond to all combinations of symbols—positive and negative, generic and token—the list of interpretive rules is necessarily quite long and complicated. (Notably, Guyote and Sternberg have provided a complete list of requisite rules in neither the body nor the appendix of their text.) Finally, like the cells in our Euler tables, any given premise chain may admit up to four different possible relations between *A* and *C*, and these too, once generated, are presumably encoded as separate propositions. In short, as compared to Johnson-Laird and Steedman's representational system, Guyote and Sternberg's provides a relatively economical means of encoding individual interpretations of the premises. But it is both less economical and less supportive for the tasks of encoding multiple interpretations of a premise and of combining the pairs of interpretations in the quest for potential conclusions.

After Guyote and Sternberg's theoretical reasoners are finished combining interpretations of the premises, they are left with some set of propositions representing possible relations between *A* and *C*. Their task at this point is to formulate a conclusion that is consistent with all such propositions. If they can think of only one consistent conclusion, they will look through the multiple-choice list, responding when they find it. (Again, the choices included only *A–C* responses despite the fact that the problems included several for which only *C–A* conclusions are valid.) If the reasoners think of more than one consistent conclusion, they choose between them on the basis of a modified version of the atmosphere principle. On the other hand, if the initial components of their candidate relations do not match, that is, if some of the propositions start with lower-case and others with upper-case letters, then with a probability of *c*, reasoners simply declare themselves confused and respond that the argument is indeterminate. At this point it is worth recalling that the propositions representing the various relations between classes in Guyote and Sternberg's system are isomorphic with the Euler diagrams. If Guyote and Sternberg had chosen to use the diagrams in the place of their system of upper- and lower-case letters, they might have found no need to posit this confusion factor.

Guyote and Sternberg offer that the major difference between Erickson's (1974) complete combination model and their own centers on his assumption that people generally encode just one interpretation of each premise. Guyote and Sternberg assume, in contrast, that people always encode all interpretations of each premise but that, for reasons of memory or processing capacity, they can combine and consider the consequences of at most four pairs of interpretations. Indeed, by modeling their assumptions mathematically and estimating the parameters from their subjects' performance, Guyote and Sternberg eventually conclude that, as often as not, people in fact combine only one pair of premise interpretations.

Note that if people generally work with just one interpretation of the premises, the contention that they recognize more than one is of no practical significance. Guyote and Sternberg further assume that the pairs of interpretations with which people will choose to work will be chosen in order of their representational complexity. It just happens that, for any given premise, the representationally simplest interpretation corresponds to one of the symmetrical Euler diagrams, that is, it is precisely the interpretation that is favored within Erickson's models.

IV. The Reasoner versus the Logic

From the preceding review of the psychology of the syllogism, we may adduce three major classes of difficulty that may beset the human reasoner: (1) inappropriate application of language comprehension heuristics; (2) incomplete processing of the premise information; and (3) the tendency to verify rather than validate working hypotheses. But difficulties in processing the syllogisms are not necessarily indicative of incompetencies with the logic that the syllogisms are intended to convey.

As was argued in Section II,D, Aristotle developed the syllogisms only as an intermediate form in his analysis of discourse. Although through history they have often been taken as the laws of logic, that was not the original intent. The syllogisms were intended only as expressions of those laws. Their import, therefore, lies not in their individual forms, but in their collective content, and that might be expressed in many other ways. In this section we will consider the extent to which people's apparent difficulties with the logic might be owed to some fault in design or presentation of the syllogisms.

A. INAPPROPRIATE APPLICATION OF LANGUAGE
COMPREHENSION HEURISTICS

Among the recurrent findings of studies on the psychology of syllogistic reasoning is that people tend to construe the premises and construct their conclusions so as to lend the arguments a degree of coherence and completeness that they do not literally possess. This, it is argued, is a consequence of the fact that the syllogisms are presented, and therefore tend to be treated as linguistic information rather than logical formalisms.

Analyses of natural language make clear that its content scarcely alludes to its meaning. Instead, accurate, efficient linguistic communication depends upon a cooperative contract between speakers or writers and their audience. Specifically, of the information that is relevant to their message, speakers or writers are to specify only as much as they think their audience might not otherwise presume or supply on their own. Within the limits thus defined, their contribution must be complete, coherent, and unambiguous. This means, of course, that in order for the message to appear complete, coherent, and unambiguous to its recipient, she or he in turn must readily supply whatever information and clarification is required to make it so.

If the syllogisms are perceived as efforts after linguistic communication, then reasoners will naturally overinterpret them. On the assumption that the information to be conveyed is expressed as succinctly but completely and unambiguously as possible given her or his own known interpretive needs and biases, the reasoner may rightfully support that "some" is intended to mean "some but not all" (see, e.g., Begg & Harris, 1982; Chapman & Chapman, 1959); if the possibility of "all" is meant to be understood, then why specify "some"? The reason dates back to Aristotle: He was concerned that, without the "some," indefinite statements were too often interpreted as *universals*. In the effort to achieve an effective compromise, psychologists have generally prefaced their experiments with the instruction that "some" is to be interpreted as "at least one and possibly all." This has been found to help (see Frase, 1966), but not a lot. It thus seems that people's difficulty in processing the ambiguity of the propositions is largely independent of how they are expressed.

As language users, reasoners further expect the arguments to reflect a certain degree of structural coherence. They thus strive to maintain whichever of the end terms has served as a subject of the premises, as the subject or topic of their conclusion (Johnson-Laird & Steedman, 1978), and, within the interpretive freedom afforded by the ambiguity of the premises, to impose consistency on the relation expressed by the separate propositions (Begg & Harris, 1982).

In contrast to the problem with particular and indefinite propositions, people's inclination to impose order on the topical and relational structure of the arguments can only be blamed on the presentation of the logic. Aristotle, after all, invented the syllogisms as a means of enabling people to extract the logically necessary information from discourse and thus to loose themselves from the interpretive acquiescence that language invites. To the extent that people nevertheless perceive and treat the syllogisms as discourse, the system cannot serve its purpose.

How could this problem be remedied? One possibility might be to make the system less seductively language-like. One might recast it on terms of, say, propositional logic. The major drawback to this solution is that the logic would remain relatively inaccessible except to reasoners with special training.

One might alternatively rid the arguments of their linguistic character by having people translate them into appropriate combination of Euler diagrams. The Euler matrices (Tables IV, VI, VII, and VIII) yield a relatively simple set of rules for identifying inconcludent premise pairs. Specifically, whenever *both* premises can be mapped onto (1) the overlap relation (diagrams M and S), (2) the exclusion relation (diagrams N and T), or (3) the relation wherein the middle term is a proper superset of the other (diagrams L and P), no valid conclusion will exist. The reason is that, in each of these three cases, the middle term, B, totally fails to mediate the relation between A and C—it provides absolutely no information or constraints on how A and C might relate to each other. The only inconcludent premise pairs that are not covered by these three rules are AO of the first figure and OA of the fourth. The includence of these premise pairs derives from the fact that from the O propositions B may be either a proper subset of or entirely distinct from the related end term: When combined with the A proposition, which asserts that B is a subset of the other end term, these two possibilities lead to conclusions that contradict each other and thereby rule out all others. The principal disadvantage to the Euler diagrams is that no such simple set of rules can be formulated for determining the permissible conclusions to valid syllogisms, and the alternate route of deducing the common conclusions to all pertinent pairs of diagrams would seem difficult to manage in one's head—although, as will be discussed later, it can be markedly simplified.

As yet another approach, contemporary logicians offer a set of rules through which one can evaluate the concludence of the arguments without even considering their meaning (see, e.g., Copi, 1961; Lemmon, 1965):

1. In a valid syllogism, no term can be distributed in the conclusion unless it is distributed in the premises.
2. The middle term of a valid syllogism must be distributed at least once.
3. If one of the premises of a syllogism is negative, its conclusion must be negative.
4. There is no valid syllogism with two negative premises.

Through the (occasionally chained and complex) application of these rules, one can identify all of the inconcludent premise pairs and generate permissible conclusions to all of the others that are recognized within the contemporary syllogistic system. My only problems with these rules, aside from the fact that they are not consistently easy to use, are (1) they do not help me understand the logic behind the deductions they prescribe, and (2) they do not work once the possibility of A–C conclusions is admitted.

As a final possibility, a solution might be had by changing the manner in which the syllogisms are presented. Instead of presenting them, as Aristotle did, as skeletal arguments into which discourse could be translated, one might present them as a set of rules through which discourse could be evaluated. For example, the essential logic of the syllogism could be developed through queries such as, "If all you know is that at least some A are B, what might you find out about the relation between B and C that would permit you to infer something definite about the way in which A and C are related?" The only possibilities are that all B are C or that no B are C. The complete set of such concludent pairs of dyadic relations is given in Table XV. This set is sufficient to identify all of the concludent premise pairs of the categorical syllogisms. If one is interested not just in identifying concludent pairs but, further, in the strongest conclusions that can be had, the relations provided in Table XVI will suffice. The relations in Table XVI are sufficient to identify all of the valid categorical syllogisms, conclusions and all.

The systems presented in Tables XV and XVI are vastly simpler than the traditional syllogistic system. Instead of 64 different pairs of premises, Table XV includes just 4, and Table XVI (ignoring the redundant pairs) includes just 6. There are two reasons why the lists of premise pairs in Tables XV and XVI are so short. The first is that inconcludent pairs are not enumerated but defined by exclusion. The second is that the figures are partially collapsed because each of t_i and t_j can represent either end term. Such flexible specification of the end terms is intended not only to reduce the requisite number of rules but, further, to eliminate the topic effect.

TABLE XV

Minimally Concludent Pairs of Dyadic Relations[a]

Relation i	Relation j	Conclusion
At least some t_i are m	All m are t_j	At least some t_i are t_j
	No m are t_j	At least some t_i are not t_j
At least some t_i are not m	All t_j are m	At least some t_i are not t_j
At least some m are not t_i	All m are t_j	At least some t_j are not t_i

[a] The two terms to be related are represented by t_i and t_j; the mediating term is represented by m.

TABLE XVI

DYADIC RELATIONS AND THEIR STRONGEST CONCLUSIONS[a]

Relation i	Relation j	Conclusions
1. All t_i are m	a. All m are t_j	$\begin{cases} \text{All } t_i \text{ are } t_j \\ \text{At least some } t_j \text{ are } t_i \end{cases}$
	b. At least some t_j are not m	At least some t_j are not t_i
	c. No t_j are m	No t_j are t_i
2. All m are t_i	a. All t_j are m^b	$\begin{cases} \text{All } t_j \text{ are } t_i \\ \text{At least some } t_i \text{ are } t_j \end{cases}$
	b. At least some t_j are m	At least some t_j are t_i
	c. At least some m are not t_j	At least some t_i are not t_j
3. No t_i are m	a. All t_i are m^c	No t_i are t_j
	b. At least some t_j are m	$\begin{cases} \text{At least some } t_j \text{ are not } t_i \\ \text{At least some } t_i \text{ are not } t_j \end{cases}$

[a] The two terms to be related are represented by t_i and t_j; the mediating term is represented by m.
[b] This pair is redundant with pair 1a.
[c] This pair is redundant with pair 1c.

B. INCOMPLETE PROCESSING OF THE PREMISE INFORMATION

Incomplete processing of the premise information is surely a major source of error in human syllogistic reasoning. In Section III, it was suggested as sufficient cause for both the atmosphere effect and the apparent phenomenon of illicit converison. In addition, it is centrally assumed in the models of Erickson (1974, 1978), Johnson-Laird and Steedman (1978), and Guyote and Sternberg (1981).

The problem derives in part from people's difficulty in recognizing the alternate interpretations of the individual premises. But having done so, the task of determining their joint implications is a challenge in itself. As is shown by the Euler matrices (Tables IV, VI, VII, and VIII), each premise of a syllogism may be translated into as many as 4 distinct set relations; each pair of premises may be translated into as many as 16 combined set relations; each combined set relation may yield as many as four different conclusions; and of all those conclusions, the only ones that follow validly from the original premises are those which are common to all of their combined interpretations. From this perspective, failures to process the premise information properly might be wholly attributed to limitations of memory or processing capacity.

On the other hand—and this point is both very important and generally overlooked—it is not necessary that the reasoner consider all interpretations of the premises. It is sufficient that he or she consider only those that bracket or capture the extremes of the range of possible relationships that can be established between the end terms. Any conclusion that is compatible with both the strongest and weakest interpretations of the premises will necessarily be compatible with any between them; if no such conclusion exists, the premises are indeterminant.

This bracketing principle substantially reduces the storage and processing requirements of the arguments. In the present context, however, it is perhaps more interesting that it renders the overlap relation entirely superfluous: As the overlap relation is itself the most neutral or intermediate interpretation of the particular propositions, so too are the conclusions it yields. Moreover, the identity relation is proved almost as useless: It can mediate extreme conclusions only when paired with itself. Recall that these two relations correspond respectively to people's preferred interpretations of particular and universal affirmative premises.

C. THE VERIFICATION FALLACY

Of the three classes of difficulties that were extracted from the theories and data on the psychology of syllogistic reasoning, this one must be owed exclusively to the reasoner. The tendency to "test" one's hypotheses by seeking out only information that fits them, or by interpreting information only so that it does fit them, is an extremely prevalent weakness of the human reasoner. In the preceding review, the verification fallacy was expressly cited for people's willingness to accept possible but unnecessary conclusions, but it may also be responsible for their reluctance or inability to properly recognize the disparate meanings of "some." More generally, the verification fallacy may spring from the very same mechanism as that which drives the necessarily presumptuous art of language comprehension. Ironically, it was precisely this presumptuousness which Aristotle intended for the logic to correct.

V. Summary

The syllogisms, as developed by Aristotle, were intended to represent the simplest of all possible implicative chains and, as such, to provide people with a simple, content-independent system for reducing and evaluating all possible argumentation. Aristotle's system, however, has eluded casual reasoners and has been disputed by scholars since its inception. The purpose of this article was to consider why this has been so: Does it reflect a fundamental irrationality of people or can it instead be ascribed to some flaw in the design or presentation of the logic?

Motivated by the disagreements among scholars as to the number of valid syllogisms that exist, the discussion was first focused on the logic itself. Most significantly, a system was invented for ascertaining which of the 64 possible pairs of premises do indeed yield necessary conclusions. Because of the transparency with which premises are mapped onto conclusions within this system, it should be an asset to students of the syllogism for practical reasons alone. In addition, however, the system was found to allow a number of valuable insights into the underlying structure of the syllogistic logic.

The results of this system were then compared with other analyses found in the literature. Excepting certain differences that were shown to be highly superficial in nature, the results of our new system were found to be in close agreement with Aristotle's text. Furthermore, the alternate counts of the syllogisms were generally seen to derive from trivial excursions from Aristotle's text. Some were traced to overly literal adoptions of parts of his original text, for example, the acknowledgment of exactly and only those valid arguments that he explicitly spelled out or the exclusion of all arguments whose conclusions contain the major (C) term as subject. Others were traced to logically inconsequential expansions of the system, for example, the formalization of the fourth figure and the separate recognition of subalternate conclusions. The final count considered, the Boolean count, additionally involved recognition of the existential fallacy which, though logically compelling in itself, may be considered peripheral to the syllogistic system.

An important coda to this discussion was the suggestion that Aristotle did not see the syllogistic system as an end in itself. To the extent that he developed the system, he consistently emphasized its internal redundancy; conversely, he frequently ignored or glossed over forms that offered no new structural or logical insights. For Aristotle, it seems that the syllogisms were but one form of expression, a convenient intermediate step in the effort to identify the basic logic of argumentation.

Consideration was then turned to theories of the psychology of syllogistic reasoning. From them we extracted three major classes of difficulty that beset the human reasoner. The first of these was the distortion of the syllogisms' content through inappropriate application of language comprehension heuristics. Inasmuch as such heuristics are crucial to making sense of natural langauge, one would not want people to remove them from their repertoire in any general way. On the other hand, in the interest of enabling logical analysis of discourse, one would like people to be able to escape from them when appropriate. The recommendation was therefore to recast the logic in a way that was less likely to trigger people's language comprehension routines. As additional desiderata, such a system should be relatively easy to understand and to translate to and from natural language. Two options were suggested: the Euler matrices and the minimal syllogistic frames of Tables XV and XVI.

The second class of difficulties was traced to the multiple possible interpretations of the premises. This class of difficulties was attributed in part to the processing load involved in managing all appropriate interpretations and their combinations. It was shown that this problem could be greatly reduced, however, if people would narrow consideration from the full range of interpretations that are possible to only those extreme interpretations that most rigidly constrain the conclusions.

The third class of difficulties was people's tendency to support rather than challenge their immediate understanding of the arguments. This was seen as a fundamental shortcoming of human reasoning and perhaps as the single most important reason why training with some digestible form of the logic may be considered so important a part of people's education. The syllogisms as developed by Aristotle represent one effort at capturing the logic in such a form. A major point of this article, however, is that they are not the only possible means of so doing. Psychologists interested in assessing people's logical abilities and educators interested in developing their logical abilities might be well advised to pay less attention to the syllogisms per se and more to the logic they were intended to convey.

ACKNOWLEDGMENTS

I would like to thank Alysia Loberfeld for her help in preparing the article. This research was supported by the National Institute of Education under Contract No. 400-80-0031.

REFERENCES

Aristotle. *Analytica Posteriora* (Translated by G. R. G. Mure). In W. D. Ross (Ed.), *The works of Aristotle*. Oxford: Clarendon, 1928.

Aristotle. *Analytica Priora* (Translated by A. J. Jenkinson). In W. D. Ross (Ed.), *The works of Aristotle*. Oxford: Clarendon, 1928.

Aristotle. *De Interpretatione* (Translated by E. M. Edghill). In W. D. Ross (Ed.), *The works of Aristotle*. Oxford: Clarendon, 1928.

Begg, I., & Denny, P. Empirical reconciliation of atmosphere and conversion interpretations of syllogistic reasoning errors. *Journal of Experimental Psychology*, 1969, **81**, 351–354.

Begg, I., & Harris, G. On the interpretation of syllogisms. *Journal of Verbal Learning and Verbal Behavior*, 1982, **21**, 595–620.

Ceraso, J., & Provitera, A. Sources of error in syllogistic reasoning. *Cognitive Psychology*, 1971, **2**, 400–410.

Chapman, L. J., & Chapman, J. P. The atmosphere effect reexamined. *Journal of Experimental Psychology*, 1959, **58**, 220–226.

Eidens, H. Experimentelle Untersuchungen ueber den Denkverlauf bei unmittelbaren Folgerungen. *Archives of Psychology Society*, 1929, **71**, 1–66 (cited in Woodworth, 1938).

Erickson, J. R. A set analysis theory of behavior in formal syllogistic reasoning tasks. In R. Solso (Ed.), *Theories in cognitive psychology: The Loyola symposium*. Potomac, Maryland: Erlbaum, 1974.

Erickson, J. R. Research on syllogistic reasoning. In R. Revlin & R.E. Mayer (Eds.), *Human reasoning*. New York: Holt, 1978.

Frase, L. T. Validity judgments of syllogisms in relation to two sets of terms. *Journal of Education Psychology*, 1966, **57**, 239–244.

Grice, H. P. *Logic and communication*. Cambridge, Massachusetts: The William James Lectures, Harvard University, 1967.

Guyote, M. J., & Sternberg, R. J. A transitive-chain theory of syllogistic reasoning. *Cognitive Psychology*, 1981, **13**, 461–525.

Johnson-Laird, P. N. Ninth Bartlett memorial lecture. Thinking as a skill. *Quarterly Journal of Experimental Psychology*, 1982, **34A**, 1–29.

Johnson-Laird, P. N., & Steedman, M. The psychology of syllogisms. *Cognitive Psychology*, 1978, **10**, 64–99.

Kant, I. *Die falsche Spitzfindigkeit der vier syllogistischen Figuren*. Konigsberg: 1762 (cited in Lukasiewicz, 1957; Patzig, 1968).

Kneale, W., & Kneale, M. *The development of logic*. Oxford: Clarendon, 1965.

Langer, S. K. *An introduction to symbolic logic*. New York: Dover, 1953.

Lemmon, E. J. *Beginning logic*. London: Nelson, 1965.

Lukasiewicz, J. *Aristotle's syllogistic*. Oxford: Clarendon, 1957.

Maier, H. *Die Syllogistik des Aristoteles*. Tuebingen: 1900 (cited in Lukasiewicz, 1957; Patzig, 1968).

Mates, B. *Elementary logic*. New York: Oxford, 1972.

McGraw-Hill encyclopedia of science and technology. New York: McGraw-Hill, 1960.

Neimark, E. D., & Chapman, R. H. Development of the comprehension of logical quantifiers. In R. J. Falmagne (Ed.), *Reasoning: Representation and process*. Hillsdale, New Jersey: Erlbaum, 1975.

Patzig, G. *Aristotle's theory of the syllogism*. Dordrecht: Reidel, 1968.

Prantl, C. Ueber die Entwicklung der aristotelischen Logik aus der platonischen Philosphie. *Abhandlungen der Koeniglich Bayerischen Akademie*, 1925, **VII**, 129–211 (cited in Lukasiewicz, 1957; Patzig, 1968).

Prior, A. N. *Formal logic*. Oxford: Clarendon, 1973.

Revlin, R., & Leirer, V. O. The effects of personal biases on syllogistic reasoning: Rational decision from personalized representations. In R. Revlin & R. E. Mayer (Eds.), *Human reasoning*. New York: Holt, 1978.

Revlis, R. Syllogistic reasoning: Logical decisions from a complex data base. In R. J. Falmagne (Ed.), *Reasoning: Representation and process*. Hillsdale, New Jersey: Erlbaum, 1975. (a)

Revlis, R. Two models of syllogistic reasoning: Feature selection and conversion. *Journal of Verbal Learning and Verbal Behavior*, 1975, **14**, 180–195. (b)

Sanford, A. J., & Garrod, S. C. *Understanding written language*. New York: Wiley, 1981.

Simpson, M. E., & Johnson, D. M. Atmosphere and conversion errors in syllogistic reasoning. *Journal of Experimental Psychology*, 1966, **72**, 197–200.

Waitz, T. (Ed. & Trans.). *Aristolelis Organon graece*. Leipzig, 1846 (cited in Lukasiewicz, 1957; Patzig, 1968).

Wason, P. C., & Johnson-Laird, P. N. *Psychology of reasoning.* Cambridge, Massachusetts: Harvard Univ. Press, 1972.

Woodworth, R. S., & Sells, S. B. An atmosphere effect in formal syllogistic reasoning. *Journal of Experimental Psychology,* 1935, **18,** 451–460.

Woodworth, R. S. *Experimental psychology.* New York: Holt, 1938.

SOME EMPIRICAL JUSTIFICATION FOR A THEORY OF NATURAL PROPOSITIONAL LOGIC

Martin D. S. Braine

NEW YORK UNIVERSITY
NEW YORK, NEW YORK

Brian J. Reiser

CARNEGIE-MELLON UNIVERSITY
PITTSBURGH, PENNSYLVANIA

Barbara Rumain

NEW YORK UNIVERSITY
NEW YORK, NEW YORK

I. Introduction

There has long been a controversy about the relation of logic to the ordinary deductive reasoning of subjects untutored in logic. Twentieth century philosophy has generally held that logic has only a normative relation

THE PSYCHOLOGY OF LEARNING
AND MOTIVATION, VOL. 18

to reasoning (e.g., Cohen, 1944): Logic specifies the correct responses, but says nothing about how they are achieved. From a psychological standpoint, however, it is often hard to explain correct responses if one cannot assume that the reasoner is following logical principles.

Within psychology, there have been three approaches to the issue of the relation of logic to reasoning. One approach has emphasized nonlogical processes and biases (e.g., Evans, 1972, 1982), of which the best known example is the atmosphere theory of syllogistic reasoning (Woodworth & Sells, 1935). Historically, however, this approach has usually focused on explaining errors rather than correct responses. No comprehensive theory has ever been presented for any kind of deductive reasoning which purports to explain correct responses as well as errors in terms of entirely nonlogical processes and biases.

The second approach posits that subjects proceed by constructing a mental model of the information given and reason from the model. For instance, given the premises *A is inside B* and *B is inside C,* a subject imagines a state of affairs corresponding to the premises; the conclusion that *A* is inside *C* can then be read off from the image. According to Johnson-Laird (1980, 1982), reasoning consists of forming a model, reading off a tentative conclusion, and then testing the conclusion by trying to construct alternative models consistent with the premises. Most errors arise from a failure to test conclusions. This kind of theory has been extensively developed to account for responses to categorical syllogisms (e.g., Erickson, 1974; Johnson-Laird, 1980, 1982; Johnson-Laird & Steedman, 1978), as well as for inferences about spatial and lexical relations (Johnson-Laird, 1980, 1982). It has been urged that it may suffice for all deductive reasoning (Johnson-Laird, 1982, 1983). The proposals for propositional reasoning (Johnson-Laird, 1983, Chs. 2 and 3), however, are sketchy. They appear to combine a truth-table algorithm for computing the semantic informativeness of propositions with a procedure that progressively substitutes truth values for the propositions in premises. The procedure is not well specified and appears to include principles that are equivalent to inference schemas, that is, that exemplify the third approach. In any case, it does not involve the construction of mental models. Thus, no clear mental model theory of propositional reasoning has yet been proposed.

The third approach assumes that reasoning includes logical principles and has been the starting point for a substantial body of work in recent years, including that reported here. It follows the lead of Henle (1962), who urged a return to the theoretical position of an earlier generation of logicians (e.g., Boole, 1854; Mill, 1874), that natural reasoning incorporates a mental logic of some sort. Since then, several theories of propositional reasoning have been proposed that include a "natural logic" specifying a repertory of the elementary deductive steps that can take a reasoner from one step to the next in a chain of reasoning (Braine, 1978; Johnson-Laird, 1975; Osherson, 1975a; Rips, 1983). In these theories, the elementary deductive steps are defined through inference schemas. An inference schema specifies the form of an inference: Given information whose semantic representation has the form specified in the schema, one can infer the conclusion whose form is also specified. In a common notation, the form of the input information is represented above a horizontal line, and the form of the conclusion below. For instance, Schema 1 is an inference schema:

$$\frac{p \ or \ q; \ not \ p}{q} \tag{1}$$

It states that given a compound proposition of the form *p or q,* and given also that one of the alternatives is false (*not p*), one can conclude the other proposition, *q.* Since an inference schema specifies a way of moving from one step to another in a chain of reasoning, a logic that consists of a set of schemas can offer an hypothesis about the repertory of deductive steps available to people in a given type of reasoning.

There have been some forays in the direction of developing inference schema theories for reasoning from quantified premises (e.g., Braine & O'Brien, 1984; Braine & Rumain, 1983; Osherson, 1976). Most work of this sort has concentrated on propositional reasoning, however, and recent theoretical accounts of propositional reasoning have usually taken this form. The main purpose of the present work was to obtain empirical evidence on the repertory of the kinds of valid inferences made by subjects in propositional reasoning. The repertory that is taken as the hypothesis to be tested is shown in Table I. These schemas are a revision of those of Braine (1978), which in turn attempted to improve on those of Osherson (1975a) and Johnson-Laird (1975). Since the present work was done well before Rip's (1983) article appeared, the choice of schemas could not be influenced by his model. Our primary goal was to obtain systematic data to assess whether the schemas of this set define the kinds of valid inferences made by subjects in propositional reasoning.[1]

---

[1]The schemas in Table I allow *n* propositions to be coordinated in conjunctions and disjunctions, rather than just two as in schemas in textbooks of logic. That is because English coordinations appear to be *n*-ary rather than binary (Gleitman, 1965; McCawley, 1981). The work reported here, however, does not bear on the distinction between *n*-ary and binary coordination.

Table I differs somewhat from Table 2 in Braine and Rumain (1983) which came from an earlier version of this article. Apart from a notational change for negation, the need to express Schema P6 as an equivalence rule became clear to us, and the transitivity of *if* is dropped here. The changes are not relevant for the experiments reported.

TABLE I

The Proposed Set of Inference Schemas
for Natural Propositional Logic[a]

P1. $\dfrac{p_1; p_2; \ldots p_n}{p_1 \text{ AND } p_2 \text{ AND } \ldots \text{ AND } p_n}$ $(.34; 1\%)$[b]

P2. $\dfrac{p_1 \text{ AND } \ldots \text{ AND } p_i \text{ AND } \ldots \text{ AND } p_n}{p_i}$ $(.41, 0\%)$

P3. $\dfrac{p; F(p)}{\text{INCOMPATIBLE}}$ $(.20; 1\%)$

P4. $\dfrac{F(p_1) \text{ AND } \ldots \text{ AND } F(p_n); p_1 \text{ OR } \ldots \text{ OR } p_n}{\text{INCOMPATIBLE}}$ $(.66; 0\%)$

P5. $\dfrac{F[F(p)]}{p}$ $(1.09; 1\%)$

P6. $p \text{ AND } (q_1 \text{ OR } \ldots \text{ OR } q_n) \ \Xi \ (p \text{ AND } q_1) \text{ OR } \ldots \text{ OR } (p \text{ AND } q_n)$ $(.16; 4\%)$

P7. $\dfrac{\text{IF } p_1 \text{ OR } \ldots \text{ OR } p_n \text{ THEN } q; p_i}{q}$ $(.49, 0\%)$

P8. $\dfrac{p_1 \text{ OR } \ldots \text{ OR } p_n; F(p_i)}{p_1 \text{ OR } \ldots \text{ OR } p_{i-1} \text{ OR } p_{i+1} \text{ OR } \ldots \text{ OR } p_n}$ $(1.38, 2.5\%)$

P9. $\dfrac{F(p_1 \text{ AND } \ldots \text{ AND } p_n); p_i}{F(p_1 \text{ AND } \ldots \text{ AND } p_{i-1} \text{ AND } p_{i+1} \text{ AND } \ldots \text{ AND } p_n)}$ $(1.39; 4\%)$

P10. $\dfrac{p_1 \text{ OR } \ldots \text{ OR } p_n; \text{ IF } p_1 \text{ THEN } q; \ldots; \text{ IF } p_n \text{ THEN } q}{q}$ $(.16; 0\%)$

P11. $\dfrac{p_1 \text{ OR } \ldots \text{ OR } p_n; \text{ IF } p_1 \text{ THEN } q_1; \ldots; \text{ IF } p_n \text{ THEN } q_n}{q_1 \text{ OR } \ldots \text{ OR } q_n}$ $(.47; 0\%)$

P12. $\dfrac{\text{IF } p \text{ THEN } q; p}{q}$ $(.47, 2\%)$

P13. Given a chain of reasoning of the form

$\Sigma; \{p\}$

--- $(.02)$

q

One can conclude: If p THEN q

P14. $\dfrac{*}{p \text{ or } F(p)}$

P15. $\dfrac{*}{\{p\}}$

P16. Given a chain of reasoning of the form

$\{p\}$

INCOMPATIBLE

One can conclude $F(p)$

(continued)

A complete theory of propositional reasoning obviously must include more than a logic of inference schemas. The logic specifies only the repertory of steps available to the reasoner; it does not itself generate a chain of reasoning. A complete theory requires at least two further components. One is a comprehension mechanism which understands natural language in terms of the semantic representations of the schemas. Note that the schemas use a set of semantic elements—AND, OR, F, and IF–THEN—which are distinct from the corresponding English words (*and, or,* etc.). Given this distinction between the surface structure in which propositions are expressed and the semantic representations provided in the schemas, it follows that before schemas are used in reasoning there must be a comprehension step in which the given verbal information is decoded into the representations used in the schemas.

The second component is a heuristic reasoning program consisting of routines and strategies that can put together a chain of inferences, selecting the schema that is to be applied at each point in the reasoning. A possible third component is a set of nonlogical or quasi-logical fallback procedures that determine a response when the reasoning program fails to deliver a solution to a problem.

While we believe that it is useful to think of all these components (i.e., the schemas, the comprehension mechanism, the reasoning program, and the fallback procedures) as functionally distinct, we do not mean to imply that they are not interrelated and cannot interdigitate. For instance, a particular reasoning heuristic may be associated with a certain schema; a fallback procedure might lead to a reconstruing of a premise, leading in turn to a new cycle of the reasoning program. Of these components, however, it is primarily the schemas and the nature of the reasoning program that

---

(*Table I footnote*)

[a] The order of conjuncts and disjuncts and of the propositions in numerators is immaterial. Where there are subscripts, i indicates any one of the subscripted propositions. F (...) indicates that "..." is false. [F( ) is commonly realized as negation in the case of atomic propositions.) "INCOMPATIBLE" blocks a chain of reasoning, except as provided for in P16. Schema P6 is formulated as an equivalence to indicate that propositions of these forms can be substituted for each other freely, including when they occur within a longer proposition. "*" indicates that the denominator can be introduced at any point in an argument. {p} marks p as a supposition. (Thus P16 says that a supposition leading to an incompatibility is false.) Any proposition derived with the help of a supposition is itself a supposition, except as provided for in Schemas P13 and P16. In P13, Σ is starting information (e.g., premises); thus, P13 says that if q can be proved from the supposition p and the premises Σ, one can conclude IF p THEN q. The trivial inference that a proposition entails itself ($p, \therefore p$) is taken to be a special case of Schema P2.

For simple examples of Schemas P1–P12, see Appendix, Problems iii and iv for P1 and P2, Problem ii for P3, and Problems v through xiv for P4 through P12.

[b] The decimal fraction in the parentheses after each of the first 13 schemas is the difficulty weight that STEPIT estimated for the schema. The percentage in the parentheses is the percentage of errors on one-step problems involving the schema.

are the concern of the present work. The work is designed to minimize the roles of differential comprehension and of fallback procedures in determining responses, in order that the contribution of these components to response variance can be neglected. We hoped thus to permit the components we wished to study to be addressed with as much precision as possible.

We used reasoning problems that consist of one or more premises and a proposed conclusion, and the subject evaluated the truth of the conclusion given the premises. A central part of the methodology consists in testing the prediction that, for a large class of reasoning problems, the difficulty of a problem for subjects can be predicted from the schemas of this repertory that are used in solving the problem, together with certain assumptions about how the subjects' reasoning program selects the schemas used, and some performance assumptions. Before explaining the methodology in more detail, we consider these assumptions, beginning with what the theory has to say about mistakes in reasoning.

The theory allows three sources for reasoning errors. We shall call them *comprehension* errors, *heuristic inadequacy* errors, and *processing* errors, respectively. A comprehension error is an error of construal of the premises or of the conclusion: The starting information used by the subject is not that intended by the problem setter. Heuristic inadequacy errors occur when the subject's reasoning program fails to find a line of reasoning that solves a problem, that is, the problem is too difficult for the subject. Processing errors comprise lapses of attention, errors of execution in the application of schemas, failure to keep track of information in working memory, and the like. We assume that the probability of a processing error increases with problem complexity, but overall tends to be low and essentially vanishes in the simplest problems where processing load must be assumed to be minimal.

The work reported is designed so that the expected sources of error are always known. First, we sought to eliminate comprehension errors entirely, by avoiding problems that are likely to give rise to them. In particular, we did not use problems in which the premises might have "conversational implicatures" (Grice, 1975) that would lead to error. Thus, it is well known that a conditional (*If p then q*) invites the inference *If not p then not q* (Geis & Zwicky, 1971), which leads to the standard fallacies of conditional reasoning. In our problems, understanding a conditional as its invited inference could never lead a subject to an evaluation of the problem conclusion. Similarly, we avoided certain problems in which interpreting *or* inclusively versus exclusively could make a difference. In addition, in premises where the relative scopes of negations and connectives had to be understood, we did pilot work to discover a wording that subjects construed in the intended manner. Thus, all situations that could plausibly lead to comprehension errors were avoided, hopefully eliminating this source of response variance.

Second, we tried to localize processing and heuristic inadequacy errors by dividing the problems into two main types. Most of the problems are of a type that we call *direct reasoning* (defined below): These problems are of low-to-moderate complexity, on which we expect all subjects to find the shortest line of reasoning, probably using much the same reasoning routine to do so. On these problems we expect all errors to be of the processing type. The other type of problem is referred to as *indirect reasoning*. The purpose of these problems is to find out whether subjects are indeed all able to find the solutions, and these problems may give rise to heuristic inadequacy errors.

The distinction between direct and indirect reasoning is important for the work reported. We define *direct reasoning* as follows: The reasoner starts with the premises, makes an inference from the premises, and then successively makes further inferences from the premises together with the propositions already inferred, until the conclusion or a proposition incompatible with it is reached. (We assume that a response of "false" is triggered by the discovery of an incompatibility among the premises, inferred propositions, and conclusion; thus, all responses of "false" involve either Schema P3 or P4). In the special case in which the conclusion to be evaluated is an *if-then* statement, we also consider the reasoning direct if the reasoner first adds the antecedent of the conclusion to the premises as an additional starting formula, taking the consequent as the conclusion to be reached, and then solves the reformulated problem by successive inferences as above, starting with the premises together with the antecedent. It follows that direct reasoning contains no lemmas, and, with one exception, does not use suppositions. (The exception is the adding of the antecedent of an *if-then* conclusion to the premises, as noted above; technically, the antecedent becomes a supposition; however, since the choice of this supposition is dictated by the conclusion, making it is a routine matter that we count as part of direct reasoning, unlike other uses of supposition as in reductio ad absurdum arguments). Certain schemas are characteristic only of indirect reasoning, notably Schema P14 of Table I which introduces a starting point for reasoning that is always outside the problem premises, P15 which introduces suppositions, and P16 which is involved only in reductio ad absurdum arguments. In general, indirect reasoning may require some "intelligent" heuristics to find the successful line of reasoning, and the difficulty of the problem will likely reflect the difficulty of finding that line of reasoning. Hence problems that require indirect reasoning may show heuristic inadequacy errors. (Of course, direct reasoning problems could be made very long and complicated and might then also elicit heuristic inadequacy errors. We tried, however, to avoid that level of complexity.)

This distinction between direct and indirect reasoning seemed to us an intuitively useful one to draw. In addition, there is developmental evidence that indirect reasoning is a later-appearing and more sophisticated phenomenon than direct reasoning (see Braine & Rumain, 1983, for a review).

The only assumption about subjects' reasoning programs that is crucial for the present work is that their programs routinely find the shortest line of reasoning that solves our direct reasoning problems using the Schemas of Table I. That assumption specifies uniquely the sequence of inferences made in solving each problem, information needed to predict problem difficulty. Later (see Table III) we outline the program that we propose that subjects bring to bear on the problems. The program provides an operational definition of direct reasoning (reasoning generated by the *direct reasoning routine*) and solves the direct reasoning problems by the shortest line of reasoning possible with the schemas of Table I. The program is discussed later.

We now outline our methodology. We examined the set of schemas in two principal ways. First, if a schema is one of a universal repertory, and if processing errors are minimal on easy problems, then performance on the simplest reasoning problems demanding a schema should be essentially error-free. Therefore, we sought to discover whether this condition was satisfied for the schemas investigated.

Second, we used the set to predict the difficulty of problems requiring short chains of direct reasoning. The methodology was a modified version of that used by Osherson (1974, 1975a, 1976) and Rips (1983). Osherson assumed that when a problem requires a chain of reasoning steps to get from the premises to the conclusion, its difficulty should be predictable from the sum of the difficulties of the component inferences that make up the chain. In our version of Osherson's methodology, many deductive reasoning problems were presented to subjects, and empirical measures of the difficulty of each problem were obtained. We used two prediction schemes. In Scheme 1, one set of data was used to estimate difficulty weights for each schema, the difficulty weights of a schema begin an index of the difficulty of adopting and using that schema in solving a problem. We then inquired whether it was possible to predict systematically the empirically measured difficulty of a problem from the sum of the difficulty weights of the component inferences claimed to be used in solving the problem, together with some difficulty contributed only by problem length. The second prediction scheme is simpler. We assigned equal difficulty weights to all the schemas, thus taking the difficulty of an argument as proportional only to the number of reasoning steps, not to their nature. Thus, Scheme 2 examines how well problem difficulty can be predicted just from problem length and the number of steps needed to solve it.

In general in this article, we shall use the word *theory* to refer to our claims about the nature of subjects' inference schemas and reasoning program. We shall use the term *model* to refer to the theory taken with a particular prediction scheme. Thus, Model 1 is the theory combined with Scheme 1, and Model 2 is the theory taken with Scheme 2.

To the extent that these models predict successfully, we take it as evidence that the inference schemas of Table I are psychologically real, that is, actually used by the subjects in solving the problems. The difference between the effectiveness of the models provides information about the relevance of kind of inference to problem difficulty.

Three measures of problem difficulty were used. First, we obtained difficulty ratings: Subjects did each problem and rated its difficulty on a 9-point scale. Two sets of difficulty ratings were obtained, one set being used to estimate difficulty weights for the schemas and the other for cross-validation. A second measure of problem difficulty was derived from the time taken to solve a problem, as estimated from reaction time measures. Errors provided a third measure of problem difficulty.

In the case of the difficulty ratings, we assume that in doing a problem the subject forms a subjective impression, reflected in the rating, of the amount of processing the problem demanded, and that this processing is in turn a function of the number and kind of mental steps required to solve the problem. Although the difficulty rating is the least orthodox of the measures, it is likely that it reflects subjects' inferential operations in solving a problem as well as either the reaction time or error measures. The reaction times are of the order of seconds and tens of seconds and thus much longer than in most studies in cognitive psychology that use latency measures. Some of the response time is undoubtedly spent not on making inferences but on other things like rereading premises after the conclusion to be evaluated has been presented; consequently, the latencies cannot be taken as a good index of the time required to execute a chain of inferences. Thus, there is no principled reason for preferring latency to the difficulty rating as a measure; neither can claim to be more than a reasonable index of the overall difficulty of a problem, or of the gross amount of processing it demanded. Although errors provide a well-motivated index of difficulty, the low error probability overall meant that an unduly large number of subjects would be required for errors to provide a highly reliable index. In general, since no single measure seemed ideal, it seemed preferable to use all three. It turned out, however, that the difficulty ratings had better psychometric properties than the latencies or errors: They were the least skewed, subjects showed relatively more consensus in their ratings than in their latencies or errors, and problems were differentiated the best. So we gave relatively more weight to the ratings and used them to estimate parameters. In his work on reasoning, Osherson (1974, 1975a, 1976) also found difficulty ratings to be preferable to latencies as measures.

Three studies were conducted. In the first study the main measure was solution latency; this is referred to as the *Reaction Time Study*. The second study, referred to as *Rating Study 1,* used a new group of subjects who rated the difficulty of each problem after they had done it. Rating Study 1 and the Reaction Time Study used essentially the same set of problems. Some afterthoughts about the problem set as well as the need for cross-validation suggested a third study, *Rating Study 2.* In this study another group of subjects rated the difficulty of a new set of problems many of which differed from problems of the previous set. The method of sampling of schemas within the problems made Rating Study 2 the most appropriate study for estimating difficulty weights for the schemas. So, in the Results, the schema difficulty weights are obtained from this study and then used to postdict the data from Rating Study 1. After that, they are used in models that seek to account for the reaction time and error data. Thus, the order of presenting results will not correspond exactly to the order of conducting the experiments. The procedures are all described together.

II. Method

A. MATERIALS

1. Types of Problems

The problems used were of the following five types. The Appendix contains examples illustrating the first four types and includes a nearly complete listing of all problems of the first three types that were used in Rating Study 2. The first three types are referred to collectively as *direct reasoning* problems.

1. One-step problems. These were problems in which the conclusion could be reached from the premises in one step using one of the schemas.

2. One-step + contradiction. In these the negation of the conclusion could be reached from the premises in one step using one of the schemas.

3. Multistep problems in which the usual, or only, solution is by direct reasoning (defined earlier). The multistep problems used involved a chain of two or more inferences; those for which the expected response was "false" also involved finding an incompatibility between the premises and the conclusion. Some indication of the range of difficulty sampled can be obtained from the listing in the Appendix.

4. "Control" problems, true and false. In control problems with answers of "true," the premise and conclusion were identical and merely had to be matched. In control problems with "false" as answer, either the conclusion directly negated the premise, or vice versa. (Formally, control-false problems are one-step problems involving Schema P3.) In the Reaction Time Study, the control-true problems provided information about how long it took to find a "match" when no reasoning was involved. In the rating studies they served to anchor the low end of the difficulty rating scale.

The above four types of problems constituted a large majority of the problems used, and most analyses of the data involved only these.

5. Other problems. One other problem that occurred in both rating studies tested the possibility that subjects might use the standard logic schema, $p, \therefore p$ OR q, which we did not believe was a schema of natural logic. The remaining other problems required indirect reasoning, according to the schemas of Table I. There was a lemma, or a suppositional step was involved to set up a reductio ad absurdum, or a starting proposition of the form p OR F (p). Some of these were problems for which the schemas of Table I, and of Braine (1978), made somewhat different predictions—they required indirect reasoning using the schemas of Table I, but had short direct solutions by the schemas of Braine (1978). These problems are cited below when the results on them are presented.

2. Content and Wording of Problems

To standardize the problems as much as possible, all problems concerned the presence or absence of letters on an imaginary blackboard, as in Osherson (1975a). This served to minimize differences in length and comprehensibility between sentences of different problems and to reduce the contribution of substantive content to response variance.

The conjunctions and disjunctions used in the problems always contained exactly two coordinate propositions. Thus, although the schemas of Table I allow for more than two coordinate propositions, the work does not bear on the distinction between binary and n-ary coordination in schemas.

The same logical form was always reflected in the same wording. The wording adopted was based on the results of some pilot work in which subjects assessed the clarity and lack of ambiguity of various possible wordings. The wordings we used are illustrated in the Appendix.

3. The Set of Problems for the Reaction Time Study

There were 121 problems. The set included 10 one-step problems (apart from control-false problems), one for each of Schemas P1-2 and P4-11. Eleven problems were one-step + contradiction. There were 33 direct reasoning multistep problems, of which 13 combined a single schema with modus ponens (P12), with or without a contradiction; the other 20 involved two or more different schemas other than P12, with or without a contradiction. These types combine to a total of 54 direct reasoning problems that are of primary interest in the data analyses.

There were also 48 control problems. Twelve true and 12 false control problems were created, so that there was a control problem whose conclusion was identical in length and logical form to each different conclusion found among the 54 reasoning problems just specified. Because of their importance, two instances of each control problem were included in the stimulus set.

In addition, there were 19 other problems that involved indirect reasoning, by the schemas of Table I. Their form is specified later when the results for them are discussed.

The expected answer to exactly half the problems was "true" and to the other half "false."

To order the problems of the stimulus set, the total problem set was first divided into two equal-sized blocks. An instance of each control problem was included in each block, and all other problems were randomly assigned to a block with the constraint that for each type of problem the number of trues and falses within a block was kept as equal as possible. The problems were then placed in random order within each block, with the constraint that only three true or three false problems could occur consecutively. The problems were divided into blocks and ordered twice in this way, to generate two different problem orders. In addition, we also generated the reverse order of each of these orders, yielding four different orderings of the problem set.

Seven true and seven false "practice problems" were also designed. These included a true and a false control problem and several one- and two-step problems. None appeared in the actual stimulus set. The practice set familiarized subjects with the equipment and procedure before the start of the experiment proper. The entire set of problems and practice problems was recorded on magnetic tape for display by a computer.

4. The Set of Problems for Rating Study 1

The set comprised 99 problems. These included the same 54 problems used in the Reaction Time Study (i.e., one-step, one-step + contradiction, and multistep direct reasoning problems). They also included the same 24 control problems, now given once each instead of twice. The same 19 indirect reasoning problems were also in the set. There were 2 new problems.

One of these involved the questionable schema p, $\therefore$ p OR q, and would have been a one-step problem if subjects used that schema. The other (identified later) was a new version with changed wording of 1 of the 19 indirect reasoning problems.

The same four orderings of the set of problems were used as in the Reaction Time Study, except that half the control problems were omitted, and the two new problems were inserted at random positions into each of the four orders. The four orders of the problems were assembled into typewritten booklets.

The practice problems for the Reaction Time Study were augmented by two problems to ensure that the range of difficulty of the main problem set should be adequately sampled within the practice problems. Experience with the practice problems could then permit subjects to form a useful rough calibration of their internal difficulty rating scale prior to beginning the main set of problems.

5. The Set of Problems for Rating Study 2

There were 85 problems. These included 12 one-step problems involving the regular versions of schemas. Another 14 problems involved one step together with a contradiction. Eight of these involved modus ponens; they had the same form but varied in length from 19 to 39 words and were especially designed to explore the relation between problem length and rated difficulty, holding the reasoning process constant (see examples xxi and xxii in the Appendix). An additional 39 problems were direct reasoning, multistep problems, involving from two to four steps. Within these 65 problems specified so far, an effort was made to have adequate representation of each of the assumed set of reasoning steps. Thus, each of the schemas occurred at least eight times (except for P14–16 which cannot occur in direct reasoning problems).

In addition, there were 11 control problems and 9 other problems. Eight of the latter involved indirect reasoning (all cited later), and the sixth tested the potential schema p, $\therefore$ p OR q. Omitting that problem, the expected answer to 42 problems was "true," and to 42 "false." Of the 85 problems, 49 had the same form as problems that occurred in both the Reaction Time Study and Rating Study 1; 36 of these were direct reasoning problems, 9 were controls, and 4 were indirect reasoning problems.

Four orders of the problems were created as before and assembled into typewritten booklets preceded by the practice problems, as in Rating Study 1.

B. PROCEDURE

1. Reaction Time Study

The basic task was to read a reasoning problem, including a premise or premises and a tentative conclusion, one sentence at a time, and then to evaluate the conclusion as true or false on the basis of the premises. The task was implemented as follows. Subjects were seated before a 15-in. TV screen and a three-button response box. The buttons formed an inverted triangle, with the bottom button labeled *move,* and the top vertices labeled *true* and *false.* The subject's preferred thumb rested on the move button, and the index fingers of either hand rested on the true and false buttons. For half of the subjects, the button pressed by the dominant hand was used to respond "true," and the other to respond "false." For the other half of the subjects, this was reversed. The screen and response box were connected to a PDP-8/I minicomputer, located in an adjacent room.

It was explained that each problem would concern the presence or absence of letters on an imaginary blackboard. The problem would contain some facts, followed by a final statement about the blackboard, the tentative "conclusion." The facts or premises contained the information that was known about the blackboard and were to be accepted at face value. Each problem would begin with the word *ready* displayed on the screen. When the subject was ready to begin, a press of the move button would clear this ready signal and bring the first premise to the screen. He or she was then to read that premise as quickly and accurately as possible and then press the move button, repeating the same process for succeeding premises. (These latencies to push the move button provided reading times for the premises.) The last premise was underlined and, after the button press, was followed by the proposed conclusion. The conclusion was marked by a question mark. Upon reading the conclusion, subjects were to decide if that sentence were definitely true or definitely false, given the premises for that problem, and respond by pressing the appropriate button. The screen then cleared, and 1.5 sec later a new ready signal was displayed, indicating the start of a new problem. If the subject could not solve the problem, or thought it impossible to solve, he or she was to press move in response to the conclusion and proceed with the next problem.

Since each sentence was displayed beneath its predecessor without clearing the screen, subjects were reading for comprehension rather than memorization. The subjects were instructed that they should respond as quickly as possible, trying to commit as few errors as possible. All reaction times, including those to read the premises and those to respond true or false, were recorded by the computer. The subjects first responded to the practice trials. After the practice problems, any difficulties were discussed, and any further questions about the procedure answered. The subjects then received the first block of problems, and after a brief intermission, received the second block.

2. Rating Studies 1 and 2

Subjects were told that they were to participate in a reasoning experiment, in which they would answer each problem in the booklet provided and then judge its difficulty. The explanation of the problems was identical to that in the Reaction Time Study. The subject was told to read each problem, accepting the sentences above the line as true, and then evaluate the proposed conclusion. In addition to true and false, the response alternative of "indeterminate" was available, although its use was not encouraged: Subjects were told that there should be enough information in almost all of the problems to reach a definite conclusion. There were a few problems that were "controversial," however, in which some people thought there was enough information, whereas others thought there was no way to prove or disprove the conclusion. If they were to find such problems, they were to respond "indeterminate," rather than "true" or "false."

After solving each problem, the subject was to rate its difficulty relative to the other problems, using a 9-point scale, with 1 being the easiest, and 9 being the most difficult. They were to evaluate how difficult it was to arrive at an answer, and to try not to be unduly influenced by the length of the sentences, or of the problem itself. Subjects were instructed to try to use all the numbers on the scale, although not necessarily equally often.

Besides familiarizing subjects with the procedure, the practice problems gave them an impression of the range of difficulty of the problem set: Since the practice problems included all levels of difficulty, they would permit subjects to establish their mental scale. Difficulties or questions were discussed, and then the subjects were given the experiment proper. Subjects worked alone, undisturbed and at their own pace. We asked only that they follow the order of the problems in the booklet. For most subjects, after they had finished the written problems, introspections were gathered orally on between 15 and 36 problems, depending on time considerations and the subject's stamina. Each problem was re-presented in written form, and subjects were asked to solve it and then summarize their reasoning as best they could.

C.   SUBJECTS

1. Reaction Time Study

Twenty-eight undergraduates participated either as paid subjects or to fulfill a course requirement. Data from three other subjects were discarded, because their extremely high error rates relative to the other subjects resulted in too few usable data points and rendered their compliance with the instructions of the task suspect.

2. Rating Studies 1 and 2

There were again 28 student subjects in each study. Some were paid and some participated to fulfill an Introductory Psychology course requirement. In both studies the difficulty ratings of only 24 subjects were used. The subjects whose ratings were discarded either failed to follow the rating instructions satisfactorily (e.g., rated most problems as "1," the lowest rating, thus providing no information about problem difficulty), or they had high error rates relative to the remaining subjects.

III.   Results

We first analyze the data from the direct reasoning problems of Rating Study 2, using the prediction schemes of Models 1 and 2, described in the Introduction. The reason for beginning with Rating Study 2 is that that study was better designed for estimating the schema weights required in Model 1, since the schemas occurred with more nearly equal frequency in its problems than in those of the other studies.

Next, we investigate how far the prediction equations predict the difficulty ratings of the direct reasoning problems of Rating Study 1. Since the subjects and some of the problems used were not the same as those of Rating Study 2, this analysis provides a cross-validation of the prediction equations. Then we inquire how well the models predict the reaction time data and the error data from all studies combined.

The final section of the Results discusses the data on the indirect reasoning problems of the various studies.

A.   DIRECT REASONING PROBLEMS: RATING STUDY 2

In Model 1, each of the schemas is associated with a difficulty weight, which is the difficulty (in the subjective units of the rating scale) of adopting and applying that reasoning step in a reasoning problem. The length of a problem (measured here by the total number of words in premises and conclusion) may also contribute to the subjective difficulty independently of the reasoning process (e.g., more or longer sentences may demand more effort to comprehend), the simplest assumption being that the contribution is a linear function of the number of words. (Other measures of length, such as number of embedded simple propositions, number of logical connectives, and the like, were investigated; they were all highly correlated with number of words and did not show closer relations to problem difficulty than did number of words.) Thus the predicted difficulty of any problem is equal to the sum of the difficulty weights of each reasoning step involved in a problem, plus some constant times the number of words in the problem, plus some other constant that sets the lower end of the rating scale at 1.0.

We posit that the difficulty of a problem should depend on the *sum* of the difficulty weights of the component reasoning steps (rather than, say, their product, or some other function), because additivity is the simplest assumption to make, and no other assumption appears to have a better rationale. Also, Osherson (1975a) assumed additivity without anomalous results.

Model 2 is just like Model 1 except that all the difficulty weights are set equal.

1. Contribution of Problem Length to Rated Difficulty

It will be recalled that in eight problems, each involving modus ponens and a contradiction, problem length was deliberately varied while holding the reasoning steps constant. (See the Appendix, Problems xxi and xxii, for examples of a short and a long problem.) Problem length varied from 19 to 35 words in this set, and the difficulty ratings from 2.04 to 3.71. On these problems there was a correlation of .93 between the mean rated difficulty and the number of words. (The mean difficulty ratings used are those for correct responses, but there were in fact only four errors among the 192 responses.) The regression equation indicated that each additional word added .0728 to mean rated difficulty. The correlation of .93 was sufficiently high that we decided to adopt .0728 as the multiplying constant for problem length, rather than use the entire set of problems to estimate this parameter.

Fixing the multiplying constant for problem length permits the other constant also to be fixed, by the following line of reasoning. The low end of the rating scale is 1.0. The easiest problem possible is a control-true problem of minimum length, that is, in which both premise and conclusion are the same and are just four words long (see Problem i of the Appendix). Such a problem involves no reasoning, and so reasoning steps make no contribution to its difficulty rating. For such an eight-word problem to have a predicted rating of 1.0, the constant must be .4176. The equation predicting the difficulty of a problem for Model 1 is then:

Predicted difficulty = .4176 + .0728 (number of words)
+ Σ (difficulty weights of reasoning steps)   (2)

(When the last term is zero, and number of words = 8, the predicted difficulty is 1.0, as required.)

The prediction equation of Model 2 is:

Predicted difficulty = .4176 + .0728 (number of words) + nD (3)

where n is the number of reasoning steps on a problem, and D is the average difficulty of a reasoning step.

2. Model 1: Estimating Difficulty Weights for the Reasoning Steps

Our "natural logic" provides a set of 16 elementary reasoning steps. Three of these (P14, 15, and 16 of Table I) occur only in indirect reasoning problems, and difficulty weights cannot be estimated for them. Weights were estimated for P1–13 of Table I.

Data from 60 problems were analyzed; 57 of these were the 65 one- and multistep direct reasoning problems, minus the 8 modus-ponens-plus-contradiction problems used to estimate the problem-length parameter just fixed. In addition, 1 control-true problem was included, the one of minimum length. The other 2 problems were constituted as follows. One condensed the 8 modus-ponens-plus-contradiction problems into a single datum: the difficulty (predicted from the equation regressing rated difficulty on problem length for the 8 modus-ponens-plus-contradiction problems —*not* Equation 2) of a modus-ponens-plus-contradiction problem with a length of 19 words. The other condensed the control-false problems into a single datum; these problems involve finding a contradiction only and are one-step problems involving Schema P3 of Table I; 2 of these had just 9 words, and the average of their rated difficulties was used. (The reason for these condensations was to control the sampling of the reasoning steps: It did not seem desirable that the estimate of the difficulty of modus ponens should be heavily determined by the single type of modus ponens problem used to obtain the problem length parameter; nor did we desire that control-false problems should contribute unduly to the estimated weight of P3.)[2]

---

[2]In fact, different decisions about how to include control-false and modus-ponens-plus-contradiction problems in the problem set used to estimate difficulty weights would not have affected the weights much.

The other control problems and the indirect reasoning problems were not used in this part of the data analysis. Each hypothesized reasoning step was represented either 8 or 9 times in the 60 problems, except for P3 which occurred 23 times. (Either P3 or P4 necessarily occurred in all problems with "false" as correct response.)

Difficulty weights for the 13 reasoning steps were estimated using the program "STEPIT" (Chandler, 1969) to obtain the best least-squares fit of the predicted problem difficulties (from Equation 2) to the obtained mean difficulty ratings. (The mean difficulty ratings were based on correct responses only.) The difficulty weights yielded by the program are given in parentheses alongside each schema in Table I.

The correlation between the predicted and the obtained mean difficulty ratings for the 60 problems was .92.

3. Model 2

The same 60 problems and the same analytic procedure were used as for Model 1, except that all the reasoning step difficulty weights were set equal. Thus, only one parameter, D in Equation 3, was estimated from the data. (It turned out to be .51.)

The correlation between the predicted and obtained mean difficulty ratings was .79 for Model 2. This correlation is significantly less than that obtained with Model 1 [t (57) = 4.82, $p < .001$—the test is Hotelling's (1940) t test for $\rho_{xy} = \rho_{xz}$ on the same population].

B. DIRECT REASONING PROBLEMS: CROSS-VALIDATION WITH RATING STUDY 1

Since the predicted difficulties for Rating Study 2 were based on parameters estimated from the data of that study, we next investigated how well the model would predict the difficulties obtained in Rating Study 1, without any new estimation of parameters.

Fifty-five problems from Rating Study 1 were used. These comprised the control-true problem of minimum length, a control-false problem (as before, this was the average of 2 minimum length control-false problems, treated as a single datum), and 53 of the original 54 one-step and multistep direct reasoning problems. The other problem was omitted because 46% of the subjects made errors on it. (This problem is identified and discussed at the end of this section.)

For these 55 problems, the correlation between the Model 1 predictions and the obtained mean difficulty ratings was .95. The Model 2 predictions correlated .73 with the same ratings. Thus, in neither case was there shrinkage of correlation, despite the fact that the two rating studies used different subjects and a partially different set of problems. The correlation for Model 2 is again significantly less than for Model 1 [t (52) = 7.21, p < .01].

A subset of 38 problems had the same form in both rating studies, and this subset permits the strength of the prediction to be compared with the test–retest reliability of the mean ratings. For these 38 problems, the correlation of the mean ratings given by the subjects of Study 2 with the mean ratings of the subjects of Study 1 was .92. For the same subset, the Model 1 predictions (Equation 2) correlated .94 with the mean ratings obtained in each study. Thus, for both studies, Model 1 predicts the data slightly better than the data predict themselves. The comparable Model 2 predictions for these 38 problems correlated .76 and .71 with the ratings for Studies 2 and 1, respectively.

The other 17 problems of Rating Study 1 did not have the same form as problems of Rating Study 2, and they thus permit a test of how well the models predict to new direct reasoning problems, of forms not originally used in the estimation of the schema difficulty weights. For these 17 problems the correlation between the predicted and obtained mean difficulty ratings was .96 for Model 1 and .69 for Model 2, suggesting satisfactory generalization to new problems.

Since the Model 1 predictions are obviously excellent, it is pertinent to inquire how much of the quality of the prediction comes from problem length and how much is due to the difficulty weightings of the reasoning steps. Taken alone, the correlation of problem length (number of words) with the obtained mean difficulty ratings was .71 for the 60 problems of Study 2 and .67 for the 55 problems of Study 1. The sum of the difficulty weights for the reasoning steps involved in a problem (the problem length parameter omitted) correlated .65 and .69 with the obtained mean ratings of problems for Study 2 and Study 1, respectively. Thus, both the sum of the reasoning step weights and problem length contribute heavily and about equally to the quality of the overall model predictions. The correlations of the sum of the reasoning step weights on a problem with the length of the problem were .09 and .03 in Study 2 and 1, respectively, neither significant. When length is partialed out, the partial correlations of the sums of the reasoning step weights with the difficulty ratings are .83 and .91 in Studies 2 and 1, respectively. Thus, most of the variance in the subjective difficulty of problems that is not associated with problem length (70–80%) is associated with the sum-of-the-reasoning-step-weights parameter of Equation 2.

For Model 2, the comparable correlations are of the number of reasoning steps with the ratings. For Studies 2 and 1, respectively, these were .67 and .66, and shrank to .51 and .52 when length was partialed out. Thus, about a quarter of the variance that is not associated with problem length is associated with number of reasoning steps.

As noted earlier, one problem of Rating Study 1 was omitted from the preceding analyses because 46% of the subjects made errors on it. (No other direct reasoning problems had more than 11% errors in Rating Study 1.) The problem was also rated as very difficult by those who solved it. It was:

> *There is a G and there's not a P*
> *There is a P or there's not an L*   (4)
> *? There is an L*

The difficulty probably comes from the form *p or not q*, of the second premise. It is known that disjuncts with one negative proposition are confusing to reason with (Johnson-Laird & Tridgell, 1972; Roberge, 1976), considerably more confusing even than disjuncts in which both propositions are negative. Our model seriously underpredicts the difficulty of this problem and would need some special processing parameter to accommodate it. We might add that, although almost two-thirds of the problems used in our studies contain negatives, this problem is the only one that seems to require special treatment.

Significance of the Schema Weights

It would be desirable to be able to demonstrate that each of the weights estimated by STEPIT was significantly greater than zero, but there is no available statistical test. The smallest weight, however, that for Schema P13, is very low, only .02. We therefore did a separate test to see whether there was evidence that this step added significant difficulty to problems. The clearest comparison would involve comparing one-step problems with the same problems with a P13 inference added. There were five such pairs in each of the rating studies, the one-step problems involving Schemas P7–11 (Appendix, Problems ix and xxiv, x and xxix, xi and xxxviii, xii and xxvi, xiii and xl). Analyses of variance were conducted for each study, with the differences among Schemas P7–11 as one within-subjects variable and the distinction between one-step and one-step + P13 as the other. In both studies, the one-step + P13 problems were rated slightly but significantly more difficult than the one-step problems [$F(1, 23) = 5.39, p < .05$ in Study 1, and $F(1, 23) = 13.80, p < .01$ in Study 2]. There were also significant differences among the five schemas, but that is not relevant to the question at issue. There was no significant interaction and thus no evidence that the difference made by P13 was greater for one schema than another. Although significant, the average increment in the difficulty rating associated with P13 was quite small (.336). There was also a significant difference between the one-step and one-step + P13 problems in errors [$t(4) = 3.01, p < .05$, using the *ranked errors* measure that is discussed later], but no significant difference in reaction times. Altogether, the evidence indicates a small but real penalty associated with P13. Presumably, STEPIT's low estimate indicates that in the more complex problems, the contribution to difficulty of P13 was submerged.

C. REACTION TIME STUDY

1. Adjustment of Reaction Times

It will be recalled that the premises were presented and read seriatim, and then the conclusion to be evaluated was presented. Times to read each premise, and to evaluate the conclusion were obtained. It seemed to us that the raw latencies (i.e., the time to respond "true" or "false" after the presentation of the conclusion) must be inadequate as measures of problem difficulty, for two reasons. First, they include the time to read the conclusion and match it against the information obtained from the premises: Since the conclusions varied widely in length (from 4 to 18 words), the raw times would tend to overestimate difficulty for the problems with relatively long conclusions. We therefore adjusted the latencies for conclusion length. Second, in problems with more than one premise, it would usually be possible for subjects to do some reasoning while still reading the premises, before the conclusion had been presented; such reasoning would not be included in the raw times. We attempted to assess whether such anticipatory reasoning was occurring and to add an estimate of it to the latencies.

The conclusion length adjustment was straightforward. The control-true problems provide a baseline time for the operations of reading a conclusion, matching it against known information, and responding. It turned out that in control-true problems, the number of words in the conclusion (identical, of course, to the words in the premise, in control-true problems) correlated .98 with the latencies. A regression equation of mean latency on number of words was computed for these problems. This equation provided an estimate of the time required to read a conclusion of a given length and match it against given information. For each reasoning problem, the raw latencies were adjusted by subtracting the time required to process the conclusion, as estimated from this equation. This subtraction constituted the conclusion length adjustment.

There was evidence that subjects sometimes did significant reasoning before the conclusion was presented that is concealed in the times taken to read the premises. We compared the mean reading time for each sentence type as a function of its serial position among the premises. For those sentence types that occurred in more than one serial position, the reading time was slower the later the sentence occurred among the premises. There are two conceivable explanations of this result. As the subject is reading through the problem, successively more information must be held in active memory. Rehearsal of the preceding premises could slow the processing of each new premise. Thus, as the number of premises increases, there is more information to rehearse, and reading time for a sentence type would increase as a function of its serial position. Alternatively, the processing of the later premises could be slower because subjects are making inferences; subjects sometimes reported that while not deliberately attempting to anticipate the conclusion, they could not help but "put together" the facts as these appeared.

In an attempt to decide between these explanations, we separated the reading times for each second position premise into those where the sentence provided information about letters in previous premises and those that involved no letter previously mentioned in the problem. We shall refer to these two types of premises as *integrable* and *nonintegrable,* respectively. For instance, the sentence type *There is an X* would be integrable if it followed *If there is an X then there is a Y,* but would not be integrable when it followed *If there is a Y then there is a Z.* If the increased reading time of the later premises is due merely to rehearsal of an increasing quantity of information, integrable and nonintegrable versions of the same sentence type should not differ. If the increased reading time is due instead to some logical manipulations being performed, this should occur to a greater extent in the integrable versions. In fact, the reading times for the nonintegrable second position premises were generally quite close to the first position times, whereas the times for the integrable second premises were substantially higher. The reading times for third and fourth position premises (always integrable) were also higher than for the same sentence type in first position. For instance, the sentence type *There is an X* took 1.98 sec to read in first position; in second position when not integrable it took 2.01 sec, about the same; but in second position when integrable it took 3.02 sec, and in third position it took 3.46 sec. Similarly, the sentence type *There's not an X* was read in 2.23 sec as first premise; as second premise it required 2.57 sec when not integrable, but 3.44 sec when integrable, and as third premise 5.18 sec. Again, the form *If there is an X then there is a Y* took 3.92 sec to read in first position; in second position it took 3.99 sec when not integrable, but 5.32 sec when integrable; it took 6.84 sec in third position and 8.55 in fourth position. It seems fairly certain therefore that some time-occupying integration of information took place during the reading of the later premises. To obtain an estimate of the time spent in this anticipatory reasoning, in problems with more than one premise the observed reading time for each additional premise was compared to the mean reading time for that sentence type when it occurred in first position (averaged over all problems). If the average reading time was greater than this baseline, the excess time was taken as anticipatory reasoning time, and was added to the solution latency. Thus, the adjusted reaction time on a problem was the raw latency plus the anticipatory reasoning time, less the conclusion length adjustment.

2. Prediction of the Adjusted Latencies

Fifty-five problems were analyzed, the same 55 direct reasoning problems that were analyzed for Rating Study 1. For these problems, the adjusted latencies correlated .77 with the mean difficulty ratings assigned to the same problems by the subjects of Rating Study 1. Thirty-eight of the problems had the same form as problems of Rating Study 2: For this set, the adjusted latencies correlated .73 with the mean ratings assigned by the Study 2 subjects. Thus, these two measures of difficulty, adjusted latency and subjective rating, correlate fairly highly with each other.

Equations 2 and 3, used to predict difficulties in the rating studies, both have problem length as a predictor variable. The length measure most relevant for predicting latency is not the total length of a problem (premises plus conclusion), however, but the length of the premises only, since an adjustment for the length of the conclusion has already been subtracted in adjusting the latencies. The length of the premises (total number of words in the premises combined) correlated .74 with the mean adjusted reaction times of the 55 problems, using latencies for correct responses only.

From Model 1, the correlation of the sum of the difficulty weights of the reasoning steps with the adjusted latencies was .37 ($p < .01$). The correlation of this predictor with the number of words in the premises was low .(.13, not significant). Using both the sum of the reasoning step difficulty weights and the length of the premises as predictor variables yielded a multiple correlation with adjusted latency of .79. From Model 2, the correlation of the number of reasoning steps with the adjusted latencies was .49 ($p < .001$). This predictor, however, correlated significantly with problem length ($r = .41$, $p < .01$). Using both number of reasoning steps and premise length as predictors yielded a multiple correlation of .77. With the length of the premises partialled out, the adjusted latencies correlate .41 ($p < .01$) with the sum of the reasoning step difficulty weights, but only .24 (not significant) with the number of reasoning steps. The difference itself is not statistically significant, however.

In general, it appears that solution latency is primarily associated with problem length. Neither of the measures of reasoning complexity in the two models predicts much independent variance, but one (the sum of the reasoning step difficulty weights) is significantly associated with latency independently of length.

D. ERRORS ON THE DIRECT REASONING PROBLEMS

Our third measure of problem difficulty used errors. To obtain a measure based on as much data as possible, we considered the 38 problems that had been used in all studies. On these problems, errors range from 0 to 11% on Rating Study 1, from 0 to 13% on Rating Study 2, and from 0 to 25% on the Reaction Time Study. The greater frequency of error on the latter study is no doubt due to subjects' attempting to work fast. To obtain an error measure to which each study would contribute equally, we ranked the 38 problems for error proneness independently for each study (the three rankings correlated well with each other); we then summed each problem's three ranks and then reranked the problems. The result was a ranking of the problems from easy to hard, according to their mean relative tendency to cause the subjects of the three studies to err. We refer to this measure as *ranked errors*. (The use of ranks also eliminated the problem that the distribution of errors is heavily skewed.)

For the 38 problems, ranked errors correlated .59 with the mean ratings of Rating Study 2, .68 with those of Rating Study 1, and .57 with the adjusted latencies.

The correlation of ranked errors with problem length is only .13, not statistically significant. Thus, among the measures of problem difficulty, errors apparently have the interesting property of being essentially uncorrelated with problem length. This lack of shared covariation with problem length may be the reason why the error measure did not correlate with ratings and latency measures quite as highly as these correlated with each other.

The correlation of ranked errors with the sum of the reasoning step difficulty weights was .73. Thus, the reasoning step weights account for a little over half of the variation in ranked errors. Since errors are not significantly associated with problem length, there is no point in partialing out length, or in using it as a second predictor in a multiple correlation. The number of reasoning steps alone (Model 2) correlated .57 ($p < .01$) with ranked errors. This is not significantly less than the correlation of errors with the summed difficulty weights. [Hoteling's (1940) $t(35) = 1.39$]. Thus, both theoretical estimates of reasoning complexity predict the error proneness of the problems quite well, the better one accounting for about half the variance.

E. DIRECT REASONING PROBLEMS: SUMMARY OF RESULTS
    AND COMMENT

Two of the three measures of problem difficulty (subjective difficulty rating and latency) are fairly highly correlated with problem length, and one (error proneness) is not. Table II summarizes how well the two theory-

TABLE II

CORRELATIONS OF THEORY-BASED PREDICTORS WITH EMPIRICAL MEASURES
OF PROBLEM DIFFICULTY[a]

Type of correlation	Sum or reasoning step weights	Number of reasoning steps	Difference
Rating Study 2 ($n = 60$ problems; $r_{\text{rating} \times \text{length}} = .71$)			
Equation 2 or 3	.92	.79	$p < .001$
Partial	.83	.51	$p < .001$
Rating Study 1 ($n = 55$ problems; $r_{\text{rating} \times \text{length}} = .67$)			
Equation 2 or 3	.95	.73	$p < .001$
Partial	.91	.52	$p < .001$
Latency ($n = 55$ problems; $n_{\text{latency} \times \text{length}} = .74$)			
Multiple	.79	.77	NS[b]
Partial	.41	NS	NS
Errors (ranks) ($n = 38$ problems; $r_{\text{rank} \times \text{length}} = .13$)			
Simple	.73	.57	NS

[a] The Equation 2 or 3 correlations are of the difficulty rating with the prediction from Equation 2 (sum of weights) or 3 (number of steps). The multiple correlation uses length of the premises as second predictor, and the partials have length partialled out. The difference test is Hotelling's (1940) t test for $\varrho_{xy} = \varrho_{xz}$ on the same population.
[b] NS, Not significant.

derived indices of expected problem complexity predict these measures, both in combination with length as a predictor, and with length partialled out.

The index from Model 1, the sum of the difficulty weights of the inferences that the theory provides to solve a problem, predicts both sets of ratings excellently; it also predicts errors well, and latencies significantly. Although this index contains 13 parameters estimated from one set of ratings data, it was shown that the quality of prediction was not dependent on possible idiosyncrasies of performance for the particular problems or subjects used to estimate the weights, since excellent predictions were obtained not only for the data set used to estimate the weights but also for ratings of the same problems by fresh subjects, and for new problems with new subjects. The other index, the number of reasoning steps from Model 2, also yields significant predictions, with fairly good correlations with the ratings and error measures. The correlations are lower overall than with the sum-of-the-weights index, but are nonetheless high considering the lack of parameters estimated from the data.

One might wonder whether the sum-of-the-reasoning-step-weights index showed so much higher independent correlations with the ratings than the latencies because of our use of ratings rather than latencies to estimate parameters. It is possible that this decision played a role, but it seems unlikely that it played a large role. First, the index correlated well with the error measure, which was also not used to estimate parameters; it is only for the latency measure that the correlations are not high. Second, the Model 2 index of complexity, the number of reasoning steps, contains no parameters estimated from data, but, although the correlations are lower overall for it, it shows the same pattern of correlations with the measures as the sum-of-the-weights index—higher with the ratings and errors than with the latencies. We are inclined to think that on these problems, the length of the premises may have tended to submerge other factors contributing to latency. It seems intuitively plausible that subjects might spend much time rereading premises on the longer problems—we invite the reader to examine the longer problems in the Appendix from this point of view. Unfortunately, it is hard to find or construct nontrivial problems that are short enough that all the premise information is within most subjects' span of short-term memory.

F. THE INDIRECT AND OTHER REASONING PROBLEMS:
ALL STUDIES

The remaining reasoning problems fall into four groups. One group was designed to elicit Schema P14; the second explored some simple arguments containing lemmas; the third was concerned with reductio ad absurdum arguments; and the fourth concerned the putative schema p, $\therefore$ p OR q. We consider these in turn.

1. Schema P14. This consisted of the following three problems used in all studies:

> *If there is an M then there is a Y*
> *If there's not an M then there is a Y*   (5)
> *? There is a Y*

> *If there is an R then there's not a C*
> *If there's not an R then there's not a C*   (6)
> *? There is a C*

> *If there is an F then there is an L*
> *If there's not an F then there is a V*   (7)
> *? There is an L or a V*

In Problem 5, Schema P14 feeds P10, Problem 6 involves P3 as well, and in Problem 7 P14 feeds P11. Responses were 88% correct on these problems across the three studies; incorrect responses most often fell into the undecidable category. The average difficulty rating given to these problems in the rating studies was 4.33 and indicates that they were considered moderately hard;[3] the error rates are consistent with this rating. There was no tendency for subjects who made errors on one of these problems to make errors on the others, that is, no subjects responded consistently as if they failed to use P14. The data indicate, not surprisingly, that elementary deductions involving P14 are well within the competence of undergraduates, although not without a scattering of errors.

2. Lemmas. The simplest kind of lemma was contained in the following problem:

> *If there is an I then there is an X*
> *There is an I or an L*   (8)
> *? There is an X or an L*

One subject verbalized the solution "If there's an *I* there's an *X*; if there's *L* then there's *L*; both possibilities result in there being an *X* or an *L*." This solution uses Schema P11. To use this schema, however, the subject has to construct the proposition *If there's an L then there's an L*. Since this proposition is not given in the premises, it has to be formed as a lemma, albeit a trivially simple one. (In our system, a proposition of the form *If p then p* is formed with schemas P13 and P2.) Another line of reasoning is also possible on this problem, and was verbalized by one subject as "If there's an *I* there's an *X*; if there's not an *I* there's an *L*, so there's an *X* or an *L*." In this line P14 feeds P11, using the lemma *If there's not an I there's an L* formed with P13, P8, and the second premise. We think, however, that the first line of reasoning was the more usual one.

The reasoning of Problem 8 was embedded in three other problems. In Problems 9 and 10 it fed a contradiction (P3 or P4), and in Problem 11 it was combined with P13:

---

[3]For purposes of comparison: The mean difficulty rating for all the direct reasoning problems of Rating Study 2 was 3.38, range 1.06 to 6.00—see the Appendix for the problems with their rated difficulties.

> *If there is an F then there is an X*
> *There is an F or an H*   (9)
> *? It's not true that there is either an X or an H*

> *There is an H or a C*
> *If there is an H then there is a P*   (10)
> *? There's not a C and there's not a P*

> *If there is a C then there is a Y*
> *? If there is either a C or a D, then there is either a Y or a D*   (11)

All of these problems were comparatively hard. Problem 8 was easiest with 6% errors and a rating of 4.15; the others had ratings of 4.95, 5.50, and 5.14, respectively, and averaged 16% errors, a very high error rate for our problems. It is possible to use Equation 2 to predict a difficulty rating for these problems based on their length and the schemas needed to solve them (e.g., Problem 8 has 24 words and taking it as using Schemas P11, P13, and P2, Equation 2 predicts a difficulty of 3.07 units). Each problem was rated very significantly more difficult by the subjects than the prediction for it from Equation 2 ($p < .01$ by t test in all cases). This fact together with the high error rate suggests that the need to construct the lemma is itself a source of difficulty over and above the particular schemas used.[4]

A different lemma was involved in Problem 12:

> *There is a P or an S*
> *If there is either a P or a K then there is a D*   (12)
> *If there is an S then there is an N*
> *? There is a D or an N*

In order for Schema P11 to be used, the lemma *If there is a P then there is a D* has to be formed, using P13 and P7. A similar lemma was also needed in two other problems. The three problems were all fairly difficult, with 5% errors and difficulty ratings from 3.96 to 5.96. Another problem re-

---

[4]Braine (1978) had a schema (p_1 OR . . . OR p_i OR . . . p_n; IF p_i THEN q; $\therefore$ p_1 OR . . . OR q OR . . . OR p_n) which would solve Problem 8 in a single step. This schema is not in our present set (Table I), for several reasons. First, the evidence summarized of a relatively high failure rate on these problems suggested that the argument is not universally immediate among our subjects. Second, self-reports of methods of solution (e.g., the two cited in the text) indicate that problems of the form of Problem 8 need not be solved in a single step but may involve a chain of inferences (as Table I assumes). Finally, the high subjective difficulty (e.g., Problem 8 is rated much more difficult than other one-step problems—see Appendix, Problems iii–xiv) also suggests that the solution is not immediate for subjects but involves a chain of inferences.

quired two lemmas, one like Problems 8–11, and the other like Problem 12. It has 21% errors and a rating of 6.10, harder on both indices than any direct reasoning problem used.

In general, these arguments involving lemmas were within the reach of most subjects, although they generally found them harder and made more errors on them than on direct reasoning problems involving the same schemas.

3. Reduction ad absurdum arguments. Our reductio problems fell into two groups. One was specially designed to explore the use of such arguments. The other group involved deriving a statement that a conjunction or disjunction was false; with the schemas of Table I they require reductio arguments, but would not necessarily do so in other systems. We begin with the first group, that more certainly demand reductio solutions.

In the reaction time and first rating study we sought to investigate the use of the reductio ad absurdum with the two following problems, which we thought might exemplify P16 straightforwardly:

If there is a C then there is an N
If there is a C then there's not an N   (13)
? There's not a C

If there is an E then there is a G
If there is an E then there's not a G   (14)
? There is an E

In the Reaction Time Study, responses of "true" to Problem 13 and of "false" to 14 occurred in only about half the subjects, and in the first rating study a majority of subjects voted both problems undecidable. The problems were given average difficulty ratings of 7 and 7.5, respectively, the highest ratings of the entire set of problems. Thus, most subjects did not see, or did not accept, the reductio solution to these problems.

In the second rating study, we discarded this pair of problems and substituted a pair of modified modus tollens problems:

If there is a G then there is a P
If there's not a G then there may or may not be a P;
you can't tell   (15)
There's not a P
? There's not a G

If there is an A then there is a D
If there's not an A then there may or may not be a D;
you can't tell   (16)
There's not a D
? There is an A

A normal modus tollens problem consists of the first and third premises together. The purpose of the second premise was to block the inference invited by the first premise [i.e., for Problem 15, *If there's not a G then there's not a P* (Geis & Zwicky, 1971)]. A normal modus tollens problem has two solutions, one primitive and the other involving a reductio (Wason & Johnson-Laird, 1972). The primitive solution consists of accepting the invited inference and concluding, for Problem 15, that *G* and *P* are either both present or both absent (which is tantamount to taking *if* as the biconditional); thus, the primitive solution has the same basis as the standard fallacies (i.e., *If p then q, not p, ∴ not q* and *If p then q, q, ∴ p*). Our extra premise blocks this solution and forces the reductio solution. (The reductio solution of 15 might be verbalized as "Suppose *G* were present, then *P* would have to be, but *P* isn't, so *G* must be absent.")

Problem 15 was solved by 71% and 16 by 67% of the subjects. All but one of the other responses was "indeterminate." Subjects who solved the problems gave them average difficulty ratings of 6.94 and 7.38, respectively, again the highest ratings of the set. Thus, reductio solutions did not come easily to subjects in any of Problems 13–16.

Turning now to the second group of reductio problems, those that required deriving the falsity of a conjunction or disjunction, we consider first the following pair:

> *There's not an R*
> *? It is not true that there is both an R and a U*   (17)

> *There's not a J*
> *? There's not both a J and a Q*   (18)

These are both solved without a reductio in some systems, for example, Osherson (1975a), and Braine (1978) has a schema that would solve them in one step.[5] They proved surprisingly difficult, however, with 27% and 21% errors and ratings of 4.76 and 4.38, respectively, suggesting that not all subjects have a schema that carries from premise to conclusion in a single step.

The relative difficulty of these problems makes an interesting contrast with the simplicity of a formally related problem:

> *There's not a C*
> *? There is a C and an H*   (19)

---

[5] The schema of Braine (1978) is: $F(p_i)$, ∴ $F(p_1 \text{ AND } p_2 \text{ AND } \ldots \text{ AND } p_n)$, $1 \leq i \leq n$, with notation as in Table I. Osherson (1975a) has the similar schema: $\sim A \lor \sim B$, ∴ $\sim (A \text{ and } B)$.

Subjects made no errors at all in saying the conclusion was false, and they rated the problem easy [1.96, very significantly easier than both of Problems 17 and 18—t (20) = 9.02, p < .001, and t (21) = 7.34, p < .001, respectively]. The greater simplicity of Problem 19 cannot be accounted for merely in terms of the greater ease of falsifying affirmative over verifying negative propositions (e.g., Carpenter & Just, 1975; Clark & Chase, 1972), because the difference is too large. Thus Problem 17 had an adjusted reaction time of 5.81 sec as opposed to 1.25 sec for 19 [t (17) = 5.57, p < .001], a difference of over 4.5 sec and an order of magnitude greater than the usual difference between falsifying affirmative and verifying negative sentences, which is less than half a second (Carpenter & Just, 1975).

In the present theory, subjects solve Problem 19 by inferring the presence of C from the conclusion and noting its incompatibility with the premise. Problems 17 and 18 involve a suppositional process: In 17 the subject has to suppose the proposition embedded in the conclusion (that there is both an R and a U), carry out the reasoning of Problem 19, conclude that the supposition is false (by P16), and then conclude that the conclusion given is true. Thus, Problems 17 and 18 involve a supposition leading to a reductio, wheras 19 does not.

The reasoning of Problems 17 and 18 was combined with another schema in two other problems and occurred as a lemma in two further ones. Problems 20 illustrates the latter:

> *If there is not both a B and a C, then there's not a W*
> *There's not a B*   (20)
> *? There is a W*

The proposition *There's not both a B and a C* has to be derived as a lemma. All these problems were rather difficult, with error rates from 9 to 23% and ratings from 4.05 to 6.50.

Problems 21 and 22 required deriving the falsity of a disjunction, and another problem combined that with another schema. This set raised issues similar to 17–20.

> *There's not an M and there's not a Q*
> *? It is not true that there is either an M or a Q*   (21)
>
> *There's not an S*
> *There's not a P*   (22)
> *? It's not true that there is either an S or a P*

Braine (1978) had a schema that would solve these problems directly.[6] Like Problems 17–18, however, they proved quite difficult, with a mean error

---

[6]The schema was: F(p_1) AND . . . AND F(p_n), ∴ F(p_1 OR . . . OR p_n), with notation as in Table I.

rate of 17% and a mean rating of 4.93, suggesting that they were not solved in one step by a universally available schema. On the other hand, the formally similar direct reasoning Problems 23 and 24 proved fairly easy:

> *There's not an A and there's not a V*
> *? There is an A or a V* (23)

> *There's not a T*
> *There's not a U* (24)
> *? There is a T or a U*

There were only 2% errors and the difficulty ratings (2.79 and 2.38) were each very significantly less than both of 21 and 22 (all comparisons, $p <$ .001). The reaction time differences (5.70 and 5.31 sec for 21 and 22, respectively, against 1.10 and 1.01 sec for 23 and 24, respectively, were significant [t (18) = 4.55, $p <$ .001 for 21 versus 23, and t (17) = 3.76, $p <$ .01 for 22 versus 24]; as in the similar case of Problems 17 and 18, these differences are too large to be accounted for simply as the difference between falsifying affirmative and verifying negative sentences.

In the present theory, Problems 23 and 24 are easy because they feed directly into Schema P4 which declares premises and conclusion incompatible. Problems 21 and 22 are a good deal harder because they involve a suppositional step (supposing the proposition embedded in the conclusion), proving it false (by P4 and P16), and concluding that the given conclusion is true.

Although these problems that involve deriving the falsity of a conjunction or disjunction require a reductio in our system, and were hard relative to the direct reasoning problems, they were nevertheless considerably easier than the first set of reductio problems discussed (Problems 13–16)—there is no overlap between the two sets, in either error rates or difficulty ratings. In the Discussion, we consider a possible reason for this difference in difficulty in terms of subjects' reasoning strategies.

4. $p,\ \therefore\ p$ OR q? The final problem to be discussed was:

> *There is an H*
> *? There is an H or an M* (25)

If the schema $p,\ \therefore\ p$ OR q was a natural one for subjects, then Problem 25 would be a one-step problem; it is of the simplest type that could be designed to elicit this schema. In the two rating studies, 52% of the subjects responded "true," 25% "false," and 23% "indeterminate." Those who responded "true" gave the problem an average difficulty rating of 4.30, harder than most problems and substantially harder than all the one-step problems. Thus, about half the subjects thought that the conclusion does not follow from the premise, and those who thought that it does follow found the inference to be relatively difficult. We argue later that p, $\therefore$ p OR q is not a natural schema for subjects.

IV. Discussion

We used two theory-based indices of expected problem complexity—the number of reasoning steps needed to solve a problem in our system and the sum of the difficulty weights of these steps. The results indicate that these indices were highly predictive of empirical measures of the difficulty of direct reasoning problems. Correlations ranged up to .95, for the joint prediction of rated difficulty from the weighted-sum index combined with problem length. There were high correlations with both errors and rated difficulty that were independent of problem length. These relationships make a case that in solving these problems, subjects do in fact go through the mental steps that the theory claims that they do, and thus that the schemas of Table I are a psychological reality. This claim, however, is affected by a number of topics that require discussion. In what follows, we first consider whether nonlogical processes or response biases could account for subjects' responses. Second, we discuss the variable of problem length—how it is measured and how it relates to problem difficulty. Third, we consider the processing assumptions of our prediction models, and particularly, the kind of reasoning program that subjects may bring to the task. Fourth, we discuss whether there are alternative logical models that could predict difficulty equally well. Fifth, we consider how far the postulated mental processes may generalize to propositional problems using other kinds of content. Finally, we present the claims we wish to make about natural propositional logic and consider how far these data support them.

A. Can Nonlogical Models Explain the Results?

Evans (1972, 1982) has claimed that subjects' responses on reasoning problems are often determined by various responses or matching biases, not by reasoning. Although this kind of explanation has been contested for some of his type cases (van Duyne, 1973, 1974; Evans 1975), let us consider whether such processes could explain the present results. We consider first whether biases could have determined subjects' responses of "true" or "false," and then whether they could have affected reaction times or ratings.

Since half the problems have "true" and half "false" as correct response, simple yea- and nay-saying biases are controlled for. Many matching or "atmosphere" type biases are conceivable. For example, subjects could have tended to say "true" to affirmatively phrased conclusions and "false" to negative ones, or they might have had the opposite bias; they might have tended to say "true" if all propositions were affirmative and "false" if any of the premises or conclusion were negative; or perhaps they tended to say "false" if the problem contained an odd number of negatives and "true" if an even number. For each of these biases there were a substantial number of problems on which the bias would lead to error, and any considerable prevalence of the bias among subjects would lead to large error percentages for these problems. Since errors were few on all the direct reasoning problems (the median percentage of error on the Appendix problems was 3%, range 0 to 13%), it follows that subjects' responses could not have been controlled by these response biases. The same argument would presumably apply against other response biases.

Latencies and ratings could be affected by biases that do not determine the choice of response, since a subject might take longer or consider a problem more difficult when a bias has to be overcome. We have no evidence that biases did not affect the latencies. On the ratings, however, the excellent cross-validated prediction of rated difficulty from the sum of reasoning step weights together with problem length suggests that response or matching bias was not a factor with which one should be concerned.

B. LENGTH AS A FACTOR AFFECTING DIFFICULTY

There are two kinds of questions to be discussed about length, one, as it were, tactical, and the other strategic. The tactical question has to do with the choice of a length measure to use in computing correlations with indices of problem difficulty, the strategic with whether length does affect the real difficulty of problems, how it does so, and how it should be brought into a prediction model.

The tactical question can be dealt with briefly. Number of words proved to be an effective measure of problem length in this work; however, one would certainly not expect it always to be so. For example, Osherson (1975a) used content very similar to ours; in one experiment (Chapter 8) he included some "wordy" problems in which proposition length was increased without effectively changing content (e.g., *There is a C* became *A C has been written down on the paper* in one of the wordy problems, an immaterial change that more than doubles the number of words). He found that such changes had no effect on problem difficulty. Obviously, number of words was a good measure of length in our work only because the content was highly stereotyped, and we adopted a constant format for expressing it in English. In any work with different content, the appropriate measure of problem length would have to be determined for that content.

On the more theoretical issues, we should first note that our results do not prove that length affects the real difficulty of problems. Length was not significantly related to errors. The relationship to the difficulty ratings shows that longer problems are perceived as more difficult; it does not prove that they actually are more difficult. The relationship of length to adjusted latency could plausibly be because the longer the premises, the more difficult they are to hold in mind, and so the more likely it is that subjects will need to spend time rereading them. Thus, it is clear that length is not related to all indices of difficulty and may be related to different indices for different reasons.

What is it about length that affects difficulty ratings? A problem can be made long in several ways. One way is by increasing the number of words used to express an idea. Osherson's (1975a) result on his wordy problems, cited above, indicates that merely padding propositions does not affect perceived difficulty. A second way of varying length occurs in the problems of Rating Study 2 in which length was manipulated while holding the reasoning steps constant: We varied the length and compositeness of the propositions that had to be substituted for the ps and qs in the schemas (cf. Problems xxi and xxii of the Appendix). Let us call this variable *substitution complexity*. The results for these problems demonstrate that this substitution complexity does affect perceived difficulty. A third way in which a problem can be long is by involving a large number of propositions or connectives or both (without complex substitutions): This was the most frequent way in which our longer and shorter problems differed. Length brought about in this way is inevitably confounded with reasoning complexity: Most problems that involve a chain of reasoning of several steps have to contain a fairly large number of propositions and connectives, and certain schemas (e.g., P6, P10, P11) necessarily involve fairly long problems just in order to present the information used in the schema.

Our method of analysis has tacitly assumed that length affects perceived difficulty to the same degree regardless of whether it is caused by substitution complexity or by the number of propositions and connectives used in a problem. This assumption has worked, in the sense that it proved consistent with good predictions of problem difficulty ratings. But other assumptions were possible, and they might have "worked" too. For instance, we could have assumed that length only affects difficulty ratings when it is brought about by substitution complexity. The prediction equation would then have had a parameter for substitution complexity but none for length per se. Any effect of length (other than substitution complexity) on difficulty ratings would then be absorbed into the difficulty weights for the schemas: The weights of schemas that necessarily involve many or long propositions (e.g., P6, P10, P11) would be relatively greater than with our present procedure. These are essentially the assumptions and prediction strategy used by Osherson (1975a).

We chose not to follow Osherson's predictive strategy for two reasons. First, with this strategy, the sum of the difficulty weights of the reasoning steps on a problem would be highly correlated with the length of the problem [as it is in Osherson's (1975a) studies], and it would be hard to be sure how much of the observed difficulty of problems could be due to length and how much *had* to be due to the difficulty of the reasoning steps. We viewed this uncertainty as a troublesome feature of Osherson's studies. Our prediction strategy is conservative, in that it results in reasoning step difficulty estimates that are not significantly influenced by problem length. Hence the correlation of a difficulty measure with the sum of the reasoning step weights cannot be due to length under any assumptions about how length really affects difficulty; it represents a minimum estimate of the covariation of the difficulty measure with reasoning complexity. It may underestimate this covariation, because if the assumption is correct that length only affects difficulty through substitution, then some possibly large fraction of the covariance of difficulty measures with length that we found is really caused by aspects of reasoning complexity that are inextricably confounded with length.

A second reason for preferring our prediction strategy was that it seemed to offer some hope of obtaining weight estimates for the schemas that would be independent of subject matter. If length is not factored out, then the schema difficulty weights that result from STEPIT's procedure must depend on the particular way that the propositions are expressed in English (since that affects length): Any change in subject matter will change length measures and require new schema weight estimates. By eliminating the influence of length, however, we can hope to have obtained weights for schemas that apply to propositions as they are understood, independently of the precise expression in English. That is, they may exclude any difficulty contributed by encoding factors. Our prediction scheme would then apply to new direct reasoning problems with a different subject matter, using just the same set of weights; it would require only that a suitable length-cum-complexity parameter be estimated from the data to take account of difficulty contributed by length and encoding factors connected with the content, but not with the form of the reasoning. But of course we cannot tell from the present work how far this hope has been realized.

That the error measure is correlated with the reasoning step weights but not with length provides, we think, some after-the-fact support for a prediction strategy that ensures weight estimates that are substantially independent of length.

C. Processing Implications and Subjects' Reasoning Program

The results imply a substantial uniformity among subjects in the way their comprehension and reasoning programs apply to the direct reasoning problems we used. Moreover, the subjects' program finds the shortest solutions (for our problems) without getting lost in blind alleys. Wide variation in how premises were understood, or in how a line of reasoning was selected, would make it unlikely that our methodology could be used to predict problem difficulty successfully. Uniformity in comprehension is plausible because as noted in the Introduction, we did not use problems that contained propositions which could easily be misconstrued, because of conversational implicatures (Grice, 1975) or for other reasons.

We suggested in the Introduction that subjects might have a direct reasoning routine that matches premises (plus the antecedent of the conclusion, when that is an *if-then* statement) with the numerators of schemas and applies any of the direct reasoning schemas that fit. If the conclusion or some proposition incompatible with it is not reached, the process is repeated on the newly created problem that consists of the original premises plus the new proposition produced by applying the schema. The program outlined in Table III contains a direct reasoning routine that works in this way. The program uses the schemas of Table I and consists of a direct reasoning routine supplemented by strategies for use when the routine fails;[7] it provides a concrete hypothesis about subjects' reasoning procedures. The direct reasoning routine solves all the Appendix problems using the line of reasoning given there.

For the reductio ad absurdum strategy, Table III proposes both a *limited form* and a *stronger form;* the limited form is assumed to be more widely available to subjects than the stronger form. In particular, the limited form would solve our easier reductio problems (e.g., Problems 17–18 and 20–22—see Section III,F), whereas a stronger strategy is needed to solve the more difficult reductio problems (13–16). We do not have the data to formulate the stronger form more precisely. In general, a skilled reasoner would have a more elaborate and powerful set of strategies than those proposed, but we estimate that the program (without the stronger form of the reduc-

---

[7]The routine goes beyond the intuitive conception of direct reasoning in containing processes that prevent useless operations, such as the duplication of propositions in the premise set, or the pointless iteration of Schema P1 (cf. Rips, 1983). Thus, the use of P1 is confined to positions where it would be useful and cannot iterate. In addition, Schema P2 is made available in Part B of the evaluation procedure to account for the simplicity of the solution of Problem 19 (cited in Section III,F), in which subjects clearly must use P2 to make an inference from the problem conclusion.

TABLE III

OUTLINE OF PROPOSED REASONING PROGRAM OF SUBJECTS

Program begins with the direct reasoning routine. The direct reasoning routine fails when Step 3 fails to generate fresh propositions for evaluation, although no determinate response has yet been made. When routine fails, apply indirect reasoning strategies.
Program stops when a response of "true" or "false" is made.

Direct reasoning routine

Step 1. Evaluate the conclusion against the premises, using the evaluation procedure (conclusion = given proposition; premise set = original premises). If the evaluation is indeterminate, then:

Step 2^a. If the conclusion is an *if-then* statement, add the antecedent to the premise set and treat the consequent as the conclusion to be tested; use the evaluation procedure to test the new conclusion against the augmented premise set. If the evaluation is indeterminate (or if Step 2 did not apply), then:

Step 3. Match the premise set (the original premises, or as augmented at prior processing steps) to the conditions of application of schemas as specified in the schema numerators. Apply any of Schemas P2 and P5 through P12 whose conditions of application are satisfied, or whose conditions of application can be satisfied by first applying P1 to propositions of the premise set. Add the proposition(s) generated to the premise set and use the evaluation procedure to test the conclusion against the augmented premise set. If the outcome of the evaluation is indeterminate, repeat Step 3. (In repeating Step 3, however, no schema that has already been applied to proposition(s) in the premise set is reapplied to the same propositions; nor is any schema applied whose only effect would be to duplicate a proposition already in the premise set.)

Evaluation procedure: to test a given proposition against a premise set (i.e., the original premises or as augmented in prior processing). (A) If the given proposition is in the premise set, or is equivalent to some conjunction (by Schema P1) of propositions in the premise set, then consider it true; if the given proposition was the conclusion, respond "true." (B) If the given proposition, or an inference from it by P2, is incompatible (by P3 or P4) with a proposition in the premise set, or with some conjunction (by P1) of propositions from the set, then consider it false; if the given proposition was the conclusion, respond "false."

Examples of indirect reasoning strategies

Lemma-producing strategy. If the premise set contains a disjunction, and some of the propositions of the disjunction do not occur as antecedents of conditionals in the premise set, then suppose each of these in turn and try to derive a conditional with it as antecedent, using P13 and the procedure of Step 3, with the goal of feeding Schema P10 or P11. If successful, add the conditionals to the premise set and return to Step 3.

(*continued*)

TABLE III *(Continued)*

Strategies of enumerating alternatives a priori. If the premise set contains one or more conditionals of the form *If p then . . .* or *If not p then . . .*, apply Schema P14 to add the appropriate proposition of the form *p or not p* to the premise set and return to Step 3. If there is a proposition, *p,* that is mentioned in the premise set (perhaps as a component of another proposition) but not mentioned in the conclusion, then use Schema P14 to add the proposition of the form *p or not p* to the premise set, and return to Step 3.

Reductio ad absurdum strategy. Limited form: If there is a conjunction or disjunction embedded within a premise proposition or within the conclusion, then suppose the conjunction or disjunction as per Schema P16 and use Part B of the evaluation procedure to test its compatibility with the premise set (the conjunction or disjunction = given proposition; premise set = premises + all added propositions); if the evaluation is "false," add the proposition that the conjunction or disjunction is false to the premise set; use the evaluation procedure to test the conclusion against the augmented premise set, and if the evaluation is indeterminate, return to Step 3. Stronger form: To test the falsity of the conclusion or of any proposition embedded within a premise, add the negation of that proposition to the premise set and try to derive an incompatibility as per Schema P16, using Step 3 and Part B of the evaluation procedure.

---

a For the two prediction models, Step 2 is a usage of Schema P13.

tio) comes close to representing the skill of our average subject as we have seen it.

We should point out that there is one situation in which the theory as a whole (i.e., the schemas of Table I, taken in conjunction with the program of Table III) predicts responses that are at variance with those dictated by standard logic. When a problem has a conditional as a conclusion, the program categorizes that conclusion as "false" when the assumption of the antecedent leads to denial of the consequent. That is, a conclusion *If p then q* will be identified as "false" when *not q* is derivable from the problem premises together with *p*. According to standard logic, *If p then q* is not decidable under these circumstances (since *p* might be false). Appendix problems xxx, xxxvi, and xxxix illustrate the situation. The program predicts a response of "false," although standard logic demands "indeterminate." The subjects agree with the program (95% of responses were "false" and hardly any were "indeterminate"). It is Step 2 of the program taken with the evaluation procedure that is responsible for the prediction, not the schemas.

It may be noted that the program will draw inferences when there is no conclusion to be tested (i.e., when only a set of premises is given and the task is to say what follows from them). Steps 1 and 2, and the evaluation procedure, are then inoperative. The inferences drawn are just the succession of propositions added to the premise set at successive cycles of Step 3.

Table III may not be the only program consistent with our results. There is developmental evidence (Braine & Rumain, 1983), however, that the schemas involved in direct reasoning tend to be available to children at least by the early school years, considerably before P14–16. Thus, a direct reasoning routine may be developmentally earlier than other reasoning strategies. Moreover, our adult subjects made few errors on the direct reasoning problems, fewer than on the indirect reasoning ones. These considerations suggest that subjects' reasoning problems have a two-part structure, as in Table III. The direct reasoning routine would be largely shared among subjects; individual differences in the strategies available would account for variation in reasoning skill.

In addition to having a two-part structure that seems well motivated, the program in Table III (without the stronger reductio strategy) meets the following conditions: (1) it uses the schemas of Table 1; (2) it solves all the problems that the great majority of subjects solve; (3) it predicts that the direct reasoning problems will be easier than the indirect ones; and (4) it predicts that the difficulty of a direct reasoning problem will be a function of the length of the chain of inferences of Table I needed to solve it. To apply to the ratings, predictions (3) and (4) require the assumption that subjects have some gross awareness of the amount of processing a problem has demanded. The direct reasoning problems usually demand more processing than the indirect ones (becaue the program runs through the direct reasoning routine before initiating strategies), and the amount of processing on direct reasoning problems depends mostly on the number of cycles of Step 3, which is a function of the length of the chain of inferences. Our program-writing efforts have convinced us that any program meeting conditions (1)–(4) would be quite similar to that of Table III.

The primary research goal was to discover subjects' repertory of schemas. The support that the results provide for the schemas of Table I does not depend on the program in Table III. So far as support for Table I is concerned, the only crucial processing assumption is that subjects' programs, whatever they are, routinely find the shortest line of reasoning with these schemas that solves the direct reasoning problems—this is the only assumption needed to specify the sequence of inferences for each problem. On the other hand, support for the program of Table III does depend on the accuracy of Table I—different schemas might require a different kind of program.

D. ALTERNATIVE LOGICAL THEORIES

Johnson-Laird (1975), Osherson (1975a), and Rips (1983) all present theories that include sets of propositional schemas for which psychological reality is claimed. We first discuss one putative schema that is common to all three theories as well as to standard logic, but missing in our system, and then we consider the theories in turn.

1. The Schema p, $\therefore$ p OR q

As we have seen, one-step inferences based on this schema were often rejected by subjects as invalid. The schema is, of course, not valid for exclusive *or*. One cannot, however, explain subjects' rejection on the simple grounds that they interpret *or* exclusively or are uncertain whether to take *or* inclusively or exclusively, because Schema P7 is also valid for inclusive *or* only; yet subjects make no errors on simple problems involving this schema (e.g., Problems ix, xvii, xxiv in the Appendix). It seems that the inferences that are valid only for inclusive *or* that subjects regularly make (e.g., the appendix problems cited) are well captured by P7. It would be a theoretical nuisance to assume that p, $\therefore$ p OR q was in the subjects' repertory, since that assumption predicts responses whose failure to occur would need to be explained away.

The inconsistency of subjects' responses to problems of the form $p/$? p *or* q, concords with the fact that the program in Table III would not deliver a solution to such problems. (p OR q can be derived from p using the schemas of Table I, but the program in Table III is not adequate to finding a derivation.)

Let us consider what information might be contained in subjects' lexical entry for *or*. There are two theories of the meanings of the connectives that are formally adequate to explain inferences: truth tables and schemas. Recent years have seen a consensus against the truth-table theory (e.g., Braine & Rumain, 1983; Osherson, 1975b; Wason & Johnson-Laird, 1972). In the case of *or*, the idea that the basic meaning relevant for reasoning is given by schemas is consistent with the fact that many simple inferences sanctioned by schemas (e.g., P7, P8, P10) occur developmentally earlier than truth judgments and are made much more consistently than truth judgments by adults (Braine & Rumain, 1981). If the schema p, $\therefore$ p OR q were part of the essential meaning of *or* for subjects, then it should not be possible for them to reject the inference on simple problems.

2. Johnson-Laird's Model

Johnson-Laird's (1975) set of schemas is fairly similar to ours, but lacks schemas equivalent to P3, P4, P6, P7, P10, and P14 of Table I. The inferences defined by these schemas can be achieved in his system, but only by relatively long chains of reasoning. For example, the effect of P4 can be achieved by a line of reasoning involving P8 and a reductio, and with further reasoning and another reductio, P14 can be derived; the effect of P6 and P10 can be achieved by lines of reasoning involving P11. If one-step problems that involve P4, P6, and P10 were solved with Johnson-Laird's schemas, then one would have to predict several errors and high subjective difficulties for them. But the data indicate that they are very simple, about as easy as problems solved in one step in both systems. In addition, problems involving P6 and P10 are not more difficult than comparable problems involving P11, as his derivations would have to predict. In general, it is not surprising that our system fits the evidence better than Johnson-Laird's, since the present system was arrived at by starting with a set like his and successively altering the system where indicated by introspective reports or data on relative difficulties of problems.[8]

3. Osherson's Model

This model (Osherson, 1975a) contains 22 schemas listed in the Appendix to Osherson (1975a), apart from modus ponens. The set includes schemas similar to only P2, P5, P6, P7, and P8 of Table I. None of the 22 schemas contains more than one formula in the numerator, so that many very simple lines of reasoning (e.g., those that use P10) are not covered. Osherson stresses that his system is both logically and psychologically incomplete. In fact, only a few of our problems can be solved with his system.[9] Some of these are solved in quite counterintuitive ways. For example, consider:

> It is not true that there is both an L and an S
> ? If there is an L, then there's not an S

His system would first infer *Either there's not an L or there's not an S;* it would then convert this into *If it is not true that there's not an L, then there's not an S* and thence into the conclusion. Such roundabout derivations would force his model to predict unduly high difficulties for some problems that subjects do not rate particularly hard.

Of Osherson's schemas that are not in our set, some (e.g, the schema *p,* ∴ *p* OR *q* and some derivatives of it) are omitted for reasons discussed.

---

[8]Johnson-Laird (1983) does not now agree with his 1975 model, but not for our reasons.

[9]Of the 59 noncontrol, direct reasoning problems in the Appendix, only 8 are solvable in Osherson's system. This is in part because his system lacks a mechanism, like Schema P3, for generating a response of "false." If one granted such a mechanism, 7 additional problems would be solved. The poor coverage is also in part because Osherson associates his schemas with "helping conditions" (i.e., constraints on the problem context in which the schema is permitted to apply). Eliminating these constraints would permit another 12 problems to be solved.

Other schemas are omitted because we do not believe the inferences are performed in one step by subjects. For instance, the effects of Osherson's schema IF p THEN q AND r, $\therefore$ IF p THEN q are obtained by applying P13, P12, P2 (i.e., by positing p, inferring q and r, and then q). Some of his schemas involve indirect reasoning in our system, using either P14 or P16. For example, the effects of IF NOT p THEN q, $\therefore$ p OR q are obtained by P14 feeding P11.

Osherson presented subjects with one-step and multistep problems and also some problems using invalid arguments. Subjects decided which conclusions were valid and then rated the difficulty of the problem. Correlations were computed between the average difficulties of the multistep arguments and the sum of the average difficulties of the one-step arguments required to solve them. The correlations were generally fairly high, ranging from .54 to .89, over eight experiments. These correlations are consistent with our theory. Although the line of reasoning to solve a problem in our theory is usually not the same as it is in his, it is often the case that the operations our theory provides to solve an Osherson multistep problem are the sum of the operations used to solve his component one-step arguments. Thus, if his subjects consistently solve his problems our way, one would still expect the difficulties of his multistep problems to correlate with the sum of the difficulties of the supposed component one-step inferences.

In assessing our model against Osherson's data, Experiments 4 and 5 of Osherson (1975a) were used. These experiments used a wider range of schemas than his earlier experiments and employed the same kind of wording and subject matter (letters on an imaginary blackboard) as our studies. The experiments included 38 different problems (14 one-step and 24 multistep in Osherson's system, all but 1 multistep in ours). Five problems were omitted that involve modus tollens (or contraposition) because such problems invite an easy solution based on misinterpretation of the intent of the premises (see the earlier discussion of modus tollens). That left 33 problems. Where the same problem occurred in both experiments, the percentages of errors and the difficulty ratings were each averaged over the two experiments; for problems occurring in one experiment we used the data from that experiment.[10]

The direct reasoning routine of Table III solves 13 of the 33 problems; the full program including the strategies (without the stronger reductio strategy because of its imprecise formulation and doubtful use by many subjects) solves a further 8; the program fails to solve 12 problems. Osherson's subjects' error rates for these sets of problems were 21, 34, and

---

[10]Treating each experiment separately, at the cost of a smaller n, does not change the import of the analysis.

51%, respectively. To obtain a rough measure of the program's ability to predict problem difficulty, an ordinal index of predicted difficulty was created by assigning the values of 0, 1, and 2 to these three categories of problems, respectively. This index correlated .66 with errors and .32 with the difficulty ratings. The index has a nonsignificant negative correlation with problem length. Length correlated only .19 with errors, but .78 with ratings. (The low correlation of errors with length is an interesting replicaton of our finding that error probability is largely independent of problem length.) With length partialled out, the index correlated .71 with errors and .69 with the ratings ($p < .001$ in both cases). We conclude that Osherson's data do not conflict with our theory.

4. Rip's Model

A natural deduction system (ANDS; Rips, 1983) is based on 11 inference schemas. In ANDS, however, the application of a schema can be made conditional on a subgoal as well as on the propositions whose form is specified in the schema. Similarly, the action taken in applying a schema can include the setting of subgoals in addition to making an inference. For example, the schema of ANDS that corresponds to our Schema P10 (Rips, 1983, p. 46) is:

R11.   Conditions: (1) Current subgoal $= r$.
        (2) Assertion tree (i.e., premises + inferred propositions) contains p OR q.
    Actions: (1) Add new subordinate node to assertion tree with assumption p.
        (2) Set up corresponding subgoal node to deduce r.
        (3) If Subgoal 2 is achieved, add new subordinate node to assertion tree with assumption q.
        (4) Set up corresponding subgoal node to deduce r.
        (5) If Subgoal 4 is achieved, add r to assertion tree.

Thus, R11 cannot come into action without a current subgoal, and the subgoals set by Actions 2 and 4 have to be identical to that in Condition 1. ANDS also contains backward and forward versions of certain schemas. The backward version sets a new subgoal and incorporates an element of planning, for example, given *IF p then q* and a current subgoal *q,* the backward version of modus ponens sets a new subgoal, *p*. (The forward version is just like Schema P12 of Table I).

This conditionality of inferences on subgoals places ANDS on a very short leash that has counterintuitive consequences. For example, consider the following premises:

> *There is an F or an R*
> *If there is an F then there is an L*
> *If there is an R then there is an L*

It seems intuitively obvious that there has to be an *L*. If ANDS is given the conclusion *There is an L,* then ANDS makes the deduction. But if the conclusion given is anything else (e.g., *There is an X,* or *There is not an L*), ANDS will not notice that there has to be an *L*. The direct reasoning routine of Table III makes such deductions in any environment, and subgoals appear only in the strategies component.

Nine of ANDS's schemas correspond to schemas of Table I (P1, P2, P7, P8, P10, P12, P13, P14, and P16). Our schemas P3, P4, P5, P6, P9, and P11 are without analogs in ANDS. ANDS has two schemas not in Table I [*p*, ∴ *p* OR *q*, already discussed, and De Morgan's ~ (*p* AND *q*), ∴ ~ *p* OR ~*q*, discussed later].

Schemas like P3 and P4 are needed by ANDS. As described by Rips, ANDS cannot prove a conclusion false. One could easily add this capability without P3 and P4 by allowing ANDS two attempts at a problem, first trying to derive the given conclusion, then its negation; ANDS would then respond "false" if the negation of the conclusion was derived. (We assume this procedure later, in discussing how ANDS fares with our problems.) Rips himself notes, however, that subjects respond "invalid" immediately on detecting a contradiction among the premises and conclusion (1983, p. 67), and schemas like P3 and P4 are needed to define "contradiction."[11]

ANDS fails to solve one-step problems involving Schemas P5 and P9 (Problems vii and xi of the Appendix). ANDS would solve them if the conditions of application of certain of Rips's schemas were loosened, but even then, the derivations would be quite roundabout and would thus predict that these problems should be more difficult than they are. In part because ANDS fails problems involving P5 and P9, it solves only 42 of the 61 problems of the Appendix.

Although ANDS can solve problems involving P6 and P11 (e.g., viii and xiii of the Appendix), for both problems, the solution has several steps and

---

[11]Schema P4 is logically redundant in that its effects could be obtained just with P3 and the other schemas. One-step problems involving P4 are sufficiently simple, however, to indicate that the contradiction is immediately apparent to subjects. Much greater difficulty would be predicted if subjects used the roundabout reasoning that would be needed if P4 were not in their repertory.

includes use of the schema p, $\therefore$ p OR q. These problems would therefore be predicted to be more difficult than they are. In particular, since Rip's own data indicate a low availability of p, $\therefore$ p OR q (a probability of usage of only .197 in problems involving it—an implicit confirmation of our critique of this schema), his system would have to predict huge numbers of errors on these problems, on which there were hardly any. In sum, ANDS would need to incorporate our schemas to account for the simplicity of many problems, as well as responses of "false."

In Rip's main supporting experiment,[12] adult subjects received 32 problems soluble by ANDS with all its schemas available, together with 32 invalid problems (and some filler problems). Subjects judged whether the conclusion had to be true when the premises were ture. Subjects judged valid problems to be valid 51% of the time and Rips attempted to predict the proportion of valid responses to each such problem, using a prediction model with 11 parameters. The model assumed that each schema has a certain probability of being "available" to subjects on any trial, and 10 such probabilities were estimated from the data. (One schema was not used.) An additional parameter was the probability of guessing; this was obtained from the proportion of valid responses to invalid problems and turned out to be quite high (.46). With 10 parameters estimated from 32 data points, predicted and obtained proportions correlated .93.

The direct reasoning routine of Table III solves 9 of Rips's problems; the routine together with the strategies (omitting the stronger reductio strategy) solves a further 6; the program fails to solve 17. On these three sets, respectively, 73.2, 44.4, and 40.8% of responses were that the conclusions followed from the premises. The ordinal index of predicted difficulty used with Osherson's problems (values of 0, 1, and 2 assigned to the three problem categories, respectively) correlated $-.61$ with the proportion of judgments of valid. The correlation is considerably less than Rips's .93, but has no parameters estimated from the data. The main reason the correlation is not higher is that the program fails to solve three problems that use Rips's schema from De Morgan, $\sim(p$ AND $q)$, $\therefore$ $\sim p$ OR $\sim q;$ these were solved by most subjects. This inference can be made with our schemas, but it requires several steps and needs cleverer strategies than those in Table III. Rip's data suggest that the De Morgan inference is simpler for subjects than our theory predicts, and that provision should be made for it. We return to this issue later.

[12]A second experiment analyzed introspective data and showed that subjects' lines of argument on some of Osherson's problems resembled ANDS's somewhat more than Osherson's models. A third experiment on memory for arguments was consistent with ANDS but also does not uniquely support it.

If the *n*-ary version of De Morgan's schema [i.e., $F(p_1$ AND . . . AND $p_n)$, $\therefore$ $F(p_1)$ OR . . . OR $F(p_n)$] were added to Table II, then the correlation of $-.61$ would jump to $-.81$. Also, the proportion of conclusions rejected for problems soluble by the direct reasoning routine (26%) and the proportion accepted on problems not soluble by the program at all (34%) would both be close to the proportion expected from Rips's estimate of guessing (23%).[13] Thus, amended to provide for the De Morgan inference discussed, our theory concords well with Rips's subjects' judgments, without estimating parameters.

E. GENERALIZATION ACROSS PROPOSITIONAL CONTENT

Merely changing the subject-matter of propositions does not seem to change subjects' reasoning. For example, Rips (1983) used two kinds of content and found no difference; Osherson's books (1974, 1975a, 1976) replicated several experiments changing the subject-matter of propositions without finding evidence for changes in reasoning. Thus, there is good reason to believe that the theory proposed is general across subject matter.

The theory does not include a comprehension mechanism, however. It describes subjects' reasoning from the information given, as it is understood; but what a subject understands may not always be identical with what the problem-setter intended that they understand. Thus, if the information given is presented in a verbal form that has conversational implicatures (Grice, 1975), some subjects will reason from an expanded premise set that includes the conversational implicature. Similarly, if the subject-matter concerns factual knowledge, some subjects may expand the premise set from which they reason to include relevant information they know. The theory only accounts for reasoning from the premise set used, and to predict behavior in such cases it would need parameters estimating the effective premise set.

F. IMPLICATIONS FOR "NATURAL" PROPOSITIONAL LOGIC

We now conclude by trying to make precise what we are claiming about schemas of natural propositional logic and the ground for the claims. A set of schemas for a natural propositional logic should satisfy three conditions,

---

[13]Surprisingly, many of Rips's subjects rejected conclusions on problems where the conclusion seems to follow transparently from the premises, for example, *p; q or r/* ? *If not q then p and r*. (With one type of content used, this could have read: *Mary is in New York; Jane is in Detroit or Barbara is in Washington/* ? *If Jane is not in Detroit, then Barbara is in Washington and Mary is in New York.*) One third of the subjects responded "not necessarily true." So high a failure rate on transparent problems suggests that the experiment often failed to engage the reasoning procedures of subjects.

we believe. Let us consider each condition in turn and assess how far it is satisfied by the schemas of Table I.

First, the schemas should be logically and psychologically valid. That is, for the inferences the schemas define, the conclusions should follow from the premises, and essentially all adult subjects should reason as if they did on straightforward problems. Note that our notion of psychological validity implies some degree of universality. Obviously, a claim of universality becomes more interesting the broader it is, but the present data limit us to discussing it with respect to our subject population. Questions of logical validity can be raised about five of the schemas of Table I: P5, P7, P13, P14, and P16. For the others, we do not see how any question could be raised about their logical validity, and the low error rates reported, especially for the one-step problems, confirm their psychological validity. Let us consider the debatable schemas. The validity of P13 has been questioned in some philosophical work on the meaning of *if* (Stalnaker, 1968; Lewis, 1973), which we will not discuss here having done so elsewhere (Braine, 1979a,b; Braine & Rumain, 1983). Suffice it to say now that P13, as used in Step 2 of the program, appears to have been an easy schema for our subjects. Schema P7 is valid for inclusive but not for exclusive *or*. Although our subjects did not consistently take *or* inclusively—witness their performance on problems involving the rejected schema $p, \therefore p$ OR q—they did all use P7 in their reasoning, making no errors at all on one-step problems involving this schema. As discussed in Braine (1978), the logic, through P7, contains a concealed commitment to inclusive *or*. The validity of the other three schemas, P5, P14, and P16, depends on the number of truth values of natural logic: They must be logically valid for two truth values only. The data show that P5 and P14 were in the subjects' repertories, indicating that they reasoned as if there were just two truth values. The availability of P5 is also indicated in work on comprehension models for negations (e.g., Carpenter & Just, 1975). On the other hand, the general availability of P16 could be questioned on the basis of these data. It could reasonably be argued, however, that P16 can enter into subjects' reasoning at two levels. The most primitive and routine level occurs at Part B of the evaluation procedure in Table III, when encountering an incompatibility triggers a response of "false." That use is universal among subjects. What is not universal is the strategic use in reductio ad absurdum strategies. P13 also has a routine use at Step 2, and a strategic use in the lemma-producing strategy.[14] In sum, all the schemas meet the first condition, although P13 and

---

[14]For both these schemas, the distinction between supposition and premise is much clearer for the strategic use than for the routine one. From a strict logical point of view, the response of "false" to a conditional conclusion when the antecedent taken with the premises are found to be incompatible with the consequent—a response universally made by subjects—implies a failure to mark the suppositional status of the antecedent that was posited at Step 2.

P16 can claim universality only in their routine use at Step 2, and Part B of the evaluation procedure, respectively.

Second, the schemas should be psychologically elementary as well as valid. That is, each reasoning step defined should be carried out as a single inferential step by subjects, not as a chain of inferences. For many of our schemas, it is hard to see how they could be other than elementary, because of the difficulty of imagining a chain of more elementary schemas that achieve the same effect. Where competing hypotheses about what is elementary are imaginable, we conclude that a schema is elementary if (1) it is psychologically valid (i.e., one-step problems involving it are solved essentially without error), and (2) its difficulty is substantially less than the sum of the difficulties of any chain of putative more elementary schemas which could conceivably be used to solve one-step problems involving it. Examples of how the kind of data collected bear on elementariness are provided in various parts of the article (e.g., the arguments in Footnote 4 and in the discussion of other logical theories). In general, evidence on difficulty cannot directly prove the elementariness of a schema, but can lead it to be questioned and should permit a decision between rival hypotheses. The schemas of Table I are those that have survived this sifting process of comparison with rival hypotheses. The work shows that good predictions of behavioral data on difficulty can be obtained from the schemas proposed, especially when taken with the difficulty weights associated with them.

The third condition is that the set of schemas should be psychologically complete: It should contain all the psychologically valid elementary schemas that there are. One candidate schema missing from Table I is De Morgan's schema from the model of Rips (1983). That schema was clearly available to most of Rips's subjects. In one-step problems involving it, however, surprisingly many of Osherson's (1975a) subjects rejected the conclusion (41% in one experiment and 34% in another). It may be a common derived schema rather than elementary, as we discuss shortly. The transitivity of *if* (IF *p* THEN *q*, IF *q* THEN *r*; ∴ IF *p* THEN *r*) is another possible elementary schema. Apart from these possibilities, the argument that the set is psychologically complete is indirect. First, we may note that the set is *logically* complete, in the sense that all the schemas of propositional logic found in standard works in logic are either contained in this set or derivable from it. So the question of psychological completeness reduces to the following: Are there any schemas logically derivable from this set, but not included in it, that are in the repertories of our subjects, and elementary by our criterion? In the course of this article we have examined a number of candidate schemas—for example, some of our former schemas (cf. Footnotes 5, 6, and 7) and some of Osherson's—and found them not to be elementary by our criterion. We do not know of other plausible candidates and tentatively conclude that the set is probably complete (apart from the question of De Morgan's schema and the transitivity of *if*). It may be noted that our set of schemas is not logically a minimum set; that is, there are several cases, as we have noted, where one schema could be logically derived from others. As exemplified in our discussion of other theories, however, in these cases of potential redundancy, the schemas meet the criterion of elementariness: One-step problems involving them are solved without error, and their subjective difficulty is much smaller than would be anticipated if they were actually carried out as chains of inferences, not as a single step.

It is possible that there are individual differences among subjects with respect to derived schemas. Some subjects may be more practiced in propositional reasoning than others and, after going through the same sequence of steps many times, might become able to treat the chain as a single step. Common observation suggests that this conflation of multiple steps into one often occurs in mathematical reasoning with increasing practice. The difficulty of the conflated sequence might then become less than the sum of the difficulties of its components. It is doubtful, however, that this sort of conflation has occurred to any great extent among our subjects; if it had, subjective difficulty would presumably have been less predictable than it was. Nevertheless, the sampling of potential schemas in our problems has no claim to completeness and there may well be some derived schemas not sampled in our problems, which have become unitary steps for many subjects. The De Morgan schema discussed and the transitivity of *if* are obvious candidates.[15]

We conclude that there are residual questions about the status of certain schemas, notably the De Morgan schema discussed, but that otherwise the data reported provide support for the schemas proposed here as constituting Natural Propositional Logic. Of course, true universality—cross cul-

---

[15]It is also likely that, to serve elaborated strategies of enumerating alternatives a priori, most undergraduates have, alongside P14, a schema:

$$\frac{*}{(p \text{ and } q) \text{ OR } [p \text{ AND } F(q)] \text{ OR } [F(p) \text{ AND } q] \text{ or } [F(p) \text{ and } F(q)]}$$

Such a schema would provide a theoretical link to the "formal operations" (Inhelder & Piaget, 1958). [See Braine & Rumain (1983), however, for a review of problems with Piaget's logic.] The derived status of this schema is suggested by the fact that studies of the formal operations imply that this schema, and elaborated alternative-enumerating strategies associated with it, are a product of development in adolescence, whereas there is evidence for most of the schemas in Table I well before that age (Braine & Rumain, 1983).

tural—remains to be investigated. In addition, questions remain about the nature and organization of subjects' reasoning strategies.

Finally, we would recall that it was a central point of Braine (1978) that people do not have direct introspective access to their schemas as such. They have introspective access to the products of reasoning, the propositions that are the output of a reasoning step and may be the input for another, for example, a subject can often report the succession of propositions derived in a chain of reasoning. Subjects do not have access to the schemas by which the propositions are derived, however. They never see them neatly arrayed as in Table I. Thus, they cannot access the information that would permit them to play metalogician to their own logic. Consequently, it is consistent with our theory that subjects should be ignorant of, and their behavior and judgments uninfluenced by, very many facts, for example, certain truth tables, that a logician could prove from or about Table I.

V. Summary

We have provided evidence supporting a particular repertory as the repertory of the kinds of inferences basic to the propositional reasoning of adults untutored in logic. It was found that measures of the difficulty of direct reasoning problems can be predicted from the number of inferences of this repertory needed to solve a problem, and very well predicted if one also takes into account problem length and the kind of inference. Correlations with difficulty measures ranged up to .95, and up to .91 with problem length partialled out. The repertory was incorporated into a reasoning program that consists of a direct reasoning routine, coupled with some strategies to be used when the routine fails to solve a problem. The routine is largely shared among subjects; intersubject variation in the strategies component would account for differences in reasoning skill. Problematical features of other models, and the logical, psychological, and universalistic claims of the present model were discussed.

VI. Appendix: The Problems of Rating Study 2

The list is complete, except that is includes only one example each of the control-true and control-false problems, two examples of the modus ponens + contradiction problems (one short and one long—numbers xxi and xxii) used to obtain the relation between problem length and rated difficulty, and none of the indirect reasoning problems. After each problem, we list the schemas from Table I that it was anticipated the subjects would use and then the mean of the difficulty ratings given by all subjects who solved the problem correctly.

Control-true

i.   *There is a W*
        ? There is a W? (—) (1.06)

Control-false

ii.   *There's not an M*
        ? There is an M ? (P3) (1.18)

One step

iii.   *There is a G*
        There is an S
        ? There is a G and an S? (P1) (1.57)

iv.   *There is an O and a Z*
        ? There is an O? (P2) (1.42)

v.   *There's not an R, and there's not a W*
        ? There is an R or a W? (P4) (2.79)

vi.   *There is a J or a Q*
        ? There's not a J and there's not a Q? (P4) (2.71)

vii.   *It is false that there's not a W*
        ? There is a W? (P5) (2.37)

viii.   *There is a B, and there is an L or an R*
        ? There is a B and an L, or there is a B and an R? (P6)
        (2.81)

ix.   *If there is either a C or an H, then there is a P*
        There is a C
        ? There is a P? (P7) (2.50)

x.   *There is a D or a T*
        There's not a D
        ? There is a T? (P8) (2.35)

xi.   *It is not true that there is both a G and an I*
        There is a G
        ? There's not an I? (P9) (3.10)

xii.   *If there is an F, then there is an L*
        If there is an R, then there is an L
        There is an F or an R
        ? There is an L? (P10) (2.61)

xiii.   *If there is an I, then there is an N*
        If there is a B, then there is a T
        There is an I or a B
        ? There is an N or a T? (P11) (2.98)

xiv.   *If there is a T, then there is an L*
            There is a T
            ? There is an L? (P12) (1.71)

One step + contradiction

xv.   *There is an F, and there's not an L*
            ? There is an L? (P2, P3) (2.15)
xvi.   *It is false that there's not an M*
            ? There's not an M? (P5, P3) (2.64)
xvii.   *If there is either a D or a J, then there's not a Q*
            There is a D
            ? There is a Q? (P7, P3) (2.88)
xviii.   *There is a Q or an N*
            There's not a Q
            ? There's not an N? (P8, P3) (2.96)
xix.   *It is not true that there is both a V and an H*
            There is a V
            ? There is an H? (P9, P3) (3.25)
xx.   *If there is an E, then there's not a V*
            If there is an O, then there's not a V
            There is an E or an O
            ? There is a V? (P10, P3) (3.17)
xxi.   *If there is an E, then there's not a K*
            There is an E
            ? There is a K? (P12, P3, short) (2.04)
xxii.   *If there is either an E and a K, or an O and a V, then there*
            is a Y
            There is either an E and a K, or an O and a V
            ? There is not a Y? (P12, P3, long) (3.46)

Multistep (direct reasoning)

xxiii.   *There's not an R*
            There's not a W
            ? There is an R or a W? (P1, P4) (2.38)
xxiv.   *If there is either an E or an O, then there is a K*
            ? If there is an E, then there is a K? (P13, P7) (2.52)
xxv.   *There is a D*
            There is a J and an X
            ? There is a D and a J? (P2, P1) (2.71)
xxvi.   *If there is an A, then there is a G*
            If there is an S, then there is a G
            ? If there is either an A or an S, then there is a G? (P13,
            P10) (2.71)

xxvii.   *If there is either a B or an R, then there is a Z*
         There is a B
         ? There is a B and a Z? (P7, P1) (2.71)

xxviii. *If there is both an A and an M, then there's not an S*
         There is an A
         There is an M
         ? There is an S? (P1, P12, P3) (2.79)

xxix.   *There is an F or a C*
         ? If there's not an F, then there is a C? (P13, P8) (2.86)

xxx.   *If there is a C, then there is an H*
         If there is a P, then there is an H
         ? If there is either a C or a P, then there's not an H? (P13, P10, P3) (3.00)

xxxi.   *It is false that there's not a C*
         There is an H
         ? There is a C and an H? (P5, P1) (3.04)

xxxii.   *If there is a C, then there is either a P or an H*
         There is a C
         ? There's not a P, and there's not an H? (P12, P4) (3.13)

xxxiii. *There is a J*
         There is a Q or an X
         ? There is a J and a Q, or there is a J and an X? (P1, P6) (3.17)

xxxiv.   *There is a B*
         If there is a T, then there is an N
         There is a T
         ? There is a B and an N? (P12, P1) (3.17)

xxxv.   *If there is either an E or a K, then there is an O*
         There is an E and a V
         ? There's not an O? (P2, P7, P3) (3.43)

xxxvi.   *It is not true that there is both a U and a D*
         ? If there is a U, then there is a D? (P13, P9, P3) (3.46)

xxxvii. *There is an E*
         ? If there is a K, then there is an E and a K? (P13, P1) (3.50)

xxxviii. *It is not true that there is both an L and an S*
         ? If there is an L, then there's not an S? (P13, P9) (3.50)

xxxix.   *There is an N or a P*
         ? If there's not an N, then there's not a P? (P13, P8, P3) (3.60)

xl.   *If there is a D, then there is a J*
         If there is a Q, then there is an X

? If there is either a D or a Q, then there is either a J or
an X? (P13, P11) (3.63)

xli.   *There is a B, and there is an I or an N*
If there is both a B and an I, then there is an X
If there is both a B and an N, then there is a Z
? There is an X or a Z? (P6, P11) (3.65)

xlii.   *It is not true that there is both a J and a Q*
There is an X and a J
? There is a Q? (P2, P9, P3) (3.74)

xliii.   *There is an L, and there is an R or a W*
If there is both an L and an R, then there is a Z
If there is both an L and a W, then there is a Z
? There is a Z? (P6, P10) (3.86)

xliv.   *There is a B, and there is a T or a Z*
If there is both a B and a T, then there is an N
If there is both a B and a Z, then there is an N
? There's not an N? (P6, P10, P3) (3.91)

xlv.   *If there is a B, then there is a T*
It is false that there's not a B
? There is a T? (P5, P12) (3.96)

xlvi.   *There is an H, and there is an R or an S*
If there is an R, then there's not a Z
If there is an S, then there's not a Z
? There is a Z? (P2, P10, P3) (4.06)

xlvii.   *It is false that there's not a J*
There is a D or an X
? There is a J and a D, or there is a J and an X? (P5, P1,
P6) (4.08)

xlvii.   *If there is either a K or an O, then there is an N*
It is false that there's not a K
? There's not an N? (P5, P7, P3) (4.48)

xlix.   *If there is an R, then there's not an X*
It is false that there's not an R
? There is an X? (P5, P12, P3) (4.50)

l.   *There is a G or an S*
If there is a G, then there is a Z
If there is an S, then there is a Y
? There's not a Z, and there's not a Y? (P11, P4) (4.57)

li.   *If there is both an N and an I, then there's not a B*
It is false that there's not an N
There is an I
? There is a B? (P5, P1, P12, P3) (4.73)

lii. *If there is a P, then there is a C*
 There is a P
 It is not true that there is both a C and an M
 ? There's not an M? (P12, P9) (4.78)

liii. *If there is an A, then there is a G and there is an M or an S*
 There is an A
 ? There is a G and an M, or there is a G and an S? (P12,
 P6) (4.83)

liv. *There is a Y or an L*
 There's not a Y
 If there is either an L or an R, then there's not a W
 ? There is a W? (P8, P7, P3) (5.00)

lv. *If there is an R, then there is an F*
 If there is a W, then there is an L
 There is an R or a W
 If there is either an F or an L, then there's not a Z
 ? There is a Z? (P11, P12, P3) (5.11)

lvi. *It is not true that there is both a C and an H*
 There is a C
 There's not a P
 ? There is an H or a P? (P9, P1, P4) (5.13)

lvii. *There is a P, and there is a Q or an R*
 If there is both a P and a Q, then there is an S
 If there is both a P and an R, then there is a T
 ? There's not an S, and there's not a T? (P6, P11, P4) (5.27)

lviii. *There is a B or a Z*
 There's not a Z
 It is not true that there is both a B and an R
 ? There's not an R? (P8, P9) (5.33)

lix. *It is not true that there is both a K and an L*
 It is false that there's not a K
 ? There is an L? (P5, P9, P3) (5.76)

lx. *There is an L or a W*
 If there is an L, then there's not an E
 If there is a W, then there's not an E
 There is an E or an O
 ? There is an O? (P10, P8) (5.80)

lxi. *There is an E or an X*
 If there is an E, then there's not an H
 If there is an X, then there's not an H
 There is an H or a T
 ? There's not a T? (P10, P8, P3) (6.00)

ACKNOWLEDGMENTS

The research was partially supported by a grant (MH 30162) from the National Institute of Mental Health, Martin D. S. Braine, Principal Investigator. We thank Mark Dobson and Elizabeth Fonseca for their assistance in running the rating studies and David O'Brien, Lance Rips, James McCawley, and Jonathan St. B. T. Evans for comments on earlier versions of the article.

REFERENCES

Boole, G. *An investigation of the laws of thought.* London: Walton & Maberly, 1854.

Braine, M. D. S. On the relation between the natural logic of reasoning and standard logic. *Psychological Review,* 1978, **85,** 1–21.

Braine, M. D. S. *If–then* and strict implication: A response to Grandy's note. *Psychological Review,* 1979, **86,** 154–156. (a)

Braine, M. D. S. On some claims about *if–then. Linguistics and Philosophy,* 1979, **3,** 35–47. (b)

Braine, M. D. S., & O'Brien, D. P. *Categorical syllogisms: A reconciliation of mental models and inference schemas.* Unpublished manuscript, 1984.

Braine, M. D. S., & Rumain, B. Development of comprehension of "or": Evidence for a sequence of competences. *Journal of Experimental Child Psychology,* 1981, **31,** 46–70.

Braine, M. D. S., & Rumain, B. Logical reasoning. In J. H. Flavell & E. M. Markman (Eds.), *Handbook of child psychology* (Vol. III). *Cognitive development.* New York: Wiley, 1983.

Carpenter, P. A., & Just, M. A. Sentence comprehension: A psycholinguistic processing model of verification. *Psychological Review,* 1975, **82,** 45–73.

Chandler, J. P. STEPIT: Finds local minima of a smooth function of several parameters. *Behavioral Sciences,* 1969, **14,** 81–82.

Clark, H. H., & Chase, W. G. On the process of comparing sentences against pictures. *Cognitive Psychology,* 1972, **3,** 472–517.

Cohen, M. R. *A preface to logic.* New York: Holt, 1944.

Erickson, J. R. A set analysis theory of behavior in formal syllogistic reasoning tasks. In R. L. Solso (Ed.), *Theories in cognitive psychology: The Loyola symposium.* New York: Academic Press, 1974.

Evans, J. St. B. T. Interpretation and "matching bias" in a reasoning task. *Quarterly Journal of Experimental Psychology,* 1972, **24,** 193–199.

Evans, J. St. B. T. On interpreting reasoning data. A reply to van Duyne. *Cognition,* 1975, **3,** 387–390.

Evans, J. St. B. T. *The psychology of deductive reasoning.* London: Routledge & Kegan Paul, 1982.

Geis, M., & Zwicky, A. M. On invited inferences. *Linguistic Inquiry,* 1971, **2,** 561–566.

Gleitman, L. R. Coordinating conjunctions in English. *Language,* 1965, **51,** 260–293.

Grice, H. P. Logic and conversation. In P. Cole & J. L. Morgan (Eds.), *Syntax and semantics* (Vol. III). New York: Academic Press, 1975.

Henle, M. On the relation between logic and thinking. *Psychological Review,* 1962, **69,** 366–378.

Hotelling, H. The selection of variates for use in prediction, with some comments on nuisance parameters. *Annals of Mathematical Statistics,* 1940, **11,** 271–283.

Inhelder, B., & Piaget, J. *The growth of logical thinking from childhood to adolescence.* New York: Basic Books, 1958.

Johnson-Laird, P. N. Models of deduction. In R. Falmagne (Ed.), *Reasoning: Representation and process in children and adults.* Hillsdale, New Jersey: Erlbaum, 1975.

Johnson-Laird, P. N. Mental models in cognitive science. *Cognitive Science,* 1980, **4,** 71-115.

Johnson-Laird, P. N. Ninth Bartlett memorial lecture. Thinking as a skill. *Quarterly Journal of Experimental Psychology,* 1982, **34A,** 1-29.

Johnson-Laird, P. N. *Mental models.* Cambridge, Massachusetts: Harvard Univ. Press, 1983.

Johnson-Laird, P. N., & Steedman, M. The psychology of syllogisms. *Cognitive Psychology,* 1978, **10,** 64-99.

Johnson-Laird, P. N., & Tridgell, J. When negation is easier than affirmation. *Quarterly Journal of Experimental Psychology,* 1972, **24,** 87-91.

Lewis, D. *Counterfactuals.* Cambridge, Massachusetts: Harvard Univ. Press, 1973.

McCawley, J. D. *Everything that linguists have always wanted to know about logic, but were ashamed to ask.* Chicago, Illinois: Univ. of Chicago Press, 1981.

Mill, J. S. *A system of logic* (8th Ed.) New York: Harper, 1874.

Osherson, D. N. *Logical abilities in children* (Vol. 2). Hillsdale, New Jersey: Erlbaum, 1974.

Osherson, D. N. *Logical abilities in children* (Vol. 3). Hillsdale, New Jersey: Erlbaum, 1975. (a)

Osherson, D. N. Models of logical thinking. In R. Falmagne (Ed.), *Reasoning: Representation and process in children and adults.* Hillsdale, New Jersey: Erlbaum, 1975. (b)

Osherson, D. N. *Logical abilities in children* (Vol. 4). Hillsdale, New Jersey: Erlbaum, 1976.

Rips, L. J. Cognitive processes in propositional reasoning. *Psychological Review,* 1983, **90,** 38-71.

Roberge, J. J. Effects of negation on adults' disjunctive reasoning abilities. *Journal of General Psychology,* 1976, **94,** 23-28.

Stalnaker, R. C. A theory of conditionals. *American Philosophical Quarterly,* 1968, Monogr. No. 2.

van Duyne, P. C. A short note on Evans' criticism of reasoning experiments and his matching bias hypothesis. *Cognition,* 1973, **2,** 239-242.

van Duyne, P. C. Realism and linguistic complexity in reasoning. *British Journal of Psychology,* 1974, **65,** 59-67.

Wason, P. C., & Johnson-Laird, P. N. *Psychology of reasoning: Structure and content.* Cambridge, Massachusetts: Harvard Univ. Press, 1972.

Woodworth, R. S., & Sells, S. B. An atmosphere effect in formal syllogistic reasoning. *Journal of Experimental Psychology,* 1935, **18,** 451-460.

INDEX

CONTENTS OF PREVIOUS VOLUMES